THE *ARGONAUTICA*

OF

APOLLONIUS RHODIUS

BOOK III

THE
ARGONAUTICA
OF APOLLONIUS RHODIUS
BOOK III

Edited
with Introduction & Commentary

by

MARSHALL M. GILLIES
M.A. (Cantab.), Ph.D. (Edin.)

*Assistant Lecturer in Greek in the
University of Liverpool*

CAMBRIDGE
AT THE UNIVERSITY PRESS
MCMXXVIII

CAMBRIDGE UNIVERSITY PRESS
Cambridge, New York, Melbourne, Madrid, Cape Town,
Singapore, São Paulo, Delhi, Mexico City

Cambridge University Press
The Edinburgh Building, Cambridge CB2 8RU, UK

Published in the United States of America by Cambridge University Press, New York

www.cambridge.org
Information on this title: www.cambridge.org/9781107687776

First published 1928
First paperback edition 2013

A catalogue record for this publication is available from the British Library

ISBN 978-1-107-68777-6 Paperback

Cambridge University Press has no responsibility for the persistence or
accuracy of URLs for external or third-party internet websites referred to in
this publication, and does not guarantee that any content on such websites is,
or will remain, accurate or appropriate.

PREFACE

THE publication of this edition discharges on its author's behalf some portion of a debt of honour incurred in 1922–4 in respect of certain studentships for post-graduate work, which were received from King's College, Cambridge, and from two of the University Funds. Its function is to present the *Argonautica* to the student as something more than a mere happy hunting-ground, where the adventurous examiner tracks down and captures tantalizing extracts for Unseen Translation.

Voices, indeed, have occasionally been heard of scholars crying in the desert; from Ekins in 1771 to Mooney and Seaton in modern times, a small but devoted company has expended its genius in the interpretation of this poet. It is to the credit of British scholarship, that it was a Fellow of a Cambridge College who first called attention to the merits of Book III in a separate translation, and that at the present day the field is held by a text with translation and by an edition with commentary, emanating respectively from Oxford and Dublin.

This edition is not intended to compete with either of these; indeed, its debt to them, and in particular to Mr Mooney's edition, will be evident from almost every page. It is an attempt to make accessible to the student a definite section of a poem, which circumstances might otherwise prevent him from studying at all. The Introduction traces at some length the relation of the *Argonautica* to the literary standards accepted in its own times; the justification of its length is the absence of a suitable text-book in English of the literature of this period, to which summary reference might have been made[1]. In the Commentary, stress has been laid

---

[1] Mr W. W. Tarn's *Hellenistic Civilisation*, which appeared too late to admit of detailed references, has been included in the Bibliography, infr. p. xlvii.

throughout on the relation of the language to that of Homer, and references and extracts have been freely given as regards both Homer and contemporary Alexandrine poets; if apology for their detail is required, let it here be made, but with this reservation, that a proper acquaintance with this relation is essential to a sympathetic understanding of the difficulties with which Apollonius had to contend.

Here, too, apology should be made for certain outstanding omissions. Considerations of space rendered inadvisable a general discussion in the Introduction of the Homeric parallels cited individually in the Notes; likewise the prior claim of literary questions prevented the inclusion of a chapter on the metre of the *Argonautica*. In defence, it might be urged that these are more relevant to a full than to a partial edition of the poem; moreover, the appendix on metre in pp. 411—428 of Mr Mooney's edition should satisfy the requirements of all save the specialist in Alexandrine metric.

Acknowledgments due for information, advice and encouragement in the preparation of this edition are far too many to be made in full. But there are two scholars in particular to whom the thanks of the author are due. The one is a critic, whose anonymous observations on this work, when ἐν προεκδόσει as a thesis, have been of the highest value; the other is Mr A. Y. Campbell, Professor of Greek in the University of Liverpool, who has read through the greater part of the ἐπέκδοσις, and made a number of timely suggestions which have been incorporated in the final form.

The author's good fortune in having had the assistance of Mr L. J. H. Bradley, of the Liverpool University Library, in revising the final proofs, will be fully appreciated by those who have found an expert but kindly critic in a similar time of need.

M. M. G.

CONTENTS

INTRODUCTION

THE IMPORTANCE OF APOLLONIUS

THE mist which for centuries has shrouded the literature of Alexandria seems at last to be lifting. An age that is critical of time-worn dogma, that presumes to test tradition by the touchstone of reason and to form its own judgment of the past, has fired with a divine discontent the student of the classics also, and stimulated him to a new independence of outlook. No longer is it thought that the study of Greek literature should end with the death of Demosthenes, and that of Roman literature begin only with the Punic Wars. The pioneers who forced their way into the literary No-Man's Land have been followed in recent years by specialists in all departments, and the reports which they have made are such as no scholar can afford to ignore.

For the most part, these have been faithfully studied, but the inevitable tendency has been to look at them through the old spectacles. To one man, Alexandrine literature is the child of the Golden Age of Greek letters, and he is interested in it only in so far as it reproduces the virtues, and still more the vices, of its great progenitor. To another, it is the parent of Roman literature, and his concern is to discover to what extent it foreshadows the characteristics of its more famous offspring. Only seldom has its independent existence in its own right been recognised; it has suffered a fate like that of Cornelia, who has gone down to history as the daughter of Scipio Africanus and the mother of the Gracchi.

This tendency has been particularly marked in the case of the *Argonautica* of Apollonius Rhodius, the largest extant poem of purely Alexandrine origin. This is an epic poem in four books, of nearly six thousand lines in length, a little less, that is to say, than the first twelve books of the *Odyssey*. The theme is the Quest of the Golden Fleece; the language is Alexandrine in the extreme; the style and the diction are obviously on the model of Homer. Scholars throughout the ages have ransacked its ample stores, and the fruits of their labours are manifest in the many articles and pamphlets on this author[1]. But these for the most part are by-products of Homeric and Vergilian studies. Overshadowed in his own time by the sacred and inimitable Homer, Apollonius was destined next to be bound as an insignificant captive to the chariot of Vergil. The glory of the past and the glamour of the future have blinded critics to his own undeniable merits.

So it will be the function of this preface to study the question from a new standpoint. Let Apollonius himself be called into court, to stand his trial for once in his own person. Let us for our part forget the past and ignore the future, and let us make the evidence of his own times, circumstantial as much of it inevitably is, the dominant factor in forming our judgment of this pedant turned poet.

I. A SHORT SURVEY OF ALEXANDRINE LITERATURE

(a) THE ALEXANDRINE LIBRARY AND ITS LIBRARIANS

The death of Alexander the Great was destined to resolve once more into its component parts the mighty empire which he alone had been able to maintain. His generals divided up his conquests, and established themselves each as an autocrat in his separate kingdom. Intrigue, murder, and strife prevailed once more, till order was restored to a weary and uneasy world by the victorious legions of Rome, and unity achieved among its warring elements through common obedience to a master.

To Ptolemy the son of Lagus was assigned the satrapy of Egypt. Had he been no more than a soldier, the history of Alexandria might have been a matter of little moment; but fortunately he was a statesman too, and while others wrangled, he kept peace and made his own position sure. He restored the finances of his province, put commerce and industry on their feet, and raised Alexandria to be the greatest commercial city of the world; and it was not a satrapy, but a throne, that he resigned to his son Philadelphus in 285.

Next, emulating perhaps the tyrants of ancient Greece, or at any rate following a tradition already established in the

---

[1] For which v. standard works of reference *s. v. Apollonius* and Bibliography, infr. p. xlvi.

Macedonian royal family, he aimed at making his city a centre
of culture as well. The great Alexandrine Library was founded
towards the end of his reign, under the inspiration apparently
of Demetrius of Phalerum, the "last of the Attic Orators," who
was living at his court at the beginning of the 3rd century B.C.
It was completed by his successor Philadelphus, who founded
also the minor Library of the Serapeum. Ptolemy I also
built in the royal quarter of the city a "Temple of the Muses,"
the Alexandrine Museum, consisting of a large building in
which the members met for their meals, and a covered walk
or περίπατος on the model of the school of Aristotle. It was
endowed by the royal exchequer, and the appointment of the
President, the "Priest of the Museum," was in the power of
the king. The Museum had a long and vigorous life, and was
famous till far into the Roman period.

The Head of the Library was always a scholar of eminence.
There are some who maintain that this position was first held
by Demetrius himself; but it is fairly certain that the first
Librarian was Zenodotus of Ephesus, the tutor of Philadelphus
and the earliest editor of Homer. About his successors there
have been endless conjectures, and our authorities have hitherto
led us to believe that he was followed by Eratosthenes and
then by Apollonius[1]. Recent discoveries, however, have established the fact that the position was next held by Apollonius
the Rhodian, and after him by Eratosthenes, Aristophanes,
Apollonius ὁ εἰδογράφος, Aristarchus and Cydas[2]. The chrono-
logy of the whole Alexandrine school is a matter of the greatest
uncertainty, and most dates are at the best only approximate.
Certain points, however, can now be established which are of
the greatest importance in the study of Apollonius.

In the first place, Callimachus himself was never Chief
Librarian; all statements to this effect are based on a misunderstanding of a Plautine scholium[3], and can now be discarded. Apollonius, on the other hand, undoubtedly held this
office. Secondly, we must reject any theory depending on the
juniority of Apollonius to Callimachus, which places them in

[1] v. Mooney, *Argonautica*, pp. 1—2, and refs. *ad loc.*
[2] *Ox. Pap.* Vol. 10, 1241.
[3] v. esp. Callimachus, ed. Mair (Loeb edition), introd. pp. 6—11.

the position of pupil and master; we are now on safe ground in treating them as comparative equals. Thirdly, as a result of this, we must revise completely our ideas of their famous quarrel, and be prepared for an entirely different interpretation of it in the light, not only of their altered status, but also of the tendencies of the age.

It is, of course, possible to account for the feuds of these two poets on purely historical grounds. Magas, the half-brother of Philadelphus, was viceroy of Cyrene under Ptolemy Soter, and on the death of the latter took the title of King. The wars in which he engaged against Philadelphus were finally ended by a treaty which left him in possession of the Cyrenaica, while his infant daughter was betrothed to Ptolemy, the son of Philadelphus. On the latter's accession to the throne of Egypt in 247–6, Cyrene was added to the kingdom in right of his wife. At such a time, the Cyrenaic origin of Callimachus and his reputed descent from Battus, the mythical founder of Cyrene, would stand him in good stead; Cyrene, too, would be a constant and profitable theme of court poets. The treatment in the *Argonautica* of the legend of the nymph Cyrene[1], and of the famous clod of earth[2], would carry little weight in comparison with the more subtle compliments implied in the Hymns of Callimachus[3]; and it might be argued that the ascendancy of the latter at this period was a purely political matter.

Yet it may be that these are but ripples on the surface of deeper waters. There is reason to believe that the quarrel was academic in origin, and that the opposition to the *Argonautica* led by Callimachus was caused by its writer's grave departure from accepted literary standards. In view of the scant treatment afforded to Alexandrine literature in our text-books, it will be necessary first to trace in outline the tendencies of this age, and to determine the literary environment in which the *Argonautica* came to birth.

---

[1] *Arg.* 4. 1552 f.   [2] *Arg.* 4. 1731 f.
[3] *H. Ap.* 73 f.; *H. Art.* 206 f.

(b) PHILOSOPHY

The gravest disadvantage under which Alexandrine literature laboured was the absence of national unity and the spur
of a common endeavour. The people of Alexandria were a
strange mixture. There were the native Egyptians, for whom
Ptolemy I is said to have established the worship of Serapis;
there was a colony of Jews, at whose request Philadelphus is
said to have authorised a translation into Greek of the Scrip-
tures, the *Septuagint*; there were, too, a large number of
Greeks, who were encouraged in every way. It was no small
achievement on the part of Ptolemy to have designed a system
of administration to accord with the varied religious and social
prejudices of these peoples. Yet the essential stimulus was
wanting. There was no common danger to fire a second
Tyrtaeus to an appeal for unity; no national pride to demand
an *Iliad*, or tradition to evoke an *Aeneid*; no family dignity
to inflate the conceit of a clan and the purse of a Pindar; no
civic consciousness to inspire and encourage a national drama.

Perhaps the safest clue to the literature of a period is the
character of its philosophy; for, as the pulse of a patient is
to the physician a guide to the physical condition of an individual, so philosophy to the student of an era can indicate the
moral and intellectual standard of a people. The significant
feature of the new philosophy is its straightforward and
practical nature. Gone is the intellectual arrogance which
sought an outlet for the creative impulse in magnificent
generalisations and lofty philosophic ideals; the sage has now
to cater for a motley public, weary of theories and anxious
only to attain to peace of mind through adherence to doctrines
which it can easily comprehend.

The Minor Socratics led the way. The Old Academy
abandoned idealism and turned to practical ethics; the Cy-
renaics sought virtue simply in the gratification of desire; the
Megarians turned to Cynicism; and the Cynics found virtue
and happiness in freedom from all needs and desires. Hard
on these followed the Peripatetics, with their doctrine that
virtue lay only in knowledge acquired by the study of facts.
The researches and classifications of this school were first the
inspiration, and then the bane, of Alexandrine scholarship,

the former while regarded as the means to an end, the latter when they became an end in themselves. Finally, there are the doctrines of the later schools; the Stoic belief that virtue was happiness, attainable only through a life directed by reason; the Epicurean theory that pleasure was the sole good, virtue simply a means to pleasure, and wisdom the proper choice of pleasures; the Sceptic striving after happiness through suspense of judgment; and the pseudo-Sceptic doctrine of the Middle and New Academies, that knowledge was unattainable and reasonable probability the safest guide.

All these philosophies are aiming by different means at a common end. The Stoic interest in action rather than result; the Cyrenaic enjoyment of the present, and the saner Epicurean advice to remember also the past and observe the future; the Cynic suspense of judgment and acceptance of conventions as they stand—these are endeavouring to set up for the individual the single aim of αὐτάρκεια, independence, trying to create for a distracted world the ideal figure of the Wise Man who takes things as they are, and moves serenely in an atmosphere of blissful calm.

It is no part of this enquiry to consider how far the change from lofty idealism to practical doctrine is progress, and how far decline; but a recognition of the change of outlook will enable us to see a deeper meaning in the parallel developments of literature. Literature is the child of the human mind, but its creative force is the human relation to the material world.

(c) DRAMA: TRAGEDY, COMEDY, AND THE MIME

The change is most clearly marked in the decline of the drama. The liberty of Athens had been the inspiration of Greek tragedy, and the passing of that freedom was the signal for decay. Hopeless efforts to recapture the glory that was Greece caused the tragic masterpieces of the fifth century to be reproduced again and again. Tragedians had to compete, not only with their own contemporaries, but with the old favourites as well. Worse still, the art of tragic composition became a trade secret of the schools, or a family tradition[1];

---

[1] *e.g.* in the family of Aeschylus, where it descended through two sons and a nephew to the third generation of the latter.

and such public performances as took place were more for the glorification of a master than for the edification of a people. It was in vain that Alexander, in an imperial imitation of the culture of freedom, caused tragedies to be written for his festivals and performed at them; it was in vain that similar performances took place throughout the Greek world right up to the Roman conquest. The star of Greek tragedy was slowly but surely setting.

Yet the output was enormous. It is clear from records such as those of Suidas, that almost every Alexandrine author, whatever his own particular sphere of work might be, wrote tragedies, and often comedies, as well[1]. At the foundation of the Great Library, the arrangement of the tragedies was entrusted to Alexander Aetolus, and that of the comedies to Lycophron of Chalcis; both these names were included in the *Pleiad* of the seven shining stars of tragedy in the time of the first two Ptolemies. The names of the others are of slight importance, and indeed the very constitution of the order is uncertain[2]; but it is significant to notice from what widely distant parts of the Greek world they were drawn.

No complete tragedy of this period has survived; but from the hand of Lycophron himself there has come down to us the *Alexandra*, a most extraordinary elaboration of the conventional " messenger's speech." It is a report by a slave, in 1474 tragic iambics, of the prophecies of Cassandra, surely the most amazing feat of memory on record. Suidas[3] justly calls it τὸ σκοτεινὸν ποίημα; for it is a product of demented pedantry, couched in riddling language, and packed with the obscurest references to unfamiliar mythology. It cannot be taken as representative of contemporary tragedy; but it is significant of the perverted standards of scholarship which were to prove the curse of Alexandrine literature.

Equally to the fore in the case of comedy are the difficulties, which prevent us from forming even a general impression of

[1] For details, v. Susemihl, *Gesch. der gr. Litt. in der Alexandrinerzeit*, pp. 269 f.

[2] Sositheus of Alexandria in the Troad, Homerus of Byzantium, Philiscus of Corcyra, Euphronius of Chersonnese, and Sosiphanes of Syracuse; with Aeantides of Alexandria (?) and Dionysiades of Mallos as rivals for the last two places.

[3] *s. v.* Λυκόφρων.

Alexandrine tragedy. Comedies innumerable were written in Alexandria, but they have not survived; our information refers almost exclusively to the New Comedy of Athens. How far Alexandrine comedy had any distinctive features of its own, is a point which cannot be determined ; probably it departed little, if at all, from the type of the New Comedy.

The New Comedy cannot be altogether ignored in this connection, although it was Athenian in origin, and not Alexandrine in the strictest sense. Unlike tragedy, it did not decline but by adapting itself to altered circumstances took on a new lease of life. First it discarded the chorus, and with it the personal satire and free comment on public affairs that distinguished the "Old" Comedy. Then as it evolved, it abandoned the supernatural and mythical plots of the transition period, sometimes known as the "Middle" Comedy. The "New" Comedy takes for its theme the affairs of ordinary life, and deals with them in the language of ordinary life; and it has a directness and lack of artificiality to which it would with difficulty have attained, had it developed under the patronage of the Museum.

It attracted through its admirable delineation of character, and its didactic and sententious nature; in this it clearly shews its descent from the drama of Euripides. But its distinctive feature is the treatment of family life and love affairs. Everywhere there are in evidence slaves and members of the family, and, above all, lovers; almost every comedy depends for its action on a strong love interest[1]. The commonest theme is that of a slave who helps the son behind his father's back to win the lady of his choice. Frequently, too, there is an old bawd or nurse, another legacy from Euripides, who provokes the confidences of the heroine; she has a similar, but more unsavoury, part to play in the mime. We shall have cause to remember her function, when we come to study the Medea of the *Argonautica*.

There was a further dramatic development in this period in the case of the mime. This was Sicilian in origin, and now became a recognised form of literature in vogue at Alexandria as well. To the lower classes, it was a popular form of dramatic

---

[1] A notable exception is the *Captivi* of Plautus.

entertainment, while to the educated it served as a medium for the presentation of chamber drama. There was a definite distinction between the literary and the theatrical mime. The former was intended to be read rather than staged; its performance, if indeed it ever took place, would have required an audience of unusual culture. This is particularly true of the Mimes of Herodas, eight of which are extant. As far as the ordinary reader is concerned, the antique dialect, the unfamiliar metre, and the obscure allusions—this last a typical Alexandrine weakness—take away a great deal of the interest. The types are clearly borrowed from the New Comedy, and their principal value lies in their repulsive realism combined with rare dramatic skill, in their humour and pathos, and especially in the delicate portrayal of characters like the old and drunken, yet curiously pious, bawd of the first mime.

These objections do not hold good in the case of Theocritus, several of whose Idylls rank properly as literary mimes. We can trace in these the influence of two great Sicilian precursors, Stesichorus, the first of the Romantics, and Sophron, the first of the Realists; from the former comes the romantic treatment of the little epics, to the native Sicilian drama represented by the latter is due the form of the dramatic idylls.

Theocritus had a two-fold aim, to translate the motifs of the old poetry into modern terms, and to bring into his new poetry the common things of life. With Apollonius in particular he shared a desire to purge Romance of its baser elements, and to elevate it to its proper position in literature; in this sense he is Alexandrine in the highest sense of the word. To select among so few is rather arbitrary; perhaps the most representative are the 15th, describing the adventures of two women at the feast of Adonis, and the 2nd, which tells of the magic spells and tortures of the love-sick Simaetha. This wretched maiden, fired with a passion which she fears is not returned, anxiously invoking the goddess of magic, and desperately revealing her most secret thoughts, is a true sister to the Medea of the *Argonautica*.

For the theatrical mime, our authorities are not so good. We are dependent to a large extent on inscriptions referring to famous actors, on references in Athenaeus, and on the denunciations of the moralists. Something of the popular taste can be inferred from a burlesque and a mime which have been preserved in a papyrus of the 2nd century A.D.[1]; the date of the composition is variously estimated as early Imperial or late Ptolemaic. The burlesque is some 230 lines long, mostly in prose, though there is a medley of metres towards the end. It is an obvious parody of the tragic theme represented by the *Iphigeneia in Tauris* of Euripides. A Greek maiden is rescued from barbarians by her brother, who plies them with liquor; the introduction of these barbarians speaking unintelligibly in their own language is an instance of unimaginative pedantry typical of a scientific and academic age. The mime is some 180 lines in length, written, except for the first line, in prose in the language of the Κοινή. It consists of six or seven short scenes; but the rapidity of the action and the obscurity of the details suggest that what we possess is only an outline, on which the actors would improvise as the action proceeded. It is full of themes familiar from Herodas and the New Comedy, and like the latter depends for its plot on intricate conspiracies of masters and slaves. Further light is thrown on the character of the popular mime by the fate of Sotades, whose satires were full of personalities and indecencies, and who, for his rashness in satirizing Philadelphus, was sewn up in a sack and drowned.

For the rest, we are dependent on fragmentary lyric inscriptions, and on remnants of παρακλαυσίθυρα, songs sung by a lover at his lady's door. The best features of the mime are seen in the *Fragmentum Grenfellianum*[2], an erotic fragment of the 2nd or 3rd century, preserving forty from a total of some sixty lines in a metre like that of a tragic chorus, and akin to the mime in that it clearly contained some action. It is the speech of a woman deserted by her lover, and though the language is that of common life, there is vivid realism and deep feeling, and an exquisite portrayal of the emotions of passion, tenderness, and jealousy. It is the solitary relic of a noble type, and it is of particular interest because of its treat-

---

[1] *Ox. Pap.* 3. 413; Powell and Barber, *New Chapters in Greek Literature*, pp. 120—3.

[2] Powell, *Collectanea Alexandrina*, p. 177.

ment, though in a humbler medium, of those passions whose conflict in the breast of Medea as depicted by Apollonius is one of the greatest things in the whole of ancient Greek literature.

(d) EPIC, EPYLLION, AND PASTORAL

It is hardly surprising to find that an age which had lost the spirit of the drama could not maintain the dignity of the epic. It was not that the epic had fallen into disrepute, for at no time can the reputation of Homer have stood higher than it did among the Alexandrines. But Homer to them was the great and inimitable master[1], who overshadowed by his very greatness the puny warblers of a day.

The decline of the epic is further due, in part to the absence of national pride[2], and in part to the academic environment. The erudition of the writers swamped their sense of poetry; narrative was sacrificed to a catalogue, and anxiety to parade the obscurest details made it impossible to sustain the interest of a poem on the scale of the *Iliad*. Euphorion is too much concerned with aetiology; Nicander is Hesiodic, or Hippocratean; the *Phaenomena* of Aratus, so much admired by Callimachus[3], is Homeric in vocabulary but Hesiodic in content, of interest principally for its skill in adapting technical terms to verse. Yet it had many imitators in Roman times, and there are clear indications in the *Argonautica* that it had been closely studied by Apollonius[4].

The hexameter came to be regarded as a convenient medium for the compilation of a catalogue in verse. Long poems on bees and agriculture were written by Menecrates, the tutor of Aratus, and by Nicander. There are extant the latter's *Theriaca* and *Alexipharmaca*, long hexameter poems on venomous animals and poisons. Historical works, too, were cast in this mould, as for example the epic of Rhianus on the Messenian War, with Aristomenes as the hero; geographical works, on the other hand, seem to have been more commonly written in prose. A common form of historical poem was the

---

[1] ἅλις πάντεσσιν Ὅμηρος, Theoc. 16. 20.   [2] v. supr. p. xiii.

[3] *Anth. Pal.* 9. 507: χαίρετε, λεπταὶ Ῥήσιες, Ἀρήτου σύμβολον ἀγρυπνίης.

[4] Mooney's edition, intr. p. 24.

Κτίσις, a short hexameter poem tracing back the history of a city to its foundation, usually, of course, by some god or hero. Such poems were written by Apollonius[1], in particular on the places with which he was especially associated, Alexandria, Naucratis, and Rhodes.

The difficulties of the large scale poem resulted in the popularity of little epics, *epyllia*. Except for those of Theocritus, we are dependent mostly on fragments and second-hand information. But two papyrus fragments recently discovered give some idea of the style of Euphorion. One[2] describes how Heracles brought up Cerberus from Hades; the other[3] is a list of obscure imprecations on some person unknown. There is at least enough of them to shew his crabbed style and love of recondite mythology.

Even Theocritus as a writer of short epics is still the conventional Alexandrine. To this class belong the *Marriage-Song of Helen*, two poems on the birth and miraculous infancy of Heracles, and a particularly graceful account of the loss of Hylas and the grief of Heracles[4]. The *Hymn to the Dioscuri*, describing the fights of Polydeuces with Amycus and of Castor with Lynceus, is a fusion of epic narrative and dialogue; the former theme, along with that of the Hylas Idyll, is also used in the *Argonautica*[5]. To this class may also be assigned the *Song of the Cyclops*, which it is instructive to compare with the semi-dramatic treatment in another Idyll of the same theme[6].

Lyrics are represented by the last three Idylls[7], of which one is a poem intended to accompany the present of a distaff, while the others are love poems on the model of the early lyric. There are two panegyrics[8], a request for the patronage of Hiero, and a still more blatant Hymn of Praise to Ptolemy; doubtless these were a necessary part of the progress of a court poet, but beside the other Idylls they make but a poor show.

The short poems of Callimachus are represented by six Hymns, of which five are in hexameters and one in elegiacs.

---

[1] Powell, *Coll. Alex.* pp. 4—8. [2] *ib.* p. 40, *frag.* 51.
[3] *ib.* p. 31, *frag.* 9. [4] *Idylls* 18; 24, 25; 13.
[5] *Idyll* 22; cf. *Arg.* 1. 1207, 2. 1 f. [6] *Idylls* 11, 6.
[7] *Idylls* 28, 29, 30. [8] *Idylls* 16, 17.

Poetry was now expressed in the forms most suitable for recitation, the hexameter, elegiac, and iambus; the lyric was little
cultivated, and survives for the most part in ceremonial hymns,
skolia, and occasional fragments. The *Hymns* of Callimachus
are a typical product of their age, narrative in form and full
of learned allusions, yet graceful in spite of their pedantry.
But they are marred by fulsome praises of the poet's patron
Philadelphus; in one Hymn, his promotion over his brothers
is illustrated from the rise to power of Zeus over his elder
brothers, in another the extent of his dominions is prophesied
by Apollo[1]. It is uncertain how far these Hymns were intended
for public recitation; at any rate, their immediate interest is
in their form. They are short poems from the hand of one
who is said to have laid it down that the day of the great epic
was past, and that the short poem was the only proper medium
for a writer of taste.

In this connection, the recently discovered fragments of the
Hecale of Callimachus are of more than usual interest. The
orthodox theory, based on the none too sacred authority of
a scholiast[2], is that Callimachus first attempted to maintain
his opposition to the "big poem," as represented by the *Argonautica*, but was finally driven to the composition of the *Hecale*.
It may well be that, in writing even so short an epic as this,
he was using a form which did not commend itself to his
deliberate judgment. The poem at any rate is typically
Alexandrine in its *genre* character, and equally Alexandrine
in its partiality to the obscurer legends. It deals with the tale
of the old crone Hecale, who entertained Theseus in her hut
on the evening before his fight with the Marathonian bull.
There is one passage which is typical of Alexandrine realism
at its best, a description of the bustle in a little town at dawn[3];
it makes an effective contrast with the magnificent description
in the *Argonautica* of the stillness of night[4].

The most striking development of the short poem in this
period is the rise of the pastoral. Theocritus as a writer of

---

[1] Call. *H. Zeus* 58 f., *H. Del.* 165 f.   [2] Schol. on Call. *H. Ap.* 106.
[3] v. text and transl. in Powell and Barber, *op. cit.* p. 104, Call. ed. Mair,
p. 252.
[4] *Arg.* 3. 744.

mimes and epyllia may be the conventional Alexandrine; as a pastoral poet he was not only unique in his own time, but is without peer among the poets of every age. The pastoral was the great and original discovery of Theocritus himself; with him it flourished, but with his death it too died away. It is nothing more than a brief description of rustic life in dialogue or monologue, enlivened perhaps by a song or singing-match. The finest of all is the *Harvest Home*[1], rightly called by Sainte-Beuve the "Queen of Eclogues." It begins with a meeting of friends and ends with the description of a feast; a song of Lycidas on the sorrows of Daphnis and the praises of Comatas is followed by one from Simichidas on the love of his friend Aratus; from beginning to end it re-creates the sounds and scents of summer. The 1st, where Thyrsis on the challenge of a goatherd sings a lament for Daphnis, was used as a model by Bion and Moschus[2]; the 8th, an exquisite tale of the singing-match of two shepherds, would seem to be the work of an unknown imitator.

Bion and Moschus are but inferior imitators. The one was an Asiatic, whose *Lament for Adonis*, oriental in its passionate extravagance and wearisome in its artificiality, has reduced to commonplaces the finest inspirations of Theocritus. The other was a Syracusan, whose *Lament for Bion* has been truly described as a lament for all Greek poetry; as is so often the case with the Alexandrines, there is one passage at least[3] where he rises above the common level to the heights of real poetry. These three poets, if we except a few isolated pieces like Meleager's little idyll on the coming of spring[4], are our sole representatives of Greek pastoral poetry.

It is easy enough to understand the appeal of the pastoral to the Alexandrines. Addressed to a people whom altered times have herded together into great cities and cut off from the joys of country life, it ministers to their instinctive yearning for those vanished delights by a rustic poetry which is dominated throughout by the note of homesickness. Time and again in Alexandrine poetry, sometimes in the most unexpected places, we are stopped short by sudden expressions

---

[1] *Idyll* 7.   [2] Bion 1; Moschus 3.   [3] 3. 99 f.
[4] *Anth. Pal.* 9. 363.

of the same longing[1]. What the new philosophy was doing for the restless, troubled souls of men, was being attempted also by poetry through the medium of this new and transient form.

While yet it flourished, the pastoral had every opportunity of success. Its brevity, polish and descriptive powers commended it to the exponents of the shorter poem; its freshness and lack of erudition attracted the favourable notice of the wider public. Its peaceful melancholy and distinctively Alexandrine preoccupation with love; its reflection of the softer side of country life, in contrast on the one hand with contemporary catalogues of agricultural data, and on the other with later poems addressed to the working farmer, like Vergil's *Georgics*; its appeal to the rustic that is in the heart not only of the Alexandrine but of every true son of Adam; its own peculiar yet scarcely definable beauties—these are but a few of the reasons which caused it to prosper in its own time, and to send down its masterpieces through the ages to us. Yet it died with its inventor; for the very nature of its function implied an artificiality which was fatal to its development in the hands of less competent imitators.

(e) ELEGY AND EPIGRAM

There remain two forms of poetry which were not in any way peculiar to this period, the elegy and epigram. It was in pre-Alexandrine times, in the school of Colophon, that the elegy was first associated with erotic poetry. Mimnermus led the way with a poem named after a female flute-player, *Nanno*. Antimachus, a contemporary of Plato, followed with the *Lyde*, an account of the misfortunes of all the mythical heroes who, like himself, had been saddened by the early death of their beloved. This poem was praised by Asclepiades[2], but Callimachus would rather appear to have hit the mark in calling it a "dull composition, and obscure[3]," for it seems to have been deficient alike in art, arrangement and form, and to have been prematurely "Alexandrine" in the use of obscure words

---

[1] Cf. *Arg.* 2. 541 f.

[2] *Anth. Pal.* 9. 63: τὸ ξυνὸν Μουσῶν γράμμα καὶ Ἀντιμάχου.

[3] Call. ed. Mair, p. 236, *frag.* 5: Λύδη καὶ παχὺ γράμμα καὶ οὐ τορόν.

and little-known legends. Yet Antimachus had a great influence on later elegiac poetry, and it is significant that on
one occasion Ovid[1] links him with Philetas as representative
of amatory elegy.

Philetas was the earliest of the strictly Alexandrine elegiac
poets, greatly admired by Theocritus[2], and preferred by Propertius[3] to Callimachus. Of the amatory elegies addressed to
his mistress Bittis little has survived, but they would seem
to have contained a good deal of obscure mythology. This is
still more true of his pupil Hermesianax of Colophon, who
wrote three books of elegies under the title *Leontion*. There
is extant from the third book a fragment of nearly a hundred
lines, giving a list of poets throughout the ages, from Orpheus
to Philetas, who had been crossed in love, and ending with
three examples from the philosophers, Pythagoras, Socrates
and Aristippus[4]. A similar list of youths who had been
loved was composed by Phanocles, under the title Ἔρωτες
ἢ Καλοί; a fragment of 28 verses is extant which deals with
Orpheus[5].

But the great majority of Alexandrine elegists are represented by still smaller fragments. The elegies of Parthenius
have not survived, though there is extant a prose work, *The
Sufferings of Love*, a series of romances which usually end in
the death or metamorphosis of the principal characters. Suf-
ficient, however, of the type has been preserved to shew its
distinctive features. There is the Alexandrine tendency to
erudition, fatal to the composition of real poetry; there is the
consequent degeneration in character of the poetry, which
tends to become a mere catalogue of parallels. But more
important still, there must have been a real and increasing
interest in romantic legends, to account for the steady pro-
duction of lists of love-sick heroes and heroines. This fact
borne in mind will throw some light on the problem of the
Argonautica. The third book is less of a mystery, if considered
as the product of an age that gave birth to the novel, that
appreciated the plots of the New Comedy, and found an interest
even in catalogues of romantic deaths and suicides.

---

[1] *Trist.* 1. 6, 1.   [2] *Idyll* 7. 39.   [3] 2. 34, 31.
[4] Powell, *Coll. Alex.* pp. 98—100.   [5] *ib.* pp. 106—7.

In this same connexion, it is significant that the elegies of Callimachus seem to have been of a somewhat different character. His *Aitia* was so learned that it was given in the schools as an exercise in exegesis, along with the works of Euphorion and his own *Ibis*[1]. The latter was a poem of studied abuse and obscurity, devoted to a comparison of Apollonius with the scavenger-bird of Egypt. *The Lock of Berenice* was a typically Alexandrine account of the disappearance of a lock of hair dedicated by the wife of Ptolemy III, and of its discovery as a celestial body which thenceforth bore that name. There is nothing in this, nor in the list of his known works, to suggest that the romantic held any appeal for Callimachus. This is a point of which the importance will shortly be shewn.

The epigram, like the elegy, dates from very early times, and enjoyed an even longer vogue. Here too the Alexandrine mania for cataloguing resulted in the formation of various collections, in which, so far as they have come down to us, most Alexandrine poets are represented by a few pieces and some by a larger number. Asclepiades is represented by 43; from Callimachus there are 64; and to Theocritus 20 are ascribed, some inscriptions, others descriptive and almost little idylls. Leonidas of Tarentum is represented by over a hundred; he has aptly been called the "poor man's poet," for his verses are full of the pathos of the hardworked. Two of his epigrams deserve particular mention; one[2] describes a fisherman dying in his hut, "going out like a lamp," the other[3] a spinning woman toiling away in her 80th year. The latter is of unusual interest as shewing in a new dress a favourite simile of the epic, familiar from Homer[4] and Vergil[5], and used with effect, though with typical wealth of irrelevant detail, in the *Argonautica*[6]. Meleager, the compiler of the first *Anthology*, is represented by over a hundred epigrams, mostly erotic.

Last, but not least, there are some epigrams written by women. From Nossis there are 12, but, unfortunately, only one[7] has survived of the erotic epigrams for which she was so

---

[1] Clem. Alex. *Str.* 5. 511 C.   [2] *Anth. Pal.* 7. 295.
[3] *ib.* 7. 726.   [4] *Il.* 12. 433.   [5] *Aen.* 8. 408.
[6] *Arg.* 3. 291; cf. 4. 1062.   [7] *Anth. Pal.* 5. 170.

highly esteemed by Meleager[1]. Erinna flourished probably in the 4th century; at any rate, she is Alexandrine to the extent that she was one of the principal founders of the school of short poems[2]. Anyte was probably an early Alexandrine; her epigrams are interesting because of the great tenderness which they shew towards animals[3], and there are three of particular charm on girls who had died in childhood[4]. Of the epigrams recently found in the papyri, the most interesting is one[5] composed in iambics and in high tragic style, on a hound which attacked and killed a boar, but died of wounds; it is clearly influenced by the new declamatory school of rhetoric.

(f) GRAMMAR, RHETORIC AND PROSE

The scientific study of grammar was an important feature of Alexandrine scholarship. γραμματικός in the Golden Age of Greek literature meant nothing more than "one who has learned to read," and τέχνη γραμματική was simply "the art of reading." Even in the Alexandrine age, the words are often ambiguous, and include not only grammar in our limited sense of the word, but literary criticism as well.

The origin of language is discussed in the *Cratylus* of Plato, where three points of view are put forward; that the origin of all names is in convention, that they are "natural" in origin (every word being either the perfect expression of a thing or meaningless), and a reconciliation of these opposing views in the claim of Socrates, that language is founded on nature but modified by convention. The dispute was continued by Aristotle, who adhered to the "conventional" theory, while Epicurus supported the view of Socrates; the extreme of the former theory was reached by the Megarian philosopher Diodorus, who claimed to invent his own language, and called his slaves by the names of the Greek particles.

---

[1] *Anth. Pal.* 4. 1, 10: Νοσσίδος, ἧς δέλτοις κηρὸν ἔτηξεν Ἔρως.

[2] It is a disputed point whether there was one Erinna only, or two: the only epigrams extant in her name are *Anth. Pal.* 6. 352, 7. 710, 712; cf. Meleager, *ib.* 4. 1. 12: καὶ γλυκὺν Ἠρίννης παρθενόχρωτα κρόκον.

[3] *Anth. Pal.* 6. 312; 7. 190, 202, 208, 215; 9. 745.

[4] *Anth. Pal.* 7. 486, 646, 649.

[5] Powell and Barber, *op. cit.* p. 108.

The Stoic school of Pergamum, on the other hand, regarded language as a product of nature, and studied grammar as an essential part of their system of dialectics. There was considerable conflict between the schools of Alexandria and Pergamum, with their rival doctrines of *analogy* and *anomaly*; the former deals with the rules which govern the formation of words, the latter with the exceptions. The principle of *anomaly* was formulated by Chrysippus, and developed by Crates, an opponent of Aristarchus; that of *analogy* was supported by Aristophanes and Aristarchus.

The earliest Greek grammar was written by Dionysius Thrax, a pupil of Aristarchus; it was a standard work for thirteen centuries and is still extant. Grammar is there defined as a "practical knowledge of the usage of writers of poetry and prose," but it is significant of the change in meaning that the book contains not a word on syntax or style.

An appreciation of the importance attached to grammatical studies in the Alexandrine period will enable us to regard with greater indulgence certain unwelcome features of the *Argonautica*. The etymological digressions, the inclusion of approved Homeric forms and reproduction of undecided alternatives, the addition to the Homeric of later forms and constructions and occasional preference of the later to the earlier —all these represent the critical spirit of a less creative age, and must not be judged solely from the standpoint of literary criticism.

Little need be said of the rhetoric of this period; despotic Alexandria offered little scope to orators, and declamations were safer than political speeches. Elsewhere there was a struggle between the Attic and Asiatic styles; by the latter is meant the abandonment of the periodic style in favour of short sentences, and excessive use of rhythm, antithesis and assonance. Its full development is commonly attributed to Hegesias of Magnesia in the middle of the 3rd century; his fragments shew typical instances of forced and unusual metaphors, artificial correspondence of clauses, pompous circumlocutions, and false antitheses. The reaction to Atticism at the end of the 2nd century, led mainly by Hermagoras of Temnos, is unexpectedly supported in an extract from the fifth book of Agatharchides, *On the Red Sea*[1]. In it the geographer inveighs against Asianists in general, and Hegesias in particular, and holds up as an example the merits and ability of Demosthenes.

Of the many histories written in this period, not one has survived entire, but several new developments can be observed. Criticism gave birth to biography, which had no place in earlier Greek literature; in this connection the recent fragments of Satyrus' *Life of Euripides*[2] are of interest, as containing some new information and some excellent literary criticism. There arose, too, a "romantic" or philosophical type of history, familiar from the names of Hecataeus and Euhemerus; in this, the writer started from a pre-conceived idea, in the light of which all evidence was interpreted, accepted, or rejected. Another form of "history," largely developed by Callimachus, consisted simply in the collection and classification of marvels[3]; their value can be judged from the extant work of Antigonus of Carystos, ἱστοριῶν παραδόξων συναγωγή.

Geographical works were as numerous as histories, and cannot always be distinguished from them. The first to treat geography in a scientific manner was Eratosthenes, who measured approximately a geographical degree, and made a reasonable estimate of the circumference of the earth. His principal work, the Γεωγραφικά, is cited on several occasions in the scholia to the *Argonautica*, and his influence on his successors can hardly be over-estimated.

It was undoubtedly in science that the Alexandrine passion for facts produced its greatest triumphs, and more than justified the precepts of Aristotle. Important advances were made alike in astronomy, geometry, mathematics, mechanics and medicine; but a catalogue of these achievements is beyond the scope of this enquiry. For the most part our evidence consists in references and extracts in later writers, for capricious fortune has preserved only too few of these valuable treatises. Doubtless their literary value would be small; for the most part, at any rate, she has preserved the literary parerga of the scientist, and condemned to oblivion the works which brought him fame.

---

[1] *Geographici Gr. Min.*, ed. Müller, Vol. 2, pp. 119 f.
[2] *Ox. Pap.* 9. 1176.   [3] Cf. *Arg.* 3. 201, etc.

II. THE *ARGONAUTICA*

(a) THE NARRATIVES OF THE VOYAGE

The *Argonautica* begins, not with the departure of Jason from Iolcus, but like a modern serial story, with a rapid synopsis of preceding events. Hard on the conventional invocation and statement of theme, there follows an explanation of Pelias' fear of the one-sandalled man, a brief account of the arrival of Jason in this condition, and a sinister version[1] of the means by which Pelias forced on Jason the Quest of the Golden Fleece. For the building of the Argo, a general reference is given to previous works on the subject, followed by a catalogue of the fifty-two heroes who made up the crew. The preliminaries to the expedition are quickly reviewed—the hopes and fears of the people, the parting of Jason from his parents, the choice of a leader, the launch of the Argo, the sacrifice to Apollo, the quarrel of Idas and Idmon, and the song of Orpheus. Dawn comes at last, and the Argo puts out to sea.

The account of these preliminaries takes up more than a twelfth part of the whole four books, five hundred lines and more of paramount structural importance, which should contain the very essence of the poem. It is only too clear how little they are in keeping with epic standards, and it must be candidly admitted that they are a sorry *farrago*. The summary of the relations of Jason and Pelias is a wicked adaptation of that last infirmity of Greek drama, the tragic prologue[2]. The catalogue is a mere parade of information obscurely gleaned; tedious in itself, by virtue of its prominent position it further acts as a drag on the narrative proper. The scene between Jason and his parents is neither heroic nor dignified; and the simile of the lonely maiden, the first deliberate piece of ornament in the poem, loses much of its force through the irrelevance of its detail. The appointment of Jason to the command only after the refusal by Heracles of the office, and under threat of violence from the latter if the choice should be opposed, is an insult to the dignity of the hero; the situation

---

[1] This is given at greater length in 3. 333 f.
[2] Mackail, *Lectures on Greek Poetry*, p. 255; cf. *Arg.* 1. 609 f.

is brought about by the anxiety of the poet to combine with the usual account a late legend[1], which actually did give the leadership to Heracles. The vulgar brawl of Idas and Idmon is an unworthy means of drawing attention to the magic powers of the music of Orpheus. It is little wonder that many who have set out conscientiously to read the *Argonautica* have at this point closed the volume in disgust for ever.

It must be already evident how deeply the style of Apollonius is tainted by the vices of Alexandrianism. The poet is vanquished by the historian, and strict chronological sequence takes the place of the Homeric way of plunging straightway *in medias res non secus ac notas*. The historian, too, is in conflict with the dramatist; this is shewn, not only in the prologue and succession of five detached incidents, but also in the constant recurrence of a similar form, sometimes modified, sometimes more than obvious. The reproduction of variant legends, the intrusion of scholarly but unpoetic detail, the use of improper ornament, and striving after immediate effect by ruinous means, the emphasis on *minutiae* and general disregard of narrative dignity—all these shew clearly the cloven hoof of the pedant beneath the mantle of the poet.

The account of the outward voyage is a detailed description, complete except for a map, of the route naturally taken by a Greek vessel from Pagasae to Colchis, through the Golden Horn and along the northern coast of Asia Minor. In striking contrast with this, the narrative of the return throws all geographical possibility to the winds. The Argo sails up the Danube and down a mythical second arm to the Adriatic, up the Po and down the Rhone, and back to Pagasae via the northern coast of Africa, Crete and Aegina. The background of this amazing account is a wealth of conflicting legends, some of which must belong to the earliest stratum of the myth. The poet is attempting to reconcile the Homeric[2] and Pindaric[3] versions with those of the colonists who identified their new homes in the west with the mythology of their native land. Political reasons[4] made it particularly advisable for Apollonius to refer to the connection of the Argo with

---

[1] Preller-Robert, *die gr. Heldensage*, pp. 840 f.   [2] *Od.* 12. 70.
[3] *Pythian* 4.   [4] v. supr. p. xii.

Cyrene; but it is hard to avoid invidious comparisons of his account with that of Pindar.

The actual details of these voyages are beyond the scope of this enquiry; but a rough analysis will shew how, in the account of the outward voyage, the dramatic form is still predominant. There is a sharp division between the sections which deal with the known waters of the Aegean, and the less familiar geography of the Euxine. In each section, five main incidents are treated at length, and separated by short narrative interludes:

First Section.

The Visit to Lemnos ...	...	619– 908.	290	lines
Narrative	...	909– 935.	27	„
The Fight with the Doliones ...		936–1152.	217	„
Narrative	...	1153–1171.	19	„
The Loss of Hylas ...	...	1172–1357.	186	„
Narrative	...	1358–1362.	5	„
The Fight with Amycus	...	II. 1– 163.	163	„
Narrative	...	164– 177.	14	„
The Visit to Phineus ...	...	178– 536.	359	„
Narrative	...	537– 548.	12	„

Second Section.

The Symplegades ...	...	549– 647.	99	„
Narrative	...	648– 668.	21	„
Apollo Eoos	...	669– 719.	51	„
Narrative	...	720– 751.	32	„
The Visit to Lycus ...	...	752– 898.	147	„
Narrative	...	899– 910.	12	„
Sthenelus, Sinope and Amazons		911–1001.	91	„
Narrative	...	1002–1029.	28	„
The Island of Ares ...	...	1030–1230.	201	„
Narrative	...	1231–1285.	55	„

It can hardly be doubted that here is an obvious affinity with the stereotyped structure evolved by the drama in its decline from the Golden Age, of five acts separated by brief choral interludes.

(b) THE THIRD BOOK

In contrast with the rapid narratives of the voyage, the action of the third book is almost stationary. The scene is laid at Colchis throughout, and changes only within the narrowest of limits. The theme is indicated in the invocation of Erato as patroness of Love; to her Apollo, the patron proper of the quest, for the moment gives place[1].

Here and Athene plan together to aid Jason, and go to secure the aid of Cypris, who bribes her son Eros to fire Medea with love for Jason. Meanwhile the Argonauts in council are persuaded by Jason to postpone the use of force, until they have first approached Aeetes with a formal demand for the Fleece. The routine of Ptolemaic court ceremonial is duly observed; Jason as captain of the expedition leads an embassy to the palace, where on his behalf Argus, the grandson of Aeetes, explains the position to the king. Aeetes at first gives way to anger, but on reflection resolves to appoint an ordeal which shall be the ruin of Jason. This ordeal, in keeping with the best traditions of mythology, is threefold, the yoking of the fiery bulls, the ploughing of the Field of Ares, and the battle with the Earth-born Men. Jason reluctantly consents, and on his return to the ship explains the situation to the crew. Various heroes offer to perform the tasks if Jason himself should feel unequal to them; but Argus persuades them first to let him find if his mother Chalciope can secure the aid of her sister, the sorceress Medea. To this end, he returns to the palace, while Aeetes orders a watch to be kept on the Argo, and devises treachery against the crew.

But meanwhile Eros, in obedience to his mother's request, had played his part. Medea, the younger daughter of Aeetes, had by the divine purpose of Here been kept from her usual attendance as priestess at the temple of the goddess, and was the first person to be seen by Jason and his companions as they crossed the outer court on arrival at the palace. When she saw them, she cried aloud, and her cry brought forth from the palace Chalciope to welcome her sons, the attendants of Chalciope, and last of all Aeetes, and Eidyia the queen. During the ensuing turmoil, Eros entered unseen and fired his

---

[1] *Arg.* 3. 1; 1. 1.

shaft at Medea; the effect is immediate, "all remembrance left her, and her soul was melted with the sweet pain":

> As when a woman, toiling with her hands
> At weaving, rises early from her sleep
> And piles dry twigs around a smouldering brand
> To furnish light under her roof by night;
> And as the fire out of the tiny brand
> Wakens to wondrous size, and utterly
> Consumes both torch and twigs together—thus,
> Crouched in Medea's heart, burned secretly
> Love the Destroyer, and her tender cheeks
> Ever were changing colour, now were pale,
> Now red, in the distraction of her soul[1].

Medea was present throughout the formal audience in the palace, but her thoughts were fixed on Jason alone; and as he retired from the palace, "her soul, creeping like a dream, flitted in his footsteps as he went[2]." Chalciope, in fear of the wrath of Aeetes, went straightway with her sons to the sanctuary of her own chamber; Medea too went to hers, "and brooded in her soul on the many cares that the Loves awaken":

> Before her eyes the vision still appeared,
> Himself just as he was, the clothes he wore,
> The words he spoke, how he had sat, and how
> He moved towards the door. Thus pondering,
> She thought no man like him had ever been;
> Ever his voice was ringing in her ears,
> And the words, sweet as honey to the mind,
> That he had spoken[3].

Fearing that he is doomed to be slain, either by the bulls or at the hand of Aeetes himself, she mourns for Jason as one already dead; in the privacy of her chamber she reveals her feelings in a moving prayer:

> Wretched am I! Why comes this grief to me?
> Be he the best of heroes, or the worst,
> Who is about to perish, let him go.
> Yet, too, I would he had escaped unharmed!
> Yes, may this be so, goddess reverend,
> Daughter of Perses; may he reach his home,
> Saved from destruction. But if he is doomed
> To perish, overmastered by the bulls,
> Then may he first learn this, that I at least
> Rejoice not in his cruel calamity[4].

---

[1] 289—298; but v. notes for ἀνεγρόμενον and οὖλος.
[2] 446—7.   [3] 451—8.   [4] 464—470.

It is tempting to speculate how far Apollonius meant the reader to remember the presence of Medea throughout the proceedings in the palace, and, if he did, how far Medea was moved, apart from the mere celestial mechanism of the shaft of Eros, by anything deeper than the mere nobility and fine appearance of Jason. A modern writer, with the modern passion for psychological analysis, would hardly have missed the opportunity offered by lines 422–425, of describing how Medea's wavering emotions were finally fixed by the sight of the hero in a moment of ordinary human hesitation before so terrible an ordeal. But the genius of Apollonius did not consist in psychological subtleties of so advanced a character; subtle indeed he is within his own limits, but beyond these he must not be pressed.

At last deep sleep relieves Medea from her waking sorrows, but even in sleep her senses are alert to her undoing. She dreams that she herself is the real object of Jason's quest; that she performs the tasks in place of him; and that her parents accordingly refuse to carry out their promise. Strife arises, and the final decision is laid on her; she sets aside her parents, and chooses the stranger. Her parents cry aloud in anger; and with the cry, Medea awakes from sleep. Once more she vainly tries to assure herself of her purely impersonal concern for Jason; and in the hope that Chalciope, on behalf of her sons, will implore the aid of Medea's magic drugs, she resolves to visit her sister:

> Ah, miserable me,
> What gloomy dreams have frightened me. I fear
> That from the heroes' voyage there may come
> Some great calamity. My heart with dread
> Is trembling for the stranger. Let him woo
> Some maid of the Achaeans, far away
> In his own country. Mine be maidenhood,
> Mine be my parents' home. Yet with my heart
> Made reckless, I shall stay no more aloof,
> But I shall put my sister to the test,
> In hope that she, through grief for her own sons,
> May beg my succour in the ordeal. This
> Might quench the bitter pain within my heart[1].

With this intention, time and again Medea tries to make her way to her sister's room, and time and again shame forces

[1] 636—644.

her to return. At last, worn out by the conflict of modesty and desire, she throws herself upon her bed, and gives way to a storm of tears. One of her handmaidens sees her in this condition, and hastens to tell Chalciope, who at that very moment was sitting with her sons, trying to devise some means of approach to Medea to win her aid. She hastens in dismay to her sister's room, and, all unconscious of her feelings towards Jason, assumes that her terror is on behalf of her own sons. Medea, whose emotions had been too much centred on Jason to have had a single thought for them, seizes the heaven-sent excuse. Urged on by a passion beyond her control, she tells of her awful dream; but with the cunning of despair she tints the whole account with gloomy forebodings for their safety. Chalciope, in terror for her sons, begs her sister, for their sake, to help the stranger; and Medea promises to bring her charms at dawn to the temple of Hecate, and give Jason instructions for their use.

But with the departure of her sister, Medea is left once more a prey to shame and fear. In the stillness of night she wavers to and fro, resolved now to help Jason, now to end her misery, now to withhold her aid and to endure her fate in silence. She pictures the destruction of Jason, and a fresh sorrow added to her burden; she imagines her own suicide, and the taunts of the Colchian women after her death. Resolved at last in desperation to end her life, she takes her casket of drugs and begins to unloosen the bonds. " But suddenly over her soul there came an awful fear of hateful Hades. For a long time she held back in speechless horror, while around her thronged visions of all the pleasing cares of life. She thought of all the pleasant things that are among the living; she thought, as a maiden does, of her happy comrades; and the sun grew sweeter than ever to behold, the more she weighed each prospect in her mind. She put the casket once more from off her knees, all changed by the promptings of Here[1]." Dawn comes at last, and Medea takes her charms and drives with her maidens to keep her tryst with Jason.

In this scene, the genius of Apollonius reaches its highest point. It is by far the longest passage in the whole *Argonautica*

[1] 809—818.

of real and living poetry; its subtle balance and symmetry are such as only the closest analysis can reduce to a formal pattern[1]; and it is executed with a delicacy of feeling which it is almost an impertinence to praise. The Medea of Apollonius stands self-revealed, as a modest maiden caught in the toils of a new and overmastering passion, and in following the development of her character, we are impressed above all with her essential humanity. We forget the formal intervention of Eros, we forget her formal allegiance to Here and the occasionally inartistic workings of the divine mind of her patroness; we see portrayed, in a manner undreamt of in the Golden Age, the eternal conflict of love and family, love and duty, love and self, and the inevitable victory at every stage of the greater passion.

The decision once made, the reaction sets in; from the uttermost depths of despondency, Medea is borne with a rush to the heights of impatient assurance: "there in her chambers she sped to and fro, and trod the ground forgetful of the awful agony that had been hers, and heedless of sorrows to come, destined to be greater still[2]." Accompanied by her maidens, she goes to keep her tryst, like Artemis driving in her chariot to the chase; and as she goes, such people as meet her on the way, partly in deference to royalty, partly through fear of her magic glance, "give way, shunning the eyes of the royal maiden[3]." On arrival at the shrine, Medea reveals her intentions to her companions, and begs them to withdraw when Jason comes. Jason, accompanied by Mopsus, sets forth; but the latter is warned off by a crow, in obedience, as the poet is rather too prone to insist at every stage[4], to the purpose of Here, and Jason goes on alone.

At last Medea sees him come, and at the sight "her heart leapt from her bosom, a mist came over her eyes, and a hot blush covered her cheeks. She had no strength to move her knees this way or that, but her feet were rooted to the ground.... Silent and speechless the two stood face to face. Like oaks or lofty pines, that stand side by side deep-rooted on the mountains, peaceful when the wind is still, but again, when stirred by the breath of the wind, murmur unceasingly—so too, stirred

[1] v. notes on 616 f. [2] 835—7. [3] 886.
[4] 931, cf. 818, 922, 1134.

by the breath of Love, they two were destined to tell their tale at length[1]." Jason, though his heart is as yet untouched by Love, shews himself none the less to be a considerate and courteous gentleman. Realising the embarrassment of the maiden, he proceeds at once to speak, and to urge his plea for her assistance, tactfully reminding her of a precedent already established in the annals of her family by Ariadne, daughter of Helios, who had rescued Theseus from the Minotaur[2]. Medea, unable yet to speak, gives him the charm without a word; "and truly in her joy she would have drawn the very soul from her breast and given it to him, had he but needed it...[3]." "For a while in modesty both kept their eyes fixed on the ground, but ever were casting glances at each other, smiling beneath their radiant brows the smile of Love[4]." At last Medea finds words, and explains the use of the charms; then, after a silence, she adds: "Remember, then, if ever thou shalt return to thy home, Medea's name, as ever shall I remember thine, though thou be far away[5]." She urges him to speak further of her kinswoman Ariadne, and of his home, and at her tears, Love at last steals over Jason too, and he replies.

He describes his fatherland, but says little more of Ariadne than to express a hope that, as Minos her father was once reconciled to Theseus for her sake, so too Aeetes may be joined in friendship to himself and Medea. But Medea assures him that any such hope is vain, and threatens in her misery, should Jason forget her, to appear some day as a suppliant in his home. By one delicate suggestion after another she makes it clear to Jason that her assistance will involve her, has indeed already involved her, in irreconcilable enmity with her father; and thus she leads him up at last to a formal proposal of marriage. Formal indeed it is: "If thou shalt come to my home and to the land of Hellas, honoured and reverenced shalt thou be by men and women. They shall worship thee as a goddess, since by thy counsel to some their sons came home again, and to some their brothers, kinsmen and stalwart husbands were saved from a dread calamity. In our bridal chamber shalt thou prepare our couch, and nothing shall come

---

[1] 962—972.   [2] 997 f.   [3] 1015—6.
[4] 1022—4.   [5] 1069—1071.

between us and our love until the doom of death shall enfold us[1]."

Then, calm as ever, Jason announces that the hour is late, and the lovers part; Jason returns to the ship, and Medea to her companions. "But these she noticed not as they thronged around, for her soul had soared aloft among the clouds; of their own accord her feet mounted the swift chariot...[2]." When she reached the palace, Chalciope in grief for her sons rushed forth to question her; "but Medea, distraught by swiftly changing thoughts, neither heard her words nor was willing to answer her questions. She sat on a low stool at the foot of her couch, and leant her cheek on her left hand; her eyes were wet with tears as she pondered in what an evil deed she had resolved to share[3]."

Thus ends Medea's share in the narrative of the third book; but Jason, as instructed by her, sacrifices to Hecate and anoints himself and his weapons with the charms. Thus protected, he goes to the ordeal, yokes the bulls and ploughs the field, sows the dragon's teeth and slays the Earth-born Men. Aeetes returns to the palace, and at this point the third book ends; the slaying of the dragon, the actual winning of the Fleece, the departure of Medea with the Argonauts and her marriage with Jason, belong to the narrative of the fourth book.

This theme has clearly the material for great poetry, and, within his own limitations, Apollonius has made good use of it. The first thing that strikes the intelligent reader of the *Argonautica* is that the style of the third book is quite different from that of the preceding two, and for that matter from that of the fourth book also. The poet has a definite plot to work out, and is less prone in consequence to serial narrative, and the whole section goes somehow with a swing that is wanting in the descriptions of the voyage. There is less digression into unfamiliar mythology, less etymology, and less parade of knowledge for its own sake; at last the poet seems to have risen superior to the pedant that is in him.

It is not that the pedant is by any means dead. Witness still the etymologies of proper names[4], the accumulation of

---

[1] 1122—1130. [2] 1150—2. [3] 1157—1162.
[4] 5, 245—6 and note *ad loc.*

titles in a simile[1], and mere parade of knowledge[2]; the elaborate descriptions of buildings[3], customs[4], and marvels[5]; the digressions into magic and religious ritual[6], and use of conventional devices like mist and sudden omens[7]; the use of *oratio obliqua*, anatomical details, and plural Erotes[8]. The taint of the Museum is in the blood of all her sons, and not even the Alexandrine leopard can change his spots. But on the other side of the account, we can credit Apollonius with innumerable beauties of detail, such as the bird's-eye view from Olympus, the simile of the aged woman, the description of the peace of night, and the curious but effective introduction of the abusive crow[9].

Nor is the third book immune from the disturbing influences of other forms of Alexandrine literature. There is a typical example of the "messenger's speech," in the explanation by Argus of Jason's quest[10], while the long speech of Aeetes in *oratio obliqua* is prosaic and inartistic in the extreme[11]. It is particularly noticeable that many of the best episodes can be detached completely from their context without injury to the narrative, and resemble in form the idyll or the *epyllion*; this is especially true of the visit to Cypris, the account of Eros and Ganymede at dice, and the fine description of Medea's turmoil of doubt and indecision[12].

The most striking feature of the third book is the departure from Homeric standards in the introduction of romance. To some extent this is inherent in the character of the legend, which is of a type familiar from the folklore and mythology of every people. A hero sets out for a mystic country at the end of the world to win a prize; he travels there on a wonderful ship, and on arrival is set some task or tasks quite beyond his powers. The difficulty is overcome in one of three ways; either a god takes pity on him, or members of the animal kingdom come to his aid in grateful remembrance of some earlier service, or it may be that the daughter of his taskmaster

---

[1] 1241. [2] 277. [3] 235 f. [4] 200 f.
[5] 137, 220, 854. [6] 846 f., 1030 f. [7] 210, 541.
[8] 579 f., 761, 687. [9] 164, 291, 744, 930.
[10] 332, cf. pp. xv, xxix supr. [11] 579 f.
[12] 6—110, 111—166, 616—824.

is herself fired with pity for the hero in his distress, and gives him secret aid[1].

It is this third and most romantic form that is developed in the *Argonautica*. The principal result is to concentrate interest on Medea to the exclusion of Jason, which is in itself a departure from earlier epic standards. Female characters in the Homeric poems, however sympathetically drawn, are always subordinate to the male; Jason, on the other hand, is never quite equal to the emergency, and can never rise above his immediate troubles[2]. This weakness of character is to some extent the fatal result of Alexandrine erudition. Earlier poets were content to rely on divine intervention or supernatural explanations in times of stress; the Alexandrine tries at the same time to observe the conventions and to trace troubles to natural causes, and falls between the stools of poetry and science.

It was the tragedy of Medea to love passionately without being loved in return. Her destiny was fixed in legend and literature, and it was not for Apollonius to alter it. But to him she is primarily a maiden tortured by the pains of love, though there are occasional glimpses of the more familiar Medea. There is an echo of Euripides in her appeal to Jason in this book[3], and a still more bitter tone in the fourth book, in her denunciation of the treachery of Jason, and her appeal to the heroes at Phaeacia against their decision to surrender her to the pursuing Colchians[4]. It is by design of Here that Medea is fired with love for Jason, and she is no more than an instrument of the divine vengeance to be wreaked on a king in distant Thessaly who had insulted the goddess[5]. Thus tradition thrust upon the poet the ironical situation, that the Queen of Heaven, the Patroness of Marriage and Divine Example of conjugal fidelity, sacrifices the love of a maiden to the safety of her *protégé*, and binds them in a marriage that is doomed to failure.

---

[1] K. Meuli, *Odyssee und Argonautika*, pp. 1—24, *Argonautensage und Helfermärchen*.

[2] Cf. Sonnenburg in *Neue Jahrbücher* 33 (1909), pp. 715 f.

[3] 1111 f.   [4] 4. 355 f., 1031 f.   [5] 60—5, 1134—6.

(c) ROMANCE AND THE EPIC

It is difficult to be sure how far Apollonius is original in his treatment of the romantic issue. Much of our information cannot be traced further back than to one or other of the many contemporary catalogues of unhappy love affairs[1]. There was a promising situation in the *Aethiopis*, in the love of Achilles for the Amazon Penthesileia; but we cannot take the later[2] romantic versions as evidence, nor build too much on the curt statement of Proclus[3], that Achilles killed Thersites ὀνειδισθεὶς τὸν ἐπὶ τῇ Πενθεσιλείᾳ λεγόμενον ἔρωτα.

But Stesichorus in the Καλύκη would seem to have anticipated the romantic movement by several centuries, as witness Athenaeus[4]: "Calyce was depicted as pure and modest in character, not anxious at all costs for intercourse with her lover, but as praying, if so it might be, to become his lawful wife, and if this might not be, to die." This has something in common with the *Argonautica*; it recalls Medea's dream that Jason had come solely to win her as his lawful wife[5], and her passionate prayer that she had died before meeting him[6]. The characters of Stesichorus, like those of the *Argonautica*, were purely mythological; but he lacked the tradition which gave some sanction to the methods of Apollonius, of Sappho and the personal lyric.

The position with regard to tragedy is well summed up by Ovid[7]: "Omne genus scripti gravitate tragoedia vincit; Haec quoque materiam semper amoris habet." Even Euripides, the most romantic of the tragedians, was never quite free of the idea that a romantic situation was a means to the end of developing a plot, and could not be an end in itself. But the New Comedy, which drew its inspiration from Euripides, found the material for nearly all its plots in the love adventure; but this soon came to be formed to a conventional pattern, and lost its freshness and appeal.

It is in the third book of the *Argonautica*, for the first time in all Greek literature, that romance is treated objectively as

[1] v. supr. p. xxiv.
[2] Prop. 3. 11, 13; Qu. Sm. 1. 659 f.; Nonnus *Dion*. 35. 27 f.
[3] *Chrestomathy*, ap. Kinkel *E. G. F.* p. 33.
[4] 14. 618 D, Bergk 4, *frag*. 43; cf. also Mimnermus, supr. p. xxiii.
[5] 3. 619 f.   [6] *ib*. 774.   [7] *Trist*. 2. 381—2.

a definite end in itself. Apollonius has rejected the conventions of an earlier age, and has developed his theme in its simplest and noblest form. He has discarded the nurse whom Euripides first made familiar in his tragedies as the confidante of a love-sick mistress, and the recipient of her guilty confessions. He has dispensed with the attendant of the New Comedy, whose furtive services were essential to the consummation of even the most romantic union. He has risen above the atmosphere of secrecy and guilty repression in which the old bawd of the mime performed her similar function. The Medea of Apollonius turns for sympathy to her own sister, and uses the fears of a mother for the accomplishment of a purpose which she is too modest to reveal. The storm of passion takes place in the breast of the maiden, and in the privacy of her own chamber; it is only by accident that her handmaiden intrudes upon her grief; and she, instead of conspiring with her mistress to form a secret plan, reports the matter to Medea's sister, and herself withdraws from the action.

This extinction of the go-between was a simple, but a great, achievement. What Terpander is said to have done for the lyric by the discovery of the octave; what Aeschylus did for the drama by the introduction of a second actor; what Aristophanes did for Comedy by the rejection of the Megarian farce—no less was done for romance by Apollonius in this purifying of the conventional form. Through the medium of the *Argonautica*, Greek romance was elevated to the epic in an atmosphere of purity, dignity, and wholesomeness, which the greater Vergil, greater in much else but inferior in this, would have done well to emulate.

It is not within the scope of this introduction to analyse at greater length the processes by which the character of Medea is developed; the third book of itself should make these evident to the reader. There is an impressiveness in the strangely modern tone of the whole treatment, and the loss is indeed ours if we fail to appreciate its signal merits. The fault is as much in ourselves as in Apollonius, if the blatant pedantry of occasional passages can blind us to the insight and daring of a pioneer, who took a legend with all the limitations of earlier tradition, with all the hindrances of familiarity and famous predecessors, with all the conventions inherited and respected by an age in which the spirit of creative literature was all but dead, and yet by the infusion of a new romantic spirit made the dry bones live.

(d) CALLIMACHUS AND THE *ARGONAUTICA*

The enquiry thus ends where it began, with the crucial problem of the *Argonautica*, and of Alexandrine literature in general, the relations of Apollonius and Callimachus. It is more than doubtful if there is real authority for referring to epic poems in general, and to the *Argonautica* in particular, the famous statement of Callimachus that "a great book was a great evil[1]"; this may be no more than the petulant comment of a librarian on the inconvenient size of a papyrus roll. There would seem to be some reference to Apollonius in the final lines of Callimachus' *Hymn to Apollo*[2]; but little can be founded on the assumed resemblance in the *Argonautica*[3], and it is dangerous to take too seriously the comment of a scholiast that the passage was directed against those who had mocked at the inability of Callimachus to compose a large poem, and so finally drove him to the composition of the *Hecale*[4].

It is reported[5] that Apollonius, while still a youth, recited his poem at Alexandria, and was received with such derision that he retired to Rhodes. There, in the more congenial atmosphere of a school which was famous for its studies in rhetoric, and which had produced among others the epic poet Antagoras, he gave with great success a recitation of his poem in a revised form. From Rhodes he returned[6], as is now known also from an independent source[7], to assume the office of Librarian at Alexandria, where a final recitation of the revised work was received with applause by a community which had derided its earlier form.

So far our authorities serve us, but now we come to the parting of the ways. We can support the view that the day of the great epic was past, pointing to the tendency of the times to shorter and more polished works, to the Alexandrine

---

[1] Ath. 2. 72 A. Καλλίμαχος ὁ γραμματικὸς τὸ μέγα βιβλίον ἴσον ἔλεγεν εἶναι τῷ μεγάλῳ κακῷ.

[2] 105 f. [3] 3. 932 and note *ad loc.* [4] On Call. *H. Ap.* 106, cf. supr. p. xxi.

[5] First Life in scholia of *Codex Laurentianus.*

[6] Second Life *ib.*, and Suidas, *s.v.* Ἀπολλώνιος. [7] v. supr. p. xi.

respect for Homer, and to the many shortcomings of the *Argonautica* in comparison with the Homeric poems. We can imagine a conceited youth of eighteen years, a pedant before his time, obstinately refusing to accept the verdict of his peers, angrily retiring to a more congenial environment, and there polishing up his slighted masterpiece with such effect that a second edition, well received at Rhodes, made the pendulum of time swing so quickly back at Alexandria, that the critics who had once denounced him as a feeble imitator of Homer were loud in acclaiming him as a worthy successor to the great master. This we may believe, and in so doing join the side of the big battalions.

But an appreciation of the literary tendencies of this age can help us to see the matter in a more reasonable light. We can imagine a youth of eighteen, fired alike with the spirit of Homer and the glamour of romance, determined to fuse these hitherto separate elements into one harmonious whole. We can picture the startled indignation of his learned audience, on hearing the instrument of the great Homer tuned to a strain thought proper only to the vulgar stage. We can imagine the derision which would greet the fumbling efforts of a raw youth in this new and dangerous medium, the conviction of the author that he was right, and a revision of his poem in a self-imposed exile with as much determination as Vergil spent in polishing up the *Georgics*. We can picture him in the Library at Rhodes, surrounded by textbooks and works of reference, lavishing the resources of pedantry on the narratives of the voyage, sweetening the romantic pill to the pedestrian taste of his critics. We can, finally, imagine these same critics, less opposed with the lapse of time to a form which they had once stigmatised as an impudent innovation, willing now to receive with approbation the maturer work of one whose genius they had formerly been unable to appreciate.

The careful reader of the *Argonautica* cannot fail to notice that the whole tone of the third book is different from that of the other three; the style is more fluent, the narrative runs more easily, and acts of wilful pedantry are far less frequent. On the one hand, it is tempting to infer that the writing of the third book was to Apollonius the more congenial task, as seeming to offer a fuller scope to his own peculiar abilities.

On the other hand, in the form which has come down to us the third book can hardly be in any great degree the work of a raw youth, for the psychology which it reveals is of too suggestively mature a character. Light would be thrown on the darkest problems of Alexandrine literature, if we could but be sure that the opposition to the *Argonautica* was caused only technically by the crude immaturity of a youthful experiment in the forbidden department of epic composition, and actually by the adaptation of the epic to romance. But it must be borne in mind that this is no more than a theory[1], which, though it accords with existing evidence, is based purely on speculation and inference. Yet it may be that some day the turn of a spade will reveal conclusive evidence in its support; ἄπανθ' ὁ μακρὸς κἀναρίθμητος χρόνος Φύει τ' ἄδηλα καὶ φανέντα κρύπτεται, Κοὐκ ἔστ' ἄελπτον οὐδέν.

The ancient critics[2], Quintilian and Longinus, realised that a direct comparison of the *Argonautica* with the Homeric poems could only be made through a misunderstanding of the style and aim of our poet; for Homer is unrivalled in the *genus grande dicendi*, while Apollonius conforms to the *genus medium*. But Apollonius was appreciated at Rome, and the Latin poets, more especially Catullus, Propertius and Ovid, were thoroughly familiar with his poem, and reproduce its better parts with almost monotonous frequency. Above all Vergil, whose genius surely might have freed him from dependence on his predecessors, deliberately imitates Apollonius, and that so closely that the text of a simile in this book can actually be restored from the version in the *Aeneid*[3]. But modern critics have set the fashion of disparaging this poet, and of admitting his merits only in so far as they can be shewn to be inferior to those of Homer or Vergil. It is the purpose of this edition of the third book to make the best part of the *Argonautica* more accessible to the student of the classics, to put the evidence before him from a less conventional point of view, and to stimulate him to form his own judgment of a work which is unique of its kind, and which has long been in exile from its proper place among the masterpieces of ancient Greek literature.

[1] Cf. E. A. Barber in *The Hellenistic Age*, p. 55.
[2] Mooney's introd. pp. 41 f. [3] *Arg.* 3. 756.

BIBLIOGRAPHY.

1. MSS., SCHOLIA, EDITIONS AND TRANSLATIONS.

The authorities for the text of the *Argonautica* are as follows :

(*a*) MANUSCRIPTS.

10th cent. Laurentianus XXXII, 9, in the Laurentian Library at Florence, containing also the plays of Aeschylus and Sophocles.

13th cent. Vaticanus 280, in the Palatine Library.

Guelferbytanus, at Wolfenbüttel.

Laurentianus XXXII, 16, transcribed from a common archetype with G.

15th–16th cent. 22 MSS. of less immediate value[1].

(*b*) PAPYRI.

In addition to these 26 MSS., there are five papyrus fragments of value for Book 3 :

1. *Ox. Pap.* 6, 874, early 3rd cent., lines 263–273.
2.   „ „   4, 690,   „   „   „   727–745.
3.   „ „   4, 691, 3rd or earlier,   „   908–914.
4.   „ „   10, 1243, 2nd cent.,   „   1055–1063.

These confirm Stephanus' μετά against κατά of the MSS. in 909, Porson's ναυτίλοι for ναῦται in 745, omit with the MSS. line 739 which is quoted by the schol. Flor., and indicate a distinct difference of reading in 269.

5. *Stras. Pap.* 173, 8th–9th cent., containing fragments of 145–161 ; for its bearing on l. 158, v. crit. appendix p. 138.

SCHOLIA.

There are two sets of scholia on the *Argonautica*, generally known as the Florentine and the Parisian. The former were first published with the *editio princeps* of the poem in 1496, the latter were found in a 15th cent. MS., and first published in 1813, in Schaefer's revision of Brunck's edition. Both sets have a common source in the scholia contained in L[2].

EDITIONS AND TRANSLATIONS.

The requirements of the average reader should be amply satisfied by the following[3]:

1. *The Argonautica of Apollonius Rhodius*, edited with Introduction and Commentary by George W. Mooney, M.A. (Dublin University Press, 1912).

2. *Apollonius Rhodius, The Argonautica*, with an English translation by R. C. Seaton, M.A. (Heinemann, Loeb Series, 1912, reprinted 1919).

[1] For a list of these, v. Mooney, introd. p. 53.

[2] For a discussion of the scholia, and for an estimate of their value, v. *ib.* pp. 56–60.

[3] For an exhaustive list, v. *ib.* pp. 61–64; add to translations a free version of Book 3 by the Rev. J. Ekins, London, 1771, entitled *The Loves of Jason and Medea.*

2. LIST OF BOOKS.

A bibliography of the *Argonautica*, if not strictly limited in scope, would be almost unlimited in length; the following is a somewhat arbitrary classification of the books which seemed to have a positive value in the preparation of this edition.

(a) ALEXANDRINE LITERATURE.

BARBER, E. A. and others. *The Hellenistic Age.* Cambridge, 1923.
COUAT, AUG. *La Poésie Alexandrine sous les trois premiers Ptolémées.* Paris, 1882.
MACKAIL, J. W. *Lectures on Greek Poetry*, esp. pp. 177 f. London, 1911.
POWELL, J. U., and BARBER, E. A. *New Chapters in Greek Literature.* Oxford, 1921.
ROHDE, E. *Die griechische Roman (die erotische Erzählung der hellenistischen Dichter).* Leipzig, 1900.
SUSEMIHL, F. *Geschichte der griechischen Litteratur in aer Alexandrinerzeit.* Leipzig, 1891.
TARN, W. W. *Hellenistic Civilisation.* London, 1927.
WILAMOWITZ-MÖLLENDORF, U. VON. *Hellenistische Dichtung in der Zeit des Kallimachos.* Berlin, 1924.

(b) LITERARY CRITICISM OF APOLLONIUS.

BALFOORT, D. *De Apollonii Rhodii laudibus poeticis.* Trajecti ad Rhenum, 1823.
HÉMARDINQUER, M. *De Apollonii Rhodii Argonauticis.* Paris, 1872.
MIRMONT, H. DE LA VILLE DE. *Apollonius de Rhodes et Virgile.* Paris, 1894.
MOLTZER, M. N. J. *De Apollonii Rhodii et Valerii Flacci Argonauticis.* Trajecti ad Rhenum, 1891.
NABER, S. A. In *Mnemosyne* 34 (1906), pp. 1–39.
SONNENBURG, P. E. *Zur Würdigung des Apollonius von Rhodes* in *Neue Jahrbücher* 33 (1909), 713–723.
WEICHERT, I. A. *Über das Leben und Gedicht des Apollonius von Rhodes.* Meissen, 1821.
WILAMOWITZ-MÖLLENDORF, U. VON. *op. cit.*, Vol. 2, pp. 165–256.

(c) MYTHOLOGY AND SOURCES.

BACON, J. R. *The Voyage of the Argonauts.* London, 1925.
JESSEN, O. *Prolegomena in catalogum Argonautarum.* Berlin, 1889.
KNORR, A. *De Apollonii Rhodii Argonautarum Fontibus Quaestiones Selectae.* Leipzig, 1902.
MEULI, K. *Odyssee und Argonautika.* Berlin, 1921.
PYL, C. T. *De Medeae Fabula.* Berlin, 1851.
RADERMACHER, L. *Das Jenseits im Mythos der Hellenen.* Bonn, 1903.
ROBERT, C. [PRELLER]. *Die griechische Heldensage* (pp. 758–877, *Die Argonautensage*). Berlin, 1921.

(*d*) GEOGRAPHY.

WALTHER, R. *De Apollonii Rhodii Argonauticorum Rebus Geographicis.* Halis Saxonum, 1890.

(*e*) GRAMMAR, VOCABULARY, ETC.

BOESCH, G. *De Apollonii Rhodii Elocutione.* Göttingen, 1908.

GOODWIN, C. J. *Apollonius Rhodius, His Figures, Syntax and Vocabulary.* Baltimore, 1891.

HART, A. H. *Observationes Criticae in Apollonium Rhodium.* Berlin, 1863.

LINSENBARTH, O. *De Apollonii Rhodii Casuum Syntaxi Comparato Usu Homerico.* Leipzig, 1888.

MERKEL, R. *Prolegomena to editio major of Argonautica.* Leipzig, 1854.

OSWALD, M. F. *The Prepositions of Apollonius Rhodius.* 1875.

PLATT, A. *On Apollonius Rhodius.* In *Journal of Philology*, 65 (1913), pp. 1–53.

   „   „   *Apollonius Again. ib.* 67 (1915), pp. 129–141.

   „   „   *Apollonius III. ib.* 69 (1919), pp. 72–85.

RZACH, A. *Grammatische Studien zu Apollonius Rhodius.* Vienna, 1878.

(*f*) TEXT.

DAMSTE, O. *Adversaria ad Apollonii Rhodii Argonautica.* Rotterdam, 1922.

KOECHLY, H. *Emendationes Apollonianae.* Turici, 1850.

WILAMOWITZ-MÖLLENDORF. *op. cit.*, Vol. 2, pp. 250–251.

ZIEGLER, CHR. *Observationes in Apollonii Rhodii Argonautica.* Stuttgart, 1846.

(*g*) APOLLONIUS AND CALLIMACHUS.

COUAT, AUG. *La Querelle de Callimaque et d'Apollonius de Rhodes.* Paris, 1878.

SMILEY, M. T. *The Quarrel between Callimachus and Apollonius.* In *Hermathena*, 17 (1913), pp. 280–294.

(*h*) ARCHAEOLOGY.

PECHTIES, E. *Quaestiones Philologicae de Apollonii Rhodii Argonauticis.* Regimonti, 1912.

SIGLA.

G	= Codex Guelferbytanus.
L	= Codex Laurentianus xxxii, 9.
L 16	= Codex Laurentianus xxxii, 16.
Pariss.	= Codices quinque Parisini.
Vatt.	= Codices quattuor Vaticani.
Vind.	= Codex Vindobonensis.
Vrat.	= Codex Vratislavensis.
Schol.	= Scholia Laurentiana.
Schol. Flor.	= Scholia Florentina.
Schol. Par.	= Scholia Parisina.

ΑΠΟΛΛΩΝΙΟΥ ΡΟΔΙΟΥ

ΑΡΓΟΝΑΥΤΙΚΩΝ Γ

Εἰ δ' ἄγε νῦν, Ἐρατώ, παρά θ' ἵστασο, καί μοι ἔνισπε,
ἔνθεν ὅπως ἐς Ἰωλκὸν ἀνήγαγε κῶας Ἰήσων
Μηδείης ὑπ' ἔρωτι. σὺ γὰρ καὶ Κύπριδος αἶσαν
ἔμμορες, ἀδμῆτας δὲ τεοῖς μελεδήμασι θέλγεις
παρθενικάς· τῷ καί τοι ἐπήρατον οὔνομ' ἀνῆπται.   5
Ὡς οἱ μὲν πυκινοῖσιν ἀνωίστως δονάκεσσιν

1 ἔνισπες Merkel.   4 ἄμμορες cum gl. ἀπέτυχες G.   5 τοι LG : οἱ Vatt. tres,
Paris. unus, Hoelzlin, Wellauer, reiecit Brunck.

1–5. Invocation of Erato as patroness of love affairs.

1. **Ἐρατώ.** Conventional invocation of a Muse, cf. that of Clio in Val. Flacc. *Argon.* 3. 16, 'tibi enim superum data, virgo, facultas Nosse animum rerumque vias.' Erato first appears as a Muse in the catalogue in Hes. *Th.* 78–9, and as patroness of love affairs in Plat. *Phaedrus* 259 C, τῇ δὲ Ἐρατοῖ τοὺς ἐν τοῖς ἐρωτικοῖς (*sc.* τετιμηκότας αὐτὴν ἀπαγγέλλοντες). The invocation is repeated at the beginning of Book 4 of the *Argonautica*, and is imitated, though less appropriately, in Verg. *Aen.* 7. 37. The typically Alexandrine derivation from ἐπήρατος is copied by Ovid. *Ars Amat.* 2. 16, 'Erato, nam tu nomen amoris habes.'

παρά θ' ἵστασο. Apollonius here differs from Zenodotus and Aristarchus, whom the scholia on *Il.* 10. 291 shew to have read παρίσταο, and not παρίστασο. **ἔνισπε**, 'tell me.' For Merkel's ἔνισπες, v. crit. appendix, p. 137.

2. **ἔνθεν,** *i.e.* from Colchis. The preceding book dealt with the adventures in the Euxine, and ended with the arrival of the Argonauts in Colchis itself. **Ἰωλκόν.** This form is used also infr. 89, 1109, 1135. Ἰαωλκός, the sole Homeric form, is in 1091, 1114. **ἀνήγαγε**, 'brought back the Fleece.' This recalls Mimnermus (*frag.* 11 Bergk), οὐδέ κοτ' ἂν μέγα κῶας ἀνήγαγεν αὐτὸς Ἰήσων.

3. **ἔρωτι.** Here only in this book as an ordinary substantive, cf. *Arg.* 4. 213, 569; elsewhere it refers to Eros in person, infr. 120, etc. For the plural Ἔρωτες, v. n. 452.

4. **ἔμμορες.** 'Thou dost share.' Apollonius has made the mistake of taking the Homeric ἔμμορε as an aorist, and not as a perfect, for which v. Curtius, *Greek Verb*, 2. 130. From this have arisen several false perfect forms, like 1. 646 μεμόρηται, infr. 1130 μεμορμένον, and others in late Greek.

μελεδήμασι, 'cares of love,' as in 471, 752. Like Homer, Apollonius uses this word only in the plural.

5. **παρθενικάς,** 'unwedded maidens,' a poetical equivalent of παρθένος, used from Homer onwards. Both Homer and Ap. use the termination -ικός only of proper names and nouns, Πελασγικός, ὀρφανικός, etc. Apart from proper names, Ap. uses only this noun, which also occurs as an adjective in 1. 791, 4. 909, on the analogy of παρθενικῇ νεήνιδι in *Od.* 7. 20. **τοι.** Hoelzlin and Wellauer read οἱ on the authority of inferior MSS., comparing *Arg.* 1. 893, ῥηιδίως δ' ἂν ἑοῖ καὶ ἀπείρονα λαὸν ἀγείραις, *i.e.* σαυτῷ. Brunck rightly rejects it. Ap. uses ἑοῖ of all three persons (v. n. 26), but in the 1st and 2nd it is always reflexive, though not necessarily in the 3rd, *e.g.* 37 infr.

ἐπήρατον, 'a name that tells of love.' Homer uses this only of things and places, Hesiod only of the form and voice of goddesses. It is first of persons in Aesch. *Eum.* 958, νεανίδων τ' ἐπηράτων, cf. infr. 1099, παρθενικὴν ἐπήρατον.

6–35. Here and Athene plan to aid Jason, and decide to appeal for help to Cypris.

6. **ἀνωίστως.** ἀνυπονοήτως schol., 'unsuspected.' Ap. uses both adj. and adv. with two distinct meanings: (1) 'un-

μίμνον ἀριστῆες λελοχημένοι· αἱ δ' ἐνόησαν
"Ηρη 'Αθηναίη τε, Διὸς δ' αὐτοῖο καὶ ἄλλων
ἀθανάτων ἀπονόσφι θεῶν θάλαμόνδε κιοῦσαι
βούλευον· πείραζε δ' 'Αθηναίην πάρος "Ηρη·   10
'Αὐτὴ νῦν προτέρη, θύγατερ Διός, ἄρχεο βουλῆς.
τί χρέος; ἠὲ δόλον τινὰ μήσεαι, ᾧ κεν ἑλόντες
χρύσεον Αἰήταο μεθ' 'Ελλάδα κῶας ἄγοιντο,
ἦ καὶ τόνγ' ἐπέεσσι παραιφάμενοι πεπίθοιεν

12 τίνα Platt.   14 ἠ Platt: ἦ codd. edd.

expected,' in 1.680, 4. 1661, cf. infr. 670, μῦθον ἀνώιστον, and (2) 'mysterious, unknown,' as here and infr. 800, cf. 4. 255, ἀνώιστος δ' ἐτέτυκτο Πᾶσιν ὁμῶς (sc. πλόος). Homer uses it as adj. only, and in the former sense, only in Il. 21. 39, τῷ δ' ἄρ' ἀνώιστον κακὸν ἤλυθε δῖος 'Αχιλλεύς: for adv. he uses ἀνωιστί, Od. 4. 92, which is not in Ap.

δονάκεσσιν, i.e. the reedbeds of the δάσκιον ἕλος of the Phasis, the 'shady backwater' in which the heroes spent the night of their arrival in Colchis, as explained at the end of the preceding book, Arg. 2. 1283 f.

8. "Ηρη 'Αθηναίη τε. For Here's particular interest in Jason, v. infr. 66. Athene, the patroness of shipbuilding in Homer, Il. 15. 412, is naturally found in connection with the Argo. In the earliest account of the voyage, Od. 12. 69, it was by grace of Here, the patroness of Jason, that the Argo passed through the Planctae; Athene's close connection with the Argo is probably due to the influence of the Milesian colonists, who connected with the legend their foundations on the coast of the Euxine.

9. ἀπονόσφι, 'apart from.' Homer uses both as prep. c. gen., as here, and as adverb; for the latter, cf. infr. 911, and 4. 735, ἀπονόσφιν ἄλυξεν...δείματα, 'fled far away from the terrors.'

θάλαμόνδε. Ap. uses the locative -δε of persons also, v. n. 647. De Mirmont is undoubtedly right in explaining this as a private chamber in Here's own house, and not, with Dübner, as 'Jovis conclave in quo conveniunt dei'; obviously it is just such a place that she is most anxious to avoid.

10. πείραζε, 'made trial of.' Normally c. gen., as in 1. 495, πείραζεν ἀοιδῆς, cf. Od. 23. 114, πειράζειν ἐμέθεν. It is common in the N.T. c. acc. in the sense of 'tempt'; e.g. Matt. 4. 3, ὁ Πειράζων, the 'Tempter,' ib. 19. 3, προσῆλθον οἱ Φαρισαῖοι πειράζοντες αὐτόν, Acts 15. 10, τί πειράζετε τὸν Θεόν; In this sense, Homer uses πειρητίζω c. gen., as in Od. 14. 459, συβώτεω πειρητίζων. There is a late use, 'attack by disease,' as in Cic. Att. 16. 7, 8, πειράζεσθαι παραλύσει, like Lat. morbo tentari.

Vergil seems to have had this passage in mind at Aen. 4. 90 f., where, except that Athene does not appear, there is a similar scheme of Juno plotting with Venus to use the love of Dido for her own ends.

12. τί χρέος, 'what is to be done?' cf. Aesch. Ag. 85, τί χρέος, i.e. τί χρῆμα; in 108, 131, χρέος means 'affair,' κατὰ χρέος in 189 'in seemly fashion.' χρειώ means 'need' in 33, 52, 173, 'object' in 332; in 500 it is the same as χρέος.

τινά. 'Wilt thou devise some plan?' or leave them to talk Aeetes round. Platt's τίνα spoils the balance and coherence of the question; his ἠ for ἦ in 14 is an improvement.

13. ἄγοιντο. The optative in -ντο is un-Homeric; cf. ἄγοιντο again in 4. 102, 400, φράξοιντο infr. 826, ἵκοιντο, ναυτίλλοιντο and θηήσαιντο in 1. 823, 918, 986. Ap. has only four cases of the optative in -ατο, two of which are Homeric: βιῴατο 4. 1236 and Il. 11. 467, μνησαίατο 4. 841 and Il. 2. 492, ἀραροίατο, ἀνεχοίατο 1. 369, 1005.

14. παραιφάμενοι, 'exhorting,' a little stronger than 'addressing,' cf. 554, παραιφασίῃσι, 'exhortations.' Ap. uses both in the original sense, here particularly in contrast with δόλος: 'deceit' is a

μειλιχίοις; ἢ γὰρ ὅγ' ὑπερφίαλος πέλει αἰνῶς.　　15
ἔμπης δ' οὔτινα πεῖραν ἀποτρωπᾶσθαι ἔοικεν.'
*Ὣς φάτο· τὴν δὲ παρᾶσσον Ἀθηναίη προσέειπεν·
'Καὶ δ' αὐτὴν ἐμὲ τοῖα μετὰ φρεσὶν ὁρμαίνουσαν,
Ἥρη, ἀπηλεγέως ἐξείρεαι. ἀλλά τοι οὔπω
φράσσασθαι νοέω τοῦτον δόλον, ὅστις ὀνήσει　　20
θυμὸν ἀριστήων· πολέας δ' ἐπεδοίασα βουλάς.'

15 γὰρ ὅγ' Paris. unus : γὰρ ὁ μὲν LG : μὲν γὰρ vulg.　　17 παρᾶσσον LG :
παρ' ἄσσον vulg.　　21 πολλὰς Pariss., Brunck.

secondary development, as in *Od.* 19.
5–6, αὐτὰρ μνηστῆρας μαλακοῖς ἐπέεσσι
Πάρφασθαι. The question at issue here
arises also in *Or. Arg.* 769 f., whether
Jason should go alone to Aeetes, μειλιχίοις στέρξοι τε παραιφάμενος ἐπέεσσιν,
or the heroes go in a body and use
force.

15. **γὰρ ὅγ'**. This is the reading of a
single Paris MS.; L. and G. read γὰρ ὁ
μὲν, the rest μὲν γὰρ. These are all need-
less attempts to correct the metre, which
is that of *Il.* 1. 342, τοῖς ἄλλοις· ἢ γὰρ
ὅγ' ὀλοιῇσι φρεσὶ θύει.

ὑπερφίαλος, always in the *Arg.* in an
offensive sense, here 'arrogant.' Homer
applies it without sinister meaning to
anything of unusual size or importance,
as when Antinous uses it of his fellow-
suitors in *Od.* 21. 289, ὑπερφιάλοισι μεθ'
ἡμῖν Δαίνυσαι. The Homeric ὑπερφιά-
λως, which is not in Ap., is equally
free from any strict meaning of reproach.
ὑπέρβιος, on the other hand, is used by
Homer only in an offensive sense, cf.
583 infr.; Ap. uses it as 'mighty,' as
infr. 714, ὅρκος ὑπέρβιος, cf. Pind. *Ol.* 10.
15 (20), ὑπέρβιον Ἡρακλέα. ὑπερφίαλος is
derived probably from ὑπὲρ-φυ (φύω),
'overgrown,' rather than ὑπὲρ-φιάλη,
'more than full, running over.'

16. **ἀποτρωπᾶσθαι**, 'to turn away
anything of advantage that might be
tried.' Homeric frequentative of ἀπο-
τρέπω.

17. **παρᾶσσον**. An adv. peculiar to
Ap., used like παραυτίκα and παραχρῆμα.
Here in temporal sense, 'straightway,'
as in 1. 383, 2. 961, and probably 125
infr. The only example of a spatial
sense is 969 infr., where it means 'side
by side,' akin to the Homeric ἆσσον,
'nearer,' the comparative of ἄγχι.

19. **ἀπηλεγέως**, 'outright.' Homer
uses this only in the phrase ἀπηλεγέως
ἀποειπεῖν, *Od.* 1. 373, *Il.* 9. 309. Apollonius uses it freely with cognate verbs,
and also, in extension of the Homeric
use, with verbs of 'promising,' 501 infr.,
'enquiring,' 4. 1469, and 'making angry,'
4. 864, ἀπηλεγέως ἐχόλωσας. There is a
further extension in the use with μίμνεν
4. 689, and νίσσετο 1. 785.

21. **θυμὸν ἀριστήων**. This need mean
no more than 'aid the valiant heroes.'
Yet there is justification for the more
literal 'scheme to aid the courage of the
heroes,' for the poet has been so keen to
stress the magnitude of the dangers, that
he has frequently sacrificed character
to narrative, and shewn the party as
strangely lacking in courage in the face
of danger (v. Introd., p. xl). It is in
keeping with the consistent weakness
of Jason's character, that it is not till
line 1256 of this book that he acquires
'courage awful, unspeakable, dauntless,'
and even so it is under the influence of
magic drugs.

πολέας. It is unnecessary to read
πολλὰς of the Pariss. MSS. with Brunck,
against πολέας of L. If this is a *schema
Atticum*, it is supported by 1393 infr.,
τετρηχότα βῶλον, cf. Hes. *frag.* 75
Lehrs, ap. Favorinum 781. 20, δαΐζομέ-
νοιο πολῆος : if an Alexandrine feminine,
by Call. *H. Del.* 28, πολέες ἀοιδαί, *H.
Art.* 42, πολέας νύμφας. Resolved forms
of the plural of πολύς are masculine in
Homer, and feminine first in the Alexandrines; contrast the Homeric fem.
πουλύν and v. Leaf on *Il.* 5. 776.

ἐπεδοίασα, 'I have been in indecision
over.' Ap. has formed this compound
on the analogy of ἐνδοιάζω in Thuc. 1.
36. 1, etc., which in turn is founded on

'Η, καὶ ἐπ' οὔδεος αἴγε ποδῶν πάρος ὄμματ' ἔπηξαν,
ἄνδιχα πορφύρουσαι ἐνὶ σφίσιν· αὐτίκα δ' "Ηρη
τοῖον μητιόωσα παροιτέρη ἔκφατο μῦθον·
'Δεῦρ' ἴομεν μετὰ Κύπριν· ἐπιπλόμεναι δέ μιν ἄμφω   25
παιδὶ ἑῷ εἰπεῖν ὀτρύνομεν, αἴ κε πίθηται

26 ὀτρύνωμεν L.   πίθοιτο Brunck.

the Homeric ἐν δοιῇ (sc. ἐστί) of Il. 9.
230. He has assumed also a simple
verb δοιάζω, used four times: (λεύσσειν)
δοιάζοντο 4. 576, (βουλὰς) δοιάζεσκεν
infr. 819, δοάσσατο 770, δοάσσαι 955. This
δοάσσατο is distinct from the Homeric
δοάσσατο, 'seemed,' which is used only
impersonally in the phrase δοάσσατο
κέρδιον εἶναι, Il. 13. 458, etc., except
for Il. 23. 339, ὡς ἄν τοι πλήμνη γε
δοάσσεται ἄκρον ἱκέσθαι. The Homeric
verb is variously derived from δάω, root
διϝ, 'shine,' and δοιός, δοιός.

22. ἔπηξαν, 'fixed their eyes upon
the ground before their feet.' A typical
variant of the Homeric κατὰ χθονὸς
ὄμματα πήξας, Il. 3. 217, as are also
Arg. 1. 784, ἐπὶ χθονὸς ὄμματ' ἐρείσας,
and infr. 1022, κατ' οὔδεος ὄμματ' ἔρειδον.
With the latter two cf. Eur. Iph. Aul.
1123, εἰς γῆν δ' ἐρείσασ' ὄμμα.

23. ἄνδιχα, 'apart,' as in 2. 927,
ἄνδιχα...μῆρ' ἔφλεγον: it is also in the
Arg. as prep. c. gen., 1. 908, ἄνδιχα
τοῖο ἄνακτος. Homer uses it of division
into two, ἄνδιχα δάσασθαι, Il. 18. 511,
etc., cf. Arg. 2. 973 of a river, ῥέεθρα...
ἄνδιχα βάλλων. ἄνδιχα πορφύρουσαι here
recalls Il. 1. 189, διάνδιχα μερμήριξεν,
with which cf. Hes. Op. 13, διὰ δ' ἄνδιχα
θυμὸν ἔχουσι, and infr. 819. Ap. uses
διάνδιχα infr. 991, etc.; the meaning is
disputed in 1. 934, διάνδιχα νηὸς ἰούσης.

πορφύρουσαι, 'brooding anxiously
over,' as often in Ap., cf. Il. 21. 551,
πολλὰ δέ οἱ κραδίη πόρφυρε μένοντι.
Jebb on Soph. Ant. 20 points out that in
καλχαίνω the idea of colour precedes
that of trouble, while the converse holds
good in the case of πορφύρω. Thus ὡς
ὅτε πορφύρῃ πέλαγος in Il. 14. 16 ex-
presses 'heaving motion' rather than
colour; Ap. has reproduced this in 1.
935, δίνῃ πορφύροντα διήνυσαν Ἑλλήσ-
ποντον.

25. ἐπιπλόμεναι, schol. παραγενόμεναι
καὶ ἐπελθοῦσαι, 'let us approach her.'
This is used in earlier epic of things only,

as in Arg. 4. 670, 1. 465, 1. 1080, etc.,
of ἠώς, τάρβος and νύξ. It is used again
of persons infr. 127, where, as in 1. 465,
L. and S. exaggerate the meaning to
'attack.' περιπλομένας likewise in 1150
is merely 'surrounding,' as in Il. 18. 220,
ἄστυ περιπλομένων δηίων, and the recurrent περιπλομένων ἐνιαυτῶν. περιέπλεο in 130 is unique in the sense of
περιέρχεσθαι, 'overreach,' as in Hdt. 3.
4, σοφίῃ γάρ μιν περιῆλθεν.

26. Eros in the Argonautica is a com-
posite figure, the result of a long development. Homer does not personify
him at all, and Hesiod tells merely of
his birth from Chaos. Alcman speaks
of him as a child walking over the
flowers; Sappho makes him παῖς of
Aphrodite, and Simonides of Ares and
Aphrodite. Anacreon was the first to
give him wings.

ἑῷ. Apollonius uses this both as pronoun and adjective. Like Homer, he
uses it freely as adj. of the 3rd singular;
with Hes. Op. 58, Th. 71, he has it of
the 3rd pl., as infr. 1375; it is used of
the 1st pl. in 4. 203, παῖδας ἐούς...
ἴσχομεν, of the 2nd sing. in 140, 1041 of
this book, and of the 1st sing. in 2. 226,
αὐτὸς ἐὸν λελάθοιμι νόον. The occasional
use for ἐμός and σός shews his approval
of its introduction in that sense into the
text of Homer by Zenodotus.

As pronoun, Homer uses it only of
the 3rd sing.; the plural ἕ is first in H.
Hom. Aphr. 267, τεμένη δέ ἑ κικλή-
σκουσιν. Ap. uses it as reflexive pronoun
in the forms εἷο, ἑοῦ, ἑοῖο, ἑοῖ with or
without αὐτῷ; of the 1st person, 99 infr.
ἑοῖ αὐτῇ and 2. 635 εἷο, of the 2nd pers.
1043 οἷ and 1. 893 ἑοῖ; of the 3rd, infr.
1065, 1335 ἑοῖο. Later poets use it as
the reflexive of any form or number.

σφέτερος, in its proper sense as adj.
of the 3rd pl., is in Ap. only in 1. 530,
4. 1294. It is used for ἡμέτερος in 4.
1353, for ὑμέτερος in 4. 1327, and for ἑός
infr. 186, 302, etc.; the latter two uses

κούρην Αἰήτεω πολυφάρμακον οἷσι βέλεσσιν
θέλξαι ὀιστεύσας ἐπ' Ἰήσονι. τὸν δ' ἂν ὀίω
κείνης ἐννεσίῃσιν ἐς Ἑλλάδα κῶας ἀνάξειν.'
*Ὣς ἄρ' ἔφη· πυκινὴ δὲ συνεύαδε μῆτις Ἀθήνη,   30
καί μιν ἔπειτ' ἐξαῦτις ἀμείβετο μειλιχίοισιν·
'"Ηρη, νήιδα μέν με πατὴρ τέκε τοῖο βολάων,
οὐδέ τινα χρειὼ θελκτήριον οἶδα Πόθοιο.

33 θελκτηρίου Damste.   Πόθοιο scripsi: πόθοιο codd.

are Hesiodic. Theocritus uses it for ἐμός
and σός in *Id.* 25. 163, 22. 67.

σφίσιν, which seems to be 2nd plural
in *Il.* 10. 398, is 1st plural infr. 909, 2.
1278. It is used for ἀλλήλοις in 2. 128,
where the scholiast comments that it
is a common mistake of post-Homeric
writers; cf. with this, 1023 infr., and 4.
1290, χεροῖν σφέας ἀμφιβαλόντες (*i.e.*
ἀλλήλους), and Hes. *Sc.* 403, ἀλλήλοις
κοτέοντες ἐπὶ σφέας ὁρμήσωσι.

ὀτρύνομεν. Mooney refers to this as
the only instance in the poem of a
subjunctive formed with a short vowel
from a non-sigmatic aorist, and cites
Od. 24. 89, ὅτε κέν ποτ'...Ζώννυνταί τε
νέοι καὶ ἐπεντύνονται ἄεθλα. But Seaton
shews (*Class. Rev.* 1914, 18a) that the
short vowel in Homer is peculiar, not
only to the subj. of sigmatic aorists, but
to the subj. of non-thematic tenses.
ὀτρύνομεν as subj. of non-thematic aor.
ὤτρυνα is in *Od.* 1. 85, 16. 355, *Il.* 9.
165 ; likewise ἐπεντύνονται is the regular
form of the aor. subj. The difficulty in
the latter case is that the subj. in a subordinate clause referring to past time is
not properly Homeric (Munro, *H. G.*
81. 298).

αἴ κε. Brunck consistently alters the
subj. in this construction to the optative,
as infr. 909, εἴ κεν ὀπάσσῃ, on the lines
of 4. 417, εἴ κε...πεπίθοιμι : other editors,
however, rightly follow the MSS. εἴ κε
c. opt., where it does occur, is a syn-
tactical vagary, spuriously formed from
ἄν c. opt. *in apodosi* : cf. 535, μνησάμεθα
...εἴ κε δύναιτο, and contrast 1. 623,
ἦκε...αἴ κε φύγῃ.

27. πολυφάρμακον, 'sorceress.' Used
of Circe in *Od.* 10. 276, Κίρκης...πολυ-
φαρμάκου : cf. of Medea in Pind. *Pyth.*
4. 233, παμφαρμάκου ξείνης. Homer uses
it also of physicians in *Il.* 16. 28, ἰητροὶ

πολυφάρμακοι, 'skilled in the use of
drugs.'

28. θέλξαι, 'charm.' Cf. 4 and 86 of
this book, and Eur. *Bacc.* 404, θελξί-
φρονες...'Έρωτες. Homer uses it of
Hermes, *Il.* 24. 343, of Circe, *Od.* 10.
291, etc. In early Greek, it properly
implies the use of magic, but later, as
with the word 'charm' in English, the
meaning becomes more general.

ἐπί. Depends on θέλξαι, *i.e.* 'charm
with love for Jason.'

29. ἐννεσίῃσιν, *lit.* 'suggestions,' from
ἐνίημι. It is used by Homer and Hesiod,
and is common in Ap., *e.g.* 478, 818,
942, 1364 in this book alone.

30. συνεύαδε, 'pleased Athene also.'
The aorist of the simple verb, which is
Homeric, is infr. 1083; the compound,
from the obsolete συνανδάνω, is found
only in late Greek, cf. Pseudo-Phocylides
178, οὐδ' αὐτοῖς θήρεσσι συνεύαδον ἄρσενες
εὐναί.

32. νήιδα, 'ignorant of.' This acc. is
found in *Il.* 7. 198; νῆιν 130 infr., like
πάϊν 4. 697, is by false analogy, as the
root is ἰδ-. Cf. Call. *Aitia* (*Ox. Pap.*
11. 1362, l. 32), (ναυτι)-λίης εἰ νῆιν
ἔ(χεις βίον).

τέκε, 'gave me being.' Used freely of
the father as well as the mother, cf.
1087 infr., Soph. *O.C.* 1108, τῷ τεκόντι,
Hes. *Th.* 208, Aesch. *Ch.* 690, τὸν
τεκόντα.

τοῖο, *i.e.* 'Έρωτος. For the sentiment,
cf. of Athene in H. Hom. *Aphr.* 9, οὐ
γάρ οἱ εὔαδεν ἔργα πολυχρύσου Ἀφροδίτης.

33. χρειώ, 'need,' as in 52, 173, v. n.
12. χρειὼ οἶδα, 'I feel a need,' is not
a violent extension of χάριν οἶδα, 'I
acknowledge a sense of favour.'

θελκτήριον. Contrast Athen. 220 F (5.
63), πόθων θελγήτρα, Eur. *Hipp.* 509,
φίλτρα...θελκτήρια 'Έρωτος. In English,

εἰ δέ σοι αὐτῇ μῦθος ἐφανδάνει, ἤ τ' ἂν ἔγωγε
ἐσποίμην· σὺ δέ κεν φαίης ἔπος ἀντιόωσα.'   35
'Ἦ, καὶ ἀναΐξασαι ἐπὶ μέγα δῶμα νέοντο
Κύπριδος, ὅ ῥά τέ οἱ δεῖμεν πόσις ἀμφιγυήεις,
ὁππότε μιν τὰ πρῶτα παραὶ Διὸς ἦγεν ἄκοιτιν.
ἔρκεα δ' εἰσελθοῦσαι ὑπ' αἰθούσῃ θαλάμοιο
ἔσταν, ἵν' ἐντύνεσκε θεὰ λέχος Ἡφαίστοιο.   40

the adj. would agree with πόθοιο. On the text, and for Πόθοιο rather than πόθοιο, v. crit. appendix, p. 137.

34. ἐφανδάνει, 'pleases.' Homeric, as is also infr. 171, ἐπιανδάνει.

35. ἀντιόωσα, 'on meeting her.' Both gen. and dat., which Ap. uses frequently with this verb (588, 1337, etc.), are Homeric in this sense. In the sense of 'beseech,' he uses acc. (643, 694, 717), or gen. (1. 703); the latter instance is translated by some as 'meet.' ἀντιάζω is used in the sense of 'beseech' in tragedy, likewise ἄντομαι, which is used by Homer, in the *Iliad* only, of 'meeting in battle'; Ap. uses the original sense, *e.g.* 1. 771, the tragic in 77, 149, 391 of this book.

36–110. Cypris is discovered at her toilet. Here explains the situation, and Cypris promises the assistance of Eros.

36. ἀναΐξασαι, 'rising quickly up.' Always used of rapid or impulsive movement, cf. *Il.* 3. 216, ὅτε ἀναΐξειεν, 'whenever he started up to speak,' and of Thetis in *Arg.* 4. 842, ἀναΐξασα κατ' αἰθέρος ἔμπεσε δίναις Κυανέου πόντοιο.

37. ἀμφιγυήεις. This is usually a substantive in Homer; Ap. may have had in mind *Il.* 14. 239, Ἥφαιστος...ἐμὸς παῖς ἀμφιγυήεις, where an Alexandrine would have omitted the proper name and used the *epitheton ornans* adjectivally in a periphrasis. The word is used always of Hephaestus, and is variously explained: (1) 'lame in both feet,' from the Alexandrine γυιός, 'lame,' which would be a violation of the rule that adjectives in -εις are formed only from nouns. (2) 'with a crooked limb on either side,' from an assumed γύη, 'crook.' (3) 'strong in both arms,' on the assumption that γυῖα refers properly to the hands, as in 63 infr., cf. ἐγγύη, ἐγγυαλίζω; the latter is probably correct.

38. ἄκοιτιν. In *Il.* 18. 383, the wife of Hephaestus is Charis, but in Hes. *Th.* 945, Aglaia. This is in accordance with *Od.* 8. 266 f.: Apollonius is dealing with the period before the Trojan war, and avoids reference to the post-Argonautic complications of this couple. It was for the sake of Hephaestus that Aphrodite was anxious to repopulate Lemnos after the massacre, in *Arg.* 1. 851.

39. ἔρκεα. The Homeric ἔρκος was the wall enclosing the courtyard, αὐλή, and could be used for the courtyard as well, cf. 215 infr.

αἰθούσῃ, 'portico,' running from either side of the entrance, and so called because it lay open to the sun; αἴθειν (cf. 1304), αἶθος) is used especially of the Sun and his horses, expressive of dazzling light or speed. The house of Aphrodite is simpler than the Homeric type; there is no πρόδομος, as infr. 278, and the chamber opens directly on to the colonnade.

40. ἐντύνεσκε, 'was wont to prepare,' a euphemism for 'sharing,' cf. Eur. *Supp.* 55, φίλα ποιησαμένα λέκτρα πόσει σῷ, *Hel.* 59, λέκτρ' ὑποστρώσω τινί, Theoc. *Id.* 6. 33, στορεσεῖν καλὰ δέμνια. Similarly λέχος ἀντιόωσαν in *Il.* 1. 31 must be interpreted as εὐτρεπίζουσαν, not literally 'sharing,' which would take a direct genitive. The meaning develops from such phrases as *Od.* 24. 56, παιδὸς τεθνηότος ἀντιόωσα, 'coming to attend upon her son'; the acc. is more natural than the gen. with reference to a thing. Similarly with πορσύνω: it means ηὐτρέπιζε in *Od.* 3. 403, τῷ δ' ἄλοχος δέσποινα λέχος πόρσυνε καὶ εὐνήν, but the preposition in *Od.* 7. 347 shews that it involves 'sharing' as well, πὰρ δὲ γυνὴ δέσποινα λέχος πόρσυνε καὶ εὐνήν: cf. 840 infr., and Jason's promise to Medea infr. 1128–9.

ἀλλ' ὁ μὲν ἐς χαλκεῶνα καὶ ἄκμονας ἦρι βεβήκει,
νήσοιο πλαγκτῆς εὐρὺν μυχόν, ᾧ ἔνι πάντα
δαίδαλα χάλκευεν ῥιπῇ πυρός· ἡ δ' ἄρα μούνη
ἧστο δόμῳ δινωτὸν ἀνὰ θρόνον, ἄντα θυράων.
λευκοῖσιν δ' ἑκάτερθε κόμας ἐπιειμένη ὤμοις   45
κόσμει χρυσείῃ διὰ κερκίδι, μέλλε δὲ μακροὺς

42 πλωτῆς schol. Flor.

41. χαλκεῶνα, 'forge.' This is a reminiscence of *Od.* 8. 273, where Hephaestus, on hearing of the conduct of Aphrodite, βῆ ῥ' ἴμεν ἐς χαλκεῶνα.

42. νήσοιο. In *Il.* 18. 369 f., this forge is in Heaven, in *Od.* 8. 283, in Lemnos; later writers found it in one of the seven volcanic islands of Aeolus off the west coast of Italy (cf. *Arg.* 4. 928, 956), usually Hiera, but Lipara according to Call. *H. Art.* 47, νήσῳ ἐνὶ Λιπάρῃ...ἐπ' ἄκμοσιν Ἡφαίστοιο. Ap. combines all three versions: Hephaestus has his home in Heaven, his forge in a western isle, but still has a connection with Lemnos.

πλαγκτῆς. Not from πλήσσω, like the Symplegades, but 'wandering,' like the rocks which are passed on the return; these are properly distinct from the 'clashing' rocks, but tended to be confused with them. The trouble with the latter is to get *through*, with the former, as their course is uncertain, to get *round*. Delos, according to legend, was originally such a 'wandering' isle. νήσοιο πλωτῆς of the Florentine scholia recalls the description of the island of Aeolus in *Od.* 10. 3, πλωτῇ ἐνὶ νήσῳ, but it is more likely that Apollonius would vary the Homeric phrase.

43. δαίδαλα, 'ingenious things.' This is based on *Il.* 18. 400, where Hephaestus says of himself χάλκευον δαίδαλα πολλὰ Ἐν σπῆι γλαφυρῷ. In the *Iliad*, he makes tripods with ears and wheels which move of their own accord, golden statues endowed with intelligence, voice, and strength to act as servants, and also houses for the gods as in 37 supr.; in the *Odyssey*, he makes dogs to guard the palace of Aeetes, fountains for Calypso, etc. He also made the brazen bulls of Aeetes, and, as appears in 137 infr., he was not above making toys for his son Eros.

44. δινωτόν, cf. the δινωτὸν σάκος of Aeetes in 4. 222. The precise meaning

is uncertain. In *Od.* 19. 55, κλισίην... Δινωτὴν ἐλέφαντι καὶ ἀργύρῳ, and 23. 200, δαιδάλλων χρυσῷ τε καὶ ἀργύρῳ ἠδ' ἐλέφαντι, some consider the reference to be to rounded legs of ivory decorated with silver, others to rounded legs of wood decorated with both ivory and silver. The latter is probably correct; in any case, Apollonius seems to have believed that δινωτός in Homer meant both *round* and *inlaid*.

45–110. This description of Aphrodite surprised at her toilet is idyllic in character rather than Olympian, but Apollonius has shewn considerable good taste in keeping it free from vulgarity. The interview between the goddesses is strikingly different from the noisy councils of the gods in Homer; it seems to reflect the polished diplomacy of the Egyptian court under the sway of the Ptolemies.

45. λευκοῖσιν. Here as in Homer it is a compliment to use this adj. of the human skin; cf. of Penelope, *Od.* 23. 240, δείρης δ' οὔ πω πάμπαν ἀφίετο πήχεε λευκώ, and of Ajax in *Il.* 11. 573, as a sign of youth and beauty, πάρος χρόα λευκὸν ἐπαυρεῖν. In later writers, the adj. was used as a stigma of effeminacy.

ἐπιειμένη, 'as she threw her hair over her white shoulders.' It is best with Platt to take this from ἐφίημι, cf. 4. 179 ἐπιειμένος ὤμῳ, 'throwing it over his shoulder'; for the form, cf. 830 infr. καταειμέναι and 1. 939 καταειμένος from καθίημι, and 2. 372 διαειμένος from δίημι. In Homer, ἐπιειμένος is from ἐπιέννυμι, and is used only in such metaphorical senses as ἀναιδείην ἐπιειμένε, *Il.* 1. 149, 'clothed in shamelessness.' Mooney takes it here in the Homeric sense, with ὤμοις as local dative, which is quite unparalleled.

46. κερκίδι. Here only of a comb for the hair. The shape is indicated by the use of κερκίς for the wedge-shaped blocks

πλέξασθαι πλοκάμους· τὰς δὲ προπάροιθεν ἰδοῦσα
ἔσχεθεν, εἴσω τέ σφ' ἐκάλει, καὶ ἀπὸ θρόνου ὦρτο,
εἷσέ τ' ἐνὶ κλισμοῖσιν· ἀτὰρ μετέπειτα καὶ αὐτὴ
ἵζανεν, ἀψήκτους δὲ χεροῖν ἀνεδήσατο χαίτας.   50
τοῖα δὲ μειδιόωσα προσέννεπεν αἰμυλίοισιν·
  ''Ηθεῖαι, τίς δεῦρο νόος χρειώ τε κομίζει
δηναιὰς αὔτως; τί δ' ἱκάνετον, οὔτι πάρος γε

of seats in the theatre, Lat. *cunei*; cf.
Pollux 9. 44. 2, Vitr. 5. 68, Suet. *Aug.*
44. 2, and Alexis, *Gynocratia* ap. Poll.
loc. cit., δεῖ ἐνταῦθα περὶ τὴν κερκίδα Ὑμᾶς
καθιζούσας θεωρεῖν ὡς ξένας. In Homer,
it is the rod which the weaver used to
draw home the woof; Calypso uses a
golden κερκίς in *Od.* 5. 62. For the
plural, cf. κερκίσιν τ' ἐφεστάναι in Eur.
Hec. 363 as the equivalent of the
Homeric ἱστὸν ἐποίχεσθαι, *Il.* 1. 31, etc.
Hence it is used in general for a rod of
any kind; and from the rustling noise
made by the original in action, the name
is given to a kind of poplar in Theoph.
Hist. Pl. 3. 14. 2.

διά...κόσμει, *in tmesi*, 'was arranging':
cf. *Il.* 2. 476, of arranging the ranks of
an army, ἡγεμόνες διεκόσμεον ἔνθα καὶ
ἔνθα.

48. ἔσχεθεν, 'ceased,' 'stayed her
hand.' In Homer, this is usually transitive; Ap. may have had in mind *Il.* 12.
460–1, οὐδ' ἄρ' ὀχῆες Ἐσχεθέτην, 'nor
did the bars hold fast.'

49. κλισμοῖσιν. A variation of *Il.* 9.
200, εἷσεν δ' ἐν κλισμοῖσι, and of *Od.* 4.
136, ἕζετο δ' ἐν κλισμῷ. The κλισμός
was a seat of honour, superior to the
θρόνος in that it had a rest for the
shoulders. Thus it was to a κλισμός
placed opposite to his hostess that Jason
was led when he went to pay his first call
on Hypsipyle in Lemnos, *Arg.* 1. 788.

50. ἀψήκτους, schol. ἀκτενίστους,
'uncombed.' It is used in Arist. *Lys.*
657 of a κόθορνος, where the scholiast
explains it as σκληρός, 'rough,' or
ἀμάλακτος, 'unsoftened.'

ἀνεδήσατο, 'gathered up *with* her
hands the uncombed locks,' *i.e.* she
completed the toilet of the hair without
troubling to comb the rest, cf. infr. 829,
ἀνήψατο χερσὶν ἐθείρας. It does not
mean, as some have taken it, that
Aphrodite held the uncombed hair *in*
her hands during the interview, like a
slattern answering the door in curl
papers; after all, she was the goddess
of beauty. See S. Reinach, *Rép. des Vases
Peints,* 2. p. 301. 4, for vases shewing
Aphrodite at her toilet; *ib.* p. 301. 2, in
presence of Eros and a maid. For women
alone, v. *ib.* 1. p. 52. 3, p. 440. 4, 5, 6;
for two women and Eros, 2. p. 317. 3.

51. αἰμυλίοισιν, 'with cunning words.'
It is in the same tone that Hypsipyle
opens her interview with Jason in 1. 792,
and Jason beguiles Medea infr. 1141;
there, as elsewhere, the poet seems
deliberately to choose such words as
will shew up Jason in a weak and un-
pleasing character (cf. Introd. p. xl).

52. ἠθεῖαι. This is properly a respectful
address from a junior to a senior; and
in this connection the scholiast remarks
that, according to Homer, it would
apply here to Here only, though later
poets make Cypris older than both.
Apollonius, however, uses it merely as
a conventional term of respect; Peleus
uses it to Argos in 2. 1219, though in
all probability he is himself the senior.
Here it is an address, irrespective of
age, from an inferior to her social
superiors; Ap. makes it clear throughout that Here and Athene, the perfect
wife and the perfect virgin, consider
themselves to have come down a step
in the social scale by paying this visit, a
point which Cypris rubs in, 54 infr.

χρειώ, v. n. 12. 'What purpose, what
need brings you here?' An adaptation
of *Od.* 4. 312, τίπτε δέ σε χρειὼ δεῦρ'
ἤγαγε; χρειώ is used also of an oracular
utterance, *e.g. Arg.* 1. 491, χρειὼ
θεσπίζων μεταμώνιον.

53. δηναιάς, 'after so long'; cf. 590
infr., δηναιόν as adv. 'for long.' It means
'long-lived' in *Il.* 5. 407, ἀλλὰ μάλ'
οὐ δηναιὸς ὃς ἀθανάτοισι μάχηται: this
meaning is probable in *Arg.* 2. 183,
γῆρας δηναιόν, 'an endless old age,'
rather than 'old age at last.'

λίην φοιτίζουσαι, ἐπεὶ περίεστε θεάων;'
Τὴν δ'"Ηρη τοίοισιν ἀμειβομένη προσέειπεν·   55
'Κερτομέεις· νῶιν δὲ κέαρ συνορίνεται ἄτῃ.
ἤδη γὰρ ποταμῷ ἐνὶ Φάσιδι νῆα κατίσχει
Αἰσονίδης, ἠδ' ἄλλοι ὅσοι μετὰ κῶας ἕπονται.
τῶν ἤτοι πάντων μέν, ἐπεὶ πέλας ἔργον ὄρωρεν,
δείδιμεν ἐκπάγλως, περὶ δ' Αἰσονίδαο μάλιστα.   60
τὸν μὲν ἐγών, εἰ καί περ ἐς "Αιδα ναυτίλληται
λυσόμενος χαλκέων Ἰξίονα νειόθι δεσμῶν,
ῥύσομαι, ὅσσον ἐμοῖσιν ἐνὶ σθένος ἔπλετο γυίοις,

58 οἱ δ' ἄλλοι Paris. unus: οἵ τ' ἄλλοι Brunck.   59 μέγα Koechly, e Vat. D.
μέλας a man. pr., μέγαν a man. sec.   61 εἴ κεν Brunck.   ναυτίληται Platt.

54. **φοιτίζουσαι,** 'accustomed to come here.' This verb is first found in the Alexandrines. A frequentative of the Homeric φοιτάω is unnecessary, as the idea of frequency is in that verb; still more unnecessary is φοιτίζεσκε in H. Hom. *Dion.* 26. 8.

52–4. These lines are clearly modelled on the speech of Charis to Thetis on visiting the house of Hephaestus in *Il.* 18. 385–6, Τίπτε, Θέτι τανύπεπλε, ἱκάνεις ἡμέτερον δῶ Αἰδοίη τε φίλη τε; πάρος γε μὲν οὔ τι θαμίζεις. The same theme is in Theoc. *Id.* 15. 7, where Gorgo apologises to Praxinoe for her long absence, and in Herodas 1. 10.

54. **ἐπεί.** Not so much 'noblest of goddesses that ye are,' as 'because ye are so superior among goddesses.' Cypris is not in the least overawed by her distinguished visitors, and makes fun of them.

56. **κερτομέεις,** schol. εἰρωνεύῃ, 'You are pretending not to know.'

συνορίνεται, 'we are both stirred in heart with fear of ill.' This verb is found in tmesi in *Il.* 24. 467, σὺν θυμὸν ὀρίνῃς, 'stir up his heart as well as thine,' and in full in *Il.* 4. 332, συνορινόμεναι κίνυντο φάλαγγες, 'moved with one impulse.'

57. **κατίσχει,** 'moors': cf. *Od.* 11. 456, νῆα κατισχέμεναι.

59. **τῶν...δείδιμεν,** 'for them we fear,' an extension of the common gen. after verbs of emotion. Cf. *Arg.* 2. 635, εἷο... ἀτύζομαι, and Eur. *Tro.* 809, ἀτυζόμενος πώλων: contrast *Arg.* 4. 616, 868, χωσάμενος περὶ παιδί, χωσαμένη Ἀχιλῆος.

Merkel has accordingly emended οὔνεκεν to ὧν κάμον in 4. 1031–2, ὑμέων, ὦ πέρι δὴ μέγα φέρτατοι, ἀμφί τ' ἀέθλοις Οὔνεκεν ὑμετέροισιν, ἀτύζομαι.

59. **πέλας,** 'since the ordeal is at hand.' With Koechly's μέγα for MSS. πέλας, cf. *Il.* 13. 122, δὴ καὶ μέγα νεῖκος ὄρωρεν.

ὄρωρεν. Ap. generally uses this, and ὄρωρει 457, with no more force than ἐστί and ἦν. Homer uses them literally, as the perfect and pluperfect of ὄρνυμι; there may be this sense in *Arg.* 1. 1291, σέο δ' ἔκτοθι μῆτις ὄρωρεν, and 2. 473, ἐπ' ἤματι δ' ἦμαρ ὀρώρει.

61. **ναυτίλληται,** 'even if he tries to sail.' For Platt's ναυτίληται, v. crit. appendix, p. 137.

62. **Ἰξίονα.** Ixion was chained in the world below, νειόθι, for having attempted to violate Here. Ap. mentions only his 'bonds'; there is no reference to the 'wheel' of Pind. *Pyth.* 2. 40, τὸν δὲ τετράκναμον ἔπραξε δεσμόν, 'Ἐὸν ὄλεθρον ὅγ'· ἐν δ' ἀφύκτοισι γυιοπέδαις πεσὼν τὰν πολύκοινον ἀνεδέξατ' ἀγγελίαν. It is rather surprising that Ap. does not mention, in connection with the purification of Medea in Book 4, the legend that Ixion was the first murderer, and the first suppliant to be purified by Zeus (schol. Pind. *ad loc.*).

63. **γυίοις,** 'hands,' rather than 'limbs,' v. n. 37. This is mere bravado on the part of Here, for only on one occasion does she personally interfere with the action, to give a warning cry in 4. 640, when the Argonauts were about to take a wrong route.

ὄφρα μὴ ἐγγελάσῃ Πελίης κακὸν οἶτον ἀλύξας,
ὅς μ' ὑπερηνορέῃ θυέων ἀγέραστον ἔθηκεν.   65
καὶ δ' ἄλλως ἔτι καὶ πρὶν ἐμοὶ μέγα φίλατ' Ἰήσων
ἐξότ' ἐπὶ προχοῇσιν ἅλις πλήθοντος Ἀναύρου
ἀνδρῶν εὐνομίης πειρωμένῃ ἀντεβόλησεν
θήρης ἐξανιών· νιφετῷ δ' ἐπαλύνετο πάντα
οὔρεα καὶ σκοπιαὶ περιμήκεες, οἱ δὲ κατ' αὐτῶν   70
χείμαρροι καναχηδὰ κυλινδόμενοι φορέοντο.
γρηὶ δέ μ' εἰσαμένην ὀλοφύρατο, καί μ' ἀναείρας

65. ἀγέραστον, 'unhonoured in his sacrifices.' Here only c. gen.; Homer uses it once without case, *Il.* 1. 118–9, ὄφρα μὴ οἶος Ἀργείων ἀγέραστος ἔω, which Ap. may have taken to mean 'unhonoured of the Argives.' There is an account of a sacrifice in which Pelias deliberately slighted Here at the beginning of the *Arg.*, 1. 13–14, εἰλαπίνης ἣν πατρὶ Ποσειδάωνι καὶ ἄλλοις 'Ρέζε θεοῖς, Ἥρης δὲ Πελασγίδος οὐκ ἀλέγιζεν. The tale of Jason's courtesy and the rudeness of Pelias must belong to a very old stratum of the legend; cf. Grimm, *Kinder- und Hausmärchen*, 13, where the politeness of one sister and the rudeness of the other are appropriately rewarded.

66. φίλατο. This passive use is first in Ap.; cf. *Anth. Pal. append.* 317, Μούσαις ἔξοχα φιλαμένῳ. For the ordinary Homeric use, cf. *Il.* 5. 61, ἔξοχα γάρ μιν ἐφίλατο Παλλὰς Ἀθήνη, and infr. 1002.

67. προχοῇσιν, *lit.* 'at the place where the river pours forth,' cf. Moschus, *Europa*, 31, προχοῇσιν ἀναύρων. This recalls *Il.* 17. 263, ὡς δ' ὅτ' ἐπὶ προχοῇσι διιπετέος ποταμοῖο: for ἅλις, v. n. 272.

πλήθοντος. Used abs. of a river in flood from Homer onwards, *e.g. Il.* 5. 87, ποταμῷ πλήθοντι ἐοικώς. The passive of 1392 infr. is first in Ap.

Ἀναύρου. A river of Thessaly, known to Simonides, which flows past Iolcus into the bay of Pagasae; the name is also used of a mountain torrent in general, *e.g.* Lyc. *Alex.* 1424, ἅπας δ' ἀναύρων νασμὸς αὐανθήσεται. Later versions combine this incident with the loss of the sandal, for which v. *Arg.* 1. 7 f.; but here, Jason is returning from the chase, there, he is making his way to a sacrifice.

68. εὐνομίης, 'as I made trial of men's righteousness.' For this old epic idea that the gods walk the earth in human shape, cf. *Od.* 17. 485, καί τε θεοὶ ξείνοισιν ἐοικότες ἀλλοδάποισι Παντοῖοι τελέθοντες, ἐπιστρωφῶσι πόληας, Ἀνθρώπων ὕβριν τε καὶ εὐνομίην ἐφορῶντες.

69. νιφετῷ, 'snow': this recalls *Il.* 10. 7, ἢ νιφετόν, ὅτε πέρ τε χίων ἐπάλυνεν ἀρούρας.

70. σκοπιαί. Here and in 883, as in Homer, of a mountain peak. It is used more literally in *Arg.* 1. 999 of a peak from which to survey the country; contrast *Od.* 8. 302, Ἥλιος γάρ οἱ σκοπιὴν ἔχεν, 'kept a look out,' and Arat. *Phaen.* 833, τοῦ γὰρ σκοπιαὶ καὶ ἄρισται, 'scanning him is best.'

περιμήκεες, 'the mighty peaks,' a typically Alexandrine adaptation of *Il.* 13. 63, πέτρης περιμήκεος.

71. χείμαρροι, 'winter torrents.' Homer uses this as adj., *Il.* 5. 87–8, ποταμῷ πλήθοντι ἐοικὼς Χειμάρρῳ, *Il.* 4. 452, χείμαρροι ποταμοὶ κατ' ὄρεσφι ῥέοντες, etc. It is first found as a substantive in Attic prose; σὺν Χειμάρρῳ, in Pind. *frag.* 90 (Schroeder), appears to be a proper name.

καναχηδά, 'with a roar.' Homer uses the noun καναχή, and the verbs καναχέω and καναχίζω. This adv. is first in Hes. *Th.* 367, ποταμοὶ καναχηδὰ ῥέοντες. There is a later καναχηδόν, first used in Dion. Peri. 145; cf. Qu. Sm. 14. 5–6, χειμάρροις ποταμοῖσιν ἐοικότες, οἵ τε φέρονται Ἐξ ὀρέων καναχηδὸν ὀρινομένου ὑετοῖο, *ib.* 2. 217, and *Or. Arg.* 1054.

72. εἰσαμένην, 'in the likeness of.' Ap. also uses ἐειδόμενοι infr. 968, and ἐείσατο, εἰδόμεναι 4. 855, 978, all of which are Homeric forms.

ὀλοφύρατο, 'pitied,' as in *Il.* 8. 245,

αὐτὸς ἑοῖς ὤμοισι διὲκ προαλὲς φέρεν ὕδωρ.
τῶ νύ μοι ἄλληκτον περιτίεται· οὐδέ κε λώβην
τίσειεν Πελίης, εἰ μή σύ γε νόστον ὀπάσσῃς.'   75
῾Ως ηὔδα· Κύπριν δ' ἐνεοστασίη λάβε μύθων.
ἄζετο δ' ἀντομένην ῞Ηρην ἔθεν εἰσορόωσα,
καί μιν ἔπειτ' ἀγανοῖσι προσέννεπεν ἥγ' ἐπέεσσιν·
῾Πότνα θεά, μή τοί τι κακώτερον ἄλλο πέλοιτο
Κύπριδος, εἰ δὴ σεῖο λιλαιομένης ἀθερίζω   80

73 διεκπροαλὲς L, vulg.: διὲκ προαλὲς Vrat.: δι' ἐκ προαλὲς Pariss. duo.
75 ὀπάσσεις G: ὀπάσσῃς vulg.: ὀπάσσοις Paris. unus, Brunck.   76 δ' ἐνεοστασίη
Ruhnken: δὲ νεοστασίη vulg.   θυμόν Ruhnken.

τὸν δὲ πατὴρ ὀλοφύρατο δάκρυ χέοντα.
It is commoner, either trans. or intr., in the sense of 'lament,' *e.g.* infr. 806.

73. διέκ, 'right across,' *lit.* 'through and out.' The force of both prepositions is required; Homer uses διέκ only c. gen. **προαλές.** This is in the nature of a gloss on *Il.* 21. 262, where χώρῳ ἔνι προαλεῖ is used of rapidly falling ground. Apollonius, *Lex. Hom.* s.v. explains the latter as τῷ καταφερεῖ καὶ προαλίζοντι τὸ ὕδωρ, Hesychius as προπετής and πρόχειρος. Our Apollonius appears to derive it from προάλλομαι, *i.e.* 'rapids'; cf. of horses leaping forward at the starting post, Qu. Sm. 4. 510, ὅππως τις προάλοιτο. The comparative adverb is in Strabo 12. 549 B, πλησιάζειν τῇ γῇ προαλέστερον.

φέρεν. There is an interesting parallel in a legend of the 6th cent. A.D., of how St. Christopher received the title of χριστοφόρος for carrying the infant Christ over a stream; v. *Catholic Encyclopaedia*, s.v. *Christopher.*

74. ἄλληκτον, 'unceasingly,' cf. 805. The adjective is Homeric, *Od.* 12. 325, μῆνα δὲ πάντ' ἄλληκτος ἄη Νότος.

περιτίεται, 'is greatly honoured.' This compound is peculiar to Ap. Its use here may indicate that in *Il.* 8. 161, περὶ μέν σε τίον Δαναοί, he took περί in *tmesi* with the verb, and not adverbially; cf. *Or. Arg.* 161, περὶ δ' αὖ τίεν... Μελέαγρον. For Here's love for Jason, cf. *Od.* 12. 72, and *Or. Arg.* 64.

λώβην, 'his insulting conduct.' Homer uses also in sense of 'disgrace,' with which cf. the Alexandrine adj. λωβήεις, 801 infr., and Tryphiod. 261, ἴχνια λωβήεντα.

75. ὀπάσσῃς, 'if thou wilt not grant Jason his return.' For the subj. after κέν, cf. infr. 437; for the text v. crit. appendix, p. 138.

76. ἐνεοστασίη, 'speechless amazement.' This is a restoration by Ruhnken from the gloss in Hesychius ἐνεοστασίη· θάμβος: it is formed from the Platonic ἐνεός, 'dumb,' and means *lit.* 'standing dumb.' μύθων is strictly redundant, but it is unnecessary to alter to θυμόν, as infr. 284, τὴν δ' ἀμφασίη λάβε θυμόν. There, as in 811, 1372, Ap. uses ἀμφασίη for the Homeric ἀμφασίη ἐπέων, *Od.* 4. 704, *Il.* 17. 695; but it does not by any means follow that the same principle holds good here.

77. ἀντομένην, 'supplicating her,' v. n. 35.

ἔθεν. Apollonius uses this as the genitive of the 3rd person reflexive pronoun, both singular and plural; for the latter, which is un-Homeric, cf. *Arg.* 4. 279, οἵ δή τοι γραπτῦς πατέρων ἔθεν εἰρύονται. He has five forms of the genitive, ἔθεν, εἷο, ἑοῖο, ἑοῦ, and οὗ, the last only in the combination οὗ ἔθεν; but the use of the Attic οὗ may shew that he followed Zenodotus in reading it in *Il.* 24. 293, φίλτατος οἰωνῶν, καὶ εὖ κράτος ἐστὶ μέγιστον. For other pronouns, v. n. 26.

78. ἀγανοῖσι. Apollonius seems here to reject the derivation of Eustathius and others from ἀ-γάνυμαι, *i.e.* 'friendly,' and to suggest a root ἀγ-, as in the *Et. Mag.* from ἀγάζω, *i.e.* 'respectful.' The other seems to be followed 937 infr.

80. λιλαιομένης, 'if I scorn thy earnest wish.' Homeric verb, of which only the present and imperfect are extant.

ἢ ἔπος ἠέ τι ἔργον, ὅ κεν χέρες αἴγε κάμοιεν
ἠπεδαναί· καὶ μή τις ἀμοιβαίη χάρις ἔστω.'
Ὣς ἔφαθ'· Ἥρη δ' αὖτις ἐπιφραδέως ἀγόρευσεν·
'Οὔτι βίης χατέουσαι ἱκάνομεν, οὐδέ τι χειρῶν.
ἀλλ' αὔτως ἀκέουσα τεῷ ἐπικέκλεο παιδὶ   85
παρθένον Αἰήτεω θέλξαι πόθῳ Αἰσονίδαο.
εἰ γάρ οἱ κείνη συμφράσσεται εὐμενέουσα,

81 αἴδε Platt.

λελίημαι, of which Homer uses only the participle, is used by Ap. c. gen. 1. 1164, λελιημένοι ἠπείροιο, 'eager to reach the mainland,' and in the ppf. λελίητο, infr. 646, 1158. These are both peculiar to late epic.

ἀθερίζω, 'make light of.' This genitive, as in 94 and 625 infr., is un-Homeric; for the Homeric accusative, cf. 4. 1101, οὐδὲ μὲν Αἰήτην ἀθεριζέμεν. For the subjunctive of the protasis and optative of apodosis, cf. crit. appendix on 75 supr. ὀπάσσῃς.

81. αἴγε. ὅγε in Homer is substantival, and regularly either resumptive, as in *Il.* 2. 664, cf. infr. 112, or marking a contrast, as in *Il.* 3. 409, εἰσόκε σ' ἢ ἄλοχον ποιήσεται, ἢ ὅγε δούλην, cf. infr. 399. Here it is adjectival, and the -γε has no force at all; so Platt's αἴδε, though not strictly necessary, is attractive.

82. ἠπεδαναί, 'weak,' used in Homer of a servant, *Il.* 8. 104, of Hephaestus, *Od.* 8. 311, cf. H. Hom. *Ap.* 316. Commentators derive it either from ἀ-πέδον, 'not firm,' or from ἤπιος (cf. οὐτιδανός and οὖτις). Ap. seems to favour the latter, as does also the schol. on *Od. loc. cit.*, who explains it as ἀσθενής: cf. ἠπεδανοῖο λέοντος (Suidas, *Lex.* s.v.), of a lion whose paw was maimed by a thorn.

ἀμοιβαίη, 'let there be no favour in return'; cf. Leonidas ap. *Anth. Pal.* 7. 657. 12, εἰσὶν ἀμοιβαῖαι κἂν φθιμένοις χάριτες. This adj. is not in Homer; cf. however Pind. *Ol.* 1. 39 ἀμοιβαῖα δεῖπνα, Theoc. *Id.* 8. 31 ἀμοιβαίαν ἀοιδάν, *ib.* 61 δι' ἀμοιβαίων, and the curious use in *Arg.* 2. 1240–1, of how Philyra bore Chiron as a monster, owing to Zeus changing his form at the critical moment: (Φιλύρη) ἦλθ', ἵνα δὴ Χείρωνα πελώριον, ἄλλα μὲν ἵππῳ, Ἄλλα θεῷ ἀτάλαντον, ἀμοιβαίῃ τέκεν εὐνῇ. Cf. also

Soph. *El.* 134 παντοίας φιλότητος ἀμειβόμεναι χάριν.

83. ἐπιφραδέως. Adverb peculiar to Ap., founded on the Homeric ἐπιφράζομαι. Hesychius explains the comparative ἐπιφραδέστερον as συντομώτερον, *i.e.* 'briefly,' or συνετώτερον, *i.e.* 'carefully.' Ap. seems to use the former here and in 1. 1336, 2. 1134 with προσέειπεν and ἐρέειψεν, the latter in 1. 1021, νῆσον ἐπιφραδέως ἐνόησεν Ἔμμεναι, thus giving alternative meanings even to a word which he alone uses.

84. χατέουσαι, 'in need of.' Homer uses either abs., or as here c. gen. τι as acc. of respect; but Ap. uses χατέω also with a direct accusative, 4. 1556–7, οἷά τε πολλὰ Ἄνθρωποι χατέουσιν, unless indeed these οἷά τε is for ἅτε, and πολλά adverbial, 'as so often men have need.'

85. αὔτως, 'just as you are,' *i.e.* do no more than merely bid.

ἀκέουσα, 'without a word.' Homer has ἀκέων, ἀκέουσα, and the dual ἀκέοντε, but no plural forms; ἀκέων can stand adverbially even with a feminine or plural, *e.g. Il.* 4. 22, Ἀθηναίη ἀκέων ἦν: *Od.* 21. 89, ἀκέων δαίνυσθε. Probably ἀκέων was originally an adverb, and came to be regarded as the nom. masc. of a participle; Ap. forms a verb ἀκέω, 1. 765, κείνους κ' εἰσορόων ἀκέοις, which must be distinguished from the Homeric ἀκέομαι, 'heal,' in 2. 155–6 ἕλκεά τ' ἀνδρῶν Οὐταμένων ἀκέοντο.

86. παρθένον, *i.e.* the 'unwedded' daughter, cf. 27 supr. Except for the invocation (3 supr.), which is quite apart from the narrative proper, Medea is not mentioned by name until an appropriate time, 247 infr.

87. συμφράσσεται, as in Homer, to 'join in deliberation,' *i.e.* to impart advice, cf. 918 infr. In the sense of

ῥηιδίως μιν ἑλόντα δέρος χρύσειον οἴω
νοστήσειν ἐς Ἰωλκόν, ἐπεὶ δολόεσσα τέτυκται.'
'Ὡς ἄρ' ἔφη· Κύπρις δὲ μετ' ἀμφοτέρῃσιν ἔειπεν·   90
'"Ηρη, Ἀθηναίη τε, πίθοιτό κεν ὔμμι μάλιστα,
ἢ ἐμοί. ὑμείων γὰρ ἀναιδήτῳ περ ἐόντι
τυτθή γ' αἰδὼς ἔσσετ' ἐν ὄμμασιν· αὐτὰρ ἐμεῖο
οὐκ ὄθεται, μάλα δ' αἰὲν ἐριδμαίνων ἀθερίζει.
καὶ δή οἱ μενέηνα, περισχομένη κακότητι,   95
αὐτοῖσιν τόξοισι δυσηχέας ἆξαι ὀιστοὺς

'counsel within one's self,' *i.e.* 'devise,' it is first in Hes. *Th.* 471, λιτάνευε τοκῆας...μῆτιν συμφράσασθαι: this appears to be the meaning in 698 infr. With the whole line, cf. *Od.* 6. 313, εἴ κέν τοι κείνη γε φίλα φρονέῃσ' ἐνὶ θυμῷ.

εὐμενέουσα, intrans. 'of her good will.' First in Pindar, *Pyth.* 4. 127, and there transitive, εὐμενέοντες ἀνεψιόν, 'with kindly feeling for their cousin.'

91. μάλιστα ἤ. Apollonius may have had in mind *Od.* 11. 482–3, σεῖο...οὔτις ἀνὴρ προπάροιθε μακάρτατος οὔτ' ἄρ' ὀπίσσω, where the text is disputed. For the comparative use of μάλιστα ἤ, cf. Eur. *Iph. Aul.* 1594, ταύτην μάλιστα τῆς κόρης ἀσπάζεται, and *Ox. Pap.* 7, p. 113, l. 21, τῷ σ' ἐπὶ τοῖσι μάλιστα γεραίρομεν ἤ περ ἐκείνοις.

92. ἀναιδήτῳ, 'shameless as he is.' This extended form of the Homeric ἀναιδής is first in Ap.; cf. 4. 360, ἀναιδήτῳ ἰότητι, and Nonnus, *Dion.* 48. 342, τολμηροῖς βλεφάροισιν ἀναιδήτοιο προσώπου. The Homeric form is used in *Arg.* 2. 383, 407.

93. ἐν ὄμμασιν, 'in his eyes,' rather than 'face to face,' for which sense, however, cf. 1115 infr. ἐν ὀφθαλμοῖσιν. For the eyes as the indicators of emotion, cf. *Anth. Pal.* 7. 661. 1–2, φυσιογνώμων ὁ σοφιστής, Δεινὸς ἀπ' ὀφθαλμοῦ καὶ τὸ νόημα μαθεῖν: *Script. Physiog.* ed. Foerster, 1. 305. 9–11, τὰ δὲ πολλὰ τῶν σημείων καὶ τὰ σύνολα τοῖς ὀφθαλμοῖς ἐνίδρυται καὶ ὥσπερ διὰ πυλῶν τούτων ἡ ψυχὴ διαφαίνεται: and further refs. in *Class. Rev.* 1903 (17), p. 244 a. Cf. also Ach. Tat. 1. 4. 4, ὀφθαλμὸς γὰρ ὁδὸς ἐρωτικῷ τραύματι, and Soph. *Aj.* 139–40, πεφόβημαι Πτηνῆς ὡς ὄμμα πελείας.

94. οὐκ ὄθεται, 'for me, he does not care.' A purely epic word, used only in the present and imperfect, and always with a negative; for the gen., cf. *Il.* 1. 180–1, σέθεν δ' ἐγὼ οὐκ ἀλεγίζω Οὐδ ὄθομαι κοτέοντος, 'I care not for thy anger.'

ἀθερίζει, 'ever slights me in contentious mood.' Still governing the gen., v. n. 80. Compare the description of Cupid in Vergil (?), *Ciris*, 133–4, 'malus ille puer, quem nec sua flectere mater Iratum potuit.'

95. μενέηνα, 'in my anger with him, I came near to breaking.' For the dative, cf. infr. 369, μενέαινε δὲ παισὶ μάλιστα. It combines two meanings, μενέηνά οἱ, 'I was angry with him,' and μενέηνα ἆξαι, 'I threatened to break.'

κακότητι. This is probably in the Homeric sense of 'wickedness,' *i.e.* 'plagued with his naughtiness,' rather than in the un-Homeric sense in which it elsewhere occurs, as 182, 423, 476, 608, 1127 infr., of 'misfortune,' *i.e.* 'overwhelmed with my misfortune.' It is a strong word, but Cypris feels strongly about the matter; and Ap., moreover, is prone to use both meanings of a word where possible.

96. αὐτοῖσιν, 'to break his arrows and his bow as well,' the so-called 'sociative' dative; cf. *Il.* 8. 24, αὐτῇ κεν γαίῃ ἐρύσαιμ' αὐτῇ τε θαλάσσῃ, and Soph. *Phil.* 1027, πλεύσανθ' ἑπτὰ ναυσί.

δυσηχέας, 'evil-sounding,' used by Homer, only in the genitive, of πόλεμος, θάνατος. It occurs metaphorically in H. Hom. *Ap.* 64, where Delos complains of its poor fame, ἐτήτυμόν εἰμι δυσηχὴς Ἀνδράσιν. It is used technically of gold and silver giving forth a dull sound, Plut. *Quaest. Conviv.* 8. 3. 7,

ἀμφαδίην. τοῖον γὰρ ἐπηπείλησε χαλεφθείς,
εἰ μὴ τηλόθι χεῖρας, ἕως ἔτι θυμὸν ἐρύκει,
ἔξω ἐμάς, μετέπειτά γ' ἀτεμβοίμην ἑοῖ αὐτῇ.'
᾽Ως φάτο· μείδησαν δὲ θεαί, καὶ ἐσέδρακον ἄντην   100
ἀλλήλας. ἡ δ' αὖτις ἀκηχεμένη προσέειπεν·
'᾽Αλλοις ἄλγεα τἀμὰ γέλως πέλει· οὐδέ τί με χρὴ
μυθεῖσθαι πάντεσσιν· ἅλις εἰδυῖα καὶ αὐτή.
νῦν δ' ἐπεὶ ὕμμι φίλον τόδε δὴ πέλει ἀμφοτέρῃσιν,
πειρήσω, καί μιν μειλίξομαι, οὐδ' ἀπιθήσει.'   105

97 τοῖον δ' ἄρ O. Schneider.   99 κ' Madvig.   101 ἀλλήλας aut ἐπέδρακον
ἀλλήλαις Ziegler: ἀλλήλαις codd., edd.

χρυσὸς μὲν γὰρ καὶ λίθος ὑπὸ πληρότητος
ἰσχνόφωνα καὶ δυσηχῆ.
ἄξαι. The aorist is usual with μενεαίνω,
as in 2. 262, 4. 233-4: but Homer uses
also the pres. and fut. inf. This recalls
Pandarus' threat to burn his bow in *Il.*
5. 215-6, ...εἰ μὴ ἐγὼ τάδε τόξα φαεινῷ
ἐν πυρὶ θείην Χερσὶ διακλάσσας· ἀνεμώ-
λια γάρ μοι ὀπηδεῖ.
97. ἀμφαδίην, 'openly,' as in Homer.
Properly it is the fem. acc. of the
adjective used as adverb. ἀμφαδόν, infr.
570, is also Homeric; cf. Arat. 771
ἀναφανδόν, and *Arg.* 4. 84 ἀναφανδά,
which are both Homeric, though in
Homer the latter is adj., not adverb.
ἀμφαδὰ ἔργα πέλοιτο, infr. 615, is
adapted from *Od.* 19. 391, ἀμφαδὰ ἔργα
γένοιτο. It is uncertain in the latter
whether ἀμφαδά is adj. or adv., and Ap.
has repeated the dubious words without
committing himself.
χαλεφθείς, 'in his anger.' In Homer,
χαλέπτω means 'oppress,' as in *Arg.* 4.
1506, 1675. This is a later meaning,
'provoke to anger,' and in middle, 'be
angry'; cf. 109, 382 infr., Call. *H.
Dem.* 48.
99. ἀτεμβοίμην, 'later, I should have
my own self to blame.' For the threat,
cf. Hdt. 5. 106. 2, ὅρα μὴ ἐξ ὑστέρης
σεωυτὸν ἐν αἰτίῃ ἔχῃς. In Homer, the
active means 'maltreat,' the passive 'be
bereft of.' Here, infr. 938 and 2. 56, it
is in the sense of μέμφεσθαι: in 2.
1199, c. acc. and inf., it means 'vexed
that,'—ἀτεμβόμενος τοῖον στόλον ἀμφιπέ-
νεσθαι.
ἑοῖ αὐτῇ, 'myself,' v. n. 26. Madvig

read κε for γε; but it is best, with Fitch,
to regard this as an 'imperative' optative (cf. Gildersleeve, *Syntax of Classical
Greek*, 394, 430).
100. ἄντην, adv. peculiar to epic;
it is used as a prep. c. gen. in late
epic. This phrase is adapted from *Il.*
24. 223, νῦν δ' αὐτὸς γὰρ ἄκουσα θεοῦ καὶ
ἐσέδρακον ἄντην: cf. 923 infr., and *Il.*
19. 14-5, οὐδέ τις ἔτλη ᾽Αντην εἰσιδέειν.
It is best, with Ziegler, to read ἀλλήλας
in the next line, for ἀλλήλαις of the MSS.
102. οὐδέ τί με χρή, 'I should not
tell them to the world': cf. *Od.* 19. 118,
Il. 19. 67, οὐδέ τί με χρή.
103. ἅλις κ.τ.λ. 'it is enough that I
myself know them': cf. Soph. *O. T.*
1061, ἅλις νοσοῦσ' ἐγώ.
105. μειλίξομαι. In 613, 985, this
word means to 'implore'; but Cypris
has just pointed out the futility of en-
treaty. In 531, it means 'beguile,' in
1035 'propitiate'; here likewise Ap.
seems to be following schol. *Il.* 7. 410,
πυρὸς μειλισσέμεν· χαρίζεσθαι τοῦ πυρός,
i.e. 'I will propitiate him (with a
present).'
ἀπιθήσει, 'he will not disobey.' Epic
word, used once in anapaests in tragedy,
Soph. *Phil.* 1447, οὐκ ἀπιθήσω τοῖς σοῖς
μύθοις. Like Homer, Ap. uses it with a
negative, cf. 669. It takes a gen. instead
of the Homeric dat. in H. Hom. *Dem.*
448, οὐδ' ἀπίθησε θεὰ Διὸς ἀγγελιάων. It
is used in *Arg.* 1. 149-50, οὐδ' ἀπίθησεν
Νισσομένοις, in the sense of ἀπιστέω,
which conversely is used in Attic in the
sense of 'disobey,' *e.g.* Aesch. *Prom.*
640, ὑμῖν ἀπιστῆσαι.

*Ὡς φάτο· τὴν δ' Ἥρη ῥαδινῆς ἐπεμάσσατο χειρός,
ἦκα δὲ μειδιόωσα παραβλήδην προσέειπεν·
'Οὕτω νῦν, Κυθέρεια, τόδε χρέος, ὡς ἀγορεύεις,
ἔρξον ἄφαρ· καὶ μή τι χαλέπτεο, μηδ' ἐρίδαινε
χωομένη σῷ παιδί· μεταλλήξει γὰρ ὀπίσσω.'   110
Ἦ ῥα, καὶ ἔλλιπε θῶκον· ἐφωμάρτησε δ' Ἀθήνη·
ἐκ δ' ἴσαν ἄμφω ταίγε παλίσσυτοι. ἡ δὲ καὶ αὐτὴ
βῆ ῥ' ἴμεν Οὐλύμποιο κατὰ πτύχας, εἴ μιν ἐφεύροι.
εὗρε δὲ τόνγ' ἀπάνευθε, Διὸς θαλερῇ ἐν ἀλωῇ,

109 ἐρίδηνε L : ἐρίδηνον Pariss., Brunck.   112 ἡ δὲ Vatt. duo, Paris. unus :
ἠδὲ LG.   114 ita interpunxi.

106. **ῥαδινῆς**, 'slender, delicate.' This adj. is used in *Il.* 23. 583 of a whip. Theognis 1002 is the first to use it of hands, though Hes. *Th.* 194–5 applies it to feet, ἀμφὶ δὲ ποίη Ποσσὶν ὑπὸ ῥαδινοῖσιν ἀέξετο. The schol. gives examples of application to horses, pillars, etc. from the lyric poets.

ἐπεμάσσατο, 'took her by the hand,' on the analogy of χειρὸς ἑλεῖν τινα, cf. 4. 18, λευκανίης ἐπεμάσσατο, 'seized her neck.' In Homer, c. gen. it is 'desire,' c. acc. 'feel'; this is reversed in 816 infr., νόῳ ἐπεμαίεθ' ἕκαστα, 'lay hold of with the mind,' *i.e.* 'desire.' The use c. dat. in *Or. Arg.* 932 depends on a false reading for ἐπιμαίνεται; but there is a curious use *ib.* 121 ἐπεμαίετο πάντοθεν ὄρφνη, 'darkness prevailed everywhere.'

107. **παραβλήδην.** Ap. seems to interpret this in Homer not as 'interrupting,' but simply 'in answer'; cf. 1078 with ἔπος ηὔδα, 2. 448 with ἀγόρευον, 2. 60 with ἐρίδηνεν, 'gave back no taunt in answer.' In 4. 1608, χαλινὰ παραβλήδην κροτέονται must mean 'ring loud as the horse throws the bit from side to side in the mouth.' ὑποβλήδην likewise, which some take as 'interrupting' in *Il.* 1. 292, τὸν δ' ἄρ' ὑποβλήδην ἠμείβετο δῖος Ἀχιλλεύς, is used by Ap. infr. 400, 1119 and 1. 699 in the same sense as παραβλήδην; the schol. on 1. 699 takes the opposite view: ὑποβλήδην κυρίως σημαίνει, ἐπειδὰν λέγοντός τινος ἕτερος περικόψας τὸν ἐκείνου λόγον λέγῃ. Καὶ ὑποβάλλειν ἐπὶ τοῦ αὐτοῦ.

108. **Κυθέρεια.** This name is not in the *Iliad*; but it occurs in the *Odyssey, Hymns* and elsewhere later.

109. **χαλέπτεο**, 'be not angry,' v. n. 97.

110. **μεταλλήξει**, 'he will cease,' *i.e.* from his naughtiness; cf. 951 infr. μεταλλήγεσκεν, 'she was for ever stopping.' The Homeric use c. gen. in 1. 1271, μεταλλήγων καμάτοιο.

111–166. Cypris goes in search of Eros, and finds him at dice with Ganymede; she bribes him to fire Medea with love for Jason.

111. **θῶκον**, a pompous word for a 'seat,' used in Homer especially of the gods, or of a solemn session in council; here it is a κλισμός, the seat of honour, v. n. 49 supr.

ἐφωμάρτησε, 'accompanied.' Here, as in Homer, used without case, but c. dat. in 1. 201, ἐφωμάρτησε κιόντι.

112. **παλίσσυτοι**, 'hastening back,' from πάλιν, σεύω. It is common in Ap., *e.g.* 306, 373 infr., but first found in tragedy, Soph. *O.T.* 193, παλίσσυτον δράμημα, Eur. *Supp.* 388–9, παλίσσυτος Στεῖχε.

113. **πτύχας**, 'glens,' *lit.* 'folds.' Note the typical difference of order from *Il.* 11. 77, κατὰ πτύχας Οὐλύμποιο, and cf. *Il.* 4. 88, *Od.* 5. 439, εἴ που ἐφεύροι.

114f. This scene, like 45–110 supr., is almost a little idyll; but here, in striking contrast with the disjointed episodes at the beginning of the first book, Ap. has worked it well into the main fabric. As in the ball of 139 infr., 'the seams are hidden.'

εὗρε κ.τ.λ. A variant of *Od.* 24. 226, τὸν δ' οἶον πατέρ' εὗρεν ἐυκτιμένῃ ἐν ἀλωῇ. It may be meant to support Zenodotus on *Il.* 4. 88–90, Πάνδαρον ἀντίθεον διζημένη, εἴ που ἐφεύροι. Εὗρε Λυκάονος

οὐκ οἶον, μετὰ καὶ Γανυμήδεα, τόν ῥά ποτε Ζεὺς 115
οὐρανῷ ἐγκατένασσεν ἐφέστιον ἀθανάτοισιν,
κάλλεος ἱμερθείς. ἀμφ' ἀστραγάλοισι δὲ τώγε
χρυσείοις, ἅ τε κοῦροι ὁμήθεες, ἑψιόωντο.
καί ῥ' ὁ μὲν ἤδη πάμπαν ἐνίπλεον ᾧ ὑπὸ μαζῷ
μάργος Ἔρως λαιῆς ὑποΐσχανε χειρὸς ἀγοστόν, 120

119 ἐπὶ Brunck.   κόλπον ἐνίπλεον...ἀγοστῷ Hemsterhuis.   120 ἀγοστόν Vat.
unus, Pariss.: ἀγοστῷ vulg.

υἱὸν ἀμύμονά τε κρατερόν τε Ἐσταότ'. Zenod. read εὗρε δὲ τόνδ' in 88, and omitted 89 entirely: Ap. at any rate reproduces both views here.

ἀπάνευθε, 'apart, in the glorious garden of Zeus'; this is best taken as an adv., as the rhythm suggests. The schol. prefers it as prep., 'apart from Zeus,' as in 333, 1169–70 infr., and is followed by de Mirmont. Both uses are Homeric.

115. οὐκ οἶον κ.τ.λ., cf. Od. 6. 84, οὐκ οἴην, ἅμα τῇγε, I. 331, 19. 601, οὐκ οἴη, ἅμα τῇγε, etc.

Γανυμήδεα. A combination of Homeric and later legend. In Homer, Ganymede was carried off by all the gods, Il. 20. 234–5, τὸν καὶ ἀνηρείψαντο θεοὶ Διὶ οἰνοχοεύειν Κάλλεος εἵνεκα οἷο, ἵν' ἀθανάτοισι μετείη: he is carried off by Zeus in H. Hom. Aph. 202–3, ἤ τοι μὲν ξανθὸν Γανυμήδεα μητιέτα Ζεὺς Ἥρπασε ὃν διὰ κάλλος, ἵν' ἀθανάτοισι μετείη, cf. Pind. Ol. I. 43. Il. 20. 235 is repeated of Cleitus in Od. 15. 251, but was rejected by Aristarchus.

116. οὐρανῷ ἐγκατένασσεν, 'set to dwell in Heaven.' The same phrase is used by the poetess Moero, ap. Ath. II. 80, of the eagle which bore nectar to the infant Zeus, and was set in Heaven as a reward.

117. κάλλεος ἱμερθείς. The schol. remarks that in Homer, Ganymede was taken οὐδὲ δι' ἔρωτα καὶ πόθον, ἀλλ' ὥστε Διὶ οἰνοχοεύειν, and cites Il. 20. 234, as though the following line, as in Od. 15. 251, were absent from his text.

ἀμφί. Seaton translates this 'for,' explained by 124; but it is probably local, 'at dice,' lit. 'around the dice,' cf. Arg. I. 458–9, παρὰ δαιτὶ...ἐψιόωνται, and 623 infr., ἀμφὶ βόεσσιν, where it is properly adverbial. Ap. is probably repeating the dubious ἀμφ' ἀστραγάλοισι

χολωθείς of Il. 23. 88, without committing himself.

ἀστραγάλοισι, 'knucklebones.' These were first used in their natural state, then superseded by dice with four flat marked and two round unmarked sides, which were known as ἀστράγαλοι, as opposed to κύβοι with six marked sides. Anacreon, ap. schol. Il. 23. 88, used a feminine, ἀστραγάλαι δ' Ἐρωτός εἰσιν μανίαι τε καὶ κυδοιμοί, whence some have introduced the f. into the text. Eros and his dice are a favourite theme of the epigrammatists; e.g. Meleager ap. Anth. Pal. 12. 47, μητρὸς ἔτ' ἐν κόλποισιν ὁ νήπιος ὀρθρινὰ παίζων Ἀστραγάλοις, τοὐμὸν πνεῦμ' ἐκύβευσεν Ἔρως: Asclepiades, ib. 12. 46. 3–4, Ἔρωτες Ὡς τὸ πάρος παίξεσθ' ἄφρονες ἀστραγάλοις.

118. ὁμηθέες, 'of like character,' Alexandrine for the Platonic ὁμοηθής; cf. Nicander, Th. 415, προλιπὼν καὶ ἕλος καὶ ὁμηθέα λίμνην.

ἐψιόωντο, 'were playing.' Two derivations of this stem are recognised, (1) play, cf. ἔψεια· παίγνια (Hesych.), and (2) mock, cf. schol. Arg. I. 459, ἐψίαν, ἤ ἐστι διὰ λόγων παιδιά. The former is followed here and infr. 950, the connection with ἔπος seems to be stressed in 1. 459, 2. 811. Similarly in Homer, ἐφεψιόωντο and καθεψιόωνται in Od. 19. 370, 372 mean 'mock,' ἐψιάασθων and ἐψιάασθαι in Od. 17. 530, 21. 429 mean 'play.'

119. ἐνίπλεον, 'full.' This form of the Homeric ἐνίπλειος is found only here and in the Orphic Lithica 192; ἔμπλειος infr. 1281 is also Homeric.

120. μάργος. The scholiast rightly explains this as ὁ μαργαίνειν ποιῶν, comparing τακερὸς δ' Ἔρως of Anacreon, and the Homeric χλωρὸν δέος. Alcman frag. 38 uses μάργος of Eros; he is not only full of turmoil himself, 276, but

ὀρθὸς ἐφεστηώς· γλυκερὸν δέ οἱ ἀμφὶ παρειὰς
χροιῇ θάλλεν ἔρευθος. ὁ δ' ἐγγύθεν ὀκλαδὸν ἧστο
σῖγα κατηφιόων· δοιὼ δ' ἔχεν, ἄλλον ἔτ' αὔτως
ἄλλῳ ἐπιπροΐείς, κεχόλωτο δὲ καγχαλόωντι.
καὶ μὴν τούσγε παρᾶσσον ἐπὶ προτέροισιν ὀλέσσας   125
βῆ κενεαῖς σὺν χερσὶν ἀμήχανος, οὐδ' ἐνόησεν

the cause also of turmoil in others. Mooney takes it here as simply 'greedy,' with which cf. Eust. on *Od.* 16. 421, 23. 11; the latter takes μάργε in Homer to mean μαινόμενε.

ἀγοστόν. Here Ap. follows Eustathius on *Il.* 11. 425, ὁ δ' ἐν κονίησι πεσὼν ἕλε γαῖαν ἀγοστῷ, in interpreting ἀγοστῷ as τὸ πλατὺ τῆς χειρός. In 1394 infr., οἱ δ' ἐπ' ἀγοστῷ Καὶ πλευροῖς, he follows the meaning ἄγκων as in *Et. Gaud.* 697; the latter gives also κόλπος, which seems to be founded on Antip. Sid. (*Anal.* 2. 35 no. 104) βρέφος φορέειν ἀγοστῷ.

121. ἐφεστηώς, 'standing upright.' In Homer, when the -ώς of a perfect participle follows a vowel, either or both of the vowels may be long, *e.g.* κεκμηότα, κεκμηῶτα; v. Monro *H.G.* 26. 1. In ἑσταότας, however, both are short, cf. infr. 1276, and Arat. 782; the resolved -αο- is now read for the contracted -αω- in 11 places in the *Od., e.g.* 11. 583. Ap., however, infr. 1384 has ἑστηῶτας; in *Arg.* 1. 517, Mooney rather convincingly restores ἑστηῶτες, for the MSS. ἐστι τέως ἐπί τε γλώσσῃσι χέοντο.

παρειάς, 'cheeks.' Aristarchus read neut. plural παρειά in Homer (schol. A. *Il.* 23. 291, Eust. 377), though in *Il.* 18. 123 both he and Aristophanes read the fem. παρειάων (schol. A. *Il.* 3. 35). Ap. favours the feminine, cf. 149, 297 infr., etc.

122. ἐγγύθεν, 'near at hand,' cf. 2. 1121, 'from near at hand'; both are Homeric. Like Homer, Ap. uses ἐγγύθι both abs., 2. 35, and c. gen., infr. 927; it is also c. dat. in *Il.* 22. 300, νῦν δὲ δὴ ἐγγύθι μοι θάνατος κακός.

ὀκλαδόν, ἀντὶ τοῦ ὀκλάσας, schol.: here only. ὀκλάξ infr. 1308 (schol. ἐπὶ τὰ γόνατα) extends the meaning, 'on to its knees.' The latter is first in Pherecrates (Κοριανν. 10 Meineke) ὀκλὰξ καθημένη; cf. Arat. 517, ταύρου τε σκελέων ὅσσον περιφαίνεται ὀκλάξ.

123. κατηφιόων, 'with downcast eyes,' cf. *Arg.* 1. 461, κατηφιόωντι ἐοικώς; an Alexandrine form of the Homeric κατηφέω. The aor. κατηφήσας in 2. 443, the noun κατηφείη infr. 1402, and the adj. κατηφέες infr. 504, are all Homeric. Grammarians derive this group in various ways, Doederlein in particular from καταί, φάϵα.

δοιώ, *sc.* ἀστραγάλω. They have been lost sight of in the digression; cf. schol. *ad loc.,* λείπει τὸ ἀστραγάλους.

124. ἐπιπροΐείς. Homer uses this of sending forth arrows or persons; for the latter, cf. infr. 379. Here the literal meaning, 'throwing forward on top of,' seems to point to an ordinary game of dice; but Seaton suggests that it is 'staking,' and that the game is ἀρτιασμός, *odd and even,* for which cf. Arist. *Rhet.* 3. 5. 4.

κεχόλωτο, 'was annoyed with him.' Homer uses this word c. dat., with ἀμφί, and with ἐκ. Ap. has it again c. dat., infr. 493. With *Arg.* 4. 8, στυγερῷ ἐπὶ θυμὸν ἀέθλῳ Αἰήτης ἄμοτον κεχολωμένος, cf. *Batrachomyomachia* 109, Τρωξάρτης ἐπὶ παιδὶ χολούμενος. The transitive active is Homeric, as in 4. 863, μή με χολώσῃς.

καγχαλόωντι, 'as he laughed aloud with satisfaction': Homeric word, cf. 286 infr., etc. Leaf on *Il.* 3. 43, ἦ πού καγχαλόωσι κάρη κομόωντες Ἀχαιοί, takes it to mean 'mock'; but that is rather implied in the word, and is hardly a distinct meaning. ἐπικαγχαλόων is used c. dat. in Qu. Sm. 1. 161, τῷ ἐπικαγχαλόωσα τάχ' ἤλυθεν ἔκτοθι πύργων, etc.

125. παρᾶσσον. Here in the sense of 'straightway,' rather than 'side by side,' v. n. 17 supr.

126. κενεαῖς, 'empty.' Ap. has also κεινάς 1346, but not κενός; all three are Homeric. The spondee is required by metre in *Il.* 3. 376, κεινὴ δὲ τρυφάλεια ἅμ' ἕσπετο χειρὶ παχείῃ, whence Platt

GA   2

Κύπριν ἐπιπλομένην. ἡ δ' ἀντίη ἵστατο παιδός,
καί μιν ἄφαρ γναθμοῖο κατασχομένη προσέειπεν·
'Τίπτ' ἐπιμειδιάᾳς, ἄφατον κακόν; ἦέ μιν αὔτως
ἤπαφες, οὐδὲ δίκῃ περιέπλεο νῆιν ἐόντα;   130
εἰ δ' ἄγε μοι πρόφρων τέλεσον χρέος, ὅττι κεν εἴπω·
καί κέν τοι ὀπάσαιμι Διὸς περικαλλὲς ἄθυρμα
κεῖνο, τό οἱ ποίησε φίλη τροφὸς Ἀδρήστεια
ἄντρῳ ἐν Ἰδαίῳ ἔτι νήπια κουρίζοντι,
σφαῖραν ἐυτρόχαλον, τῆς οὔ σύγε μείλιον ἄλλο   135

129 ἐπιμειδάεις Pariss. tres.

reads κεινὴν with L. for κοινὴν in *Arg.*
1. 103, Πειρίθῳ ἐσπόμενον κεινὴν ὁδόν.
127. ἐπιπλομένην. ἀντὶ τοῦ ἐπελθοῦ-
σαν, schol. For the use of persons, v. n.
25 supr.
    ἀντίη, 'she stood before her son,' cf.
Il. 17. 31, μηδ' ἄντιος ἵστασ' ἐμεῖο. Ap.
uses this word as adjective, abs. 1. 320
or as here c. gen.; as adverb, ἄντιον 2.
682 and perhaps infr. 287 ἄντια (but v.
note *ad loc.*); as preposition c. gen., 1.
790. All these are Homeric.
    128. κατασχομένη, 'seizing him by
the chin': ἔχεσθαι is commoner in this
sense. Homer uses κατέχεσθαι, but not
in this sense nor c. gen., *Od.* 3. 284, ὡς
ὁ μὲν ἔνθα κατέσχετ', 'so he tarried there.'
    129. ἐπιμειδιάᾳς, 'why smilest thou
in triumph?' This compound is first
found in prose; Homer has ἐπιμειδάω
only in the phrase τὸν δ' ἐπιμειδήσας
κ.τ.λ., which is not in the *Argonautica*.
The simple μειδιάω is used by both, but
only in the present participle, 51 supr.,
etc.
    130. περιέπλεο, 'overreached,' οὐδὲ
δικαίως αὐτοῦ περιεγένου, schol. A
unique equivalent of the Attic περιέρχεσθαι, v. n. 25 supr.
    νῆιν, 'and him so innocent!' For the
false form, cf. 4. 697 πάιν, and v. n. 32
supr.
    132. ὀπάσαιμι κ.τ.λ. This recalls
the bribing by the goddesses of Eily-
thyia to attend the birth of Apollo, H.
Hom. *Ap.* 103–4, ὑποσχόμεναι μέγαν
ὅρμον, Χρυσείοισι λίνοισιν ἐερμένον, ἐννεά-
πηχυν.
    περικαλλές, cf. *Od.* 18. 300, περι-
καλλὲς ἄγαλμα. The whole line is an
adaptation of *Od.* 8. 430, καί οἱ ἐγὼ τόδ'
ἄλεισον ἐμὸν περικαλλὲς ὀπάσσω: cf. also

H. Hom. *Herm.* 40, ἂψ εἴσω κίε δῶμα
φέρων ἐρατεινὸν ἄθυρμα.
    ἄθυρμα, 'toy.' Homer has the pl.
ἀθύρματα in *Il.* 15. 363, *Od.* 18. 323:
ἀθύρειν is also Homeric, cf. infr. 949.
    133. Ἀδρήστεια, *i.e.* Nemesis, sister
of the Curetes and nurse of Zeus when,
as told in *Arg.* 1. 509 f., he dwelt in the
Idean cave; she is first in Alexandrine
poetry, cf. Call. *H. Zeus* 45–6, Ζεῦ, σὲ
δὲ Κυρβάντων ἑτάραι προσεπηχύναντο
Δικταῖαι Μελίαι, σὲ δ' ἐκοίμισεν Ἀδρήστεια.
    135. σφαῖραν. It is not certain how
the toy of Zeus came to be regarded as
the symbol of the universe; late Cretan
coins shew the child Zeus seated upon
it. For Eros as ball-player, cf. in literature, Anacreon ap. *Ath.* 13. 599C, and
Meleager, *Anth. Pal.* 5. 214, σφαιριστὰν
τὸν Ἔρωτα τρέφω· σοὶ δ', Ἡλιοδώρα,
Βάλλει τὰν ἐν ἐμοὶ παλλομέναν κραδίαν;
in art, cf. S. Reinach, *Rép. de la Stat.
gr. et rom.* 2. 429. 7.
    ἐυτρόχαλον, 'round.' Cf. 889 infr., of
a chariot with good wheels, 4. 907, of a
'rippling' melody, and Eur. *Bacc.* 268,
εὔτροχον γλῶσσαν. Homer uses ἐύ-
τροχος, cf. *Arg.* 4. 1326, 1355; ἐυτρό-
χαλος is first in Hes. *Op.* 599 of a 'well-
rounded' threshing floor, χώρῳ ἐν εὐάέι
καὶ ἐυτροχάλῳ ἐν ἀλωῇ.
    μείλιον. Homer uses μείλια in the
sense of 'gifts to soothe' a god or man,
cf. infr. 594, ἐοικότα μείλια τίσειν 'suitable recompense.' Here and 146, it is
extended to mean 'gifts to soothe a
child,' *i.e.* 'toys.' μείλιον ἁπλότης in
Call. *H. Art.* 230, 'a charm against ill-
weather,' is on Homeric analogy; but
μείλια χρυσοῖο in *Arg.* 4. 1190, in the
sense of 'ornaments,' is a new use.

χειρῶν Ἡφαίστοιο κατακτεατίσσῃ ἄρειον.
χρύσεα μέν οἱ κύκλα τετεύχαται· ἀμφὶ δ' ἑκάστῳ
διπλόαι ἀψῖδες περιηγέες εἰλίσσονται·
κρυπταὶ δὲ ῥαφαί εἰσιν· ἕλιξ δ' ἐπιδέδρομε πάσαις
κυανέη. ἀτὰρ εἴ μιν ἑαῖς ἐνὶ χερσὶ βάλοιο,   140
ἀστὴρ ὥς, φλεγέθοντα δι' ἠέρος ὁλκὸν ἵησιν.

136. Ἡφαίστοιο. The maker of wonderful things, v. n. 43 supr.

κατακτεατίσσῃ. Here only for the Attic κατακτάομαι, used like δέχεσθαι c. gen., 'to receive at another's hands.' The simple verb is Homeric.

137. κύκλα here is used in a spatial sense; Zeno, for example, ap. Diog. Laer. 7. 155, uses the word of the 'zones' of heaven and earth. A κύκλον is nothing more than the space occupied by two semicircular ἀψῖδες, like the golden band on a fountain pen if it were put on in two halves and not entire; the κύκλον is 'golden' in that the ἀψῖδες of which it consists are golden..

8'. This δέ is explanatory, with the force of γάρ; cf. Od. 1. 433, εὐνῇ δ' οὕποτ' ἔμικτο· χόλον δ' ἀλέεινε γυναικός. The contrast is between χρύσεα μέν, and κρυπταὶ δέ.

138. διπλόαι. Simply 'two' numerically, not necessarily 'double'; cf. Soph. O. T. 20-1, Παλλάδος διπλοῖς Ναοῖς, κ.τ.λ.

ἀψῖδες. ἀψίς is used in Homer only in Il. 5. 487, ἀψῖσι λίνοι', of the meshes of a net; it does not recur in this sense till Oppian. After Homer, it is used of anything forming a circle or arc; e.g. of the sun, Eur. Ion 87-8, τὰν ἡμερίαν Ἀψῖδα, and of the rainbow, Arist. Meteor. 3. 2. 3. The scholiast here explains ἀψῖδες as αἱ συναφαί, seams, which makes the description unintelligible.

περιηγέες, 'circular,' a purely Alexandrine word. It is used infr. 1032 of a trench, 1365 of a rock, and in Call. H. Del. 198, of the islands lying round Delos in a circle, Κυκλάδας ὀψομένη περιηγέας. The description in Arat. 401 of the stars of the Corona Australis, δινωτοὶ κύκλῳ περιηγέες εἰλίσσονται, may indicate that this ball is cosmic.

139. ῥαφαί, 'seams.' In Homer only in Od. 22. 186, of the shield of Laertes, ῥαφαὶ δὲ λέλυντο ἱμάντων.

ἕλιξ. The spiral as a mathematical

figure was at this time a recent discovery of the court astronomer Conon, and is a distinctive feature of contemporary Alexandrine art. The actual word is found in Aesch. Prom. 1083, ἕλικες στεροπῆς, cf. in Arg. 1. 438, of smoke rising πορφυρέαις ἑλίκεσσιν.

ἐπιδέδρομε, 'over them all runs a dark blue spiral'; cf. ἐπιδέδρομεν αἴγλη in Od. 6. 45, and Arat. 80. Here again δέ is explanatory; the seams are hidden, for over all there runs a spiral.

140. κυανέη. Properly 'dark blue,' as here; infr. 1031 and 1205 it means 'dark black.' Both are Homeric; e.g. the former of a serpent in Il. 11. 26, the latter in Il. 24. 94 of the mourning veil of Thetis.

It is essential to understand that there is no question of construction, but only of ornament in explanation of περικαλλές, Hephaestus took a ball already made, and covered it with a number of semicircular gold bands; these were so arranged that the joins were each directly above the other. Then the bands were stitched to the main fabric at the point where the two semi-circles met each other, i.e. once on each side of the ball; and it was accordingly possible to conceal the seams by a single line of blue, running once, and once only, round the ball, meander-pattern. See further in Classical Review 1924, pp. 50–51, The Ball of Eros.

ἑαῖς, i.e. 'thy,' v. n. 26 supr.: cf. Il. 21. 104, ἐμῆς ἐν χερσὶ βάλῃσι.

βάλοιο, a somewhat involved condition; 'you would see how pretty the ball is if ever you should have a chance to throw it, which you won't unless you do as I say.' For a general condition, Ap. uses the subj., 2. 1028, ἢν γάρ πού τι θεμιστεύων ἀλίτηται...ἔχουσιν.

141. ὁλκόν, 'furrow,' post-Homeric. ὁλκοῖσιν is used infr. 413 of ordinary furrows made by the plough. With this passage, cf. 1378 infr., of a star ὁλκὸν

τήν τοι ἐγὼν ὀπάσω· σὺ δὲ παρθένον Αἰήταο
θέλξον ὀιστεύσας ἐπ' Ἰήσονι· μηδέ τις ἔστω
ἀμβολίη. δὴ γάρ κεν ἀφαυροτέρη χάρις εἴη.'
*Ὡς φάτο· τῷ δ' ἀσπαστὸν ἔπος γένετ' εἰσαΐοντι.   145
μείλια δ' ἔκβαλε πάντα, καὶ ἀμφοτέρῃσι χιτῶνος
νωλεμὲς ἔνθα καὶ ἔνθα θεᾶς ἔχεν ἀμφιμεμαρπώς.
λίσσετο δ' αἶψα πορεῖν αὐτοσχεδόν· ἡ δ' ἀγανοῖσιν
ἀντομένη μύθοισιν, ἐπειρύσσασα παρειάς,
κύσσε ποτισχομένη, καὶ ἀμείβετο μειδιόωσα·   150
'Ἴστω νῦν τόδε σεῖο φίλον κάρη ἠδ' ἐμὸν αὐτῆς,
ἦ μέν τοι δῶρόν γε παρέξομαι, οὐδ' ἀπατήσω,

147 ἔχετ' Brunck.   149 ἐπειρύσσασα Brunck : ἐπειρύσασα vulg.

ὑπαυγάζων, 4. 296 for a ὁλκὸς Οὐρανίης ἀκτῖνος, and the imitation of the latter in Verg. Aen. 2. 697, of the shooting star, 'longo limite sulcus Dat lucem.' These and other passages illustrate the Alexandrine interest in astronomy as a proper science.

144. ἀμβολίη, 'delay,' a late epic form of ἀναβολή, cf. ἀμβολιεργός for ἀναβολεργός, a 'man who puts off work,' in Hes. Op. 413. Similar new forms in Ap. are 593 ἐπιδρομίη, 830 ἀτημηλίη, 1157 παλιντροπίη, and 676, 974 θευμορίη. The latter is used by Callimachus, who likewise invents, e.g. H. Zeus 91 ἀπημονίη, H. Ap. 78 τελεσφορία, H. Art. 7 πολυωνυμίη, ib. 11 φαεσφορίη, Lout. Pall. 139 εὐαγορίη, frag. 15 Mair (120), 2 αὐταγρεσίη.

ἀφαυροτέρη, schol. ἐλάσσων, 'fainter.' Homeric word, closely connected with φαῦλος; in Arg. 2. 453, ὅτι καὶ ἀφαυρὸς ἵκοιτο, it means probably 'feeble' as here, rather than 'poor.'

145. εἰσαΐοντι, 'as he heard.' Alexandrine for Homeric and Attic εἰσακούω, cf. Il. 8. 97 ἐσάκουσε. Apollonius uses it abs. 368 infr. ; with ἐκ, infr. 903; with acc., infr. 330, and with gen. 1. 764, εἰσαΐων κριοῦ, cf. Theoc. 7. 88, φωνᾶς εἰσαΐων. The metre of this line recalls Od. 8. 295, ὡς φάτο, τῇ δ' ἀσπαστὸν ἐείσατο.

147. νωλεμές, like νωλεμέως, 346 infr., 'unceasingly.' Both are Homeric, and the derivation is quite uncertain.

ἔχεν. Brunck reads ἔχετ', and says that the text is a solecism; but surely it means 'tried to hold her back' (im-

perfect), and governs neither of the genitives?

ἀμφιμεμαρπώς. 'Seizing the goddess by her robe on this side and that.' This compound of the Homeric μάρπτω is first here and recurs in later epic. Mooney takes the construction as θεᾶς ἀμφιμεμαρπὼς ἔχεν τοῦ χιτῶνος.

148. αὐτοσχεδόν, 'forthwith,' as infr. 398, etc.; but Arg. 1. 594, 4, 969, it has the Homeric meaning 'close at hand,' except that Homer uses it always of close fight, Latin cominus. Arat. 901 uses it as prep. c. gen., meaning 'near,' ἀστέρες ἀλλήλων αὐτοσχεδὸν ἰνδάλλονται.

149. ἀντομένη, 'beseeching,' v. n. 35 supr.

ἐπειρύσσασα, 'drawing his cheeks near her,' cf. Apul. Met. 6. 22, 'tunc Juppiter prehensa Cupidinis buccula.' The quantity of the -υ- varies, as in Homer, through confusion of the two roots Fερυ- (protect), and Fερυσ- (drag); e.g. Od. 1. 441 ἐπέρυσσε, and ib. 12. 14, ἐπὶ στήλην ἐρύσαντες. Both H. and Ap. have the vowel short in the aor., e.g. Arg. 2. 586, ἀνείρυσε τηλόθι νῆα: Od. 9. 77, ἀνά θ' ἱστία λεύκ' ἐρύσαντες.

151. ἴστω, 'be my witness,' a regular formula in oaths; cf. Il. 10. 329, ἴστω νῦν Ζεὺς αὐτός. For use to emphasise a statement, cf. Hdt. 4. 76, ἴστω ὑπὸ τοῦ ἀδελφεοῦ ἀποθανών.

ἐμὸν αὐτῆς. Cf. Od. 2. 45, ἐμὸν αὐτοῦ χρεῖος, Eur. Andr. 107, τὸν ἐμὸν μελέας πόσιν. For oaths sworn by the head, cf. Aen. 4. 357, 'testor utrumque caput,' i.e. 'I swear by thy head and mine,' etc.

εἴ κεν ἐνισκίμψῃς κούρῃ βέλος Αἰήταο.'
Φῆ· ὁ δ' ἄρ' ἀστραγάλους συναμήσατο, κὰδ δὲ φαεινῷ
μητρὸς ἑῆς εὖ πάντας ἀριθμήσας βάλε κόλπῳ.   155
αὐτίκα δ' ἰοδόκην χρυσέῃ περικάτθετο μίτρῃ
πρέμνῳ κεκλιμένην· ἀνὰ δ' ἀγκύλον εἵλετο τόξον.
βῆ δὲ Διὸς μεγάλοιο θέων πάγκαρπον ἀλωήν.
αὐτὰρ ἔπειτα πύλας ἐξήλυθεν Οὐλύμποιο
αἰθερίας· ἔνθεν δὲ καταιβάτις ἐστὶ κέλευθος   160
οὐρανίη· δοιὼ δὲ πόλον ἀνέχουσι κάρηνα

158 μεγάλοιο Gerhard: Διὸς (διὲκ suprascriptum) μεγάλοιο θ... *Stras. Pap.* 173:
διὲκ μεγάροιο Διὸς codd.   161 πόλον Platt: πόλοι codd.

153. **ἐνισκίμψῃς**, 'if thou wilt strike
with thy shaft.' Here and infr. 765,
this verb is transitive, as in *Il.* 16. 611–
2, δόρυ μακρὸν Οὔδει ἐνισκίμφθη. Ap. does
not use the passive, but ἐνισκίμψασα in
4. 113 is intransitive, like ἐμπεσοῦσα,
cf. Eur. *Hipp.* 438, ὀργαὶ δ' εἰς σ' ἐπέ-
σκηψαν θεᾶς.
154. **συναμήσατο**, 'gathered together.' This compound of the Homeric
ἀμάω is extant only in Ap., though
συναμησάμενος is cited in the *Et. Mag.*
155. **βάλε κόλπῳ**, 'threw into her
lap.' Ap. is fond of this Homeric use of
the dative, cf. infr. 542.
157. **κεκλιμένην**, 'which was leaning
against a tree.' For the dative, cf. *Od.*
6. 307, κίονι κεκλιμένη of Arete, and 17.
97, κλισμῷ κεκλιμένη of Penelope.
158. For the text, v. crit. appendix,
p. 138. βῆ δὲ θέων is a characteristic
variant of the Homeric βῆ δὲ θέειν, *Il.*
2. 183, etc.; for the participle, cf. also
Il. 1. 391, ἔβαν κήρυκες ἄγοντες, etc.
For the acc. ἀλωήν, rather than the
Homeric genitive (*e.g.* πεδίοιο *Il.* 22.
23), cf. *Anth. Pal.* 7. 273· 4, μέσσα
θέων πελάγευς, *ib.* 10. 23. 4, μέσσα θέει
πελάγη, and Soph. *Aj.* 30, πηδῶντα
πέδια. θέων is a good touch, fortunately
preserved; the impetuous Eros when he
has gained his point does not walk
sedately away, but *runs*. The whole
passage, according to the scholiast, is
based on a poem of Ibycus on the rape
of Ganymede.
πάγκαρπον. Post-Homeric. It can
mean either 'producing all fruits,' *e.g.*
χθών, Pind. *Pyth.* 9. 58 (101), cf.
Soph. *El.* 634–5, θύματα...πάγκαρπα,

or, 'covered with fruit,' as in Soph.
O. T. 83, παγκάρπου δάφνης. Here it is
presumably the latter, unless ἀλωή is
used in the broader sense of 'garden'
rather than 'vineyard.'
159. **αὐτὰρ ἔπειτα**. The use of such
epic tags as this is denounced in an epigram of Pollianus, *Anth. Pal.* 11. 130;
τοὺς κυκλίους τούτους, τοὺς 'αὐτὰρ ἔπειτα'
λέγοντας, Μισῶ, λωποδύτας ἀλλοτρίων
ἐπέων,...Οἱ δ' οὕτως τὸν Ὅμηρον ἀναιδῶς
λωποδυτῶσιν, Ὥστε γράφειν ἤδη 'μῆνιν
ἄειδε θεά.' See further in *Prolegomena*
to Merkel's larger edition of Ap., pp.
34 f.
ἐξήλυθεν. This Homeric use c. gen.
is in 1. 844–5, 2. 202. For the accusative with ἐξέρχομαι, cf. Hdt. 7.
29, 1, ἐξήλυθον...χώρην, and Latin
egredi.
160. **καταιβάτις**, 'a downward path
from Heaven.' For this Alexandrine fem.
of the masc. and fem. adj. καταιβά-
της (or καταιβατός -ή -όν), in *Od.* 13. 110
θύραι...καταιβαταί, cf. *Arg.* 2. 353, Lyc.
90–1, 497. It is quoted as transitive
from Sosiphanes by schol. 533 infr.,
Θεσσαλὶς κόρη, Ψευδὴς σελήνης αἰθέρος
καταιβάτις, *i.e.* 'a false bringer-down of
the moon from the air.'
161. **ἀνέχουσι κ.τ.λ.** 'Two peaks of
lofty mountains uphold the sky, the
highest points of earth, where the rising
sun reddens to a blush in the earliest
rays.' Mooney, following MSS. πόλοι,
takes ἀνέχουσι as intransitive, as infr.
851, 1383: but it is better, with Platt,
to read πόλον, and take it transitive, as
infr. 257, etc.: v. further in crit. appendix, p. 138.

οὐρέων ἠλιβάτων, κορυφαὶ χθονός, ἧχί τ' ἀερθεὶς
ἠέλιος πρώτησιν ἐρεύθεται ἀκτίνεσσιν.
νειόθι δ' ἄλλοτε γαῖα φερέσβιος ἄστεά τ' ἀνδρῶν
φαίνετο καὶ ποταμῶν ἱεροὶ ῥόοι, ἄλλοτε δ' αὖτε   165
ἄκριες, ἀμφὶ δὲ πόντος ἀν' αἰθέρα πολλὸν ἰόντι.
"Ηρωες δ' ἀπάνευθεν ἑῆς ἐπὶ σέλμασι νηὸς

163 ἐρεύθεται G, Paris. unus: ἐρεύγεται vulg.: ἐρείδεται Merkel: ἐπεύχεται
Damste.   164 ἄλλοτε Pariss.: ἄλλοθι vulg.   165 ἱεραὶ ῥοαί Spitzner.
166 ἀν' αἰθέρα Pariss. duo: ἐν αἰθέρι vulg.: ἀν' αἰθέρι LG: ἀν' αἰθέρι παπταίνοντι
prop. Platt.

162. ἠλιβάτων. Always in Homer of a rock, and meaning apparently 'steep,' except in *Od.* 9. 243, of the rock which the Cyclops put at his door, where it must mean 'huge.' Ap. uses it always of mountains, except in 2. 360–1, ἄκρη... Πάντοθεν ἠλίβατος. From the idea of 'steep,' as with Latin *altus*, develops that of depth, hence it is applied to caves in Hes. *Th.* 483, and by Euripides and Stesichorus. For the explanations of the old grammarians, v. Mooney on 1. 739; the commonest but least likely is from ἥλιος and βαίνω, *i.e.* 'where even the sun cannot go.'

ἧχί τε, 'where,' cf. Arat. 1009, *Or. Arg.* 744. Homer uses ἧχι alone, which is reproduced in *Arg.* 4. 925. Callimachus, *H. Zeus* 10, wrote it without *iota subscript*, as Aristarchus and Dionysius did in their Homer, v. schol. *Il.* 1. 607. ἧχί τε is a late use, on the analogy probably of the apparently otiose τε in the Homeric phrase ἔνθα τε; definitely otiose particles are occasionally found in the vulgate of Homer replacing a lost digamma.

163. ἐρεύθεται, 'grows red,' Homeric verb. The noun ἔρευθος, which is un-Homeric, is used of a robe in *Arg.* 1. 726, of the Fleece 4. 173, and of a blush infr. 298, 963, cf. 122. Damste objects to the idea of the sun growing red with his own rays, and reads ἐπεύχεται.

164. νειόθι 'below,' cf. 62, 706: the Homeric use c. gen. is in 1. 63, 255. Apollonius alone has the compound ἐπινειόθι, 4. 1615. He uses νειόθεν with ἐκ in 1. 385, cf. *Il.* 10. 10, νειόθεν ἐκ κραδίης: elsewhere it is abs., as infr. 383, 1358.

φερέσβιος, 'life-giving,' used also of γαῖα in 4. 1509, cf. Hes. *Th.* 693, γαῖα φερέσβιος. It is not Homeric, but occurs in the *Hymns, e.g. H. Dem.* 450, φερέσβιον οὖθαρ ἀρούρης, cf. *Or. Arg.* 311, 323.

165. ἱεροί, cf. 4. 134 ἱερὸν ῥόον. Rivers are called sacred from Homer onwards, *e.g. Il.* 11. 726, ἱερὸν ῥόον Ἀλφειοῖο.

166. ἄκριες, 'peaks,' as in 1192. Homer uses it only in the *Odyssey*; the singular is found only in an inscription. For αἰθέρα, v. crit. appendix, p. 138.

This is an attractive bird's eye view, which is typical of Ap.'s fidelity to nature, and must arise from something deeper than mere academic striving after accuracy. Similarly in *Il.* 13. 13, Poseidon ascends a peak, ἔνθεν γὰρ ἐφαίνετο πᾶσα μὲν Ἴδη, Φαίνετο δὲ Πριάμοιο πόλις καὶ νῆες Ἀχαιῶν. Such descriptions make one of the best features of Alexandrine poetry. This has some points in common with the description in H. Hom. *Dem.* 380f., of the bringing back of Persephone from Hades; ῥίμφα δὲ μακρὰ κέλευθα διήνυσαν· οὐδὲ θάλασσα Οὔθ' ὕδωρ ποταμῶν οὔτ' ἄγκεα ποιήεντα Ἵππων ἀθανάτων οὔτ' ἄκριες ἔσχεθον ὁρμήν, Ἀλλ' ὑπὲρ αὐτάων βαθὺν ἠέρα τέμνον ἰόντες, cf. also Moschus *Europa* 132–3, φαίνετο δ' οὔτ' ἀκτή τις ἀλίρροθος οὔτ' ὄρος αἰπύ, Ἀλλ' ἀὴρ μὲν ἄνωθεν, ἔνερθε δὲ πόντος ἀπείρων.

167–209. The Argonauts meet in council. Jason decides to go in person with a few companions to Aeetes, in the hope that peaceful counsels may prevail.

167. ἀπάνευθεν, adv., 'apart,' v. n. 114. This recalls us to the main theme

ἐν ποταμῷ καθ᾽ ἕλος λελοχημένοι ἠγορόωντο.
αὐτὸς δ᾽ Αἰσονίδης μετεφώνεεν· οἱ δ᾽ ὑπάκουον
ἠρέμας ᾗ ἐνὶ χώρῃ ἐπισχερῶ ἑδριόωντες·   170
'Ὦ φίλοι, ἤτοι ἐγὼ μὲν ὅ μοι ἐπιανδάνει αὐτῷ
ἐξερέω· τοῦ δ᾽ ὕμμι τέλος κρηῆναι ἔοικεν.
ξυνὴ γὰρ χρειώ, ξυνοὶ δέ τε μῦθοι ἔασιν
πᾶσιν ὁμῶς· ὁ δὲ σῖγα νόον βουλήν τ᾽ ἀπερύκων
ἴστω καὶ νόστου τόνδε στόλον οἶος ἀπούρας.   175
ὤλλοι μὲν κατὰ νῆα σὺν ἔντεσι μίμνεθ᾽ ἔκηλοι·
αὐτὰρ ἐγὼν ἐς δώματ᾽ ἐλεύσομαι Αἰήταο,
υἷας ἑλὼν Φρίξοιο δύω δ᾽ ἐπὶ τοῖσιν ἑταίρους.
πειρήσω δ᾽ ἐπέεσσι παροίτερον ἀντιβολήσας,

170 ἠρέμα G, vulg.

of the poem, after a digression of 160
lines.

168. λελοχημένοι, *lit.* 'having placed
themselves in ambush.' This is formed
from the Homeric λοχήσασθαι, just as
from the Homeric βιάω, βεβίηκεν, there
is formed βεβιημένοι infr. 1249. The
latter is passive in *Anth. Pal.* 9. 546.
3 πῦρ βεβιημένον, cf. *Arg.* 4. 1390
ἀναγκαίῃ βεβιημένοι, and Opp. *Hal.* 1.
224.

170. ἠρέμας, 'quietly.' Homeric, like
4. 1314 ἠρέμα.
ἐπισχερῶ. Homer uses this word in
Il. 11. 667, etc. where some take it to
be 'on the shore,' ἐπὶ σχερῷ, citing
Hesychius σχερός· αἰγιαλός. Ap., however, seems definitely to interpret it as
'in order,' 'one after the other'; cf. 4.
451 τὸ γὰρ ἡμιν ἐπισχερὼ ἦεν ἀοιδῆς,
'for this is the next theme of our song.'
It takes a dative in 1. 528, ἐπισχερὼ
ἀλλήλοισιν.

171. ἐπιανδάνει, v. n. 34. ἐπιανδάνω
and ἐφανδάνω are used by both Homer
and Apollonius. The substance of this
speech is reproduced in Jason's address
to the heroes in Val. Flacc. 5. 37 f.

172. ἔοικεν. 'It is for you to bring it
to fulfilment.' For τέλος κρηῆναι, cf. *Il.*
9. 625–6, δοκέει μύθοιο τελευτή...κρανέ-
εσθαι.

173. χρειώ, schol. rightly, κοινὴ γὰρ
ἡ χρεία, 'common is our need'; some
take it here in the sense of 'object,' for
which v.n. 12. Compare Jason's words
at the departure from Iolcus, *Arg.* 1.

336, ξυνὸς γὰρ ἐς Ἑλλάδα νόστος ὀπίσσω,
Ξυναὶ δ᾽ ἄμμι πέλονται ἐς Αἰήταο κέλευθοι;
and Theoc. *Id.* 7. 35, ξυνὰ γὰρ ὁδός,
ξυνὰ δὲ καὶ ἠώς.

174. ἀπερύκων. Homer uses this in
the sense of 'keeping off,' *e.g. Od.* 18.
105, σύας τε κύνας τ᾽ ἀπερύκων. Here it
is to 'keep back,' cf. infr. 384, and the
unique use in 327 infr., 'kept them there.'

175. ἀπούρας. Homeric aorist of
ἀπαυράω, 'let him know that he, and
he alone, deprives our company of its
return.'

178. υἷας κ.τ.λ. This refers to *Arg.*
2. 1090 f. The four sons of Phrixus
were on their way from Colchis to
Orchomenos, when they were wrecked
on the island of Ares; there the
Argonauts landed in obedience to the
instructions of the blind prophet Phineus,
and persuaded them to act as guides to
Colchis; cf. infr. 320 f. In Val. Flacc.
5. 325, Jason simply chooses nine
companions by lot; 'Scythicam qui
se comitentur ad urbem Sorte petit,
numeroque novem ducuntur ab omni.'

179. ἀντιβολήσας, probably the
Homeric sense, as infr. 941, 'on
meeting him'; it seems to have the
post-Homeric sense of 'entreating,' infr.
482. The gen., as in *Arg.* 1. 12,
ἀντιβολήσων Εἰλαπίνης, is Homeric, in
the sense of 'partaking,' cf. *Il.* 4.
342, μάχης καυστείρης ἀντιβολῆσαι; the
dative is rarer in the sense of 'being
present at,' *e.g. Od.* 11. 416, φόνῳ
ἀνδρῶν ἀντεβόλησας, cf. infr. 1213. In

εἴ κ' ἐθέλοι φιλότητι δέρος χρύσειον ὀπάσσαι,   180
ἠὲ καὶ οὔ, πίσυνος δὲ βίῃ μετιόντας ἀτίσσει.
ὧδε γὰρ ἐξ αὐτοῖο πάρος κακότητα δαέντες
φρασσόμεθ', εἴτ' ἄρηι συνοισόμεθ', εἴτε τις ἄλλη
μῆτις ἐπίρροθος ἔσται ἐεργομένοισιν αὐτῆς.
μηδ' αὔτως ἀλκῇ, πρὶν ἔπεσσί γε πειρηθῆναι,   185
τόνδ' ἀπαμείρωμεν σφέτερον κτέρας. ἀλλὰ πάροιθεν
λωίτερον μύθῳ μιν ἀρέσσασθαι μετιόντας.
πολλάκι τοι ῥέα μῦθος, ὃ κεν μόλις ἐξανύσειεν
ἠνορέη, τόδ' ἔρεξε κατὰ χρέος, ᾗπερ ἐῴκει
πρηΰνας. ὁ δὲ καί ποτ' ἀμύμονα Φρίξον ἔδεκτο   190
μητρυιῆς φεύγοντα δόλον πατρός τε θυηλάς.
πάντες ἐπεὶ πάντῃ καὶ ὅτις μάλα κύντατος ἀνδρῶν,

189 ἐώθει Damste.   190 ὅδε vulg.

the sense of 'meet,' Ap. uses also the Alexandrine ἀβολέω, without case infr. 1145, c. dat. 2. 770; the gen. is in *Or. Arg.* 470; cf. also Call. *frag.* 129 (Mair) ἅ βάλε μηδ' ἀβόλησαν.

181. ἠὲ καὶ signifies the more probable alternative, as in 4. 205.

πίσυνος, 'trusting to his might.' This recalls *Il.* 11. 9, ἠνορέῃ πίσυνοι καὶ κάρτεϊ χειρῶν; cf. also Aesch. *Supp.* 352, ἀλκᾷ πίσυνος.

ἀτίσσει, 'will set at nought our quest.' Common in tragedy, but used by Homer only in *Il.* 20. 166, πρῶτον μὲν ἀτίζων, where the short ἀ- is an exception to the ordinary use of such compounds. Ap. has four other instances of this verb, all similarly situated at the end of the verse.

184. μῆτις ἐπίρροθος, 'helpful plan,' a phrase thrice used in *Arg.* 2. Homer uses this adj. only of persons, *Il.* 4. 390, τοίη οἱ ἐπίρροθος ἦεν Ἀθήνη, cf. *Il.* 23. 770: Ap. has also πύργον ἐπίρροθον, 4. 1045. The verb ἐπιρροθέω, which is first in tragedy, is in *Or. Arg.* 293-4, φωνῇ ἐπερρόθεεν, 'helped with all her voice.'

ἐεργομένοισιν, 'if we refrain from the battle-cry.' This is a piece of Homeric criticism; Ap. has taken *Il.* 13. 525, ἐεργόμενοι πολέμοιο, in this sense, against the scholia and Hesych. εἰργόμενοι· κωλυόμενοι. For a similar use, cf. Soph. *O. T.* 890, τῶν ἀσέπτων ἔρξεται, 'refrain from deeds of lawlessness.'

186. ἀπαμείρωμεν, 'deprive.' ἀπαμείρεται occurs as a variant in *Od.* 17. 322, ἥμισυ γάρ τ' ἀρετῆς ἀποαίνυται εὐρύοπα Ζεύς, and in Hesiod for ἀπομείρεται αἶσαν, *Op.* 578, and θεῶν ἀπομείρεται αἰὲν ἐόντων, *Th.* 801. Ap.'s opinion on Hom. *loc. cit.* may be indicated infr. 785, ζωῆς ἀπαμείρεται.

σφέτερον, 'his,' v.n. 26: cf. *Or. Arg.* 728, σφετέρῃσι δαημοσύνῃσι.

187. λωίτερον, 'better,' cf. 850: Homer uses this adj. twice only, as neuter.

188. ἐξανύσειεν, 'fully accomplish,' as infr. 788, 1190. In Homer, it is to 'kill,' ἦ θήν σ' ἐξανύω, *Il.* 11. 365.

189. κατὰ χρέος, 'in seemly fashion,' not 'in time of need,' v.n. 12. Τειρεσίαο κατὰ χρέος, in *Od.* 11. 479, seems to mean χρησόμενος, 'to consult'; with this passage cf. H. Hom. *Herm.* 138, πάντα κατὰ χρέος ἤνυσε δαίμων, 'duly finished all.'

ἐῴκει, 'as is proper,' a typical variant of *Od.* 24. 295, ὡς ἐπεῴκει. Damste objects that it is the same as κατὰ χρέος, and, on the grounds that 'oratio mitis animos lenire solet,' reads ἐώθει.

190. πρηΰνας, 'calming.' First in Hesiod: cf. *Arg.* 1. 265 καταπρήυνεν.

192. κύντατος, 'worst.' Homer has this superlative only in *Il.* 10. 503, μένων ὅ τι κύντατον ἔρδοι, elsewhere the comparative κύντερον, *e.g. Il.* 8. 483, ἐπεὶ οὐ σέο κύντερον ἄλλο. κύντατα in tragedy is used once only, in lyrics,

Ξεινίου αἰδεῖται Ζηνὸς θέμιν ἠδ' ἀλεγίζει.'
'Ὡς φάτ'· ἐπήνησαν δὲ νέοι ἔπος Αἰσονίδαο
πασσυδίῃ, οὐδ' ἔσκε παρὲξ ὅτις ἄλλο κελεύοι. 195
καὶ τότ' ἄρ' υἷας Φρίξου Τελαμῶνά θ' ἕπεσθαι
ὦρσε καὶ Αὐγείην· αὐτὸς δ' ἕλεν Ἑρμείαο
σκῆπτρον· ἄφαρ δ' ἄρα νηὸς ὑπὲρ δόνακάς τε καὶ ὕδωρ
χέρσονδ' ἐξαπέβησαν ἐπὶ θρωσμοῦ πεδίοιο.
Κιρκαῖον τόδε που κικλήσκεται· ἔνθα δὲ πολλαὶ 200
ἐξείης πρόμαλοί τε καὶ ἰτέαι ἐκπεφύασιν,

194 ἐπήνησαν Pariss. duo, Vrat., Vind.: ἐπήνυσαν L: ἐπήνεσαν G: ἐπήνεσσαν vulg. 198 ἄρα Pariss. quatt.: ἀνὰ vulg. 201 πρόμαλοι Stephanus, Et. Mag. 689, 35: πρόμαδοι codd.

τὰ κύντατ' ἄλγη κακῶν, Eur. Supp. 807.

193. **Ξεινίου**, 'the god of strangers,' cf. 986 infr. So too in Od. 9. 271, Zeus is Ξείνιος, ὃς ξείνοισιν ἅμ' αἰδοίοισιν ὀπηδεῖ.

αἰδεῖται. For the singular verb for plural after a parenthesis, cf. 950 infr., and Thuc. 1. 42. 1, ὧν ἐνθυμηθέντες καὶ νεώτερός τις...ἀξιούτω...καὶ μὴ νομίσῃ.

θέμιν, 'ordinance': cf. Or. Arg. 660, Πανομφαίου Ζηνὸς θέμιν οὐκ ἀλεγίζων.

195. **πασσυδίῃ**, 'with all speed,' common in Homer and Ap.

παρέξ, goes with ἔσκε, 'there was no one who dissented.' Mooney takes it with ἄλλο, 'any different plan,' cf. Od. 14. 168, ἄλλα παρὲξ μεμνώμεθα, ib. 4. 348, ἄλλα παρὲξ εἴποιμι. For use as preposition, v. n. 743.

196. **υἷας**. Apollonius uses forms from four different roots; (1) **υἱευ-**: υἷες 2. 1093, and υἷας here. (2) **υἱ-**: υἷος 4. 742, υἷα 2. 1144, υἷε (dual) 1. 118, υἷες 245, etc., υἷας 178, and υἱάσιν 450. (3) **υἱο-**: υἱός 443, υἱέ 2. 214, and υἱόν 357. (4) **υἱυ-**: υἱέος 604, υἱέα 2. 803, υἱέε 517, υἱέες 1. 52, υἱέας 1. 1352, υἱεῖς (voc.) 2. 288. Ap. has un-Homeric forms υἱέε, υἱῆες and υἱῆας; Homer has the following forms which are not in Ap.; υἱοῦ, υἱέι, υἱέι, υἷε (dual dat.), υἱῶν and υἱοῖσι (Rzach, Gramm. Studien, pp. 93-4).

197. Augeias, like Aeetes, was a son of Helios; he is more famous as the owner of the Augean Stables. His reason for going, as given in the catalogue of heroes in Arg. 1. 174, is Herodotean rather than epic; μέγα δ' ἵετο Κολχίδα γαῖαν Αὐτόν τ Αἰήτην ἰδέειν σημάντορα Κόλχων.

198. **σκῆπτρον**. The wand of Hermes, i.e. the herald's wand; it was originally an olive branch crowned with garlands. The crew had an official herald in the person of Aethalides, the son of Hermes; but here his services are not drawn upon, as it is necessary to bring Jason into prominence.

199. **ἐπὶ θρωσμοῦ πεδίοιο**, 'on the rising ground of the plain.' This is a slight alteration of the Homeric ἐπὶ θρωσμῷ πεδίοιο, Il. 20. 3, 10. 160; Ap. has also the plural, 2. 823, ἀνὰ θρωσμοὺς ποταμοῖο, of the uneven places on a river's bank.

200. **Κιρκαῖον**, 'the plain of Circe.' Circe was a sister of Aeetes, and, according to Ap., lived in Colchis before she took up her abode in Italy, infr. 311.

201. **πρόμαλοι**. This is some kind of willow or osier; it is first mentioned in Hippocrates and Eupolis. The old lexicographers are undecided as to its exact nature: Hesychius calls it a tamarisk or willow, μυρίκην, ἄγνον, while the Et. Mag., referring to this passage, calls it εἶδος ἀγρίας δρυός.

ἰτέαι, 'willows.' Properly this word should have the digamma, as in Od. 10. 510, αἴγειροι καὶ ἰτέαι (Curt. Et. no. 593). But in Il. 21. 350, all MSS. but L. Lips. read πτελέαι τε καὶ ἰτέαι, which Ap. has reproduced here with typical alteration; cf. also Arg. 4. 1428, δ' ἰτείης.

τῶν καὶ ἐπ' ἀκροτάτων νέκυες σειρῇσι κρέμανται
δέσμιοι. εἰσέτι νῦν γὰρ ἄγος Κόλχοισιν ὄρωρεν
ἀνέρας οἰχομένους πυρὶ καιέμεν· οὐδ' ἐνὶ γαίῃ
ἔστι θέμις στείλαντας ὕπερθ' ἐπὶ σῆμα χέεσθαι,   205
ἀλλ' ἐν ἀδεψήτοισι κατειλύσαντε βοείαις
δενδρέων ἐξάπτειν ἑκὰς ἄστεος. ἠέρι δ' ἴσην
καὶ χθὼν ἔμμορεν αἶσαν, ἐπεὶ χθονὶ ταρχύουσιν
θηλυτέρας· ἡ γάρ τε δίκη θεσμοῖο τέτυκται.

206 κατειλύσαντες G: κατειλύσασι Samuelsson.   208 ἐπεὶ Pariss.: ἐπὶ vulg.
209 τε Brunck: κε codd.

203. ἄγος, 'an abomination.' This is properly something which, if committed, would bring religious pollution upon the community. It is un-Homeric, and must be distinguished from the Homeric ἀγός, 'chief,' infr. 1245.

205. στείλαντας. This use for περιστέλλειν, 'bury,' is unique. The latter is properly to lay out a corpse, as in Od. 24. 292–3, οὐδέ ἑ μητήρ Κλαῦσε περιστείλασα, and comes to mean 'cherish,' as in Soph. Ph. 447, ἀλλ' εὖ περιστέλλουσιν αὐτὰ δαίμονες.

206. ἀδεψήτοισι, 'untanned.' This is a typical variant of Od. 20. 142, ἀλλ' ἐν ἀδεψήτῳ βοέῃ, cf. ib. 2, κὰδ μὲν ἀδέψητον βοέην στόρεσ'. Ap. does not use βοέη; but Homer has βοείη in Od. 22. 364, θοῶς δ' ἀπέδυνε βοείην.

κατειλύσαντε, 'wrap,' as in Il. 21. 318, κὰδ δέ μιν αὐτὸν Εἰλύσω. For the dual, cf. the doubtful βρίσαντε μιῇ of the vulg. in Arg. 1. 384, which Brunck alters to βρίσαντες ἰῇ. Apollonius seems to have believed, with Zenodotus, that Homer used the dual and the plural indiscriminately, though here he may also have had in mind H. Hom. Ap. 487, ἱστία μὲν πρῶτον κάθετον λύσαντε βοείας: cf. infr. 410, 1173, 1327; and v. also n. 673.

208. ἔμμορεν, 'has,' v.n. 4. Compare Soph. El. 87, γῆς ἰσομοῖρ' ἀήρ, and for the comparatio compendiaria, Isoc. ad Nic. 21 A, τὸ τῆς πολέως ὅλης ἦθος ὁμοιοῦται τοῖς ἄρχουσιν.

ταρχύουσιν, 'bury.' In Homer, where cremation was usual, this can have meant little more than ' perform funeral rites.' Leaf on Il. 7. 85, ὄφρα ἑ ταρχύσωσι κάρη κομόωντες Ἀχαιοί, points out

that it properly implies 'embalming,' but that this meaning must have been lost as early as Homer. The middle, as in Arg. 1. 83, 281, 4. 1500, and Lyc. 882, seems to be an Alexandrine use.

209. θηλυτέρας, simply 'the women,' cf. Od. 11. 386, γυναικῶν θηλυτεράων. Similar uses are ἀγρότερος, by implied contrast with the town dweller, κουρότεροι with the older men, etc.; cf. also στιβαρώτερον, infr. 1057, αἰπύτεροι n. 238.

δίκη, 'custom,' as often in Homer; cf. Od. 24. 255, ἡ γὰρ δίκη ἐστὶ γερόντων; Od. 18. 275, μνηστήρων οὐχ ἥδε δίκη τὸ πάροιθε τέτυκτο. This curious piece of folklore, according to the scholiast, comes from Nymphodorus; it reappears in Aelian V.H. 4, 1, and Sil. Ital. 13. 486. Burial in trees is a common Australian custom (Frazer, Golden Bough, The Magic Art 1. 102); it is also found in the Eastern Archipelago and America (Hastings, Enc. of Rel. and Eth. s.v. Death 4. 421 A). The souls of the dead were thought to reside there, and to be reborn. With the different ritual for the sexes, cf. the Australian custom of laying young men and women on platforms along the boughs of trees, to encourage the spirit to return, while aged men and women, as being useless, were buried in the ground (Frazer, op. cit.). Compare also Paus. 3. 19. 9, for the Rhodian worship of Helen of the Tree, because she caused her maidens disguised as Furies to string her up to a bough; and Frazer (Adonis p. 245), for sacrificial victims hung on trees, and yearly sacrifices of a man god on the sacred tree (ib. p. 246).

Τοῖσι δὲ νισσομένοις Ἥρη φίλα μητιόωσα   210
ἠέρα πουλὺν ἐφῆκε δι' ἄστεος, ὄφρα λάθοιεν
Κόλχων μυρίον ἔθνος ἐς Αἰήταο κιόντες.
ὦκα δ' ὅτ' ἐκ πεδίοιο πόλιν καὶ δώμαθ' ἵκοντο
Αἰήτεω, τότε δ' αὖτις ἀπεσκέδασεν νέφος Ἥρη.
ἔσταν δ' ἐν προμολῇσι τεθηπότες ἕρκε' ἄνακτος   215
εὐρείας τε πύλας καὶ κίονας, οἳ περὶ τοίχους
ἐξείης ἄνεχον· θριγκὸς δ' ἐφύπερθε δόμοιο

---

211 αἰθέρος Koechly.   217 θριγκὸς Vrat., Vind. : θριγχὸς (sup. θ scr. τ man. sec.)
L : θριγγὸς vulg.

210–248. Description of the Palace of Aeetes.

211. ἠέρα κ.τ.λ. Contrast *Arg.* 4. 647–8, ἀμφὶ γὰρ αἰνὴν Ἥρα χεῦε θεὰ πάντ' ἤματα νισσομένοισιν. These two passages may reflect the rival views of critics on *Od.* 7. 14–5, ἀμφὶ δ' Ἀθήνη Πολλὴν ἠέρα χεῦε φίλα φρονέουσ' Ὀδυσῆι; Zenodotus maintained that it was the Phaeacians who were shrouded in mist, Aristarchus that it was Odysseus. Ap. thus uses both types. It is unnecessary to read δι' αἰθέρος, or to punctuate ἐφῆκε, δι' ἄστεος ὄφρα. So too in Verg. *Aen.* 1. 411, Venus shrouds Aeneas and his companions in mist; cf. also the imitation in Val. Flacc. 5. 399–401; 'Ille autem inceptum famula duce protinus urget Aere saeptus iter, patitur nec regia cerni Juno virum, prior Aeetae ne nuntius adsit.'

214. ἀπεσκέδασεν, 'dispersed,' cf. 996. It is *in tmesi* infr. 1360; both forms are Homeric.

215. ἔσταν κ.τ.λ. Typical alteration of *Od.* 24. 392, ἔσταν ἐνὶ μεγάροισι τεθηπότες, and of *Od.* 10. 220, ἔσταν δ' ἐν προθύροισι.

προμολῇσι, 'at the entrance,' Alexandrine. It is used literally in *Arg.* 1. 260, ἐπὶ προμολῇσι κιόντων, 'as they went forth.' It occurs in *Anth. Pal.* 7. 9 for the mouth of a river, and in Call. *H. Art.* 99, 142 for the base of a hill. Mooney finds the latter meaning in *Arg.* 1. 320, στῆ δ' ἄρ' ἐπὶ προμολῆς, referring it to the base of the promontory on which Pagasae was situated; but it is probably simply the point where the road and shore met, the *vestibule* of the

shore, cf. Arat. 239, ἐν προμολῇσι νότοιο, 'in the vestibule of the south.'

ἕρκεα, 'the court,' v. n. 39.

216. τοίχους. Properly this should refer to the wall of the house; that of the court would be τεῖχος or τοιχίον. But as this court appears to contain other houses at the sides, τοῖχοι can apply to all the walls. We are to imagine a court surrounded by a row of columns; the description leads the eye from the columns facing the entrance, *i.e.* those of the αἴθουσα (237), to the wall above and the θριγκός at the top. For a plan of the palace, v. Appendix, p. 135.

217. ἄνεχον, 'pillars that stood up in order round the walls.' It is better to take it thus, than to regard περί as adverbial, 'around,' and ἄνεχον as transitive, as in 161 supr.

θριγκός, 'coping,' *i.e.* the topmost course of stones in a wall, projecting over the lower courses and supporting the roof beams. It is used in this sense in the plural in *Od.* 17. 266, ἐπήσκηται δέ οἱ αὐλὴ Τοίχῳ καὶ θριγκοῖσι, and in the singular, of the frieze along the upper part of the inner wall of a house, *Od.* 7. 86, χάλκεοι μὲν γὰρ τοῖχοι ἐληλέδατ' ἔνθα καὶ ἔνθα, Ἐς μύχον ἐξ οὐδοῦ, περὶ δὲ θριγκὸς κυάνοιο.

ἐφύπερθε, abs. 'above,' as infr. 834 and in Homer. It does not here govern the gen. δόμοιο, as in *Arg.* 2. 393 in the geographical sense 'situated above,' *i.e.* 'beyond,' Φιλύρων δ' ἐφύπερθεν ἔασιν Μάκρωνες. It is abs. also in 4. 1708, μῆῆς ἐφύπερθεν ὀρούσας, where the gen. is governed by ὀρούσας as in Pind. *Pyth.* 10. 61 (95), τῶν δ' ἕκαστος ὀρούει.

λαίνεος χαλκέῃσιν ἐπὶ γλυφίδεσσιν ἀρήρει.
εὔκηλοι δ' ὑπὲρ οὐδὸν ἔπειτ' ἔβαν. ἄγχι δὲ τοῖο
ἡμερίδες χλοεροῖσι καταστεφέες πετάλοισιν   220
ὑψοῦ ἀειρόμεναι μέγ' ἐθήλεον. αἱ δ' ὑπὸ τῆσιν
ἀέναοι κρῆναι πίσυρες ῥέον, ἃς ἐλάχηνεν
Ἥφαιστος. καί ῥ' ἡ μὲν ἀναβλύεσκε γάλακτι,
ἡ δ' οἴνῳ, τριτάτη δὲ θυώδεϊ νᾶεν ἀλοιφῇ·
ἡ δ' ἄρ' ὕδωρ προρέεσκε, τὸ μέν ποθι δυομένῃσιν   225

218 χαλκέῃσιν Pariss. quatt.: χαλκείαις LG.   221 ἐπὶ Pierson.   225 ποτὶ
δυνομένῃσιν Brunck.

218. **λαΐνεος**, 'of stone,' as in *Il.* 22. 154; Ap. has the commoner Homeric and tragic λάϊνος in 1. 668.

γλυφίδεσσιν, 'capitals.' Probably this meant originally 'carving,' *Class. Rev.* 1887 (1) p. 244 A; thence develop three meanings: (1) the 'notch' at the end of an arrow, as probably in *Il.* 4. 122, *Od.* 21. 419, cf. infr. 282. (2) 'grooves' for the feathers, or notches for the fingers; cf. Hdt. 8. 128. 2, and the second explanation *s.v.* in the *Et. Mag.*, τὰς παρὰ τοῖς πτεροῖς ἐντομὰς τοῦ βέλους. (3) 'capitals' in architecture; cf. the *Et. Mag.* with reference to this passage, γλυφὶς καὶ ἡ κεφαλὴ τοῦ κίονος.

219. **εὔκηλοι**, 'silent.' In Homer, this means 'in ease of mind,' for which cf. infr. 1172, and 1. 1290, etc. ἔκηλος is used in H. Hom. *Dem.* 450–1 of an inanimate object, οὔθαρ ἀρούρης...ἔκηλον, from which use that of 'silent' is probably derived.

οὐδόν, 'threshold,' *i.e.* of the court; cf. *Od.* 1. 103–4, ἐπὶ προθύροις Ὀδυσῆος Οὐδοῦ ἐπ' αὐλείου.

220. **ἡμερίδες**, *sc.* ἄμπελοι, 'cultivated' as opposed to 'wild' vines; cf. *Od.* 5. 69, for the ἡμερὶς ἡβώωσα, τεθήλει δὲ σταφυλῇσι in the cave of Calypso.

καταστεφέες, 'covered with.' First in tragedy, especially of suppliant boughs wreathed with wool, or of heralds wearing wreaths, as in Soph. *Tr.* 178, καταστεφῆ Στείχονθ' ὁρῶ τιν' ἄνδρα. For the dative cf. *Od.* 9. 183, σπέος...δάφνῃσι κατηρεφές: Hes. *Op.* 513, λάχνῃ δέρμα κατάσκιον. The gen. is more usual with words of this character; cf. Eur. *Supp.* 259, χλοὴν φυλλάδος καταστεφῆ: Soph. *O. T.* 83, πολυστεφὴς...δάφνης: *El.* 895,

περιστεφῆ...ἀνθέων. κατηρεφής of a wave in *Arg.* 2. 593 is borrowed from *Od.* 5. 367.

221. **ὑψοῦ κ.τ.λ.**, cf. *Od.* 13. 83, of horses ὑψόσ' ἀειρόμενοι.

222. **ἀέναοι**, 'everflowing,' cf. 860. Post-Homeric word, used by epic and lyric writers, and in trag. only in lyrics: it corresponds to the Homeric ἀενάων of *Od.* 13. 109, ἔν θ' ὕδατ' ἀενάοντα. This description is an extension of *Od.* 5. 70, κρῆναι δ' ἑξείης πίσυρες ῥέον ὕδατι λευκῷ, describing the fountains near the cave of Calypso.

πίσυρες, 'four,'cf. 1367. Like Homer, Ap. has also the ordinary τέσσαρες, *Arg.* 1. 946.

ἐλάχηνεν, 'dug.' The simple verb is Alexandrine, cf. Lyc. 624, χέρσον λαχήνῃ; Homer has ἀμφιλαχαίνω, to 'dig round,' φυτὸν ἀμφελάχαινε, *Od.* 24. 242.

223. **ἀναβλύεσκε**, 'gushed forth with milk.' Homer has only ἀποβλύζω, *Il.* 9. 491; Ap. has ἔβλυσε from βλύζω in 4. 1446. βλύω and its compounds are un-Homeric. The quantity of the -υ- varies; it is short in ἐπιβλύει 4. 1238, long in περιβλύει 4. 788 and ἐκβλύοντα 4. 1417.

224. **νᾶεν**, 'flowed': cf. *Od.* 9. 222, ναῖον δ' ὀρῷ ἄγγεα: *Arg.* 1. 1146, ὕδατι νᾶεν: Call. *H. Art.* 224, νᾶεν φόνῳ.

225. **προρέεσκε**. Homer uses this simply of a river flowing; for the cognate accusative, cf. H. Hom. *Ap.* 380, προρέειν ὕδωρ: Theoc. 5. 124, Ἰμέρα ῥείτω γάλα: Luc. *V.H.* 1. 7, ποταμῷ οἶνον ῥέοντι. With the whole description, which is typically Alexandrine, cf. Luc. *V.H.* 2. 213, πηγαὶ δὲ περὶ τὴν πόλιν ὕδατος μὲν πέντε καὶ ἑξήκοντα καὶ τετρακόσιαι, μέλιτος δὲ ἄλλαι τοσαῦται μύρου

θέρμετο Πληιάδεσσιν, ἀμοιβηδὶς δ' ἀνιούσαις
κρυστάλλῳ ἴκελον κοίλης ἀνεκήκιε πέτρης.
τοῖ' ἄρ' ἐνὶ μεγάροισι Κυταιέος Αἰήταο
τεχνήεις Ἥφαιστος ἐμήσατο θέσκελα ἔργα.
καί οἱ χαλκόποδας ταύρους κάμε, χάλκεα δέ σφεων   230
ἦν στόματ', ἐκ δὲ πυρὸς δεινὸν σέλας ἀμπνείεσκον·
πρὸς δὲ καὶ αὐτόγυον στιβαροῦ ἀδάμαντος ἄροτρον
ἤλασεν, Ἡελίῳ τίνων χάριν, ὅς ῥά μιν ἵπποις

226 Πληιάδεσσιν ἐθέρμετ' Hermann.

δὲ πεντακόσιαι, μικρότεραι μέντοι αὖται. καὶ ποταμοὶ γάλακτος ἕπτα καὶ οἴνου ὀκτώ; and the paradoxographi *passim*.

δυομένῃσιν, 'water which grew warm when the Pleiads set, but when they rose, bubbled forth cold as ice from the hollow rock.' The Pleiads set at the end of October, and rise at the end of April; so Aeetes had cold water in summer and warm in winter. The long -υ- is un-Homeric, cf. *Arg.* 1. 581, 925; Homer has it short in the present and imperfect, and long in the future participle δυσομένου, *Od.* 1. 24.

226. ἀμοιβηδίς, 'in turn,' as in *Il.* 18. 506, *Od.* 18. 310. Ap. has also the following forms, which are Alexandrine; ἀμοιβαδίς 1. 457 and c. gen. 4. 199, ἀμοιβαδόν 2. 1226, ἀμοιβηδόν 2. 1071 and ἐναμοιβαδίς c. gen. 1. 380.

227. κρυστάλλῳ. Ap. may be thinking of the two streams of Scamander in *Il.* 22. 149 f.; ἡ μὲν γάρ θ' ὕδατι λιαρῷ ῥέει, ἀμφὶ δὲ καπνὸς Γίγνεται ἐξ αὐτῆς ὡς εἰ πυρὸς αἰθομένοιο· Ἡ δ' ἐτέρη θέρεϊ προρέει εἰκυῖα χαλάζῃ, Ἡ χιόνι ψυχρῇ, ἢ ἐξ ὕδατος κρυστάλλῳ.

ἀνεκήκιε, 'gushed forth from.' Intransitive in the *Iliad*, and here only c. gen.: for the cognate acc., cf. 4. 600, ἀνακηκίει ἀτμόν, and n. 225 supr.

228. ἐνὶ μεγάροισι. Ap. uses this plural as referring to the house and palace generally; it may represent his views on *Od.* 19. 16, ἔρυξον ἐνὶ μεγάροισι γυναῖκας, which some take to refer, like *Od.* 17. 569, 19. 16, 30, specifically to the women's quarters. This may be implied, but not necessarily, infr. 251.

Κυταιέος. Typical Alexandrine for Colchian. Cyte, the modern Kutais, was associated by the Alexandrine and Roman poets with the birth of Medea; cf. Prop. 1. 1. 24, Euphorion ap. schol.

Od. 4. 228, Κυταιῖς (?)...Μήδη, and Val. Flacc. 6. 693, 'terris Cytaeis.'

229. τεχνήεις. This is probably founded on *Od.* 8. 296-7, δεσμοὶ τεχνήεντες...Ἡφαίστοιο. The adv. τεχνηέντως is used by Homer and Ap. of skill with a rudder, *Od.* 5. 270, *Arg.* 1. 561. For Hephaestus as the maker of marvels, v. n. 43 supr. This whole description is clearly modelled on those in Homer of the home of Calypso and the palace of Alcinous. From the latter comes the notion of the trees, *Od.* 7. 86 f., esp. 114 f., and from the former, that of the four fountains, *Od.* 5. 70.

θέσκελα, 'wondrous works': cf. *Od.* 11. 610, ἵνα θέσκελα ἔργα τέτυκτο: *Il.* 3. 130, ἵνα θέσκελα ἔργα ἴδηαι: and Hes. *frag.* 96 (Rzach, p. 165, l. 58), μήδετο θέσκελα ἔργα.

230. κάμε, 'wrought,' transitive as often in Homer; cf. esp. *Il.* 2. 101, σκῆπτρον ἔχων, τὸ μὲν Ἥφαιστος κάμε τεύχων. In the middle, the Homeric νῆσον...ἐκάμοντο of *Od.* 9. 130 (cf. *Arg.* 2. 718, ἱρὸν ἐκάμοντο), is extended to ἄεθλον 'perform the task,' 580 infr.

231. ἀμπνείεσκον, 'they breathed.' For the cognate acc., v. n. 225; cf. 410, 1292, 1303 and 1327 infr., and *Il.* 6. 102, δεινὸν ἀποπνείουσα πυρὸς μένος αἰθομένοιο: Pind. *Ol.* 8. 36, ἀμπνεῦσαι καπνόν.

232. αὐτόγυον, cf. 1285. This is founded on Hes. *Op.* 432-3, δοιὰ δὲ θέσθαι ἄροτρα, πονησάμενος κατὰ οἶκον, Αὐτόγυον καὶ πηκτόν. In the former, the γύης (*ploughtree*) is of a piece with the ἔλυμα (*stock*) and ἱστοβοεύς (*pole*); in the latter the three parts are all mortised together; cf. also 412 infr., τετράγυον.

233. ἤλασεν, 'forged': cf. *Il.* 12. 295-6, ἀσπίδα...ἣν ἄρα χαλκεὺς Ἥλασεν.

ἵπποις, 'in his chariot,' as often in Homer with this plural: cf. *Il.* 5. 46,

δέξατο, Φλεγραίῃ κεκμηότα δηιοτῆτι.
ἔνθα δὲ καὶ μέσσαυλος ἐλήλατο· τῇ δ' ἔπι πολλαὶ 235
δικλίδες εὐπηγεῖς θάλαμοί τ' ἔσαν ἔνθα καὶ ἔνθα·
δαιδαλέη δ' αἴθουσα παρὲξ ἑκάτερθε τέτυκτο.
λέχρις δ' αἰπύτεροι δόμοι ἔστασαν ἀμφοτέρωθεν.
τῶν ἤτοι ἄλλῳ μέν, ὅτις καὶ ὑπείροχος ἦεν,

235 ἐπὶ codd.　　　239 ἄλλῳ Paris. unus, Vrat.: ἄλλων LG : ἄλλον vulg.

ἵππων ἐπιβησόμενον. V. infr. 311 for Circe's journey in the solar chariot.

234. Φλεγραίῃ, i.e. the battle of the gods and giants at Phlegra; this was identified with various volcanic places, especially with Pallene in Chalcidice.

κεκμηότα, 'tired after the battle,' as natural for one who suffered from lameness; the scholiast objects that Hephaestus was stronger than the giants, apparently taking this as 'worsted,' as in Pind. *Pyth.* 1. 78 (151), Μήδειοι κάμον, *ib.* 80 (156).

235. μέσσαυλος. This has nothing to do with the 'inner court' of Homer, in which sense the word is either m. or neut., *Il.* 11. 548, etc. ἡ μέσσαυλος in Attic is the connecting door between two halls (Eust. on *Il.* 11. 548, Ap. *Lex. s.v.* μέσσαυλον); here it is the door between the court and the μέγαρον. Compare Lysias *Erat.* 17 ἐψόφει ἡ μέταυλος καὶ ἡ αὔλειος, and Harpocration's explanation that αὔλειος in an Attic house is the entrance from the street: v. also *Class. Rev.* 41 (1927), pp. 9–10, for fuller references.

ἐλήλατο. This responds to ἤλασεν supr., and means 'had been forged.' The entrance to the μέγαρον was a wrought metal of such magnificence as to attract the notice of strangers in the courtyard, and to call for comment by the narrator. Editors take μέσσαυλος wrongly, in the sense of an 'inner court,' and translate this accordingly 'had been built,' or, as often in Homer and Herodotus, simply 'ran.'

τῇ δ' ἔπι, not '*in*' the μέσσαυλος, but 'in addition to it.' Along the whole length of the πρόδομος, on either side of the μέσσαυλος or central door, were a number of doors of rooms, which were accessible from the outer court, or more

strictly from the πρόδομος itself, and visible through the pillars of the πρόδομος from the outer entrance.

236. δικλίδες, 'double-folding,' in Homer usually with θύραι, etc. and later, as here, used alone.

εὐπηγεῖς, 'well-built,' cf. 1235. This corresponds to *Od.* 2. 344, etc., σανίδες πυκινῶς ἀραρυῖαι Δικλίδες. Homer uses εὐπηγής only of stature, *Od.* 21. 334, οὗτος δὲ ξεῖνος μάλα μὲν μέγας ἠδ' εὐπηγής.

θάλαμοι, 'chambers.' This can be used without technical significance of any room in the Homeric house except the μέγαρον.

237. αἴθουσα, 'colonnade, portico,' as in 39 supr. This ran παρὲξ ἑκάτερθε, 'the whole way along, on either side' of the μέσσαυλος or central door.

238. λέχρις. Peculiar to Ap. (cf. 1160), formed from the tragic λέχριος: *i.e.* 'crossways, at right angles' to the portico. These buildings stood on the right and left of the courtyard, adjoining the main building of the palace, and were entered from the colonnade which ran (237) round the court.

δόμοι. Probably 'suites' rather than separate erections. For δόμος used by Homer for an apartment within the palace, cf. *Od.* 1. 330, κλίμακα δ' ὑψηλὴν κατεβήσετο οἷο δόμοιο, and *Od.* 21. 5. αἰπύτεροι need not imply that these were higher than the main building containing the μέγαρον: it may mean 'rising in successive storeys' above the αἴθουσα, or simply 'of considerable height,' cf. n. 209, 1057.

239. ὑπείροχος. The scholiast takes this as ὑψηλότερος, 'higher.' In Homer it is rather 'superior,' *e.g. Il.* 6. 208, αἰὲν ἀριστεύειν καὶ ὑπείροχον ἔμμεναι ἄλλων. Tragedy has ὑπέροχος: Aesch. *P. V.* 428, Soph. *Tr.* 1096.

κρείων Αἰήτης σὺν ἑῇ ναίεσκε δάμαρτι· 240
ἄλλῳ δ' Ἄψυρτος ναῖεν πάις Αἰήταο.
τὸν μὲν Καυκασίη νύμφη τέκεν Ἀστερόδεια
πρίν περ κουριδίην θέσθαι Εἰδυῖαν ἄκοιτιν,
Τηθύος Ὠκεανοῦ τε πανοπλοτάτην γεγαυῖαν.
καί μιν Κόλχων υἷες ἐπωνυμίην Φαέθοντα 245
ἔκλεον, οὕνεκα πᾶσι μετέπρεπεν ἠιθέοισιν.
τοὺς δ' ἔχον ἀμφίπολοί τε καὶ Αἰήταο θύγατρες
ἄμφω, Χαλκιόπη Μήδειά τε. τῇ μὲν ἄρ' ἦγε

243 Ἰδυῖαν L.   245 καὶ Κόλχων υἷές μιν Wilamowitz.   248 τὴν μὲν ἄρ
οἴγε...μετιοῦσαν Vatt. duo, Vrat., Vind.: τῇ μὲν ἄρ' οἴγε...μετιοῦσαν LG: τῇ μὲν
corr. τὴν μὲν L 16 : ἡ μὲν ἄρ' ἦει...μετιοῦσα vulg.: βῆ μὲν ἄρ' ἦγε...μετιοῦσα
Gerhard: τὴν μὲν ἄρ' εὗρον...μετιοῦσαν Damste: τῇ μὲν ἄρ' ἦγε...μετιοῦσα Platt.
Versum post 249 excidisse coniecit Wilamowitz.

240. δάμαρτι. Eidyia is the mother of Medea and wife of Aeetes in Hes. *Th.* 958; her descent from Oceanos dates from the earliest legend, when Aea was supposed to lie on the border of Ocean. Apollonius is the first to make Absyrtus the elder brother of Medea; in Euripides, etc. he is younger. His mother is variously given.

242. Ἀστερόδεια. Asterodeia as mother of Absyrtus is mentioned only here and by the Pontic historian Diophantus.

243. θέσθαι, 'before he took Eidyia as his lawful wife.' Cf. *Od.* 21. 72, γῆμαι θέσθαι τε γυναῖκα; the active is used of a third party 'arranging' a marriage, *Il.* 19. 297–8, ἀλλά μ' ἔφασκες Κουριδίην ἄλοχον θήσειν.

244. πανοπλοτάτην, 'the very youngest,' here only. Homer has ὁπλότατος, and the Homeric comparative ὁπλότερος is in *Arg.* 1. 43.

245. ἐπωνυμίην, 'by name,' the acc. of the adjective used adverbially. For the direct acc., cf. Hdt. 2. 44. 4, ἐπωνυμίην ἔχοντος Θασίου εἶναι and *ib.* 4. 15. 2. This is modelled on *Il.* 22. 506, Ἀστυάναξ, ὃν Τρῶες ἐπίκλησιν καλέουσιν.

Φαέθοντα, 'the Shining One,' cf. 1236. It is properly an epithet of the Sun, *Il.* 11. 735, and is naturally used of one of solar descent. Absyrtus-Phaethon is not, with Knaack (*Quaestiones Phaethonteae*, pp. 14 f.), to be too closely iden-

tified with the Phaethon who drove the chariot of the Sun and fell into the Eridanus, *Arg.* 4. 598. The original inspiration of these lines is probably *Il.* 6. 402–3, τὸν δ' Ἕκτωρ καλέεσκε Σκαμάνδριον· αὐτὰρ οἱ ἄλλοι Ἀστυάνακτ', οἶος γὰρ ἐρύετο Ἴλιον Ἕκτωρ. Alexandrine etymologists were very fond of such derivations (cf. Introd. p. xxvii), and the scholia to Homer abound in them. Callimachus, for instance, spelt Achilles with a single -λ-, and explained it as ἄχος τοῖς Ἰλεῦσιν (*frag.* 549 Schneider, gramm. in *Anecd. Oxon.* 4. p. 403. 29).

246. μετέπρεπεν, 'was conspicuous among,' cf. 335. This is a typical adaptation of *Il.* 2. 579, πᾶσιν δὲ μετέπρεπεν ἡρώεσσιν, cf. *Or. Arg.* 169. Homer uses this verb also with a double dative, ἔγχεϊ Τρωσὶ μεταπρέπω, *Il.* 16. 835, cf. *ib.* 194 with the infinitive. Ap. uses ἐν, infr. 443, and the simple dative when only the means of superiority is referred to, 4. 220 ἵπποισι μετέπρεπεν.

248. Ap. is following Herodorus in making Chalciope daughter of Aeetes and wife of Phrixus (schol. 2. 1123).

Μήδεια. This, except for the invocation, is the first mention of Medea by name; she has hitherto been referred to indirectly. The attention of the reader is kept on the alert by these vague references, so that her actual entrance into the action of the poem is made with considerable effect.

ἐκ θαλάμου θαλαμόνδε κασιγνήτην μετιοῦσα—
Ἥρη γάρ μιν ἔρυκε δόμῳ· πρὶν δ' οὔτι θάμιζεν 250
ἐν μεγάροις, Ἑκάτης δὲ πανήμερος ἀμφεπονεῖτο
νηόν, ἐπεί ῥα θεᾶς αὐτὴ πέλεν ἀρήτειρα—
καί σφεας ὡς ἴδεν ἆσσον, ἀνίαχεν· ὀξὺ δ' ἄκουσεν
Χαλκιόπη· δμωαὶ δὲ ποδῶν προπάροιθε βαλοῦσαι
νήματα καὶ κλωστῆρας ἀολλέες ἔκτοθι πᾶσαι 255
ἔδραμον. ἡ δ' ἅμα τοῖσιν ἑοὺς υἵηας ἰδοῦσα
ὑψοῦ χάρματι χεῖρας ἀνέσχεθεν· ὡς δὲ καὶ αὐτοὶ
μητέρα δεξιόωντο, καὶ ἀμφαγάπαζον ἰδόντες

252 θεᾶς Merkel: θεῆς codd. 254 ποδῶν om. LG. 256 τοῖσιν Vatt.,
Stephanus: τῆσιν LG.

248–274. The sons of Phrixus meet their mother, and Aeetes and the queen come from the palace.
τῇ μὲν ἄρ' ἦγε...μετιοῦσα. For the text of this passage, v. crit. appendix, p. 138. 'There was Medea, going in search of.'
250. θάμιζεν, 'was not often in the house.' This is adapted from Il. 18. 386, πάρος γε μὲν οὔ τι θαμίζεις, cf. n. 52-4 supr.
251. Ἑκάτης. This is a complete departure from Homeric ideas. Magic in the Argonautica is a definite branch of religion; Hecate is its patroness, and its priestesses are Medea and such other γυναῖκες φαρμακίδες as go in search of roots and corpses (Arg. 4. 51). Hecate is first found in Hes. Th. 411, as daughter of Perses, cf. Arg. 3. 467, 1035. It is best, with Robert (gr. Myth. 1. 321), to regard the name as being originally an attribute of Artemis, who was worshipped under that title in Athens, Delos, and Epidaurus; cf. also ἕκατος as applied to her brother Apollo. When she developed into a separate figure, Hecate like Artemis was regarded as the patroness of doors and ways, and was worshipped at places where three roads met. From the association of such places with spirits—they were regarded as the meeting places of spirits and men—have arisen the later ideas of her position as a chthonian goddess, and in particular as patroness of sorcery both benevolent and malevolent; cf. infr. 478.
πανήμερος, 'all day.' First in tragedy;
the Homeric πανημέριος is in Arg. 1. 1358, etc.
ἀμφεπονεῖτο, 'attended to.' In Il. 23. 159, some read ἀμφὶ πονήσομεθ' separately, not as a compound verb.
252. ἀρήτειρα, 'priestess,' an Alexandrine feminine of the Homeric ἀρητήρ; cf. Arg. 1. 312, Call. H. Dem. 1.
253. ὀξὺ δ' ἄκουσεν, 'Chalciope was quick to hear.' Cf. Il. 17. 256, ὀξὺ δ' ἄκουσεν Ὀιλῆος ταχὺς Αἴας, and Leaf ad loc.; 'the power of hearing, being regarded as something that goes out of a man, is naturally called keen when it penetrates to a distance.'
255. νήματα καὶ κλωστῆρας, 'yarn and spindles.' A combination of a Homeric with a later word; the former is in Homer only in the phrase μή μοι μεταμώνια νήματ' ὄληται, Od. 2. 98, 19. 143, the latter is first in drama. It is used in Theoc. Id. 24. 70 of the spindle of Fate, Μοῖρα κατὰ κλωστῆρος ἐπείγει.
ἔκτοθι, 'outside.' Here only used abs.; the Homeric use c. gen. is in 373, 1199 infr.
256. υἵηας. For the form, v. n. 196.
257. ὑψοῦ. As the scholiast points out, this should be ὑψόσε, since ὑψοῦ is properly of 'rest at' a place; but the Alexandrines are lax in this respect, cf. in 255, 261 of this book, ἔκτοθι, τηλόθι for ἔκτοσε, τηλόσε, and 1. 63 νειόθι γαίης used of motion.
258. δεξιόωντο, properly to 'greet with the right hand,' as in H. Hom. Aphr. 6. 15-6, οἱ δ' ἠσπάζοντο ἰδόντες Χερσί τε δεξιόωντο. It is not in Homer.

γηθόσυνοι· τοῖον δὲ κινυρομένη φάτο μῦθον·
'"Ἔμπης οὐκ ἄρ' ἐμέλλετ' ἀκηδείῃ με λιπόντες 260
τηλόθι πλάγξασθαι· μετὰ δ' ὑμέας ἔτραπεν αἶσα.
δειλὴ ἐγώ, οἷον πόθον Ἑλλάδος ἔκποθεν ἄτης
λευγαλέης Φρίξοιο ἐφημοσύνῃσιν ἔλεσθε
πατρός. ὁ μὲν θνῄσκων στυγερὰς ἐπετέλλετ' ἀνίας
ἡμετέρῃ κραδίῃ. τί δέ κεν πόλιν Ὀρχομενοῖο, 265

263 λευγαλέης Platt: λευγαλέης codd. φημοσύνῃσινέεσθαι L: ἐφημοσύνῃσιν
ἔεσθε G: ἐφημοσύνῃσι νέεσθαι vulg.: ἐφημοσύνῃσιν ἔλεσθε Brunck, cum quo
fortasse congruit dubia lectio ap. Ox. Pap. 6. 874. 264 ἐπετέλλετ' Ox. Pap.
6. 874: ἐπετείλατ' codd.

ἀμφαγάπαζον, cf. 1167 infr., and Od. 14.381, ἐγὼ δέ μιν ἀμφαγάπαζον, 'greeted with a warm embrace.' The middle ἀμφαγαπαζόμενος is in Il. 16.192.

259. κινυρομένη, 'in the midst of her lamentations,' cf. 664 infr. The verb is first found in lyrics in Aesch. Sept. 123, κινύρονται φόνον χαλινοί, 'the bridles chatter murder.' The adj. κινυρός is Homeric; Il. 17. 4–5, ὥς τις περὶ πόρτακι μήτηρ Πρωτοτόκος κινυρή, cf. Arg. 4. 605 of the Heliades, μύρονται κινυρὸν μέλεαι γόον. The scholiast on Arg. 1. 292 gives a desperate derivation: κυρίως ἐστὶν ἐπὶ βοός, καὶ εἴρηται παρὰ τὸ κινεῖν τὴν οὐρὰν ἐν τῷ μυκᾶσθαι.

260. ἐμέλλετε, 'ye were not destined to,' cf. 1133; this use is peculiar to epic poetry. Ap. uses μέλλε or ἔμελλε (infr. 753, 837) except in 1. 1309, a line taken from Callimachus, according to the scholia; καὶ τὰ μὲν ὡς ἤμελλε μετὰ χρόνον ἐκτελέεσθαι; in using ἤμελλε he follows Zenodotus on Il. 12. 34, ὡς ἄρ' ἔμελλον κ.τ.λ., a use which our scholia brand as a common error of post-Homeric poets.

ἀκηδείῃ, 'indifference,' post-Homeric. The plural appears to have two senses, 2. 219 as here, and infr. 298, which according to the schol. means πολυκήδειαι, λῦπαι. Homer has ἀκηδής meaning 'uncared-for,' or 'without sorrow'; Ap. has only the latter, infr. 597, and for the former uses the Homeric ἀκήδεστοι, 2. 151, cf. Il. 6. 60.

261. τηλόθι, ἀντὶ τοῦ τηλόσε, schol.: v. n. 257.

262. ἔκποθεν, 'from some infatuation,' peculiar to Ap. He is particularly fond

of ἔκποθεν ἀφράστοιο, as infr. 1289. Qu. Sm. has ἔκποθι, 9. 420.

263. λευγαλέης, 'through the dire commands.' Take with Platt as a dative; Ap. and Qu. Sm. do not qualify the gen. with ἔκποθεν, except in the latter's ἔκποθεν Ἰδαίων ὀρέων, which is simply an extension of Ἴδης. The adj. is common in Homer; the adv. λευγαλέως is in Homer only in Il. 13. 723, in Ap. only infr. 703 and 2. 129.

ἐφημοσύνῃσιν, 'solemn command,' Homeric; for the sing. v. infr. 602. This refers to the command of Phrixus to his sons in Arg. 2. 1096, to go to Orchomenos to take possession of his wealth.

ἔλεσθε, 'with what a yearning were ye seized;' v. crit. note: Ox. Pap. 6. 874 is obscure, but clearly does not conform with L. and G. For the hiatus in the weak caesura, cf. 492, 591, 737, and with a proper name in 409, 495, πεδίον τὸ Ἀρήιον.

264. ἐπετέλλετ', 'bitter sorrow was that which he continually urged.' The imperfect of the papyrus should be adopted against the aorist of the MSS.; the aorist is used in 2. 1096, referring to the same subject, but here it is the wife speaking, who was present at the death-bed, and remembers the insistent charge. The line may be modelled on Od. 11. 622, ὁ δέ μοι χαλεποὺς ἐπετέλλετ' ἀέθλους. For other uses of this verb, cf. 276–7 infr. in tmesi, unique in the sense of 'attacking,' and literally in 4. 141 of spirals, 'rising on top of one another,' ἄλλη δ' αἶψ' ἑτέρη ἐπιτέλλεται. It is used of a star rising in Hes. Op. 567, H. Hom. Herm. 371; for this Ap. uses ἀνατέλλω infr. 959.

GA 3

ὅστις ὅδ' Ὀρχομενός, κτεάνων Ἀθάμαντος ἕκητι
μητέρ' ἐὴν ἀχέουσαν ἀποπρολιπόντες, ἵκοισθε;'
Ὣς ἔφατ'· Αἰήτης δὲ πανύστατος ὦρτο θύραζε,
ἐκ δ' αὐτὴ Εἰδυῖα δάμαρ κίεν Αἰήταο,
Χαλκιόπης ἀίουσα· τὸ δ' αὐτίκα πᾶν ὁμάδοιο   270
ἕρκος ἐπεπλήθει. τοὶ μὲν μέγαν ἀμφεπένοντο
ταῦρον ἅλις δμῶες· τοὶ δὲ ξύλα κάγκανα χαλκῷ
κόπτον· τοὶ δὲ λοετρὰ πυρὶ ζέον· οὐδέ τις ἦεν,
ὃς καμάτου μεθίεσκεν, ὑποδρήσσων βασιλῆι.
     Τόφρα δ' Ἔρως πολιοῖο δι' ἠέρος ἷξεν ἄφαντος,   275

270 Χαλκιό)πην μ(... *Ox. Pap.* 6. 874, fortasse μετιοῦσα, cf. 249 supr.
271 ἀμφεπένοντο LG, *Pap.*: ἀμφιπένοντο Pariss.

266. ὅστις κ.τ.λ., cf. *Aen.* 5. 83,
'nec tecum Ausonium, quicunque est,
quaerere Thybrim.'
    267. ἐήν, *i.e.* ὑμετέρην, v. n. 26.
ἀποπρολιπόντες, 'deserting,' cf. 1.
1285. This is first in Hes. ap. Paus. 9.
36, 7; Ap. does not use the Homeric
ἐκπρολείπω. The imperf. with hiatus in
2.1230, ἀποπροέλειπον, is on the analogy
of ὑπεκπροέλυσαν in *Od.* 6. 88.
    268. πανύστατος, 'last of all,' cf. *Il.*
23. 547, πανύστατος ἦλθε διώκων. With
ὦρτο (*sc.* ἰέναι), cf. 1165, ὦρτ' ἰέναι. It
is merely a variation of the ordinary
ἦλθε of Homer.
    269. In the papyrus, this line is re-
written at the bottom of the column with
a note of an alternative reading; 270
reads (Χαλκιό)πην μ..., with Χαλκιόπης
ἀίουσα in the margin, suggestive of
μετιοῦσα, 'coming in search of,' for
which cf. 249 supr.
    271. ἐπεπλήθει, 'was filled.' This
form is here only; for the ppf. to express instantaneous action, cf. *Arg.* 1.
1329 ἐβεβήκει, and 450 infr.
    ἀμφεπένοντο. This form in L. and G.
is supported by the papyrus, cf. *Il.* 4.
220; Brunck and edd. read ἀμφι- with
4 Paris MSS.
    272. ἅλις, 'in great numbers': cf. *Il.*
3. 384, Τρωαὶ ἅλις, and 67 supr. ἄδην,
infr. 1127, seems to be an adverb, as in
Qu. Sm. 1. 796, ἄδην ἐπέχευεν ἄλειφα,
which is probably the original form. In
Homer it can govern a genitive, viz. *Il.*
19. 423, ἄδην ἐλάσαι πολέμοιο, with
which cf. Aesch. *Ag.* 828, ἄδην ἔλειξεν
αἵματος; some take it as an accusative

in Homer, 'to a satiety.' The best MSS.
give ἄδην a smooth breathing in Homer,
but Aristarchus wrote it with rough,
which is fundamentally correct.
    κάγκανα, 'dry,' cf. Hesych. καγκαίνειν·
θάλπειν, ξηραίνειν. This recalls *Il.* 21.
364, ὑπὸ δὲ ξύλα κάγκανα κεῖται, and
Od. 18. 308, περὶ δὲ ξύλα κάγκανα θῆκαν.
    273. ζέον, causal, 'made to boil,' cf.
n. 225, and *Anth. Pal.* 7. 385. 7,
θυμὸν...ἔξεσας. In *Arg.* 1. 734, ἀκτῖνα
πυρὸς ζείουσαν αὐτμήν, Mooney takes it
as in apposition to ἀκτῖνα, while Brunck
reads dat. αὐτμῇ.
    274. μεθίεσκεν, 'ceased from the toil';
this, and 4. 622 ἐξανίεσκον, are un-Homeric forms modelled on Hes. *Th.* 157
ἀνίεσκε.
    ὑποδρήσσων, 'in service to the king.'
This verb, first in Ap. and recurring in
Musaeus, seems to be formed from
Od. 15. 330, 333, ὑποδρηστῆρες, ὑπο-
δρώωσιν.
    275-298. Eros appears, and fires
Medea with love for Jason.
    275. πολιοῖο, schol. διαφανοῦς, 'clear.'
This is an epithet in Homer particularly
of the sea; cf. Eur. *Or.* 1376, πολιὸν
αἰθέρα. πολιὸν ἔαρ in Hes. *Op.* 477,
492 may be in this sense; but some
translate 'grey,' *i.e.* of the buds which
have not yet shed their iron-grey husks.
With 'clear,' however, cf. *Anth. Pal.* 7.
485, πολιὰ κρίνα, 'white lilies.' It should
be observed that here Eros in his own
person fires Medea; it is less direct and
less effective in *Aen.* 1. 710, where
Cupid takes on the guise of Ascanius to
fire Dido.

τετρηχώς, οἷόν τε νέαις ἐπὶ φορβάσιν οἶστρος
τέλλεται, ὅν τε μύωπα βοῶν κλείουσι νομῆες.
ὦκα δ' ὑπὸ φλιὴν προδόμῳ ἔνι τόξα τανύσσας
ἰοδόκης ἀβλῆτα πολύστονον ἐξέλετ' ἰόν.
ἐκ δ' ὅγε καρπαλίμοισι λαθὼν ποσὶν οὐδὸν ἄμειψεν   280
ὀξέα δενδίλλων· αὐτῷ δ' ὑπὸ βαιὸς ἐλυσθεὶς
Αἰσονίδη γλυφίδας μέσσῃ ἐνικάτθετο νευρῇ,
ἰθὺς δ' ἀμφοτέρῃσι διασχόμενος παλάμῃσιν

276. **τετρηχώς,** from ταράσσω, 'full of turmoil': cf. 1393 infr., τετρηχότα βῶλον, *Il.* 7. 346, ἀγορὴ τετρηχυῖα. The transitive sense could only be 'having caused perturbation already,' which is premature and untrue.
ἐπὶ...τέλλεται, 'rises against,' *i.e.* 'attacks'; here only in this sense, v. n. 264 supr.
φορβάσιν. This is first in tragedy, cf. Eur. *Bacc.* 168, πῶλος ὅπως ἅμα μητέρι φορβάδι. It is derived from φέρβω, and can mean either 'giving food or pasture,' as in Soph. *Ph.* 700 of γῆ, or 'out at pasture,' of animals, masc. and fem. Here and in 4. 1449 it is a noun; in 2. 89, 1024 it is adj.
277. **κλείουσι,** 'call,' cf. 357, 1003. Cf. Call. *Hec. frag.* 6, βουσσόον ὅν τε μυῶπα βοῶν καλέουσιν ἀμορβοί, and for the reverse order Aesch. *Supp.* 308, μυῶπα... Οἶστρον καλοῦσιν αὐτὸν οἱ Νείλου πέλας.
278. **φλιήν,** 'lintel.' This word occurs once as plural in Homer, 'doorposts,' *Od.* 17. 221, ὃς πολλῆς φλιῆσι παραστὰς θλίψεται ὤμους. The πρόδομος is the space covered by the colonnade, αἴθουσα, on the inner side of the court, on either side of the μέσσαυλος, the door opening into the μέγαρον, v. n. 235 supr.
279. **ἀβλῆτα,** 'not shot before': used here only and in the Homeric citation above. Contrast the Homeric ἀβλητος of *Il.* 4. 540 as opposed to ἀνούτατος; the former refers to missiles, the latter to thrusts.
πολύστονον, 'a messenger of many pains': modelled on *Il.* 15. 451, πολύστονος ἔμπεσεν ἰός. There is a Homeric use of persons, *Od.* 19. 118, which is not in Ap.: μάλα δ' εἰμὶ πολύστονος, 'a person of many sorrows.'
ἰόν, 'arrow.' This recalls *Il.* 8. 323, ἧ τοι ὁ μὲν φαρέτρας ἐξείλετο πικρὸν ὀϊστόν ; but it is probably more directly

modelled on *Il.* 4. 116, ἐκ δ' ἔλετ' ἰὸν Ἀβλῆτα πτερόεντα μελαινέων ἕρμ' ὀδυνάων. The latter line was rejected by Aristarchus; but Ap. may have accepted it. At any rate he avoids the difficulty of μελαινέων ἕρμ' ὀδυνάων by a rough paraphrase πολύστονος.
280. **ἐκ...λαθών.** It is better to take ἐκ thus than with ἄμειψεν ; *i.e.* 'utterly unnoticed.' Homer uses this verb in the active, 'to make forgetful of,' and in the middle, 'to forget utterly,' as infr. 1112.
281. **δενδίλλων,** 'looking around with sharp glances.' Compare *Il.* 9. 180, δενδίλλων ἐς ἕκαστον, and schol. ('making significant glances') τοῖς ὀφθαλμοῖς, ἢ περιβλέπων. The former of these meanings is in Hesychius, the latter in Ap. *Lex. Hom.*, and, according to our scholiast, in Sophocles. Ap. clearly uses it as περιβλέπων.
ἐλυσθείς, 'crouching with tiny form at Jason's feet' (Mooney), not 'gliding close by Aeson's son' (Seaton). This is modelled on *Il.* 24. 510, προπάροιθε ποδῶν Ἀχιλῆος ἐλυσθείς, with which cf. Archil. 103, Ἔρως ὑπὸ καρδίαν ἐλυσθείς, and εἰλυθέντος in Theoc. *Id.* 25. 246 of a lion 'gathering himself' for an attack. Homer makes a distinction between ἐλύω, εἰλυμένος meaning 'push, compress,' and εἰλύω, ἐλυσθείς, 'wrap, envelop.' Apollonius does not; ἐλυσθείς here and εἰλυμένος 296 mean 'crouching small,' εἰλυμένα and ἐλυσθείς in 1291, 1313 mean 'enveloped in.'
282. **γλυφίδας,** the 'notched end' of the arrow, v. n. 218.
ἐνικάτθετο. This and 867 infr. recall *Il.* 14. 219, τεῷ ἐνικάτθεο κόλπῳ.
283. **διασχόμενος,** 'keeping it apart,' *lit.* stretching it ; cf. Verg. *Aen.* 9. 623, 'intendit telum diversaque bracchia ducens.' Homer uses it in the active of an

ἦκ᾽ ἐπὶ Μηδείῃ· τὴν δ᾽ ἀμφασίη λάβε θυμόν.
αὐτὸς δ᾽ ὑψορόφοιο παλιμπετὲς ἐκ μεγάροιο   285
καγχαλόων ἤιξε· βέλος δ᾽ ἐνεδαίετο κούρῃ
νέρθεν ὑπὸ κραδίῃ, φλογὶ εἴκελον· ἀντία δ᾽ αἰεὶ
βάλλεν ἐπ᾽ Αἰσονίδην ἀμαρύγματα, καί οἱ ἄηντο
στηθέων ἐκ πυκιναὶ καμάτῳ φρένες, οὐδέ τιν᾽ ἄλλην
μνῆστιν ἔχεν, γλυκερῇ δὲ κατείβετο θυμὸς ἀνίῃ.   290

287 εἴκελον Stephanus: ἴκελον codd.   288 ἐπ᾽ G, Stephanus, Platt: ὑπ᾽ vulg.
290 γλυκερῇ...ἀνίῃ Pariss. duo et coni. Stephanus: γλυκερὴ...ἀνίῃ L: γλυκερὴ...
ἀνίη vulg.   θυμὸς Fitch: θυμὸν codd.

arrow piercing, *Il.* 5. 100; Ap. uses διισχάνω (ἅπ. λεγ.), in a similar sense, in 4. 1696, νύκτ᾽ ὀλοὴν οὐκ ἄστρα διίσχανεν.
284. ἀμφασίη, 'speechlessness,' v. n. 76, ἐνεοστασίη.
285. παλιμπετές, 'back'; the adv. is Homeric, but the adj. is first found in Nonnus.
286. καγχαλόων, 'laughing aloud with self-satisfaction,' v. n. 124.
ἐνεδαίετο, 'was kindled to flame within her': cf. *Od.* 6. 131, ἐν δέ οἱ ὄσσε Δαίεται, and for the active, Pind. *Pyth.* 4. 184 (328), πόθον ἔνδαιεν Ἥρη.
287. φλογί, cf. for this phrase *Il.* 13. 330, φλογὶ εἴκελον ἀλκήν, and Hes. *Sc.* 451, φλογὶ εἴκελά τ᾽ ἔγχεα πάλλων. For comparison of Love with fire, cf. *Anth. Plan.* 4. 250, ὁ πτανὸς τὸν πτανὸν ἴδ᾽ ὡς ἄγνυσι κεραυνόν, Δεικνὺς ὡς κρεῖσσον πῦρ πυρός ἐστιν, Ἔρως; and *Aen.* 4. 2, 'volnus alit venis et caeco carpitur igni,' etc.
ἀντία. Best taken as adverb, though it may be in agreement with ἀμαρύγματα; both uses are Homeric, v. n. 127.
288. βάλλεν, 'kept darting bright glances': cf. Aesch. *Ag.* 240, 742, ἔβαλλ᾽ ἕκαστον...ἀπ᾽ ὄμματος βέλει, μάλθακον ὀμμάτων βέλος.
ὑπό, 'towards,' cf. 675, 1404. This sense is un-Homeric; in Homer it means 'under,' as infr. 1077, 'stole secretly over (*lit.* "under") him.' ἐπί should be read with G., Stephanus and Platt.
ἀμαρύγματα, 'bright glances.' This is first in Hes. *frag.* 21. 3 (Rzach) of Atalante, Χαρίτων ἀμαρύγματ᾽ ἔχουσα; cf. *Et. Gen.* s.v. ἀμαρύσσω· σημαίνει τὰς τῶν ὀμμάτων ἐκλάμψεις. Homer uses

μαρμαρυγὰς ποδῶν in *Od.* 8. 265 of swift movement; cf. in the *Arg.*, infr. 1379 of a star, 4. 173 of the Fleece, 4. 728 of 'glances.' The phrase ὀφθαλμῶν ἀμαρυγαί, 1018 infr., is in H. Hom. *Herm.* 45; it is used of a star twinkling in *Arg.* 2. 42, cf. Arat. 676, Κυνὸς πᾶσαι ἀμαρυγαί. ἀμαρύσσειν of 4. 178 is first in Hesiod.
ἄηντο. This word has two meanings in Ap. In 2. 81, ἐπ᾽ ἄλλῳ δ᾽ ἄλλος ἄηται Δοῦπος (cf. schol. *ad loc.*), it seems to be connected with ἄω. Here the scholia give πνοὴν ἔπεμπον, ἡ μετεωρίζοντο, founded on *Il.* 21. 386, δίχα θυμὸς ἄητο. The former meaning is indicated infr. 688, 'my heart has been in a flutter,' cf. *Od.* 6. 131, ὑόμενος καὶ ἀήμενος, *lit.* 'tossed by the wind.' On 634 Platt cites Hesych. ἄητο· ἐφέρετο, and suggests that Ap. misunderstood *Il. loc. cit.* and took it to mean something like 'jumped,' a reasonable extension of the alternative μετεωρίζοντο supr. cit. This would be a typical reproduction of both meanings of a dubious Homeric word.
289. ἐκ στηθέων, cf. infr. 962.
καμάτῳ, 'anguish.' Homer uses this mostly of labour, or physical weariness; cf. *Arg.* 1. 104, καμάτοιο τέλος. This, and infr. 961, can be paralleled from *Od.* 9. 75, καμάτῳ τε καὶ ἄλγεσι θυμὸν ἔδοντες.
290. κατείβετο, cf. 1131, and read θυμός (Fitch) for MSS. θυμόν: 'her soul melted away in sweet sorrow.' This recalls *Il.* 24. 794, θαλερὸν δὲ κατείβετο δάκρυ παρειῶν; cf. also Alcman 36, Ἔρως κατείβων καρδίαν. Homer uses the verb also of time passing, *Od.* 5. 152, and in the active of weeping, *Od.* 21. 86. For ἔχεν v. crit. appendix, p. 139.

ὡς δὲ γυνὴ μαλερῷ περὶ κάρφεα χεύατο δαλῷ
χερνῆτις, τῆπερ ταλασήια ἔργα μέμηλεν,
ὥς κεν ὑπωρόφιον νύκτωρ σέλας ἐντύναιτο,
ἄγχι μάλ' ἐγρομένη· τὸ δ' ἀθέσφατον ἐξ ὀλίγοιο
δαλοῦ ἀναιθόμενον σὺν κάρφεα πάντ' ἀμαθύνει·   295
τοῖος ὑπὸ κραδίη εἰλυμένος αἴθετο λάθρη
οὖλος Ἔρως· ἁπαλὰς δὲ μετετρωπᾶτο παρειὰς

294 πάγχυ μάλ' Merkel: ἄγχι μάλ' ἐξομένη Hemsterhuis: ἄγχι μάλ', ἐργομένη
Damste.   295 ἀνερθόμενον Paris. unus, unde Brunck ἀνερχόμενον: ἀνεγρόμενον
vulg.: ἀναιθόμενον prop. Platt.

291. **μαλερῷ.** This in Homer is a
conventional epithet of fire, usually
translated 'raging,' 'devouring'; but
that has little force here, as the whole
simile depends on the fact that the fire
was nearly out. Ap. is surely using it
here in the sense ἀσθενής, i.e. 'smouldering,' as in Hesych. μαλερὰς φρένας·
ἀσθενεῖς καὶ ξηράς.

κάρφεα, 'dry twigs.' First in a frag.
of Aeschylus, and used in Hdt. 3. 111
of dry sticks of cinnamon.

292. **χερνῆτις,** 'a woman who labours
with her hands.' This simile is expanded
from that in Il. 12. 433 f., ὥς τε τάλαντα
γυνὴ χερνῆτις ἀληθής, Ἥ τε σταθμὸν
ἔχουσα καὶ εἴριον ἀμφὶς ἀνέλκει Ἰσάζουσ',
ἵνα παισὶν ἀεικέα μισθὸν ἄρηται.

ταλασήια, 'the work of wool-spin-
ning.' This adj. is peculiar to Ap. and
Nonnus; Xen. Oec. 7. 6 has ἔργα
ταλάσια.

293. **ὑπωρόφιον,** 'in her house,' lit.
'beneath her roof,' cf. Arat. 970, ὑπωρό-
φιοί τε κολοιοί, 'jackdaws which haunt
the roof.' The word is Homeric, and in
Arg. 4. 168 it seems to refer particularly
to the upper storey, ὑπερῴιον, where, as
in Homer, the women's chambers were.

294. **ἄγχι μάλ',** 'early,' cf. Eust. in
Od. 19. 301, 'soon.' It is usually taken
here in a local sense, 'near.'

ἐγρομένη. Assuming the above temporal sense of ἄγχι, there is no need to
alter this text to ἐξομένη, or ἐργομένη,
'protecting herself from the fire.' In
this sympathetic picture of the toiling
woman rising early to begin her labours,
and in the irrelevance of the details to
the simile proper, are reflected the best
characteristics of Alexandrine poetry,
along with the fatal erudition which

prevented it from being really great
(cf. Introd., p. xxxix).

ἀθέσφατον, 'of wondrous power,' as
often in Homer: lit. 'beyond the power
even of a god to express.' τὸ δ', sc. σέλας,
πῦρ.

295. **ἀνεγρόμενον.** With ἐγρομένη in
the preceding line, this can hardly be
right. Read, with Platt, ἀναιθόμενον, for
which v. crit. appendix, p. 139.

σὺν...ἀμαθύνει, 'destroys along with
it'; the compound is peculiar to Ap.
Homer has the simple verb, likewise of
fire, in Il. 9. 593, πόλιν δέ τε πῦρ
ἀμαθύνει.

296. **εἰλυμένος,** 'crouching small,'
v. n. 281. Compare Val. Flacc. 6. 673,
'mole dei, quem pectore toto Iam tenet;
extremus roseo pudor errat in ore.'

297. **οὖλος.** Ap. uses this word only
of Eros, here and infr. 1078. Callimachus extracts no less than four meanings from Homer: (1) 'destructive,'
schol. Il. 21. 536. (2) 'dark-haired,'
οὖλος ἐθείραις Ἔσπερος, H. Del. 302: cf.
Od. 6. 231, οὖλας ἧκε κόμας. (3) 'strong,'
H. Ap. 76, οὖλος Ἀριστοτέλης, based on
ὅλος-οὖλος in Od. 17. 343, ἄρτον τ' οὖλον
ἑλών. (4) 'vehement,' H. Zeus 51, οὖλα
...ὠρχήσαντο: cf. Il. 17. 756, οὖλον
κεκλήγοντες. In Moschus, App. Plan.
4. 200. 2, Mackail follows Hesychius,
μαλακὸς καὶ ἁπαλός, and translates
'curly-haired.' This is probably the
meaning in Ap.; in the sense of 'destructive' he uses the Homeric ὀλοός 384,
οὐλόμενος 436, and in 1402 a form
peculiar to himself, οὐλοός.

μετετρωπᾶτο, 'kept continually
changing,' cf. Prop. 1. 15. 39, 'multos
pallere colores.' Frequentative of μετατρέπω, based on the Homeric πάλιν

ἐς χλόον, ἄλλοτ' ἔρευθος, ἀκηδείῃσι νόοιο.
Δμῶες δ' ὁππότε δή σφιν ἐπαρτέα θῆκαν ἐδωδήν,
αὐτοί τε λιαροῖσιν ἐφαιδρύναντο λοετροῖς,   300
ἀσπασίως δόρπῳ τε ποτῆτί τε θυμὸν ἄρεσσαν.
ἐκ δὲ τοῦ Αἰήτης σφετέρης ἐρέεινε θυγατρὸς
υἵηας τοίοισι παρηγορέων ἐπέεσσιν·
'Παιδὸς ἐμῆς κοῦροι Φρίξοιό τε, τὸν περὶ πάντων
ξείνων ἡμετέροισιν ἐνὶ μεγάροισιν ἔτισα,   305
πῶς Αἶάνδε νέεσθε παλίσσυτοι; ἠὲ τίς ἄτη
σωομένοις μεσσηγὺς ἐνέκλασεν; οὐ μὲν ἐμεῖο

306 ἠε τίς ἄνην O. Schneider.   307 σωομένοις codd.: σωομένους ed. Flor.

τρωπᾶσθαι, *Il.* 16. 95, cf. *Il.* 18. 585 ἀπετρωπῶντο, 'shrank from.'
298. ἀκηδείῃσι νόοιο, v. n. 260. This same phrase is in Empedocles *ed.* Mullachius 441 (*frag.* 136 D), 'in the distraction of her soul.' The germ of this simile is apparently in *Od.* 5. 488; ὡς δ' ὅτε τις δαλὸν σποδιῇ ἐνέκρυψε μελαίνῃ, Ἀγροῦ ἐπ' ἐσχατιῆς ᾧ μὴ πάρα γείτονες ἄλλοι, Σπέρμα πυρὸς σώζων, ἵνα μὴ πόθεν ἄλλοθεν αὔοι.
299–366. Aeetes demands from the sons of Phrixus an explanation of their visit; Argus assures him that Jason comes peaceably and not with evil intent.
299. ἐπαρτέα, 'ready to their hand': in Homer only of persons, in Ap. only of things. The latter also invents a verb ἐπαρτίζω, 'make ready,' 1. 877.
300. λιαροῖσιν, 'warm,' cf. 876, 1064, and *Il.* 11. 830, νίζ' ὕδατι λιαρῷ. Homer also applies it by metaphor to Sleep, *Il.* 14. 164, ὕπνον ἀπήμονά τε λιαρόν τε. χλιαρός is later used by Hdt. and others.
ἐφαιδρύναντο, 'washed,' cf. 832, and for the active, 1043. It is first in Hes. *Op.* 753, χρόα φαιδρύνεσθαι.
301. δόρπῳ, 'food.' In Homer only of the evening meal; later of any meal.
ποτῆτι, 'drink.' Always used in Homer, as here, in contrast with some word for food.
ἄρεσσαν, 'satisfied.' A variant of *Od.* 5. 95, ἤραρε θυμὸν ἐδωδῇ. The form is peculiar to Ap.; the ordinary Attic is ἤρεσαν. Cf. 846 infr.
302. ἐκ δὲ τοῦ, 'thereupon.'
σφετέρης, 'his,' ἀντὶ τοῦ ἰδίας, schol.: v. n. 26.

θυγατρός, i.e. Chalciope, the wife of Phrixus and mother of Argos and his brothers.
303. υἵηας, for the form, v. n. 196.
παρηγορέων, 'addressing,' cf. 2. 1281 παρηγορέῃσι. Both words are un-Homeric, and first used in tragedy. In the proper and Homeric style, the guests are first fed, and then asked to explain their visit. Similarly in *Aen.* 1. 638, Aeneas is entertained by Dido, and then, 753, the story is demanded.
306. Αἶάνδε. The ordinary Homeric use of -δε with nouns of place: for use of persons, cf. 647 and note *ad loc.*
παλίσσυτοι, 'hastening back,' v. n. 112.
ἄτη, 'did some calamity thwart you in your haste?' It is unnecessary to read Schneider's ingenious ἄνην, 'thwart your accomplishment.' The ἀ- of this word is properly long, but is short in Call. *H. Zeus* 89, αὐτὸς ἄνην ἐκόλουσας, meant, no doubt, to indicate the fact that in Homer ἄνω is long except for *Il.* 18. 473, ἔργον ἄνοιτο.
307. σωομένοις, 'hastening.' Seaton reads the accusative, from σώω, σώζω, i.e. 'cut short your escape'; but the dative is on the analogy of verbs of opposition. Ap. uses the forms σώεσθαι, σώοντο, from the un-Homeric σώομαι, a form of σοῦμαι, σεύομαι. These are distinct from σώεσθαι 2. 610, and σώετε 4. 197, which are from the Homeric σώω, σώζω; cf. σώοντες in *Od.* 9. 430, σώεσκον in *Il.* 8. 363.
μεσσηγύς, 'in mid course,' cf. 441, etc., and μεσσηγύ *metri gratiâ* 1317; both are Homeric.

πείθεσθε προφέροντος ἀπείρονα μέτρα κελεύθου.
ἤδειν γάρ ποτε πατρὸς ἐν ἅρμασιν Ἡελίοιο
δινεύσας, ὅτ᾽ ἐμεῖο κασιγνήτην ἐκόμιζεν   310
Κίρκην ἑσπερίης εἴσω χθονός, ἐκ δ᾽ ἱκόμεσθα
ἀκτὴν ἠπείρου Τυρσηνίδος, ἔνθ᾽ ἔτι νῦν περ
ναιετάει, μάλα πολλὸν ἀπόπροθι Κολχίδος αἴης.
ἀλλὰ τί μύθων ἦδος; ἃ δ᾽ ἐν ποσὶν ὑμῖν ὄρωρεν,
εἴπατ᾽ ἀριφραδέως, ἠδ᾽ οἵτινες οἵδ᾽ ἐφέπονται   315
ἀνέρες, ὅππῃ τε γλαφυρῆς ἐκ νηὸς ἔβητε.᾽
    Τοῖά μιν ἐξερέοντα κασιγνήτων προπάροιθεν
Ἄργος ὑποδδείσας ἀμφὶ στόλῳ Αἰσονίδαο

314 ὑμιν L : ὕμμιν vulg.   316 ὅππῃ τε Pariss. duo. : ὁππότε LG : ὁππότε καὶ
Stephanus : ὁππότε τε Samuelsson.

ἐνέκλασεν, 'thwarted you,' *lit.* 'broke
in on you.' This is extended from *Il.*
8. 408, 422, ἐνικλᾶν ὅττι κεν εἴπω,
'interrupt'; cf. Call. *H. Zeus* 89, αὐτὸς
ἄνην ἐκόλουσας ἐνέκλασσας δὲ μενοινήν.
    308. πείθεσθε, 'ye did not listen.' The
gen. ἐμεῖο may be either absolute with
προφέροντος, or governed directly by the
verb; cf. Eur. *Iph. Aul.* 726, πείθεσθαι
γὰρ εἴθισμαι σέθεν: Hdt. 1. 126. 5,
ἐμέο πείθεσθαι.
    προφέροντος, 'when I put before you,'
i.e. 'explained.'
    310. δινεύσας, 'when I was whirled.'
For the intransitive use, cf. *Il.* 18. 606,
ἐδίνευον κατὰ μέσσους, and infr. 835.
    312. Τυρσηνίδος. Our scholia give
Hesiod as authority for the legend that
Circe was transported εἰς τὴν κατὰ
Τυρρηνίαν νῆσον in the solar chariot.
Hesiod likewise, in *Th.* 1011 f., tells of
the sons of Circe and Odysseus, οἳ δή
τοι μάλα τῆλε μυχῷ νήσων ἱεράων Πᾶσιν
Τυρσηνοῖσιν ἀγακλειτοῖσιν ἄνασσον. The
site was early identified with the pro-
montory of Circei in Latium. The earlier
Homeric account locates her home more
vaguely, but apparently in the East,
Od. 12. 3, νῆσόν τ᾽ Αἰαίην, ὅθι τ᾽ Ἠοῦς
ἠριγενείης Οἰκία καὶ χοροί εἰσι καὶ ἀντολαὶ
Ἠελίοιο.
    313. ναιετάει, 'dwells,' as infr. 991;
also of places infr. 1092, 'are situated.'
Both uses are Homeric; this line recalls
Od. 4. 811, μάλα πολλὸν ἀπόπροθι δώματα
ναίεις.

πολλόν. Ap. uses also πολύ and πολλά
adverbially, 798, 1263; Homer likewise
uses all three indifferently.
    ἀπόπροθι, c. gen., as in 372, 1065;
Homer uses it without case, as in *Arg.*
1. 602, τόσσον ἀπόπροθι Λῆμνον ἐοῦσαν.
    314. ἦδος, 'pleasure,' used by Ap.
only in this phrase, cf. 1. 1294, which
recalls *Il.* 18. 80, ἀλλά τί μοι τῶν ἦδος,
and *Od.* 24. 95, αὐτὰρ ἐμοὶ τί τόδ᾽ ἦδος;
    ἐν ποσίν, 'at your feet,' cf. 836 and
Soph. *Ant.* 1327, τὰν ποσὶν κακά.
    ὄρωρεν, means no more than ἐστί, v. n.
59 supr.
    315. ἀριφραδέως, 'clearly.' The adj.
is Homeric, but this adv. is Alexandrine,
cf. Theoc. 25. 176.
    ἐφέπονται, 'accompany'; common in
this sense in Homer, and once in a
hostile sense, 'pursue,' *Od.* 16. 426,
λῃστῆρσιν ἐπισπόμενος. For the active
in *Arg.* 2. 384, of birds 'haunting' an
island, cf. Pind. *Pyth.* 1. 30, ἐφέπεις
ὄρος.
    318. ὑποδδείσας, 'fearing for the
safety of.' This use with ἀμφί is exceptional. Homer uses the direct accusative,
as in *Arg.* 2. 821; Ap. has also the
infinitive, 435 infr. Homer has the
perfect, aorist and pluperfect; Ap. has
the latter two only. In *Il.* 23. 417, 425,
Aristarchus read a single -δ- against the
vulgate (schol. A. on *Il.* 15. 123); de
Ian likewise, following A. against the
other MSS., reads it thus in Call. *H. Art.*
51.

μειλιχίως προσέειπεν, ἐπεὶ προγενέστερος ἦεν·
'Αἰήτη, κείνην μὲν ἄφαρ διέχευαν ἄελλαι   320
ζαχρηεῖς· αὐτοὺς δ' ὑπὸ δούρασι πεπτηῶτας
νήσου Ἐνναλίοιο ποτὶ ξερὸν ἔκβαλε κῦμα
λυγαίῃ ὑπὸ νυκτί· θεὸς δέ τις ἄμμ' ἐσάωσεν.
οὐδὲ γὰρ αἰ τὸ πάροιθεν ἐρημαίην κατὰ νῆσον
ηὐλίζοντ' ὄρνιθες 'Αρήιαι, οὐδ' ἔτι κείνας   325
εὕρομεν. ἀλλ' οἵγ' ἄνδρες ἀπήλασαν, ἐξαποβάντες
νηὸς ἑῆς προτέρῳ ἐνὶ ἤματι· καί σφ' ἀπέρυκεν

320 διέχευσαν Stephanus.   321 ἐπὶ Madvig.   325 οὐδ' ἔτι Pariss. duo :
οὐδέ τι vulg.   326 οἶδε Wilamowitz.   327 καί σφας ἔρυκεν Herwerden.

319. προγενέστερος, 'older,' cf. Il. 2.
555, ὁ γὰρ προγενέστερος ἦεν; προγίγνο-
μαι also, as infr. 1292, is Homeric. As
before, in Arg. 2. 1122, Argos acts as
spokesman.
320. κείνην, sc. νῆα, referring to 316
supr. This speech of Argos is really in
character a 'messenger's speech,' a
legacy from the drama (v. Intr. pp. xivf.).
For a survival of this form in prose, cf.
Ach. Tat. 1. 12. 2, where the death of
Charicles is described by a servant in a
speech embodying most of the worst
characteristics of the tragic prototype.
διέχευαν, 'tore apart.' Like Homer,
Ap. uses only the aorist of this verb;
the former uses it only of cutting up an
animal, Od. 3. 456, etc., αἶψ' ἄρα μιν
διέχευαν.
321. ζαχρηεῖς, 'fierce.' Ap. uses this
always of winds, Homer also of warriors
furious in battle, ζαχρηεῖς τελέθουσι κατὰ
κρατερὰς ὑσμίνας, Il. 12. 347.
ὑπό...πεπτηῶτας. Seaton (Class. Rev.
1914. 18) rightly objects to Madvig's
ἐπί, and takes this as in tmesi from
ὑποπτήσσω, 'crouching on the beams,'
cf. Arat. 615 παραπεπτηῶτας. In Il. 2.
312, πετάλοις ὑποπεπτηῶτας must mean
'crouching under,' cf. Od. 14. 474,
ὑπὸ τεύχεσι πεπτηῶτες. In the sense of
'at,' cf. Eur. Hel. 1203, ὑποπτήξας τάφῳ.
ὑπό refers to the curled-up position of a
person crouching. Madvig considers that
the verb here is πίπτω, and that this
passage refers to Od. 12. 444, where
Odysseus comes to land sitting on
boards, ἐζόμενος ἐπὶ τοῖσιν. For the
confusion between the two perfect
participles, v. Leaf on Il. 21. 503, and

cf. Arat. 167, etc. πεπτηυῖαν in Arg. 2.
535 is from πτήσσω; πεπτηότες in 4.
1263, cf. 1298, is from πίπτω. ὑποπτήσσοντας αὐτήν, infr. 571, is a unique use;
cf. Xen. Cyr. 1. 3. 8, παῖς μηδέπω
ὑποπτήσσων, 'not yet at all shy.'
322. Ἐνναλίοιο. Jason had been
bidden by Phineus, in 2. 382 f., to land
on the island of Ares in the Euxine,
where help would come to them from
the sea; this turned out to be the ship-
wreck of the sons of Phrixus.
ποτὶ ξερόν, 'to the dry land.' Note
the variant of the Homeric ποτὶ ξερὸν
ἠπείροιο, Od. 5. 402.
323. λυγαίῃ, 'dark,' first in tragedy,
cf. 863, 1361. The grammarians derive
it from an assumed λύγη, 'twilight.'
ὑπό. This use of ὑπό is un-Homeric:
πρωῒ δ' ὑπηοῖοι should be read in Il. 8.
530, 18. 277. This phrase recurs infr.
1361, contrast 863 λυγαίῃ ἐνὶ νυκτί; they
are reminiscent of Il. 8. 529, ἀλλ' ἦ τοι
ἐπὶ νυκτί.
θεὸς κ.τ.λ., cf. 328, and Qu. Sm. 14.
627, ἐσάωσεν "Η θεὸς ἢ δαίμων: v. also
references in Headlam's note on Aesch.
Ag. 662.
325. ηὐλίζοντο, cf. 839; of persons,
lit. 'take up abode in the courtyard.'
For use of animals, cf. Od. 12. 265; of
persons, Soph. Ph. 30, καθ' ὕπνον...
καταυλισθείς: Eur. El. 304, οἵοις ἐν
πέπλοις αὐλίζομαι. These birds haunted
the island of Ares, and were able to
wound with feathers dropped from the
air, Arg. 2. 1036.
326. ἐξαποβάντες νηός, cf. 199, and
Od. 12. 306, ἐξαπέβησαν...νηός.
327. ἑῆς, 'their,' v. n. 26.

ἡμέας οἰκτείρων Ζηνὸς νόος, ἠέ τις αἶσα,
αὐτίκ' ἐπεὶ καὶ βρῶσιν ἅλις καὶ εἵματ' ἔδωκαν,
οὔνομά τε Φρίξοιο περικλεὲς εἰσαΐοντες   330
ἠδ' αὐτοῖο σέθεν· μετὰ γὰρ τεὸν ἄστυ νέονται.
χρειὼ δ' ἦν ἐθέλῃς ἐξίδμεναι, οὔ σ' ἐπικεύσω.
τόνδε τις ἱέμενος πάτρης ἀπάνευθεν ἐλάσσαι
καὶ κτεάνων βασιλεὺς περιώσιον, οὔνεκεν ἀλκῇ
σφωιτέρῃ πάντεσσι μετέπρεπεν Αἰολίδῃσιν,   335
πέμπει δεῦρο νέεσθαι ἀμήχανον· οὐδ' ὑπαλύξειν
στεῦται ἀμειλίκτοιο Διὸς θυμαλγέα μῆνιν
καὶ χόλον, οὐδ' ἄτλητον ἄγος Φρίξοιό τε ποινὰς
Αἰολιδέων γενεήν, πρὶν ἐς Ἑλλάδα κῶας ἱκέσθαι.
νῆα δ' Ἀθηναίη Παλλὰς κάμεν, οὐ μάλα τοίην,   340

337 στεῦτο schol. Par.

ἀπέρυκεν, 'kept them there,' a unique use for ἐρύκω, 250 supr., for which v. n. 174.

330. εἰσαΐοντες, 'hearing': Alexandrine for εἰσακούω, v. n. 145.

331. μετά, merely 'to,' cf. *Od.* 3. 366, μετὰ Καύκωνας...εἶμι.

332. χρειώ, 'quest,' v. n. 12.

οὔ σ' ἐπικεύσω, 'I will not conceal it from you.' In Homer, as here, always with a negative; the accusative of the person is first in Aesch. *Ag.* 800 as restored by Musgrave, οὐ γάρ (σ') ἐπικεύσω, with which contrast Headlam's οὐκ ἐπικεύσω.

333. τόνδε, sc. Ἰήσονα. In Val. Flacc. 1. 31–2, Pelias plots to kill Jason: 'ergo anteire metus iuvenemque exstinguere pergit Aesonium letique vias ac tempora versat.'

ἀπάνευθεν. Homeric as prep. c. gen.; v. n. 114.

334. περιώσιον, with ἱέμενος, 'exceedingly anxious.' Homer uses only, as here, adverbially. Post-Homeric uses are (1) adv. c. gen., *Arg.* 1. 466; (2) περιώσια as adv., infr. 1326; (3) as adj., 2. 394 περιώσια φῦλα.

335. σφωιτέρῃ, 'his,' v. n. 26, 186.

μετέπρεπεν, 'was conspicuous among': cf. *Il.* 16. 194, πᾶσι μετέπρεπε Μυρμιδόνεσσι, and v. n. 246. Aeolus had two sons, Cretheus and Athamas; Aeson and Amythaon were sons of Cretheus, and Jason was son of Aeson.

336. νέεσθαι, epexegetic, with πέμπει: cf. *Od.* 4. 8, πέμπε νέεσθαι.

ἀμήχανον, Homeric, like ἀμηχανίη 504, 893. This may be either masculine, 'powerless to refuse,' or neuter internal accusative, 'go on a hopeless quest'; cf. *Il.* 14. 262, νῦν αὖ τοῦτό μ' ἄνωγας ἀμήχανον ἄλλο τελέσσαι.

ὑπαλύξειν, 'escape.' Homer uses only the aorist; cf. *Or. Arg.* 106, οὐκ ἔσθ' ὑπαλύξαι ἃ δὴ πεπρωμένα κεῖται.

337. στεῦται, 'he declares.' Homer uses with fut. inf. of boasting, cf. 579 infr. Ap. also has the present, 2. 1204, στεῦται ἔμμεναι, 'says that he is.'

ἀμειλίκτοιο, 'relentless,' as in Homer, but here only as an attribute of Zeus.

θυμαλγέα, 'grieving the heart,' as often in Homer; *e.g. Od.* 23. 64, ὕβριν ἀγασσάμενος θυμαλγέα.

338. ἄγος, cf. 203, 'the pollution which would come from Phrixus.' Compare the words of Pelias to Jason in Pind. *Pyth.* 4. 158 f.; δύνασαι δ' ἀφελεῖν Μᾶνιν χθονίων. κέλεται γὰρ ἑὰν ψυχὰν κομίξαι Φρίξος ἐλθόντας πρὸς Αἰήτα θαλάμους, Δέρμα τε κριοῦ βαθύμαλλον ἄγειν.

339. ἱκέσθαι, cf. *Od.* 1. 21, πάρος ἦν γαῖαν ἱκέσθαι.

340. νῆα. Athene was the designer of the Argo, and Argos built it under her direction. Apollonius explicitly avoids a description of the building of the ship, *Arg.* 1. 18–19, νῆα μὲν οὖν οἱ πρόσθεν

42 ΑΠΟΛΛΩΝΙΟΤ ΡΟΔΙΟΤ

οἵαί περ Κόλχοισι μετ' ἀνδράσι νῆες ἔασιν,
τάων αἰνοτάτης ἐπεκύρσαμεν. ἤλιθα γάρ μιν
λάβρον ὕδωρ πνοιή τε διέτμαγεν· ἡ δ' ἐνὶ γόμφοις
ἴσχεται, ἣν καὶ πᾶσαι ἐπιβρίσωσιν ἄελλαι.
ἶσον δ' ἐξ ἀνέμοιο θέει καὶ ὅτ' ἀνέρες αὐτοὶ   345
νωλεμέως χείρεσσιν ἐπισπέρχωσιν ἐρετμοῖς.
τῇ δ' ἐναγειράμενος Παναχαιίδος εἴ τι φέριστον

346 ἐρετμούς Pariss. tres, Brunck.   347 φέριστον corr. φέριστοι L: οἵ τε φέριστοι
Vat. unus, Pariss. tres.

ἐπικλείουσιν ἀοιδοὶ Ἄργον Ἀθηναίης κα-
μέειν ὑποθημοσύνῃσιν: but the theme
appealed to the Latin poets, Catull.
64. 9, Val. Flacc. 1. 92.
341. νῆες. Apollonius does not follow
the legend that the Argo was the first
ship ever built; she was the first ship
of war, cf. schol. Flor. on *Arg.* 1. 4, ταύτην δέ φασι πρώτην ναῦν γενέσθαι μακράν.
342. ἐπεκύρσαμεν, schol. ἐνετύχομεν,
'obtained.' It is also used abs. 'reach'
4. 1451; this use c. gen. is first in
Pindar and Aeschylus, the dative as in
1. 1245 is Homeric, οὐδ' ἐπέκυρσεν
Ποίμνῃσιν.
ἤλιθα, 'utterly,' as in Homer, connected with ἅλις. In *Arg.* 2. 283,
possibly following Callimachus, *Lout.
Pall.* 123-4, ὄρνιχας...οἵ τε πέτονται
Ἤλιθα, Ap. seems to connect it with
ἠλιθίως of Plat. *Theaet.* 180 D, Theoc.
10. 40, and to interpret it as meaning
'in vain.'
343. διέτμαγεν. Homer uses the first
and second aorists of διατμήγω transi-
tively. This is best taken as a *schema
Pindaricum*, ὕδωρ διέτμαγεν πνοιή τε.
διέτμαγον, intr., is given by MSS. infr.
1147, and 2. 298; editors follow Spitzner
in changing to διέτμαγεν, 3rd pl. of aor.
διετμάγην. But though forms in -ην are
of passive force in spite of their active
form (Munro, *Hom. Gr.* 42), the alteration is dubious. Edd. print διέτμαγεν
(intr.) in *Il.* 1. 531, 7. 302, 12. 461,
where in all cases the scholia give
διέτμαγON-διεχωρίσθησαν. The fact that
Aristarchus wrote -εν is no evidence
that Ap. agreed; Merkel rightly keeps
-ον in both passages. Ap. here uses the
transitive διέτμαγεν; but he seems to
have believed it to have also an intransitive character in Homer.

γόμφοις. Wooden, as distinct from
metal pegs, ἧλοι. Common in Ap. and
once in Homer, *Od.* 5. 248, γόμφοισιν
δ' ἄρα τήν γε καὶ ἁρμονίῃσιν ἄρασσεν.
ἐνὶ...ἴσχεται, 'is held fast by her
bolts'; cf. Herod. 7. 128. 3, ἐνὶ θώματι
ἐνέσχετο.
344. ἐπιβρίσωσιν, 'fall heavily on':
cf. *Arg.* 1. 678, αἴ κεν ἐπιβρίσῃ Θρήιξ
στρατός. Homer uses of rain, and metaphorically of seasons 'weighing down'
the vines, *Od.* 24. 344, ὁππότε δὴ Διὸς
ὧραι ἐπιβρίσειαν ὕπερθεν.
345. ἐξ ἀνέμοιο, 'before the wind.'
For ἐκ with an intransitive or passive
verb, cf. *Il.* 2. 669, ἐφίληθεν Ἐκ Διός,
Soph. *O. T.* 854, πατρὸς ἐξ ἐμοῦ θανεῖν.
346. νωλεμέως, 'unceasingly,' v. n.
147.
ἐπισπέρχωσιν, 'urge on.' Homer
uses also intr. of winds 'sweeping down,'
Od. 5. 304, ἐπισπέρχουσι δ' ἄελλαι. For
the double dative χείρεσσιν, ἐρετμοῖς,
cf. 462, 470, 1297 infr. Thuc. uses it
also with cognate acc., 4. 12. 1, τούς τ'
ἄλλους τοιαῦτα ἐπέσπερχε.
347. Παναχαιίδος. This is Thessaly,
according to schol. 1. 243; but here, as
probably also there, it refers to Greece
as a whole. Homer does not use this
fem., but he refers to the whole of the
Greeks as Πανάχαιοι, *Il.* 2. 404. According to the schol., Ἀχαιίδες in *Arg.*
1. 284 means Thessalian women; but
probably it means women of Greece in
general. In 601, 639, 775, 1081, Ἀχαιίς
may refer either to Thessaly or Greece;
Homer uses it of the south of Thessaly,
of the Peloponnese, and of Greece as a
whole.
εἴ τι φέριστον, neut. for masc., 'the
best of the heroes'; cf. Theoc. 7. 4,
εἴ τί περ ἐσθλὸν Χαῶν.

ἡρώων, τεὸν ἄστυ μετήλυθε, πόλλ' ἐπαληθεὶς
ἄστεα καὶ πελάγη στυγερῆς ἁλός, εἴ οἱ ὀπάσσαις.
αὐτῷ δ' ὥς κεν ἅδῃ, τὼς ἔσσεται· οὐ γὰρ ἱκάνει   350
χερσὶ βιησόμενος· μέμονεν δέ τοι ἄξια τίσειν
δωτίνης, ἀΐων ἐμέθεν μέγα δυσμενέοντας
Σαυρομάτας, τοὺς σοῖσιν ὑπὸ σκήπτροισι δαμάσσει.
εἰ δὲ καὶ οὔνομα δῆθεν ἐπιθύεις γενεήν τε
ἴδμεναι, οἵτινές εἰσιν, ἕκαστά κε μυθησαίμην.   355
τόνδε μέν, οἷό περ οὔνεκ' ἀφ' Ἑλλάδος ὧλλοι ἄγερθεν,
κλείουσ' Αἴσονος υἱὸν Ἰήσονα Κρηθεΐδαο.
εἰ δ' αὐτοῦ Κρηθῆος ἐτήτυμόν ἐστι γενέθλης,

349 ὀπάσσοις Pariss. quatt., Brunck.   351 βιησάμενος vulg.: βιησόμενος Vatt.
duo et coni. Stephanus.   355 κε Brunck, Headlam : γε codd.

348. **πόλλ' ἐπαληθείς**, 'after many wanderings'; typical alteration of *Od.* 4. 81, πολλὰ παθὼν καὶ πόλλ' ἐπαληθείς, cf. *Aen.* 1. 3, 'multum ille et terris iactatus et alto.' For the accusative ἄστεα κ.τ.λ., cf. *Od.* 4. 83, Κύπρον Φοινίκην τε καὶ Αἰγύπτους ἐπαληθείς.
349. **εἰ κ.τ.λ.**, 'in hope that...': cf. *Od.* 4. 317, ἤλυθον, εἴ τινά μοι κληηδόνα πατρὸς ἐνίσποις.
350. **αὐτῷ**, i.e. σοὶ αὐτῷ, cf. 537 infr., αὐτοῖσιν for ὑμῖν αὐτοῖς.
τὼς..., cf. *Arg.* 2. 345, καὶ τὰ μὲν ὡς κε πέλῃ, τὼς ἔσσεται.
351. **μέμονεν**, 'he is anxious.' Homer uses with this verb the present, future, or aorist inf.; the genitive, as infr. 434, 509, is un-Homeric. Similarly μαιμάω is abs. 1351, but c. gen. 2. 269; the latter use dates from Sophocles. In Val. Flacc., Book 5, the Argonauts actually do fight for Aeetes, and the narrative is rather long and tedious; Aeetes thus welcomes their arrival (5. 534), 'Cuperem haut tali vos tempore tectis Advenisse meis, quo me gravis adsidet hostis...Quare age, cognatas primum defendite sedes.'
352. **μέγα**. Common as adverb with such verbs of strong feeling in Homer.
353. **Σαυρομάτας**. Situated by the sea of Azov, mentioned in Hdt. 4. 21. In Diod. 4. 45 there is a legend of Circe marrying and then poisoning their king, and thus becoming ruler of the people. Hippocrates (περὶ ἀέρων κ.τ.λ. 17) tells of the activity of their women, and how

they ride, fight and remain virgins till they have slain three enemies, and how by cautery of the right breast in childhood the strength is diverted to the right shoulder and arm.
354. **δῆθεν**. No irony intended, simply a strengthened form of δή, cf. 1119 infr.
ἐπιθύεις, 'if thou art anxious,' cf. *Arg.* 2. 1154, εἰ δὲ καὶ οὔνομα δῆθεν ἐπιθύεις δεδαῆσθαι. It is uncertain whether this compound is ἐπι-θύω with the -υ- long in arsis, or ἐπι-ιθύω with irregular lengthening of the -υ- in the present, as in *Od.* 22. 408, ἴθυσέν ῥ' ὀλολύξαι.
355. **κε**. Read this with Brunck and Headlam for γε, which is barely polite enough; contrast 99 supr. and cf. Hes. *Op.* 10, ἐγὼ δέ κε, Πέρση, ἐτήτυμα μυθησαίμην.
357. **κλείουσι**, 'call,' cf. 1003, v. n. 277 supr.
358. **ἐτήτυμον**, 'if he is truly of the race of Cretheus himself': cf. 402 infr., and for ἐτήτυμον as adv. cf. *Od.* 4. 157, κείνου μέντοι ὅδ' υἱὸς ἐτήτυμον. This is merely a rhetorical periphrasis leading up to the point of Jason's kinship. There is no doubt as to his full legitimacy as a Cretheid; it is Pelias in *Od.* 11. 254 who is the son of Poseidon and Tyro, not of Cretheus. This tradition is further developed in the Διηγήματα, where Tyro is pregnant by Poseidon when she marries Cretheus, so that her children Pelias and Neleus are consequently claimed as his own by Cretheus.

οὕτω κεν γνωτὸς πατρώιος ἄμμι πέλοιτο.
ἄμφω γὰρ Κρηθεὺς Ἀθάμας τ᾽ ἔσαν Αἰόλου υἷες·   360
Φρίξος δ᾽ αὖτ᾽ Ἀθάμαντος ἔην πάις Αἰολίδαο.
τόνδε δ᾽ ἄρ᾽, Ἡελίου γόνον ἔμμεναι εἴ τιν᾽ ἀκούεις,
δέρκεαι Αὐγείην· Τελαμὼν δ᾽ ὅγε, κυδίστοιο
Αἰακοῦ ἐκγεγαώς· Ζεὺς δ᾽ Αἰακὸν αὐτὸς ἔτικτεν.
ὣς δὲ καὶ ὧλλοι πάντες, ὅσοι συνέπονται ἑταῖροι,   365
ἀθανάτων υἷές τε καὶ υἱωνοὶ γεγάασιν.᾽
    Τοῖα παρέννεπεν Ἄργος· ἄναξ δ᾽ ἐπεχώσατο μύθοις
εἰσαΐων· ὑψοῦ δὲ χόλῳ φρένες ἠερέθοντο.
φῆ δ᾽ ἐπαλαστήσας· μενέαινε δὲ παισὶ μάλιστα
Χαλκιόπης· τῶν γάρ σφε μετελθέμεν οὕνεκ᾽ ἐώλπει·   370
ἐκ δέ οἱ ὄμματ᾽ ἔλαμψεν ὑπ᾽ ὀφρύσιν ἱεμένοιο·
    ᾽Οὐκ ἄφαρ ὀφθαλμῶν μοι ἀπόπροθι, λωβητῆρες,

---

359 κε Brunck.   370 σφε Pariss., Vrat., Vind.: σφι vulg.   ἐώλπει Stephanus:
ἐόλπει codd.   371 ὀφρύσι χωομένοιο Herwerden.

---

359. **γνωτός**, 'kinsman,' as always in Ap.; Homer has it also meaning 'well-known.'

361. **Φρίξος**. Cf. the words of Jason in Val. Flacc. 5. 476, 'ipse egomet proprio de sanguine Phrixi, Namque idem Cretheus ambobus et Aeolus auctor Cum Iove Neptunoque et cum Salmonide nympha.'

365. **συνέπονται**, 'accompany.' Common in tragedy, once in Homer *in tmesi*, cf. 881 infr. ἅμα...ἕπονται.

366. **ἀθανάτων**. Compare Medea's address to the Argonauts in Pind. *Pyth.* 4. 13, παῖδες ὑπερθύμων τε φωτῶν καὶ θεῶν, and *ib.* 184, ἡμιθέοισιν.

367-395. Aeetes furiously demands their instant departure. Jason offers service in war in return for the Fleece.

367. **παρέννεπεν**, like παραυδάω, to 'speak by way of encouragement'; the compound is here only, but the simple verb is Homeric.

ἐπεχώσατο, 'was stirred to anger at....' This compound is also peculiar to Ap.; χώομαι as in 110 is Homeric.

368. **εἰσαΐων**, 'as he heard,' v. n. 145.

ἠερέθοντο. This verb is used only in 3rd pl. present and imperfect indicative. The scholia on *Il.* 3. 108 give two

derivations, αἰωρῶ καὶ σείω, ἀείρω. Here Ap. follows the latter, 'his heart was lifted high with passion': infr. 638, 830, he adopts the former.

369. **ἐπαλαστήσας**, 'in anger at his words,' cf. 557 infr. This is modelled on *Od.* 1. 252, τόνδ᾽ ἐπαλαστήσασα προσηύδα, which the scholia interpret as δεινοπαθεῖν, ἀναστενάζειν. The latter has been wrongly illustrated from 557 infr., which Ap. clearly uses in the sense of ΔΕΙΝΟπαθεῖν. Ap. does not use the simple verb, which is in *Il.* 12. 163, Call. *H. Del.* 239. For the aorist of emotion, v. Merry and Riddell on Homer, *Od.* 1. 252, and cf. αἰδεσθείς, ἀλγήσας, χολωσάμενος κ.τ.λ.

370. **μετελθέμεν**, 'for he was sure that it was on their account that they had come.' For μετά in this sense of 'to,' cf. 348 supr., and n. 331.

371. **ἐκ**, *in tmesi* with ἔλαμψεν, 'flashed forth.'

ἱεμένοιο, 'in his impetuous anger': this implies both meanings of ἵεσθαι, 'hasten' and 'desire.'

372. **ἀπόπροθι**, v. n. 313.

λωβητῆρες, 'insulting wretches': cf. *Il.* 24. 239, ἔρρετε λωβητῆρες, ἐλεγχέες. Soph. *Ant.* 1074 uses it of the Furies 'Destroyers'; v. n. 74 λωβήν.

νεῖσθ᾽ αὐτοῖσι δόλοισι παλίσσυτοι ἔκτοθι γαίης,
πρίν τινα λευγαλέον τε δέρος καὶ Φρίξον ἰδέσθαι·
αὐτίχ᾽ ὁμαρτήσαντες ἀφ᾽ Ἑλλάδος, οὐκ ἐπὶ κῶας,   375
σκῆπτρα δὲ καὶ τιμὴν βασιληίδα δεῦρο νέεσθε.
εἰ δέ κε μὴ προπάροιθεν ἐμῆς ἥψασθε τραπέζης,
ἦ τ᾽ ἂν ἀπὸ γλώσσας τε ταμὼν καὶ χεῖρε κεάσσας
ἀμφοτέρας, οἵοισιν ἐπιπροέηκα πόδεσσιν,
ὥς κεν ἐρητύοισθε καὶ ὕστερον ὁρμηθῆναι,   380
οἷα δὲ καὶ μακάρεσσιν ἐπεψεύσασθε θεοῖσιν.᾽

373 νεῖσθαι LG.   374 versum post 374 excidisse coniecit Wilamowitz, schol.
ἀπὸ κοινοῦ τὸ ἔολπα testatus.   375 ὁμαρτήσαντε ἐφ᾽ Ἑλλάδα Brunck:
ἐφ᾽ Ἑλλάδος omisso v. 374 Ruhnken.   οὐκ Vatt. duo, Pariss. nonnulli: οὐδ᾽ vulg.
376 δὲ Pariss., v. l. in schol.: τε LG.   νέεσθε Stephanus et fort. Pariss.:
νέεσθαι LG.   379 ἀποπροέηκα Herwerden.

373. αὐτοῖσι κ.τ.λ., 'tricks and all,' sociative dat., v. n. 96.

ἔκτοθι, 'out of the land,' the usual use c. gen., v. n. 255.

374. τινα. Vague and indefinite; cf. Ar. Frogs 628, ἀγορεύω τινὶ Ἐμὲ μὴ βασανίζειν, 'I give notice to all and sundry,' and Thuc. 2. 37. 1, παράδειγμα ὄντες τισίν.

λευγαλέον, v. n. 263. De Mirmont rightly deprecates any tampering with the text, 'ere some one see Phrixus and his Fleece to his sorrow': cf. Od. 17. 448, μὴ τάχα πικρὴν Αἴγυπτον καὶ Κύπριν ἴδηαι, and Eur. Bacc. 357, ὡς ἂν...Θάνῃ πικρὰν βάκχευσιν ἐν Θήβαις ἰδών. δέρος καὶ Φρίξον is properly a hendiadys, since Phrixus, being dead, could hardly be seen; but Aeetes is in a temper and does not stop to think. Even Medea in 776 seems to believe, like Aeetes here, that the sons of Phrixus actually reached Greece and then returned; but she is not in a condition for coherent thought either. In the legend, the character of Aeetes varies in sympathy with that of Pelias; each alike puts tasks on Jason, each is thoroughly malevolent.

377. εἰ δέ κε μή. The proper formula for a condition contrary to fact is past tense of the indicative, with ἄν or κεν in the apodosis, and for Ap. preferably the aorist, and κεν. A protasis with κεν, and ἄν in the apodosis is irregular. 2. 339 has the optative in both cases; 1. 694

has κε in the protasis and not in the apodosis; in 585, 1140 infr., and in 1. 253, 4. 916, the apodosis lacks κεν altogether.

378. ἀπό. In tmesi with both ταμών and κεάσσας.

379. οἵοισιν, sociative dative, 'with your feet and nothing more.'

ἐπιπροέηκα, 'cast you forth,' lit. forward; cf. Or. Arg. 361, οὖρον ἐπιπροέηκεν, and v. n. 124 supr.

380. ἐρητύοισθε, 'be prevented': this use is on the analogy of κωλύεσθαι. Homer uses it only abs., as in Il. 8. 345, ἐρητύοντο μένοντες, cf. infr. 525; or c. acc., as in Il. 15. 723, ἐρητύοντό τε λαόν.

381. οἷα κ.τ.λ. Take with Platt along with ἐρητύοισθε, not with Mooney as a mere exclamation; i.e. 'be prevented from thus....'

ἐπεψεύσασθε. This cannot be taken as 'attribute lies to,' for they have attributed no statements, true or false, to the gods. It must mean 'belie,' i.e. in making out that the gods (366) are the ancestors of such a piratical set of rascals as Aeetes affects to consider the Argonauts; he returns to the subject infr. 402. It is correctly translated in Jac. Lectius' edition of the Greek poets (Aureliae Allobrogum 1606) 'immortales blasphemastis deos.' The word is first in Xen. Hier. 2. 16 meaning 'lie still more'; cf. Call. H. Art. 223, συνεπιψεύσονται, 'lie together.'

Φῆ ῥα χαλεψάμενος· μέγα δὲ φρένες Αἰακίδαο
νειόθεν οἰδαίνεσκον· ἐέλδετο δ' ἔνδοθι θυμὸς
ἀντιβίην ὀλοὸν φάσθαι ἔπος· ἀλλ' ἀπέρυκεν
Αἰσονίδης· πρὸ γὰρ αὐτὸς ἀμείψατο μειλιχίοισιν·   385
'Αἰήτη, σχέο μοι τῷδε στόλῳ. οὔτι γὰρ αὔτως
ἄστυ τεὸν καὶ δώμαθ' ἱκάνομεν, ὥς που ἔολπας,
οὐδὲ μὲν ἱέμενοι. τίς δ' ἂν τόσον οἶδμα περῆσαι
τλαίη ἑκὼν ὀθνεῖον ἐπὶ κτέρας; ἀλλά με δαίμων
καὶ κρυερὴ βασιλῆος ἀτασθάλου ὦρσεν ἐφετμή.   390

386 τῷ δὲ Merkel: τοῦδε στόλου ex schol. O. Schneider: ψόγου Platt.

382. χαλεψάμενος, 'in his anger,'
v. n. 97, cf. 109. Cf. Val. Flacc. 5. 519,
'Talibus orantem vultu gravis ille minaci
Iamdudum fremit et furiis ignescit
opertis.'
383. νειόθεν, v. n. 164.
οἰδαίνεσκον, 'began to swell': cf.
Arat. 909, οἰδαίνουσα θάλασσα. This
form is Alexandrine; Ap. has the
Homeric transitive οἰδάνω in 1. 477–8,
μέθυ θαρσαλέον κῆρ Οἰδάνει ἐν στήθεσσι.
ἐέλδετο, 'he longed.' This is used only
in pres. and imp. tenses, c. gen., as in
747, 1259, c. inf., as here, and abs. as
in 601, 956; Homer has also c. acc.
The contracted ἐλδομένοισι of Arg. 1. 110
is also Homeric.
384. ἀντιβίην, 'against him.' Here
and 1. 1002 without case, but c. dat. as
in Homer in 2. 758. ἐναντίβιον infr.
1234 is Homeric; but Ap. does not use
the Homeric ἀντίβιον.
ὀλοόν, v. n. 297, 'one that would
bring destruction in its train.'
ἀπέρυκεν, 'restrained,'·v. n. 174.
385. πρό, 'beforehand': cf. Od. 1. 37,
πρὸ οἱ εἴπομεν.
ἀμείψατο μειλιχίοισιν. A typical
Alexandrine variant; Homer uses
ἀμείβετο alone frequently, and four
times προσηύδα μειλιχίοισιν or μειλιχίοισι προσηύδα, but never this actual
phrase.
386. σχέο, lit. 'restrain thyself as
regards this enterprise': i.e. 'bear with
me in this enterprise.'
στόλῳ. For the dative, cf. Arg. 2.
772, ἄχος δ' ἕλεν 'Ηρακλῆι Λειπομένῳ.
From the schol. ἀνάσχου περὶ τούτου τοῦ
στόλου, Platt assumes a genitive here,

and proposes ψόγου, 'cease, I pray, from
this abuse.' But it hardly accords with
Jason's explicit wish to be tactful, to
pull Aeetes up for abuse in his very
first words.
388. ἱέμενοι, either, 'nor would we
wish to be doing so,' or with Mooney,
'through covetousness.' The former is
perhaps supported by Val. Flacc. 5. 481,
'cui non iusso tot adire voluptas Monstra
maris?'
389. ὀθνεῖον, 'belonging to a stranger,'
cf. 403, 591. First in Democritus, cf.
Eur. Alc. 532, ὀθνεῖος ἢ σοὶ συγγενής,
and the imitation in Val. Flacc. 5. 508,
'non aliena peto terrisve indebita
nostris.'
κτέρας, 'possession,' cf. Il. 24. 235,
(δέπας) μέγα κτέρας. For the pl., cf.
Arg. 1. 254, ἐνὶ κτερέεσσιν ἐλυσθείς, 'in
his shroud'; the Homeric meaning of
the plural, 'funeral rites,' is in Arg. 1.
691, κτερέων ἀπὸ μοῖραν ἑλοῦσαν.
390. ἀτασθάλου, 'presumptuous,'
Homeric. This recalls the description
of Pelias in Hes. Th. 996, ὑβριστὴς
Πελίης καὶ ἀτάσθαλος, ὀμβριμοεργός.
ἐφετμή, 'command': cf. Il. 21.
299, θεῶν ὄτρυνεν ἐφετμή, and Soph.
El. 1264, θεοί μ' ἐπώτρυναν μολεῖν.
These lines are based on Od. 5. 99, Ζεὺς
ἐμέ γ' ἠνώγει δεῦρ' ἐλθέμεν οὐκ ἐθέλοντα.
Τίς δ' ἂν ἑκὼν τόσσονδε διαδράμοι ἁλμυρὸν
ὕδωρ; 387 f. are imitated in Aen. 1. 527,
'Non nos aut ferro Libycos populare
Penatis Venimus, aut raptas ad litora
vertere praedas,' and in Or. Arg. 829,
οὔτε νυ ληιστῆρες ἱκάνομεν, οὔτε τιν'
ἄλλην Γαῖαν ἐπιστρωφῶντες ἐγείρομεν
ὕβριος αἴσῃ Ἔργ' ἄδικ' ἀνθρώποισιν.

δὸς χάριν ἀντομένοισι· σέθεν δ' ἐγὼ Ἑλλάδι πάσῃ
θεσπεσίην οἴσω κληηδόνα· καὶ δέ τοι ἤδη
πρόφρονές εἰμεν ἄρηι θοὴν ἀποτῖσαι ἀμοιβήν,
εἴτ' οὖν Σαυρομάτας γε λιλαίεαι, εἴτε τιν' ἄλλον
δῆμον σφωιτέροισιν ὑπὸ σκήπτροισι δαμάσσαι.'   395
Ἴσκεν ὑποσσαίνων ἀγανῇ ὀπί· τοῖο δὲ θυμὸς
διχθαδίην πόρφυρεν ἐνὶ στήθεσσι μενοινήν,
ἢ σφεας ὁρμηθεὶς αὐτοσχεδὸν ἐξεναρίζοι,
ἢ ὅγε πειρήσαιτο βίης. τό οἱ εἴσατ' ἄρειον
φραζομένῳ· καὶ δή μιν ὑποβλήδην προσέειπεν·   400
'Ξεῖνε, τί κεν τὰ ἕκαστα διηνεκέως ἀγορεύοις;

397 ἐνὶ Pariss. tres: ἐπὶ vulg.   399 βίην Pariss., schol.   401 ἀγορεύοις Paris.
unus: ἀγορεύεις vulg.: τί καὶ...ἀγορεύεις Wellauer.

391. ἀντομένοισιν, 'to us thy sup-
pliants,' v. n. 35; cf. Val. Flacc. 5.
491, 'tibi gratia nostri Sit precor haec
meritique locus.'
392. θεσπεσίην, cf. 837: Homer uses
this adj. of anything of exceptional size
or quality. The use of the neuter as adv.
is Alexandrine; cf. infr. 443, 1064, and
Theoc. 25. 70, θεσπέσιον δ' ὑλάοντες
ἐπέδραμον ἄλλοθεν ἄλλος.
κληηδόνα, 'fame.' This meaning
is first in tragedy; in Homer it is
'rumour,' or 'omen.'
393. πρόφρονες, 'ready' as in Homer;
but the use with infinitive is exceptional.
395. σφωιτέροισιν, 'thy,' v. n. 186.
Ap. follows Zenodotus, who took Il. 1.
216, χρὴ μὲν σφωίτερόν γε, θεά, ἔπος
εἰρύσασθαι, to refer to Athene only, and
not to include Here.
δαμάσσαι, 'subdue': note the resemblance to Il. 6. 159, Ζεὺς γάρ οἱ ὑπὸ
σκήπτρῳ ἐδάμασσεν.
396–438. Aeetes appoints an ordeal
to which Jason must first submit, and he
reluctantly assents.
396. ἴσκεν, 'he said,' cf. 439, 1. 834,
4. 410, Lyc. 574. In Homer this is
always from εἴσκω, except in the disputed passages Od. 19. 203, 22. 31; it
would appear that Ap. there read ἴσκεν
rather than ἴσπεν.
ὑποσσαίνων, lit. 'fawning like a
dog': an Alexandrine compound of
the Homeric σαίνω, first in Ap., cf. 974,
4. 410. Aelian, N. A. 17. 17, cf. 9. 1
γλώττῃ ὑποσήνας, uses it of animals.

397. διχθαδίην, Lat. ancipitem.
Compare Il. 14. 20, ὡς ὁ γέρων ὥρμαινε
δαϊζόμενος κατὰ θυμὸν Διχθάδι', ἢ...ἦε...
Ὧδε δέ οἱ φρονέοντι δοάσσατο κέρδιον
εἶναι, and Il. 1. 189, διάνδιχα μερμήριξεν.
This may be more directly based on Il.
16. 435, διχθὰ δέ μοι κραδίη μέμονε
φρεσὶν ὁρμαίνοντι.
πόρφυρεν, 'was brooding over,' v. n.
23.
398. αὐτοσχεδόν, v. n. 148: cf. Il.
13. 496, αὐτοσχεδὸν ὡρμήθησαν.
ἐξεναρίζοι. The cpd. is common in
Homer; the metre of this line recalls
Il. 1. 191, τοὺς μὲν ἀναστήσειεν, ὁ δ'
Ἀτρεΐδην ἐναρίζοι. For the emphatic use of
399. ὅγε, cf. 248, 1241, and Il. 3. 409, ἢ
ἄλοχον ποιήσεται ἢ ὅγε δούλην. Mooney,
on Arg. 1. 308, compares the use of ille
in Latin, as in Aen. 5. 457, 'nunc
dextra ingeminans ictus nunc ille
sinistra.' Cf. also n. 81 supr.
εἴσατ' ἄρειον, 'seemed better': cf.
Od. 19. 283, ἀλλ' ἄρα οἱ τό γε κέρδιον
εἴσατο θυμῷ, and Aen. 4. 287, 'Haec
alternanti potior sententia visa est.'
400. ὑποβλήδην, 'in answer': cf.
1119, and for the differences from the
Homeric use, v. n. 107.
401. διηνεκέως, 'from beginning to
end.' Homer uses this always with
ἀγορεύω: cf. Od. 7. 241, etc., διηνεκέως
ἀγορεῦσαι, Hes. Th. 627, διηνεκέως
κατέλεξε, Arat. 494, and Arg. 1. 649,
847. The adv. διηνεκές of Arg. 2. 391 is
not Homeric, though the adj. is; the

εἰ γὰρ ἐτήτυμόν ἐστε θεῶν γένος, ἠὲ καὶ ἄλλως
οὐδὲν ἐμεῖο χέρηες ἐπ' ὀθνείοισιν ἔβητε,
δώσω τοι χρύσειον ἄγειν δέρος, ἤν κ' ἐθέλησθα
πειρηθείς. ἐσθλοῖς γὰρ ἐπ' ἀνδράσιν οὔτι μεγαίρω,   405
ὡς αὐτοὶ μυθεῖσθε τὸν Ἑλλάδι κοιρανέοντα.
πεῖρα δέ τοι μένεός τε καὶ ἀλκῆς ἔσσετ' ἄεθλος,
τόν ῥ' αὐτὸς περίειμι χεροῖν ὀλοόν περ ἐόντα.
δοιώ μοι πεδίον τὸ Ἀρήιον ἀμφινέμονται
ταύρω χαλκόποδε, στόματι φλόγα φυσιόωντες·   410
τοὺς ἐλάω ζεύξας στυφελὴν κατὰ νειὸν Ἄρηος
τετράγυον, τὴν αἶψα ταμὼν ἐπὶ τέλσον ἀρότρῳ

404 ἤν κ' codd., Platt: αἴ κ' Paris. unus, edd.   410 φυσιόωντε Paris. unus,
Brunck.

adv. is used of foundations solidly laid in H. Hom. *Ap.* 255. διηνεκῶς λέγειν is only in Aesch. *Ag.* 319. Empedocles 439, Nicander *Alex.* 605, and Aratus 445 have ἠνεκές.

403. **χέρηες**, 'inferior,' used in *Od.* 15. 324; the usual Homeric form is χερείων, as infr. 465, *Od.* 5. 211.

ὀθνείοισιν. Note the characteristic variations of this phrase in 389 supr., and infr. 591.

404. **ἤν κε.** Editors, following Brunck, read αἴ κε with a single Paris. MS.; but ἤν κε is probably original, and represents Ap.'s views on the question in Homer. V. further in crit. appendix, p. 139.

405. **πειρηθείς**, 'when I have put you to the test,' cf. n. 10.

ἐπί, 'in the case of': cf. Soph. *Ph.* 806, τἀπί σοι κακά, *i.e.* τὰ σὰ κακά.

οὔτι, cf. *Od.* 8. 206, οὔ τι μεγαίρω.

μεγαίρω, 'I am not grudging,' cf. 485. This use abs., the dative of the person in 1. 288, and the genitive of the thing in 1. 289 are all Homeric. *Arg.* 4. 1670, ἐμέγηρεν ὀπωπάς, 'fascinated the eyes of,' is a unique use.

406. **τόν**, *i.e.* that (other) king: cf. the character of Pelias in Val. Flacc. 1. 23, 'iam gravis et longus populis metus.'

κοιρανέοντα. Homer uses abs., and with ἀνά or κατά of place; this use c. dat. is first in Aesch. *P. V.* 49, θεοῖσι κοιρανεῖν. The gen., as in Hes. *Th.* 331 and Aesch. *Pers.* 214, is not in Ap.

408. **περίειμι**, 'which I myself can encompass with my own hands.' In

Pind. *Pyth.* 4. 224, Jason does not have to yoke the bulls himself, as in the *Arg.*: Aeetes begins the ploughing himself and calls on Jason to complete it.

409. **Ἀρήιον**, 'the plain of Ares,' where the Fleece hung in a grove, infr. 1270. The Homeric adjective ἀρήιος is used of a horse infr. 1259. For the hiatus, v. n. 263.

ἀμφινέμονται, *lit.* 'feed around.' Homer uses this of the gods dwelling round Olympus, *Il.* 18. 186, and frequently, in the Catalogue, of men.

410. **χαλκόποδε**, 'bronze-footed,' an epithet of horses in *Il.* 8. 41, 13. 23: Pind. *Pyth.* 4. 226 describes these bulls as 'pawing the ground with their bronze hoofs.' The origin of these bulls is probably to be sought in the figure of the Cretan Talos, who was, according to Apollodorus 1. 9. 26, regarded by some as a bull, and whom Cook (*Zeus,* 1. 722) concludes to have been represented with a bovine head on a human body; cf. Gruppe, *Gr. Myth.* p. 546.

φλόγα φυσιόωντες, cf. 1303 infr. and Pind. *loc. cit.* φλόγα πνέον, etc. For the mixture of dual and plural, v. n. 206, cf. 1173, 1327: Brunck reads φυσιόωντε here with a single Paris. MS.

411. **στυφελήν**, 'hard,' cf. 1053. This is first in tragedy; cf. Soph. *Ant.* 250, στυφλὸς γῆ.

νειόν. Homeric, cf. infr. 1053, etc. It is properly land ploughed up after being fallow.

412. **τετράγυον**, cf. 1344. γύης is properly the ploughstock (v. n. 232),

οὐ σπόρον ὁλκοῖσιν Δηοῦς ἐνιβάλλομαι ἀκτήν,
ἀλλ' ὄφιος δεινοῖο μεταλδήσκοντας ὀδόντας
ἀνδράσι τευχηστῆσι δέμας· τοὺς δ' αὖθι δαΐζων   415
κείρω ἐμῷ ὑπὸ δουρὶ περισταδὸν ἀντιόωντας.
ἠέριος ζεύγνυμι βόας, καὶ δείελον ὥρην
παύομαι ἀμήτοιο.   σύ δ', εἰ τάδε τοῖα τελέσσεις,

413 ἀκτήν Vat. unus, Pariss. aliquot, Stephanus: ἀκτῇ LG.

and comes to mean a portion of ploughed land. τετράγυον in *Od.* 18. 374 is four of these, a fair day's ploughing. Pherecydes made the field πεντηκοντόγυον; but Ap. reasonably restricts it to the amount that can be ploughed in a single day. Jason could hardly be expected, on top of his other difficulties, to do 12½ days' work in a single morning. τέλσον, 'headland,' *i.e.* where the plough turns at the end of the field. Cf. *Il.* 18. 544, τέλσον ἀρούρης: *ib.* 13. 707, τέμει δέ τε τέλσον ἀρούρης.

413. σπόρον, 'seed,' cf. 498, 1173. First in Hdt. 8. 109; properly 'sowing.' Cf. Theoc. 25. 25, σπόρον ἐν νειοῖσι βάλλοντες.

Δηοῦς. Name of Demeter first in H. Hom. *Dem.* 47.

ἐνιβάλλομαι. The active would have been more natural, and the force of the middle is not quite clear. It may mean, as in Demosth. *in Timoth.* 65, to 'throw in what is one's own,' *i.e.* 'it is not ordinary seed of my own that I throw in.' For the dative, cf. *Il.* 10. 447, 23. 313 φύξιν (μῆτιν) ἐμβάλλεο θυμῷ.

ἀκτήν, cf. *Od.* 2. 355, ἀλφίτου ἀκτῆς; this is a typical variant of the Homeric Δημήτερος ἀκτήν, *Il.* 13. 322. The three phrases are fused in *Or. Arg.* 323, Δήμητρος μὲν πρῶτα φερέσβιος ἀλφίτου ἀκτή.

414. ὄφιος. There was a tradition, at least as old as Pherecydes, that the teeth of the dragon which Cadmus slew were divided equally between him and Aeetes. Cadmus sowed his, and when they grew into armed men, set them fighting with each other by throwing a stone into their midst, until only five were left; these were the first citizens of Thebes (schol. *Arg.* 3. 1179). Probably it was from this legend that the account was introduced into the story of Jason; v. n. 1179 infr.

μεταλδήσκοντας, 'teeth which grow up like armed men.' This word is here only; μετά has the force of 'changing into' something during the process. For the simple verb, cf. *Il.* 23. 599; ἀναλδήσκω, infr. 1363, is first in Ap., and recurs in Oppian *Cyn.* 2. 397. ἀλδήσκω is transitive, like ἀλδαίνω, in Theoc. 17. 78.

415. τευχηστῆσι. This is first in Aesch.; the description recalls that of the third Hesiodic generation, *Op.* 145, 150, οἷσιν Ἄρηος Ἔργ' ἔμελεν...τῶν δ' ἦν χάλκεα μὲν τεύχεα, who, like the warriors in 1374 infr., die at each other's hands, *Op.* 152, χείρεσσιν ὑπὸ σφετέρῃσι δαμέντες.

δέμας. Ap. does not have the Homeric use of δέμας as a preposition c. gen., as in *Il.* 11. 596, δέμας πυρὸς αἰθομένοιο. Here it is accusative of respect, as in *Arg.* 4. 877, πνοιῇ ἰκελὴ δέμας, and the dative is accounted for by the μετα- in the verb.

416. περισταδόν, 'standing around.' Probably Ap. read this in *Il.* 13. 551, against παρασταδόν of Zenodotus and Aristophanes.

417. ἠέριος, 'early in the morning,' cf. 915, the usual Homeric meaning, and in this sense connected with ἦρι, 'early.' Ap. seems also to connect it with ἀήρ, meaning 'misty,' as in 1. 580, ἠερίη πολυλήιος αἶα Πελασγῶν Δύετο. In *Arg.* 4. 1239, ἠερίη ἄμαθος seems to mean 'vast,' cf. schol. *ad loc.*, πᾶν τὸ πολὺ καὶ δαψιλὲς ἠερόεν λέγομεν. One meaning of the word in Hesychius is μέγα, and Diodorus, 1. 33. 3, speaks of θῖνας ἄμμου ἔχοντας μέγεθος ἀέριον.

δείελον, 'at evening.' Here as adj., and in 1. 1160 as noun; both are Homeric. For the accusative of time, cf. 899 infr., etc., Herod. 2. 2, 2 τὴν ὥραν, and *Journal of Philology* 62. 234.

418. ἀμήτοιο, 'from the reaping.' For this metaphorical sense, cf. *Il.* 19.

αὐτῆμαρ τόδε κῶας ἀποίσεαι εἰς βασιλῆος·
πρὶν δέ κεν οὐ δοίην, μηδ' ἔλπεο. δὴ γὰρ ἀεικὲς   420
ἄνδρ' ἀγαθὸν γεγαῶτα κακωτέρῳ ἀνέρι εἶξαι.'
῀Ως ἄρ' ἔφη· ὁ δὲ σῖγα ποδῶν πάρος ὄμματα πήξας
ἧστ' αὔτως ἄφθογγος, ἀμηχανέων κακότητι.
βουλὴν δ' ἀμφὶ πολὺν στρώφα χρόνον, οὐδέ πη εἶχεν
θαρσαλέως ὑποδέχθαι, ἐπεὶ μέγα φαίνετο ἔργον·   425
ὀψὲ δ' ἀμειβόμενος προσελέξατο κερδαλέοισιν·
'Αἰήτη, μάλα τοί με δίκῃ περιπολλὸν ἐέργεις.
τῶ καὶ ἐγὼ τὸν ἄεθλον ὑπερφίαλόν περ ἐόντα
τλήσομαι, εἰ καί μοι θανέειν μόρος. οὐ γὰρ ἔτ' ἄλλο
ῥίγιον ἀνθρώποισι κακῆς ἐπικείσετ' ἀνάγκης,   430
ἥ με καὶ ἐνθάδε νεῖσθαι ἐπέχραεν ἐκ βασιλῆος.'
῀Ως φάτ' ἀμηχανίῃ βεβολημένος· αὐτὰρ ὁ τόνγε

426 κηδοσύνῃσιν Spitzner.   430 ἐπικείσετ' G, Vatt. tres: ἐπικλείσετ' L:
ἐπιβήσετ' vulg.: ἐπαμείβετ' Pariss. tres, unde ἄνθρωπός γε...ἐπαμείψετ' Brunck:
ἐπινίσσετ' Gerhard, Koechly.

222, φυλόπιδος...ῆς...ἄμητος δ' ὀλίγιστος, and the comparison of fighters to ἀμητῆρες in *Il.* 11. 67. It is first found in the purely agricultural sense in Hesiod.

419. εἰς βασιλῆος sc. δόμον, a common ellipse.

420. δὴ γάρ. For this emphatic use, cf. *Il.* 15. 488, δὴ γὰρ ἴδον, *Od.* 1. 194, δὴ γάρ μιν ἔφαντο, etc.

422. πήξας, v. n. 22.

423. κακότητι, 'helpless in his evil plight,' v. n. 95.

424. ἀμφί...στρώφα, *lit.* 'turned round and round.' This compound, which is not recognised by the lexicographers, is here only. Homer has the simple verb, *e.g.*, of turning a spindle, *Od.* 6. 53, and in passive, of wandering, *Il.* 20. 422. For ἐπιστρωφῶσι v. n. 893 infr.

οὐδέ πη εἶχεν, cf. *Il.* 16. 110, οὐδέ πη εἶχεν 'Αμπνεῦσαι.

425. ὑποδέχθαι, 'accept the challenge': this recalls *Il.* 7. 93, αἴδεσθεν μὲν ἀνήνασθαι δεῖσαν δ' ὑποδέχθαι.

426. κερδαλέοισιν. This can hardly be 'cunning' (Seaton), for Hermes himself would find nothing cunning in this speech; it could be 'wily' only in the modified sense of 'tactful.' Ap. is using both meanings of a Homeric word; it is 'wily' in *Od.* 13. 291, and 'wise' in

Il. 10. 44. κερδοσύνῃσιν in *Arg.* 2. 951 is in the Homeric sense of 'craftiness,' but here, and infr. 798 κέρδιον, the reference is to prudence rather than cunning: cf. *Od.* 2. 118, φρένας ἐσθλὰς Κέρδεά θ'.

427. περιπολλόν. 'Thou dost hedge me in very closely with thy claim of right.' This compound of the Homeric adv. is peculiar to Ap.; the plural in Arat. 914, περιπολλὰ λεληκώς 'with many a scream,' is not recognised by L. and S.

428. ὑπερφίαλον, 'exceedingly great,' hence 'excessive,' v. n. 15.

430. ῥίγιον, 'worse.' This is in Homer and Hesiod, but only in the neuter; the superlative, as in *Arg.* 2. 215, is also Homeric.

ἐπικείσετ', modelled on *Il.* 6. 458, κρατερὴ δ' ἐπικείσετ' ἀνάγκη; for the whole line, cf. Arat. 126, ἔσσεται ἀνθρώποισι, κακὸν δ' ἐπικείσεται ἄλγος.

431. ἐπέχραεν, 'which forced me to come hither,' *lit.* 'was urgent that...' Homer uses only c. dat., meaning 'attack,' but Ap. has the further un-Homeric uses, abs. of winds blowing, 2. 498, and c. gen., 'touch,' 2. 283.

432. ἀμηχανίη, 'helpless plight': v. n. 336, cf. 504, 893 infr.

σμερδαλέοις ἐπέεσσι προσέννεπεν ἀσχαλόωντα·
'"Ερχεο νῦν μεθ' ὅμιλον, ἐπεὶ μέμονάς γε πόνοιο·
εἰ δὲ σύγε ζυγὰ βουσὶν ὑποδδείσαις ἐπαεῖραι,   435
ἠὲ καὶ οὐλομένου μεταχάσσεαι ἀμήτοιο,
αὐτῷ κεν τὰ ἕκαστα μέλοιτό μοι, ὄφρα καὶ ἄλλος
ἀνὴρ ἐρρίγῃσιν ἀρείονα φῶτα μετελθεῖν.'
"Ισκεν ἀπηλεγέως· ὁ δ' ἀπὸ θρόνου ὤρνυτ' Ἰήσων,
Αὐγείης Τελαμών τε παρασχεδόν· εἵπετο δ' "Αργος   440
οἶος, ἐπεὶ μεσσηγὺς ἔτ' αὐτόθι νεῦσε λιπέσθαι
αὐτοκασιγνήτοις· οἱ δ' ἦισαν ἐκ μεγάροιο.
θεσπέσιον δ' ἐν πᾶσι μετέπρεπεν Αἴσονος υἱὸς
κάλλεϊ καὶ χαρίτεσσιν· ἐπ' αὐτῷ δ' ὄμματα κούρη
λοξὰ παρὰ λιπαρὴν σχομένη θηεῖτο καλύπτρην,   445

442 ἦισαν Rzach: ἦεσαν codd.   443 ἐνὶ πᾶσι Gerhard.

433. σμερδαλέοις, 'terrible.' This is also used infr. 1215 of δράκοντες, as in *Il.* 2. 309. The adv. σμερδαλέον, 1. 524, etc., is also Homeric.

ἀσχαλόωντα, 'in his distress': common in Homer.

434. μεθ', 'to,' 'right into the middle of,' v. n. 331.

ὅμιλον, 'your comrades,' rather than 'to the ordeal' (Way), or 'to the gathering' (Seaton).

μέμονας, 'art eager for': cf. 509, v. n. 351.

435. ὑποδδείσαις. For construction and form, v. n. 318. This is the only place where Ap. uses weak aorist forms -αις, -αι, except at the end of a line.

436. ἠὲ καί, v. n. 181. This introduces the more probable alternative; 'If you are in doubt...or if (as I expect) you refuse altogether.'

μεταχάσσεαι, 'shrink from,' compound peculiar to Ap. The simple verb abs., or c. gen. as infr. 1051, is Homeric; c. inf. (4. 190), and with ὑπὲκ (1319), it is un-Homeric.

ἀμήτοιο, v. n. 418.

437. μέλοιτο, 'all this shall be my care.' This is modelled on *Il.* 1. 523, ἐμοὶ δέ κε ταῦτα μελήσεται ὄφρα τελέσσω.

438. ἐρρίγῃσιν, 'may shrink from coming to a better man than himself.' This is based on *Il.* 3. 353, ὄφρα τις ἐρρίγῃσι καὶ ὀψιγόνων ἀνθρώπων...; compare also for metre and position *Od.* 8. 241, ὄφρα καὶ ἄλλῳ Εἴπῃς.

439-470. The Argonauts return to the ship; Medea retires to her chamber full of anxious fears for Jason.

439. ἴσκεν, 'he spake,' v. n. 396.

ἀπηλεγέως, 'outright,' v. n. 19.

ὤρνυτο, a slight variation from the Homeric ἀπὸ θρόνου ὦρτο, *Il.* 24. 515.

440. παρασχεδόν, 'forthwith,' cf. 667. An Alexandrine word, corresponding to παραχρῆμα when used in a temporal sense; for use of place, cf. *Arg.* 2. 10, and c. gen., *ib.* 859.

441. μεσσηγύς, 'meanwhile,' v. n. 307.

λιπέσθαι, merely to 'remain.' For this neuter sense, cf. *Il.* 5. 154, υἱὸν δ' οὐ τέκετ' ἄλλον ἐπὶ κτεάτεσσι λιπέσθαι.

442. αὐτοκασιγνήτοις. Homer uses this freely as masc., Ap. once only; the fem. is once in Homer, and common in Ap.

ἦισαν common Homeric form, *e.g. Il.* 10. 197.

443. θεσπέσιον, 'wonderfully,' v. n. 392.

μετέπρεπεν ἐν, v. n. 246. Unlike Homer, Ap. does not use the double dative with this word; cf. *Or. Arg.* 806, ἐν πάντεσσι μ.

444. χαρίτεσσιν, cf. *Od.* 6. 237, κάλλεϊ καὶ χάρισιν. This form of the dative is in the *Iliad*, but not in the *Odyssey*.

445. λιπαρήν, as in Homer, like λαμπρός, a conventional epithet of the κρήδεμνον or καλύπτρη; infr. 835 it is

κῆρ ἄχεϊ σμύχουσα· νόος δέ οἱ ἠΰτ' ὄνειρος
ἑρπύζων πεπότητο μετ' ἴχνια νισσομένοιο.
καί ῥ' οἱ μέν ῥα δόμων ἐξήλυθον ἀσχαλόωντες.
Χαλκιόπη δὲ χόλον πεφυλαγμένη Αἰήταο
καρπαλίμως θάλαμόνδε σὺν υἱάσιν οἷσι βεβήκει.   450
αὕτως δ' αὖ Μήδεια μετέστιχε· πολλὰ δὲ θυμῷ
ὥρμαιν', ὅσσα τ' Ἔρωτες ἐποτρύνουσι μέλεσθαι.

called ἀργυφέη. It seems to have been a light, fine garment, perhaps of a semi-transparent character (Abrahams, *Greek Dress*, p. 35).

σχομένη. An involved adaptation of *Od.* 1. 334, where Penelope stands ἄντα παρειάων σχομένη λιπαρὰ κρήδεμνα, cf. 834 infr. Here Medea casts sidelong glances παρὰ λιπαρὴν καλύπτρην, 'from beside her shining veil,' σχομένη, 'as she held it aside.'

καλύπτρην. Women's dress in Homer, on which this is modelled, consisted of two garments, the πέπλος, and the καλύπτρη or κρήδεμνον, called also κάλυμμα in one passage, *Il.* 24. 93. The latter was worn either as a cloak or as a veil, put unfolded over the shoulders, and sometimes worn over the head, as in *Od.* 5. 232: cf. infr. 834.

446. σμύχουσα, *lit.* 'smouldering in her heart with grief,' *i.e.* 'with anguish smouldering in her heart': cf. 762, and *Od.* 10. 247, κῆρ ἄχεϊ μεγάλῳ βεβολημένος. Homer uses this word only in the literal sense, active in *Il.* 9. 653, κατά τε σμύξαι πυρὶ νῆας, passive in *Il.* 22. 411, ὡς εἰ ἅπασα Ἴλιος ὀκριόεσσα πυρὶ σμύχοιτο. For this sense, cf. Theoc. 3. 17, Ἔρως...με κατασμύχων.

νόος, cf. Moschus *Europa* 106, νόος δέ οἱ ἠΰτε φωτὸς Αἰσίμου ἀμφιθέει.

447. ἑρπύζων. This conveys an idea of painful and unsuccessful endeavour. Homer uses only the present part. of people thus weighed down by age or distress; cf. *Arg.* 4. 1289, ἤλυον ἑρπύζοντες.

πεπότητο, 'her soul, creeping like a dream, flitted in his footsteps as he went.' An adaptation of *Od.* 11. 222, ψυχὴ δ' ἠΰτ' ὄνειρος ἀποπταμένη πεπότηται. In *Il.* 22. 199, cf. *Aen.* 12. 908, Homer uses the comparison of unsuccessful endeavour in a dream, which does not enter into this simile.

ἴχνια, cf. Call. *H. Dem.* 9, μετέστιχεν ἴχνια κώρας.

448. ἀσχαλόωντες, 'in deep distress,' v. n. 433.

450. βεβήκει, not 'had gone' (Seaton), but the 'instantaneous' use, 'went at once,' cf. 271 supr. The sons were present in 442, and Chalciope, like Medea, was presumably present at their departure.

451. αὕτως, cf. 53, 85; either 'likewise,' or, 'just as she was,' *i.e.* dreaming of Jason.

μετέστιχε, 'went after her,' to her own chamber. Here only in this sense; this verb is first in tragedy, in the sense 'go in search of,' Eur. *Hec.* 509, ἥκω μεταστείχων σε.

452. ὥρμαιν', adapted from *Od.* 7. 82, 23. 85, πολλὰ δέ οἱ κῆρ Ὥρμαιν' : cf. *Il.* 21. 551, πολλὰ δέ οἱ κραδίη πόρφυρε μένοντι.

Ἔρωτες. Here, as Couat points out, Apollonius has descended to the banalities of the ordinary Alexandrine erotic poetry in writing of more than one Eros; every stage in the progress of Medea's passion has to be signalised by an intervention of Eros, or of an Eros, cf. Val. Flacc. 6. 457, 'volucrumque exercitus omnis amorum.' Hes. *Th.* 201 knows of Eros and Himeros as escort of Aphrodite; Ap., however, seems to have been the first to introduce the personal plural, cf. infr. 687, 765, 937, and n. 3. Impersonal ἔρωτες are found in Aesch. *Choeph.* 597; and it should be noted that the word, both in singular and plural, often denotes strong passion rather than actual love, cf. Philodemus περὶ μουσικῆς ed. Kemke, p. 81, l. 30, πᾶσαν ὁρμὴν καὶ ἐπιθυμίαν ὑπὸ τῶν παλαίων ἔρωτα καλεῖσθαι. For statues of Aphrodite with two Erotes, v. Reinach *Rép. St. gr. et rom.* 2. 377. 5, 6, 7, etc.

ἐποτρύνουσι, 'all the sorrows that

προπρὸ δ' ἄρ' ὀφθαλμῶν ἔτι οἱ ἰνδάλλετο πάντα,
αὐτός θ' οἷος ἔην, οἵοισί τε φάρεσιν ἔστο,
οἷά τ' ἔειφ', ὥς θ' ἔζετ' ἐπὶ θρόνου, ὥς τε θύραζε   455
ἤιεν· οὐδέ τιν' ἄλλον ὀίσσατο πορφύρουσα
ἔμμεναι ἀνέρα τοῖον· ἐν οὔασι δ' αἰὲν ὀρώρει
αὐδή τε μῦθοί τε μελίφρονες, οὓς ἀγόρευσεν.
τάρβει δ' ἀμφ' αὐτῷ, μή μιν βόες ἠὲ καὶ αὐτὸς
Αἰήτης φθίσειεν· ὀδύρετο δ' ἠύτε πάμπαν   460
ἤδη τεθνειῶτα, τέρεν δέ οἱ ἀμφὶ παρειὰς
δάκρυον αἰνοτάτῳ ἐλέῳ ῥέε κηδοσύνῃσιν·

454 ἔστο Brunck: εἶτο Pariss. tres: ἧστο vulg.   462 κηδοσύνῃ τε O. Schneider:
ἠδ' ὀδύνῃσιν Damste.

the Loves excite.' Homer uses this verb
both with direct infinitive, as 715, 722,
or abs., cf. 567, *Il.* 6. 439, ἐποτρύνει
καὶ ἀνώγει. μέλεσθαι is here an explanatory infinitive.

453. προπρό, like πρό, 'in front of.'
Homer uses it only in composition with
κυλινδόμενος, *Il.* 22. 221: cf. *Arg.* 2.
595, προπροκαταίγδην, 1. 386, προπρο-
βιαζόμενοι. Both as prep. and adverb
it is peculiar to Ap.; in 1013 it is
'thoroughly,' intensifying the verb, cf.
4. 1235, προπρὸ μάλ' ἔνδοθι, 'right
within.'

ἰνδάλλετο. In using this verb consistently in the sense of φαίνομαι,
Apollonius is following the Aristophanic
view on *Il.* 17. 214, ἰνδάλλετο δέ σφισι
πᾶσιν Τεύχεσι λαμπόμενος μεγαθύμου
Πηλεΐωνος, where Ven. A. and Aristarchus read the dative. The sense
'resemble' is first authentically found
in Plato *Rep.* 381 E, *Theaet.* 189 E.
There are two Latin imitations of this
passage, Val. Flacc. 7. 106: 'respexit-
que fores et adhuc invenit euntem,
Visus et heu miserae tunc pulchrior
hospes amanti Discedens; tales umeros,
ea terga relinquit'; and Verg. *Aen.* 4.
3: 'multa viri virtus animo multusque
recursat Gentis honos; haerent infixi
pectore voltus Verbaque,' and *ib.* 83,
'illum absens absentem auditque vide-
que.' In *Aen.* 4. 4, the typically Roman
addition *gentis honos* is a distinct
blemish. Compare also Ach. Tat. 1. 19.
2, ἡ μὲν οὖν μετὰ μικρὸν ἀπιοῦσα ᾤχετο...
ἐμοὶ δὲ ἐδόκει παρεῖναι, ἀπελθοῦσα γὰρ
τὴν μορφήν ἐπαφῆκέ μου τοῖς ὀφθαλμοῖς.

454. ἔστο, 'the clothes in which he
was clad'; the form, like ἔεστο 1225,
is Homeric. Curtius, *G. V.* 2. 147, con-
nects them with ϝεϝεστο.

455. θρόνου, cf. in the same position
in the line, *Il.* 24. 522, ἔζευ ἐπὶ θρόνου.

456. ὀίσσατο, cf. 926, 1189, 'she
thought.' The -σσ- is faulty, for Homer
has the -ι- long in the resolved diphthong; cf. *Od.* 1. 323, ὀίσατο: 15. 443,
ὀισάμενος. Ap. has also ᾠσάμην, 1.
291.

πορφύρουσα, cf. 397, n. 231, 'as she
brooded.'

457. ὀρώρει, simply ἦν: cf. 314, and
n. 59. A plural verb is not necessary,
as the phrase μῦθοί κ.τ.λ. follows it, and
can be considered separately from the
verb. For the 'ringing in the ears,'
cf. Plat. *Menex.* 235 C, λόγοι ἔναυλοι,
Meleager in *Anth. Pal.* 5. 212. 1, αἰεί
μοι δινεῖ μὲν ἐν οὔασιν ἦχος Ἔρωτος, and
Seneca, *epig.* 62, *de tinnitu auris* 11-12,
'Verae venit mihi vocis imago, Blandior
arguta tinnit in aure sonus.'

458. μελίφρονες, as in Homer, 'sweet
as honey to the mind.' Contrast the use
in *Arg.* 4. 1132 of Aristaeus, the dis-
coverer of honey, in the literal sense
'whose care was for honey.' There is no
parallel in Homer to this minutely
detailed, but always sympathetic description; the first trace is in the lyric
poets, particularly in Sappho.

462. αἰνοτάτῳ, 'most terrible,' cf.
342.

ἐλέῳ, 'pity,' causal dative. Once only
in Homer, *Il.* 24. 44, but common in
Attic; cf. 761.

ἦκα δὲ μυρομένη λιγέως ἀνενείκατο μῦθον·
'Τίπτε με δειλαίην τόδ' ἔχει ἄχος; εἶθ' ὅγε πάντων
φθίσεται ἡρώων προφερέστατος, εἴτε χερείων,   465
ἐρρέτω. ἦ μὲν ὄφελλεν ἀκήριος ἐξαλέασθαι.
ναὶ δὴ τοῦτό γε, πότνα θεὰ Περσηί, πέλοιτο,
οἴκαδε νοστήσειε φυγὼν μόρον· εἰ δέ μιν αἶσα
δμηθῆναι ὑπὸ βουσί, τόδε προπάροιθε δαείη,
οὕνεκεν οὔ οἱ ἔγωγε κακῇ ἐπαγαίομαι ἄτῃ.'   470
'Η μὲν ἄρ' ὡς ἐόλητο νόον μελεδήμασι κούρη.
οἱ δ' ἐπεὶ οὖν δήμου τε καὶ ἄστεος ἐκτὸς ἔβησαν
τὴν ὁδόν, ἣν τὸ πάροιθεν ἀνήλυθον ἐκ πεδίοιο,

---

464 ἔλεν ἄχος coni. Brunck.   471 ἐόλητο Vat. unus, Pariss. quatt., Et. Mag.
352. 2: αἰόλητο LG.

κηδοσύνῃσιν, 'in her yearning': cf. 1. 277, 4. 1473. The word is peculiar to Ap., and occurs only in dat. plural. Damste compares 762 and 4. 1067, and from schol. λυπουμένη needlessly alters to ἠδ' ὀδύνῃσιν. Technically ἐλέῳ is causal, and this modal, dative. For other double datives, v. n. 346, cf. 470, 1297.

463. μυρομένη. Here and in 657, 665, 1065, in the Homeric sense, 'weeping'; in 2. 372 it is used of a river 'flowing', which is found elsewhere only in Lyc. 982, ἔνθα μύρεται Σίνις.

ἀνενείκατο μῦθον, cf. 635, and Or. Arg. 76, etc. Homer uses this only in the phrase ἀνενείκατο φώνησέν τε, Il. 19. 314, 'taking a deep breath.' The Alexandrines took this to mean 'cried aloud'; v. schol. Hom. ad loc. The Homeric phrase is used in Arg. 4. 1748, a typical double use.

464. For the end of this verse, cf. Il. 3. 409, ἢ ὅ γε δούλην, closely imitated in Call. H. Art. 150, ἢ ὅ γε χλούνην.

465. χερείων, 'whether he be the worst of heroes,' v. n. 403, χέρηες.

466. ὄφελλεν. The aorist refers to a wish incapable of fulfilment because already past; the changing moods shew the rapid changes in the mind of Medea, 'would that he were now safe and had escaped the task already,' 'utinam salvus evassiset.' For the impersonal use, v. n. 678.

ἀκήριος, 'unharmed,' as always in the Odyssey. In the Iliad it means 'lifeless,' for which cf. Arg. 2. 197,

ἀκήριον ἠύτ' ὄνειρον, Il. 7. 100, ἥμενοι αὖθι ἔκαστοι ἀκήριοι, ἀκλεὲς αὔτως.

ἐξαλέασθαι, 'escape,' also used c. acc. 'avoid,' infr. 600; cf. Il. 18. 586, ἐκ τ' ἀλέοντο.

467. Περσηί, cf. 478, 1035, and v. n. 251 supr.

470. οὕνεκεν after verbs of perception means simply ὅτι, like Latin quod, as in Od. 5. 216, etc., and often in tragedy. οἱ...ἄτῃ, for the double dative, v. n. 346, cf. 462, 1297.

ἐπαγαίομαι, 'that I at least do not rejoice in,' cf. 1262. The compound seems to be peculiar to Ap., and recurs in a fragment of his 'Founding of Lesbos,' preserved in Parthenius 21, line 18 (Powell, Collectanea Alexandrina, p. 8), ὀλοῷ δ' ἐπεγάσσατο πατρίδος οἴτῳ. In Homer and elsewhere the simple verb means 'to be indignant at'; infr. 1016, cf. 1. 899, it seems to mean 'in loving admiration,' following the first explanation of schol. Od. 20. 16, ἄγαν θαυμάζειν, ἢ χαλεπαίνειν.

471-488. Argos suggests to Jason that his mother Chalciope might secure for them the aid of Medea in the trials.

471. ἐόλητο, 'was troubled in mind': cf. Moschus Europa 74, ἐόλητο θυμόν. Buttmann derives it from εἴλω, εἰλέω, 'press,' Boeck from ἐολέω; the latter reads imperf. ἐόλει for αἰόλλει in Pind. Pyth. 4. 233 (414).

μελεδήμασι, 'cares': v. n. 4, cf. 752.

473. ὁδόν, cognate acc. with βαίνειν; cf. βαίνειν κέλευθον in Pind. frag. 201.

δὴ τότ' Ἰήσονα τοῖσδε προσέννεπεν Ἄργος ἔπεσσιν·
'Αἰσονίδη, μῆτιν μὲν ὀνόσσεαι, ἥντιν' ἐνίψω;   475
πείρης δ' οὐ μάλ' ἔοικε μεθιέμεν ἐν κακότητι.
κούρην δή τινα πρόσθεν ὑπέκλυες αὐτὸς ἐμεῖο
φαρμάσσειν Ἑκάτης Περσηίδος ἐννεσίησιν.
τὴν εἴ κεν πεπίθοιμεν, ὀίομαι, οὐκέτι τάρβος
ἔσσετ' ἀεθλεύοντι δαμήμεναι· ἀλλὰ μάλ' αἰνῶς   480
δείδω, μή πως οὔ μοι ὑποστήῃ τόγε μήτηρ.
ἔμπης δ' ἐξαῦτις μετελεύσομαι ἀντιβολήσων,
ξυνὸς ἐπεὶ πάντεσσιν ἐπικρέμαθ' ἡμῖν ὄλεθρος.'
Ἴσκεν εὐφρονέων· ὁ δ' ἀμείβετο τοῖσδ' ἐπέεσσιν·
'Ὦ πέπον, εἴ νύ τοι αὐτῷ ἐφανδάνει, οὔτι μεγαίρω.   485
βάσκ' ἴθι καὶ πυκινοῖσι τεὴν παρὰ μητέρα μύθοις

475 ita interpunxit Platt.   480 δαήμεναι Stephanus.   481 ὑποστήῃ coni.
Mooney: ὑποσταίη codd.

475. ὀνόσσεαι, 'treat with scorn.'
Both Homer and Ap. use the accusative
normally with this verb; the former has
the gen. once in *Od.* 5. 379, ὀνόσσεσθαι
κακότητος. This line is best taken, with
Platt, as a question; cf. *Il.* 5. 421, Ζεῦ
πάτερ, ἦ ῥά τί μοι κεχολώσεαι, ὅττι κεν
εἴπω; For μὲν in questions without an
answering δὲ, cf. Eur. *Hipp.* 316, Plat.
Char. 153 C, etc.
476. μεθιέμεν, 'neglect': cf. *Il.* 11.
841, ἀλλ' οὐδ' ὣς περ σεῖο μεθήσω.
κακότητι, 'misfortune,' v. n. 95.
477. ὑπέκλυες, 'thou hast heard ere
this.' This compound is first in Ap., and
recurs in Qu. Sm. 1. 509, etc.
478. φαρμάσσειν, 'use magic drugs':
it can also mean 'heal with medicines,'
as in 4. 1512. The middle is used infr.
859. This verb is once only in Homer, *Od.*
9. 393, of a metal worker 'tempering,'
ὡς δ' ὅτ' ἀνὴρ χαλκεὺς πέλεκυν μέγαν ἠὲ
σκέπαρνον Εἰν ὕδατι ψυχρῷ βάπτῃ μεγάλα
ἰάχοντα Φαρμάσσων.
ἐννεσίῃσιν, *lit.* 'suggestions,' *i.e.*
'through inspiration from Hecate': v. n.
29, cf. *Il.* 5. 894, κείνης...ἐννεσίῃσι.
For Medea's connection with Hecate,
v. n. 529.
480. δαμήμεναι, 'fear for thee (of
defeat) in the contest,' a mixture of
τάρβος ἔσται (1) ἀεθλεύοντί σοι and
(2) ἀεθλεύοντά σε δαμήμεναι: cf. Eur.
Or. 1531 Μενελέων δ' οὐ τάρβος ἡμῖν

ἀναλαβεῖν εἴσω ξίφους. Perhaps δαήμεναι
should be read with Stephanus, 'fear
for thee to know in the battle.'
481. δείδω, cf. *Il.* 19. 24, ἀλλὰ μάλ'
αἰνῶς Δείδω μή μοι....
ὑποστήῃ: so Mooney reads for MSS.
ὑποσταίη. The only two places where
the optative is found with μή after a
primary tense have been altered by
editors, Soph. *Aj.* 279, Hdt. 7. 103.
This recalls *Il.* 10. 38-9, ἀλλὰ μάλ'
αἰνῶς Δείδω μὴ οὔ τίς μοι ὑπόσχηται τόδε
ἔργον.
482. ἐξαῦτις, 'back again,' frequent
in Homer as *denuo*, and thence
developing all the meanings of αὖ,
αὖτις. It is in the sense of *deinde* in
Arg. 4. 455, δέγμενος Ἄψυρτόν τε καὶ
οὓς ἐξαῦτις ἑταίρους.
ἀντιβολήσων, 'and will entreat her':
post-Homeric, v. n. 179.
483. ἐπικρέμαθ', 'hangs over us':
cf. Simonides 14, ἄφυκτος ἐπικρέμαται
θάνατος and Thuc. 7. 75. 7, ἐπικρεμά-
μενος κίνδυνος.
484. ἴσκεν, 'he spake,' v. n. 396.
485. ἐφανδάνει, for the form, v. n. 171.
οὔτι μεγαίρω, 'I am in no way
grudging,' v. n. 405.
486. βάσκ' ἴθι, 'go,' a Homeric
phrase. βάσκω is extant only in the
imperative; the plural occurs in comedy.
παρά...ὄρνυθι, 'urge on': this compound of the Homeric ὄρνυμι is here only.

ὄρνυθι λισσόμενος· μελέη γε μὲν ἧμιν ὄρωρεν
ἐλπωρή, ὅτε νόστον ἐπετραπόμεσθα γυναιξίν.'
ὡς ἔφατ'· ὦκα δ' ἔλος μετεκίαθον. αὐτὰρ ἑταῖροι
γηθόσυνοι ἐρέεινον, ὅπως παρεόντας ἴδοντο·   490
τοῖσιν δ' Αἰσονίδης τετιημένος ἔκφατο μῦθον·
'"Ω φίλοι, Αἰήταο ἀπηνέος ἄμμι φίλον κῆρ
ἀντικρὺ κεχόλωται, ἔκαστα γὰρ οὔ νύ τι τέκμωρ
οὔτ' ἐμοί, οὔτε κεν ὔμμι διειρομένοισι πέλοιτο.
φῆ δὲ δύω πεδίον τὸ Ἀρήιον ἀμφινέμεσθαι   495
ταύρω χαλκόποδε, στόματι φλόγα φυσιόωντας.
τετράγυον δ' ἐπὶ τοῖσιν ἐφίετο νειὸν ἀρόσσαι·
δώσειν δ' ἐξ ὄφιος γεννύων σπόρον, ὅς ῥ' ἀνίησιν
γηγενέας χαλκέοις σὺν τεύχεσιν· ἤματι δ' αὐτῷ
χρειὼ τούσγε δαΐξαι. ὁ δή νύ οἱ—οὔτι γὰρ ἄλλο   500

---

493 ἀντικρὺς Pariss. quatt., Brunck.   497 ὑπὸ Samuelsson.   498 ἀνίησιν
Platt, vulg.: ἀνίῃσιν L.

---

487. μελέη, 'wretched indeed is our hope, when we have entrusted our return to women.' In this sense, μελέοισι has been accepted by some in the disputed passage in Hes. *Th.* 567, οὐκ ἐδίδου μελέοισι (?) πυρὸς μένος ἀκαμάτοιο θνητοῖς ἀνθρώποις, i.e. 'wretched mortals.' The Homeric sense is like ἠλεός, 'in vain,' as in *Arg.* 1. 1249, μελέη δέ οἱ ἔπλετο φωνή, which should be translated 'his shouting was in vain,' rather than merely 'wretched was his cry.'

ὄρωρεν, as elsewhere, 'is': v. n. 59.

489–520. Jason describes the interview to those who had remained at the ship. Peleus and others offer if necessary to take his place in the trials.

489. ἔλος, v. 168 supr.

491. τετιημένος, 'in sorrow.' Homer has only this participle, the perfect τετίησθον, and the active part. τετιώς in same sense: Ap. has only this form. There is an analogous use of the perfect of χαίρω in H. Hom. *Dion.* 10, κεχαρμένοι ἦτορ, cf. *Arg.* 1. 1104, κεχαρημένος.

492. ἀπηνέος, 'cruel': cf. *Il.* 1. 340, τοῦ βασιλῆος ἀπηνέος. For the hiatus in the weak caesura, cf. 263.

φίλον κῆρ, a curious use of a stock phrase: cf. *Od.* 4. 270, οἷον Ὀδυσσῆος ταλασίφρονος ἔσκε φίλον κῆρ.

493. κεχόλωται, 'is angry': for other constructions with this verb, v. n. 124.

494. διειρομένοισι, 'question closely': cf. *Od.* 4. 492, τί με ταῦτα διείρεαι; The phrase is rather too compact to be clear; 'were you to ask me everything at length, neither you nor I would come to an end.' Compare Isoc. *Evag.* 195 C, οὐδ' ἂν ὁ λόγος ἴσως τοῖς καιροῖς ἁρμόσειεν, οὔτ' ἂν ὁ χρόνος τοῖς λεγομένοις ἀρκέσειεν, and Soph. *El.* 1294, χρόνου γὰρ ἄν σοι καιρὸν ἐξείργοι λόγος.

495. Ἀρήιον, 'the plain of Ares,' v. n. 409.

497. ἐπὶ τοῖσιν, 'with these as a condition': cf. *Il.* 21. 444, θητεύσαμεν εἰς ἐνιαυτὸν Μισθῷ ἐπὶ ῥητῷ, and contrast 178 supr., 'in addition to.' There is no need to read ὑπὸ with Samuelsson.

ἀρόσσαι. This aor. inf. of ἀρόω, 'plough,' is here only.

498. ἀνίησιν. L. gives the subj. ἀνίῃσιν; but Ap. does not use the subj. alone as a future. κ' ἀνίῃσιν would be Homeric, and in the style of Ap.; but the present can be read with G. and the other MSS. against L.

499. αὐτῷ. This use of αὐτός alone for ὁ αὐτός, 'the same,' belongs to epic and late prose; cf. *Od.* 10. 263, τὸν δ' ἂψ ἠνώγεα αὐτὴν ὁδὸν ἡγήσασθαι.

500. χρειώ, i.e. χρέον, 'I must': v. n. 12.

βέλτερον ἦν φράσσασθαι—ἀπηλεγέως ὑποέστην.'
'Ὡς ἄρ' ἔφη· πάντεσσι δ' ἀνήνυτος εἴσατ' ἄεθλος,
δὴν δ' ἄνεῳ καὶ ἄναυδοι ἐς ἀλλήλους ὁρόωντο,
ἄτῃ ἀμηχανίῃ τε κατηφέες· ὀψὲ δὲ Πηλεὺς
θαρσαλέως μετὰ πᾶσιν ἀριστήεσσιν ἔειπεν·   505
'Ὥρη μητιάασθαι ὅ κ' ἔρξομεν. οὐ μὲν ἔολπα
βουλῆς εἶναι ὄνειαρ, ὅσον τ' ἐπὶ κάρτεϊ χειρῶν.
εἰ μέν νυν τύνη ζεῦξαι βόας Αἰήταο,
ἥρως Αἰσονίδη, φρονέεις, μέμονάς τε πόνοιο,
ἦ τ' ἂν ὑποσχεσίην πεφυλαγμένος ἐντύναιο·   510

501. **ἀπηλεγέως**, 'outright,' v.n. 19. In like manner Cleon, in Thuc. 4. 28. 4, οὐκ ἔχων ὅπως τῶν εἰρημένων ἔτι ἐξαπαλλάγῃ, ὑφίσταται τὸν πλοῦν.

ὑποέστην, cf. 619. 'I undertook.' Other uses are with fut. inf. 983, which is Homeric; with περί c. dat., 905; in the sense of 'withstand,' 1232. The meaning 'undertake' is first in Attic prose and tragedy. Ap. has the rough breathing only in 619; elsewhere, as in Homer, it is smooth. The hiatus in the compound is un-Homeric, formed on the analogy of Homeric words that properly have the digamma; elsewhere in Ap. it is without hiatus, *e.g.* 983 infr. Compare the Homeric ἀπόερσε, and infr. 628, 830 ἐπιέτρεπον, καταειμέναι. Forms of ὑπείκω, which properly should have the digamma, have this hiatus in 2. 1266, 4. 41, 1676; ὑπήεργος in 1. 226 is parallel, for, as Leaf shews on *Il.* 17. 280, ἔργον properly has a digamma, though it loses it early.

502. **ἀνήνυτος**, 'one that no man could accomplish.' This form and ἀνηνύτως are first in Soph. *El.* 167, *frag.* 557; Plato uses ἀνήνυτον ἔργον in *Phaedo* 84 A of the web of Penelope. Ap. has the Homeric ἀνήνυστος in 4. 1307.

503. **ἄνεῳ**, 'silent'; note the echo of *Il.* 24. 633, αὐτὰρ ἐπεὶ τάρπησαν ἐς ἀλλήλους ὁρόωντες. This phrase is in 967 infr., and 4. 693. ἄνεῳ is Homeric, and is usually regarded as a plural adj.; but as it is sing. in *Od.* 23. 93, ἡ δ' ἄνεῳ δὴν ἧστο, it is best to follow Aristarchus in writing it consistently as an adverb in Homer. In Ap., however, it should be written ἄνεῳ, since he clearly takes it as a plural.

504. **Πηλεύς**. Peleus is by far the most cheerful member of the party. He and he alone shows courage at the meeting with the sons of Phrixus in 2. 1217, and at the recital of the coming trials; it is he who interprets to his comrades the omen in 4. 1370; and it is to him, and not to Jason, that Ancaeus pointedly addresses his offer to act as steersman in place of Tiphys in 2. 869, when the death of the latter had cast a gloom over all.

507. **ὄνειαρ**, 'good,' as infr. 900, 1051, etc., following the Homeric derivation from ὀνινάναι. It must mean 'dream,' however, in Call. *ep.* 49. 6 (*Anth. Pal.* 6. 310), where some editors read ὄνειρον; but for this sense, cf. *Anth. Pal.* 7. 42, περίπυστον ὄνειαρ, and Eust. 1877: 62, on *Od.* 19. 562, ὠνόμασέ τις ὄνειαρ καὶ αὐτὸ τὸ ὄνειρον.

κάρτεϊ, cf. *Arg.* 2. 333, ἐπεὶ φάος οὔ νύ τι τόσσον Ἔσσετ' ἐν εὐχωλῇσιν, ὅσον τ' ἐνὶ κάρτεϊ χειρῶν.

508. **τύνη**, an emphatic form of σύ, used by Homer only in the *Iliad*; cf. infr. 1109.

509. **μέμονας**, 'art anxious for,' v. n. 351, cf. 434.

510. **ἐντύναιο**, 'observe thy promise, and prepare thyself for the ordeal.' L. & S., misled by 737 infr., take this with ὑποσχεσίην. Homer uses the middle of 'getting one's self ready,' as in *Od.* 6. 33, and it takes the accusative only in phrases such as ἐντύνεσθαι δεῖπνον, ἄριστον, δαῖτα. Ap. extends this meaning to other words, which are properly cognate accusatives, in 4. 1191, ἀγλαΐην, ὅσην τε νεόζυγες ἐντύνονται: 1. 235, ὅσσα περ ἐντύνονται...νῆες.

εἰ δ' οὔ τοι μάλα θυμὸς ἐῇ ἐπὶ πάγχυ πέποιθεν
ἠνορέῃ, μήτ' αὐτὸς ἐπείγεο, μήτε τιν' ἄλλον
τῶνδ' ἀνδρῶν πάπταινε παρήμενος. οὐ γὰρ ἔγωγε
σχήσομ', ἐπεὶ θάνατός γε τὸ κύντατον ἔσσεται ἄλγος.'
    Ὣς ἔφατ' Αἰακίδης· Τελαμῶνι δὲ θυμὸς ὀρίνθη·   515
σπερχόμενος δ' ἀνόρουσε θοῶς· ἐπὶ δὲ τρίτος Ἴδας
ὦρτο μέγα φρονέων, ἐπὶ δ' υἱέε Τυνδαρέοιο·
σὺν δὲ καὶ Οἰνεΐδης ἐναρίθμιος αἰζηοῖσιν
ἀνδράσιν, οὐδέ περ ὅσσον ἐπανθιόωντας ἰούλους

511 μάλα πάγχυ θυμὸς ἐῇ ἐπὶ πέποιθεν L: ἐπέποιθεν G.   513 πάπταινε
Brunck: πάπτηνε codd.   517 υἱέε Koechly: υἱεῖς Gerhard: υἷες codd.
519 ἐπιχνοάοντας Spitzner.

511. ἐῇ, 'thy,' v. n. 26.
πάγχυ, 'much': the phrase is modelled on *Il.* 10. 99, φυλακῆς ἐπὶ πάγχυ λάθωνται, cf. Hes. *Op.* 264, δικέων ἐπὶ πάγχυ λάθεσθε.
ἐπὶ...πέποιθεν, cf. *Il.* 17. 154, ἐπιπείσεται. The intransitive perfect of the compound is first found here: cf. Qu. Sm. 5. 137, κείνοις ἐπὶ πάγχυ πεποίθει.
513. πάπταινε, 'peer round wistfully.' This use with the accusative is Homeric, cf. *Il.* 17. 115, παπταίνων Αἴαντα μέγαν, though it is more usual with a relative clause. In the sense of 'glaring,' it is first in Soph. *Ant.* 1231, τὸν δ' ἀγρίοις ὄσσοισι παπτήνας ὁ παῖς, cf. *Arg.* 1. 1170 of Heracles when he broke his oar, ἀνὰ δ' ἕζετο σιγῇ Παπταίνων.
514. σχήσομαι, 'I shall not hold back,' as in 1264 and often in Homer. The scholia take it as οὐκ ἀνέξομαι, 'I shall not allow it'; but in the first place, it is doubtful if ἔχομαι can stand for ἀνέχομαι as it does for ἀπέχομαι, and in the second it is against the sense. Peleus does not say 'you and you alone must do it, whether you like it or not,' but is obviously offering himself as a substitute.
515. Τελαμῶνι. Telamon is represented throughout as impulsive to a degree, quick to wrath and equally quick to forgive; he is well portrayed in 1. 1290, when he lost his temper with the crew for refusing to put back for Heracles, and came later to apologise to Jason. Idas too is well painted. He is impetuous and arrogant, and almost comes to blows with Idmon in 1. 462 f.:

yet he is swift in action, and it was he who slew the boar that wounded Idmon in 2. 830. In this book he is the warrior who trusts in his sword alone. He is among the first here, and again in 558 leaps up in anger at the idea of using Medea's services, and is still surly on that account in 1170; in 1252 he tries furiously to break Jason's spear to demonstrate the futility of the magic drugs with which it had been sprinkled. This whole passage is reminiscent of the account in *Il.* 7. 161 f. of the heroes who offered to fight with Hector.
517. μέγα φρονέων, 'in his pride': cf. his epithet ὑπέρβιος in the Catalogue, *Arg.* 1. 151.
υἱέε, Castor and Pollux. For the un-Homeric form, v. n. 196: this emendation of the vulgate υἷες is metrically desirable in order to avoid a violation of 'Wernicke's Law,' for which v. n. 1084, crit. appendix, p. 141.
518. Οἰνεΐδης. Meleager, of whom it was said in the Catalogue, *Arg.* 1. 190, that had he been a year older, he would have been second to Heracles alone.
ἐναρίθμιος, 'numbered among.' The dative is Alexandrine; Homer uses ἐν, *Il.* 2. 202, οὔτε ποτ' ἐν πολέμῳ ἐναρίθμιος οὔτ' ἐνὶ βουλῇ.
αἰζηοῖσιν, a word of doubtful origin, used by Homer as here of young men in their prime. Ap. extends the Homeric use in 4. 268 to men in general, 'young,' in the broadest sense of the Lat. *iuvenis.*
519. οὐδέ...ὅσσον. An Alexandrine phrase, first in Callimachus and Ap.

ἀντέλλων· τοίῳ οἱ ἀείρετο κάρτεϊ θυμός.   520
οἱ δ' ἄλλοι εἴξαντες ἀκὴν ἔχον. αὐτίκα δ' Ἄργος
τοῖον ἔπος μετέειπεν ἐελδομένοισιν ἀέθλου·
'Ὦ φίλοι, ἤτοι μὲν τόδε λοίσθιον. ἀλλά τιν' οἴω
μητρὸς ἐμῆς ἔσσεσθαι ἐναίσιμον ὕμμιν ἀρωγήν.
τῶ καί περ μεμαῶτες, ἐρητύοισθ' ἐνὶ νηὶ   525
τυτθὸν ἔθ', ὡς τὸ πάροιθεν, ἐπεὶ καὶ ἐπισχέμεν ἔμπης
λώιον, ἢ κακὸν οἶτον ἀφειδήσαντας ἑλέσθαι.
κούρη τις μεγάροισιν ἐνιτρέφετ' Αἰήταο,
τὴν Ἑκάτη περίαλλα θεὰ δάε τεχνήσασθαι

L. & S. wrongly cite Aristophanes *Wasps* 213, τί οὐκ ἀπεκοιμήθημεν ὅσον ὅσον στίλην, where οὐκ does not go with ὅσον.

ἐπανθιόωντας, 'though he had not yet grown the soft down upon his cheeks'; cf. Call. *Hec. frag.* 4 (Mair), ἀρμοῖ που κἀκείνῳ ἐπέτρεχεν ἀβρὸς ἴουλος. Apollonius follows Aratus in coining verbs in -ιάω for those in -έω; this is ἅπ. λεγ. for the post-Homeric ἐπανθέω.

520. ἀντέλλων, cf. *Arg.* 2. 44, ἰούλους ἀντέλλων of Polydeuces, *lit.* 'make to rise up.' It is once only in Homer, and transitive, *Il.* 5. 777, τοῖσιν δ' ἀμβροσίην Σιμόεις ἀνέτειλε νέμεσθαι: it is intr. in 683, 959 infr. This passage recalls the description of Apollo in Call. *H. Ap.* 37, οὔποτε Φοίβῳ θηλείης οὐδ' ὅσσον ἐπὶ χνόος ἦλθε παρειαῖς. ἀνδράσιν here in the place of the ill-chosen θηλείησ' may be a tacit criticism of Callimachus.

521–554. Argos explains his plan in detail; the omen of the dove is favourably interpreted by Mopsus.

521. ἀκήν. Frequent as adv. in Homer. Properly it is the accusative of a noun; Hesychius glosses it as ἡσυχία. It is definitely adverbial in 2. 1086, ἧνται ἀκήν, like the Homeric ἀκὴν ἐγένοντο σιωπῇ. Here, however, it may be the actual noun; cf. Hesych. ἀκὴν ἦγες· ἡσυχίαν ἦγες. For ἀκέω, v. n. 85.

523. τόδε, referring to 514 θάνατος, 'to this we may come at the last.' There seems to have been no alternative plan in the *Naupactia*, in which poem, according to our scholia, all the heroes offered to take the place of Jason, but Idmon rose up and ordered him to perform the tasks himself.

524. ἐναίσιμον, 'of good omen.' Ap. uses this word always of a definitely good omen; but in Homer it is simply 'connected with omens,' good or bad, *e.g. Od.* 2. 182 (ὄρνιθες) οὐδέ τε πάντες ἐναίσιμοι, 'are not all teachers of fate,' and schol. μαντικοί, τὸ εἱμαρμένον σημαίνοντες.

525. μεμαῶτες, 'eager as ye are': for the fem., cf. 682, 809. μεμαότες is in *Arg.* 4. 1588; both are Homeric.

ἐρητύοισθε, 'remain,' v. n. 380.

527. ἀφειδήσαντας, 'it is better to hold back, than recklessly to choose an evil fate.' In this sense of 'reckless,' cf. Eur. *I. T.* 1354, ἡμεῖς δ' ἀφειδήσαντες, ὡς εἰσείδομεν Δόλια τεχνήματ', εἰχόμεσθα τῆς ξένης. For the sense of 'neglecting,' as infr. c. gen. 630, cf. Soph. *Ant.* 414, εἴ τις τοῦδ' ἀφειδήσοι πόνου (altered by Bonitz to ἀκηδήσοι). It is abs. 1013, 'ungrudging.' The adv. ἀφειδείως in 897 is a form of ἀφειδέως, ἀφειδῶς peculiar to Ap. For the adj. ἀφειδέες c. gen. as in 4. 1252, cf. Aesch. *Ag.* 195, νεῶν τε καὶ πεισμάτων ἀφειδεῖς. All these forms and uses are post-Homeric.

529. For Hecate, v. n. 251. It is thus by Hecate that the despised and rejected Medea of Euripides (*Medea* 395) swears her revenge. It is in her name that Jason makes his appeal to Medea, infr. 985, and on her that he calls when using the magic salve, 1035; it is by her grace that Medea brings Talos to ruin, 4. 1666, and in her name that she makes her oath to Arete in Phaeacia 4. 1020. Naturally it is beside her temple, then, that the first meeting of the lovers is arranged, 738; 'it is as though she wished to present her lover to

φάρμαχ', ὅσ' ἤπειρός τε φύει καὶ νήχυτον ὕδωρ,   530
τοῖσι καὶ ἀκαμάτοιο πυρὸς μειλίσσετ' ἀυτμή,
καὶ ποταμοὺς ἵστησιν ἄφαρ κελαδεινὰ ῥέοντας,
ἄστρα τε καὶ μήνης ἱερῆς ἐπέδησε κελεύθους.
τῆς μὲν ἀπὸ μεγάροιο κατὰ στίβον ἐνθάδ' ἰόντες

531 ἀυτμή LG: ἀυτμήν vulg.

the goddess, and to put her love under
the divine protection' (de Mirmont).
περίαλλα, 'especially.' Un-Homeric,
and first in Pind. *Pyth.* 11. 5; ὡς
περίαλλα ἰαχέων of the MSS. in Soph.
O. T. 1219 has been emended to ὥσπερ
ἰάλεμον χέων. The gen. in *Arg.* 2. 217,
περίαλλα θεῶν, is unique.
δάε, 'taught,' cf. 4. 989 ἔδαε. Elsewhere in Ap. it is intransitive; in trans.
sense, Homer uses the reduplicated aor.
δέδαε, *Od.* 20. 72, ἔργα δ' Ἀθηναίη
δέδαε κλυτὰ ἐργάζεσθαι.
530. ὅσα κ.τ.λ., cf. H. Hom. *Aph.* 5,
θηρία πάντα, Ἠμὲν ὅσ' ἤπειρος πολλὰ
τρέφει ἠδ' ὅσα πόντος. With this passage
should be compared the typical description in Seneca *Medea* 707–730, of
Medea's magic charms.
νήχυτον, 'flowing,' cf. 4. 1367 of
ἅλμην, *Or. Arg.* 39, 312 ἐπινήχυτα δῶρα.
νήχυτος was formed by Philetas and
Callimachus under the mistaken idea that
the Homeric νήδυμος was derived from
νη- (*very*), and ἡδύς. Our scholia translate it as πολύχυτον, and cite an Ionian
and Sicilian expression ἀχύνετον ὕδωρ.
531. μειλίσσεται, 'is beguiled,' v. n.
105.
ἀυτμή, here 'blast of fire,' as in *Od.*
16. 290, ὅσσον πυρὸς ἵκετ' ἀυτμή. For
the use of bellows in 1301, cf. *Il.* 18.
470, φῦσαι δ' ἐν χοάνοισιν ἐείκοσι πᾶσαι
ἐφύσων Παντοίην εὐπρηστον ἀυτμὴν
ἐξανιεῖσαι. For the 'breath' of the bulls
in 1327, cf. *Od.* 11. 400, ἀνέμων ἀμέγαρτον ἀυτμήν.
532. κελαδεινά, 'in their noisy flow.'
The adverb is here only; the adjective
is used in *Il.* 23. 208 of Zephyrus, and
frequently of Artemis because of her
love of the noisy chase. This passage is
imitated in Val. Flacc. 6. 441 f.; 'Illius
adfatus sparsosque per avia sucos Sidera
fixa pavent, et avi stupet orbita Solis;
Mutat agros fluviumque vias, suus alli-
gat ignis Cuncta, sopor recolit fessos
aetate parentes Datque alias sine lege

colus.' Compare also Verg. (?) *Dirae*
67, 'Flectite currentes nymphas, vaga
flumina, retro': *Lydia* 18, 'Tardabunt
rivi labentes (sistite, lymphae)': and
Seneca *Medea* 763–5, 'Violenta Phasis
vertit in fontem vada, Et Hister, in tot
ora divisus, truces Compressit undas
omnibus ripis piger.'
533. μήνης. The moon in *Arg.* 4.
57 f. rejoices over the secret flight of
Medea, remembering the many times
when she had been 'brought down' to
make darkness for magic rites; the
Massylian witch in Verg. *Aen.* 4. 489
was equally able 'sistere aquam fluviis
et vertere sidera retro.' For a full description of a witch at work, cf. Tibullus
1. 2. 43. To draw down the moon was
an art peculiar to Thessalian witches;
cf. Plat. *Gorg.* 513 A, τὰς τὴν σελήνην
καθαιρούσας, τὰς Θετταλίδας. Hippocrates, περὶ ἱερᾶς νόσου 4, brands as
impious acts σελήνην καθαίρειν (? κατά-
γειν) καὶ ἥλιον ἀφανίζειν καὶ χειμῶνά τε
καὶ εὐδίην ποιεῖν, καὶ ὄμβρους καὶ αὐχμοὺς
καὶ γῆν ἄπορον καὶ τἄλλα τὰ τοιουτότροπα
πάντα. Compare Lucian *Dial. Mer.* 1.
2, φαρμακίς...Θετταλάς τινας ὡδὰς ἐπι-
σταμένη καὶ τὴν σελήνην καταγοῦσα, and
Aristophanes *Clouds* 748 and Blaydes
ad loc. Medea was a Thessalian by adop-
tion, and these practices were naturally
ascribed to her.
533. ἐπέδησε, a typical variant of *Od.* 4.
380, πεδάᾳ καὶ ἔδησε κελεύθου. It may be
modelled metrically on *Od.* 10. 20, ἔνθα
δὲ βυκτάων ἀνέμων κατέδησε κέλευθα: cf.
Od. 5. 383, ἥ τοι τῶν ἄλλων ἀνέμων
κατέδησε κελεύθους, and Call. *H. Art.*
230, ὅτε οἱ κατέδησας ἀήτας.
534. κατὰ στίβον, 'as we came along
the path,' cf. 927. In 1218 infr., it is
'at her tread.' The word is first in the
Homeric Hymns, and both meanings
are represented in H. Hom. *Herm.*
352–3, αὐτὰρ ἐπεὶ ψαμάθοιο μέγαν στίβον
ἐξεπέρησεν, Ἄφραστος γένετ' ὦκα βοῶν
στίβος ἠδὲ καὶ αὐτῶν.

μνησάμεθ᾽, εἴ κε δύναιτο, κασιγνήτη γεγαυῖα,   535
μήτηρ ἡμετέρη πεπιθεῖν ἐπαρῆξαι ἀέθλῳ.
εἰ δὲ καὶ αὐτοῖσιν τόδ᾽ ἐφανδάνει, ἦ τ᾽ ἂν ἱκοίμην
ἤματι τῷδ᾽ αὐτῷ πάλιν εἰς δόμον Αἰήταο
πειρήσων· τάχα δ᾽ ἂν σὺν δαίμονι πειρηθείην.᾽
  ῟Ως φάτο· τοῖσι δὲ σῆμα θεοὶ δόσαν εὐμενέοντες.   540
τρήρων μὲν φεύγουσα βίην κίρκοιο πελειὰς
ὑψόθεν Αἰσονίδεω πεφοβημένη ἔμπεσε κόλπῳ·
κίρκος δ᾽ ἀφλάστῳ περικάππεσεν. ὦκα δὲ Μόψος
τοῖον ἔπος μετὰ πᾶσι θεοπροπέων ἀγόρευσεν·
  ῾῟Υμμι, φίλοι, τόδε σῆμα θεῶν ἰότητι τέτυκται·   545
οὐδέ πῃ ἄλλως ἐστὶν ὑποκρίνασθαι ἄρειον,
παρθενικὴν δ᾽ ἐπέεσσι μετελθέμεν ἀμφιέποντας
μήτι παντοίῃ.   δοκέω δέ μιν οὐκ ἀθερίξειν,

542 Αἰσονίδαο LG.   κόλπῳ G : κόλποις supr. οι scr. ω L.   544 ἀγόρευεν
Stephanus, vulg.   548 ἀθερίξειν vulg., Headlam, Platt : ἀθερίζειν G, edd.

535. **εἴ κε δύναιτο**, for this opt.,
v. n. 26.
537. **αὐτοῖσιν**, i.e. ὑμῖν αὐτοῖσιν, v.
n. 350.
ἐφανδάνει, v. n. 34.
539. **σὺν δαίμονι**, 'with good luck':
cf. *Il.* 11. 792, τίς δ᾽ οἶδ᾽ εἰ κέν οἱ σὺν
δαίμονι θυμὸν ὀρίναις.
541. **τρήρων.** Here, as always in
Homer, epithet of πελειάς. Contrast
the omen of the eagle and the dove in
Od. 20. 243, and the imitation in *Aen.*
6. 190 f. In *Il.* 8. 247, the eagle carries
a fawn and drops it on the altar of Zeus.
It is rather surprising that Ap. does not
explain the omen in this passage; it
refers, of course, to the pursuit of Medea
by Absyrtus and the death of the latter,
as related in the fourth Book.
542. **κόλποις,** cf. 707, 155. Read
κόλπῳ here, and v. crit. note. For this
dative with ἐμπίπτω cf. *Od.* 5. 50, 2. 45,
ἔμπεσε πόντῳ, ἔμπεσεν οἴκῳ.
543. **ἀφλάστῳ,** 'the stern ornament,'
cf. *Arg.* 1. 1089, 2. 601. Homer uses
this only in *Il.* 15. 717, where it seems
to be the same as the κόρυμβα of 9. 241;
v. further in Leaf, *ad loc.*
περικάππεσεν, 'fell impaled upon':
cf. 2. 831, περικάππεσε δουρί. The
double compound is peculiar to Ap.;
Homer has ἀλὶ κάππεσε in *Od.* 5. 374, cf.
also Soph. *Ajax* 828, πεπτῶτα περὶ ξίφει.

544. **θεοπροπέων,** 'with prophetic
words': θεοπροπέων ἀγορεύειν is common in Homer. Mopsus was fully
qualified to interpret such an omen; cf.
his description in the Catalogue, *Arg.*
1. 65, ὃν περὶ πάντων Λητοΐδης ἐδίδαξε
θεοπροπίας οἰωνῶν, and in Pind. *Pyth.*
4. 190, μάντις ὀρνίχεσσι καὶ κλάροισι
θεοπροπέων ἱεροῖς Μόψος.
545. **ἰότητι,** 'by the will of the gods.'
This phrase is frequent in Homer; Ap.
has also ἐμῇ ἰότητι, infr. 786, corresponding to *Il.* 15. 41, δι᾽ ἐμὴν ἰότητα.
546. **οὐδέ πῃ ... ἐστίν.** Homeric
phrase, *e.g. Il.* 24. 71.
ὑποκρίνασθαι, 'interpret': adapted
from *Od.* 19. 555, εἰ πῶς ἔστιν ὑποκρίνασθαι ὄνειρον, cf. *ib.* 535, τὸν ὄνειρον
ὑπόκριναι.
547. **ἀμφιέποντας,** 'with all the power
of our craft': cf. *Od.* 3. 118, ἀμφιέ-
ποντες Παντοίοισι δόλοισι. For ἐπέεσσι
μετελθέμεν, cf. Eur. *Bacc.* 713, τὸν θεὸν
...Εὐχαῖσιν ἂν μετῆλθες. For other senses
in Ap., cf. 2. 761, δαίτην ἀμφίεπον:
1. 562, πηδάλι᾽ ἀμφιέπεσκε : 1. 1102,
θεὸν ἀμφιέπουσιν: 1. 571, σκοπιὰς ἁλὸς
ἀμφιέπεσκεν: 1304 infr., ἄμφεπε
δήιον αἶθος. Like Homer, he has both
ἀμφι- and ἀμφ-έπω.
548. **ἀθερίξειν,** 'she will not treat us
lightly.' Read the future with Headlam
and Platt against MSS. ἀθερίζειν, which

εἰ ἐτεὸν Φινεύς γε θεᾷ ἐνὶ Κύπριδι νόστον
πέφραδεν ἔσσεσθαι. κείνης δ' ὅγε μείλιχος ὄρνις   550
οἶτον ὑπεξήλυξε· κέαρ δέ μοι ὡς ἐνὶ θυμῷ
τόνδε κατ' οἰωνὸν προτιόσσεται, ὡς δὲ πέλοιτο.
ἀλλά, φίλοι, Κυθέρειαν ἐπικλείοντες ἀμύνειν,
ἤδη νῦν Ἀργοιο παραιφασίῃσι πίθεσθε.'

Ἴσκεν· ἐπήνησαν δὲ νέοι, Φινῆος ἐφετμὰς   555
μνησάμενοι· μοῦνος δ' Ἀφαρήιος ἄνθορεν Ἴδας,
δείν' ἐπαλαστήσας μεγάλῃ ὀπί, φώνησέν τε·
'Ὦ πόποι, ἦ ῥα γυναιξὶν ὁμόστολοι ἐνθάδ' ἔβημεν,
οἳ Κύπριν καλέουσιν ἐπίρροθον ἄμμι πέλεσθαι,
οὐκέτ' Ἐνναλίοιο μέγα σθένος; ἐς δὲ πελείας   560

549 θεᾷ Merkel: θεῇ codd.   551 οἶτον ed. Flor., Platt: πότμον L, vulg. :
μόρον G.   552 ὥς γε Brunck.

Mooney keeps as a *praesens propheti-cum* : the confusion of -ζ- and -ξ- is common. This refers to the advice of Phineus in 2. 423, φράζεσθε θεᾶς δολόεσσαν ἀρωγὴν Κύπριδος. The germ of this idea may be in Jason's words in Eur. *Medea* 526, ἐγὼ δ', ἐπειδὴ καὶ λίαν πυργοῖς χάριν Κύπρην νομίζω τῆς ἐμῆς ναυκληρίας Σώτειραν εἶναι θεῶν τε κἀνθρώπων μόνην.

550. κείνης, emphatic, 'hers was that gentle bird.'

551. οἶτον. Read this with Lascaris and Platt for MSS. πότμον, for which v. crit. appendix, p. 140. ὑπεξήλυξε, 'escaped from,' is first in Hes. *Th.* 615, ὑπεξήλυξε βαρὺν χόλον; the phrase corresponds to the Homeric ὑπέκφυγε κῆρα, *Il.* 5. 22.

552. προτιόσσεται, 'as my heart within me forebodes according to this omen, so may it come to pass': cf. *Od.* 5. 389, κραδίη προτιόσσετ' ὄλεθρον.

553. ἐπικλείοντες, 'invoking': cf. 2. 700, ἐπικλείοντες Ἑῴων Ἀπόλλωνα. In *Arg.* 1. 18 it means 'relate,' in 4. 571 'call by name,' like κλείουσι 277. In *Od.* 1. 351, τὴν γὰρ ἀοιδὴν μᾶλλον ἐπικλείουσ' ἄνθρωποι, it must mean 'applaud at the end,' but there is a hint of an alternative reading in Plat. *Rep.* 424 B. All the uses in Ap. are Alexandrine.

554. παραιφασίῃσι, 'advice, exhortations,' v. n. 14. This is an Alexandrine

form of the Homeric παραίφασις, first in Musaeus ap. Paus. 10. 9. 11, παραιφασίη δέ τις ἔσται, cf. *Arg.* 2. 324, τῷ νῦν ἡμετέρῃσι παραιφασίῃσι πίθεσθε.

555-575. Idas furiously protests against an appeal to women, but receives no support. The Argo is rowed from the backwater to the main channel of the river.

555. ἴσκεν, 'he spake': v. n. 396.

556. μνησάμενοι. Elsewhere in Ap. c. gen. The accusative is Homeric, usually of things, as in *Od.* 24. 122, μέμνημαι τάδε πάντα, but occasionally applied to persons, *Il.* 6. 222, Τυδέα δ' οὐ μέμνημαι.

ἄνθορεν, 'leapt up,' contrast 957. Homer uses this once in *Il.* 13. 140 of a stone, ὕψι δ' ἀναθρᾴσκων πέτετο; with this use, cf. Hdt. 7. 18. 2, ἀμβώσας μέγα ἀνθρώσκει. For Idas, v. n. 516.

557. ἐπαλαστήσας, 'uttering terrible threats,' v. n. 369.

558. ὁμόστολοι, 'in the company of': cf. 2. 802, ὁμόστολον ὕμμιν. The dative is peculiar to Ap. The word is first in tragedy, and c. gen., Soph. *O.T.* 212, Μαινάδων ὁμόστολος: contrast Aesch. *Supp.* 496, μορφῆς δ' οὐχ ὁμόστολος φύσις, 'is not like.'

559. ἐπίρροθον, 'helper,' v.n. 184: cf. Eur. *Hipp.* 522, Κύπρι, συνεργὸς εἴης.

560. Ἐνναλίοιο. Epithet and proper name of Ares in Homer, but only in the *Iliad.*

καὶ κίρκους λεύσσοντες ἐρητύεσθε ἀέθλων;
ἔρρετε, μηδ' ὕμμιν πολεμήια ἔργα μέλοιτο,
παρθενικὰς δὲ λιτῆσιν ἀνάλκιδας ἠπεροπεύειν.'
῾Ως ηὔδα μεμαώς· πολέες δ' ὁμάδησαν ἑταῖροι
ἦκα μάλ', οὐδ' ἄρα τις οἱ ἐναντίον ἔκφατο μῦθον.   565
χωόμενος δ' ὅγ' ἔπειτα καθέζετο· τοῖσι δ' Ἰήσων
αὐτίκ' ἐποτρύνων τὸν ἑὸν νόον ὧδ' ἀγόρευεν·
'"Αργος μὲν παρὰ νηός, ἐπεὶ τόδε πᾶσιν ἔαδεν,
στελλέσθω· ἀτὰρ αὐτοὶ ἐπὶ χθονὸς ἐκ ποταμοῖο
ἀμφαδὸν ἤδη πείσματ' ἀνάψομεν. ἦ γὰρ ἔοικεν   570
μηκέτι δὴν κρύπτεσθαι ὑποπτήσσοντας αὐτήν.'
῾Ως ἄρ' ἔφη· καὶ τὸν μὲν ἄφαρ προΐαλλε νέεσθαι
καρπαλίμως ἐξαῦτις ἀνὰ πτόλιν· οἱ δ' ἐπὶ νηὸς
εὐναίας ἐρύσαντες ἐφετμαῖς Αἰσονίδαο

567 ἀγόρευσεν G, vulg.   568 ἔαδεν Mooney: ἔαδεν L: ἔαδε G.
571 δὴν κρύπτεσθαι ὑποπτήσσοντας Pierson: δὴν κρύπτεσθαι πτήσσοντας LG:
δηθὰ κρύπτεσθαι πτήσσοντας vulg.

561. ἐρητύεσθε, 'keep back from,'
v. n. 380.
563. ἀνάλκιδας, 'cajole weak maidens
with your prayers.' This is borrowed
from Il. 5. 349, γυναῖκας ἀνάλκιδας
ἠπεροπεύεις: the adj. is used also of the
suitors, Od. 4. 334, 17. 125. For the
sentiment, cf. Hector's words to Ajax
in Il. 7. 235, μήτι μευ ἠύτε παιδὸς
ἀφαυροῦ πειρήτιζε 'Ηὲ γυναικὸς, ἡ οὐκ
οἶδεν πολεμήια ἔργα: Aesch. Ag. 940,
οὔτοι γυναικός ἐστιν ἱμείρειν μάχης, and
Supp. 749, γυνὴ μονωθεῖσ' οὐδέν· οὐκ
ἔνεστ''Αρης. Contrast Soph. El.1243, ὅρα
γε μὲν δὴ κἂν γυναιξὶν ὡς "Αρης "Ενεστιν.
ἠπεροπεύειν, epic word, used only in
pres. and imperfect: cf. Od. 15. 421,
τά τε φρένας ἠπεροπεύει Θηλυτέρῃσι
γυναιξί. For ἠπεροπῆες in 617 infr., cf.
Od. 11. 364, ἠπεροπῆά τ' ἔμεν καὶ
ἐπίκλοπον.
564. μεμαώς, 'in his eager wrath,'
v. n. 525.
ὁμάδησαν, 'muttered.' Homer uses
in the Odyssey only, always of the
suitors 'making a din'; the scholiast
on ὅμαδος in Il. 9. 573 and the Et. Mag.
derive it from ὁμοῦ αὐδᾶν. Our scholiast
here remarks ἀντὶ τοῦ ὀργιζόμενος νῦν.
οὐ γὰρ ἐπὶ κακοῖς τις πρόθυμός ἐστι. Ap.
uses it infr. 971 of trees 'murmuring,'

and 1304 of bellows; contrast Arg. 2.
638, οἱ δ' ὁμάδησαν Θαρσαλέοις ἐπέεσσι,
'shouted together with words of cheer.'
567. νόον...ἀγόρευεν, cf. the English
phrase 'to speak one's mind.' This is a
typical variant of the Homeric νόον
κατέλεξεν, Od. 4. 256.
568. ἔαδεν. Read this, the Homeric
form, here and in 1062 with Mooney v.
ἔαδεν of the best MSS., which aspirate
in 1. 867. Rzach calls the latter an
aorist; but Ap. uses the form εὔαδεν.
569. στελλέσθω, 'let him go,' un-
Homeric. στέλλειν in Homer is to array
an army, στέλλεσθαι to array one's self,
as in Il. 23. 285, ἄλλοι δὲ στέλλεσθε
κατὰ στράτον. With this use, cf. Soph.
Ph. 466, ἤδη, τέκνον, στέλλεσθε.
570. ἀμφαδὸν ἤδη, 'with no further
concealment,' v. n. 97. ἐκ is at first
sight misleading, for in Homer ἀνάπτειν
ἐκ means 'to fasten to,' Od. 12. 179,
ἐκ δ' αὐτοῦ πείρατ' ἀνῆπτον.
571. ὑποπτήσσοντας, 'crouching
from' the battle cry; v. n. 321.
574. εὐναίας. Formed from εὐνή, like
σεληναία from σελήνη. This plural, and
the singular 1. 955, are used for the
Homeric εὐνά, which is in 4. 1713, 'the
mooring stone.' Eur. I.T. 432 uses it as
adj. εὐναίων πηδαλίων, 'guiding the ship.'

τυτθὸν ὑπὲξ ἔλεος χέρσῳ ἐπέκελσαν ἐρετμοῖς.   575
Αὐτίκα δ' Αἰήτης ἀγορὴν ποιήσατο Κόλχων
νόσφιν ἑοῖο δόμου, τόθι περ καὶ πρόσθε κάθιζον,
ἀτλήτους Μινύῃσι δόλους καὶ κήδεα τεύχων.
στεῦτο δ', ἐπεί κεν πρῶτα βόες διαδηλήσωνται
ἄνδρα τόν, ὅς ῥ' ὑπέδεκτο βαρὺν καμέεσθαι ἄεθλον,   580
δρυμὸν ἀναρρήξας λασίης καθύπερθε κολώνης
αὔτανδρον φλέξειν δόρυ νήιον, ὄφρ' ἀλεγεινὴν
ὕβριν ἀποφλύξωσιν ὑπέρβια μηχανόωντες.
οὐδὲ γὰρ Αἰολίδην Φρίξον μάλα περ χατέοντα
δέχθαι ἐνὶ μεγάροισιν ἐφέστιον, ὃς περὶ πάντων   585

577–8 om. G.   578 Μινύῃσι Merkel : Μινύαισι vulg.   579 διαδηλήσωνται
Stephanus : διαδηλήσονται LG, vulg.

575. ἐπέκελσαν, 'drove to land.'
Homer uses also of a ship 'running to
shore of itself,' Od. 13. 114, ἡ μὲν
ἔπειτα Ἠπείρῳ ἐπέκελσεν. For τυτθὸν
ὑπέξ, 'a little out from,' cf. Arg. 1. 1166,
τυτθὸν ὑπὲκ Φρυγίης: Il. 21. 604, τυτθὸν
ὑπεκπροθέοντα.
576–615. Aeetes holds a council of
the Colchians and threatens to burn the
Argo and its crew. Argos goes to plead
with his mother.
578. Μινύῃσι, so called because of
their descent from Minyas : cf. Arg. 1.
229, τοὺς μὲν ἀριστῆας Μινύας περιναιετά-
οντες Κίκλησκον μάλα πάντας, ἐπεὶ
Μινύαο θυγατρῶν Οἱ πλεῖστοι καὶ ἄριστοι
ἀφ' αἵματος εὐχετόωντο Ἔμμεναι. For
the direct descendants of Minyas among
the Argonauts, v. Mueller, Orchomenos,
pp. 253 f.
579. στεῦτο, 'he declared': the usual
Homeric use with fut. infinitive, v. n.
337. This is modelled on Hector's threat
in Il. 9. 241, στεῦται γὰρ νηῶν ἀποκόψειν
ἄκρα κόρυμβα Αὐτάς τ' ἐμπρήσειν μαλεροῦ
πυρός, αὐτὰρ 'Αχαιοὺς Δηώσειν παρὰ τῇσιν
ὀρινομένους ὑπὸ καπνοῦ. This long passage in oratio obliqua, extending to 608,
is not in the style of Homer, and is
thoroughly prosaic and tedious : cf.
Introd. p. xxxix.
διαδηλήσωνται, 'tear to pieces': cf.
Od. 14. 37, κύνες διεδηλήσαντο, and Arg.
2. 284, Theoc. 24. 85.
580. καμέεσθαι ἄεθλον, 'perform the
task,' v. n. 230.

582. αὔτανδρον, 'men and all,' first
in Ap. It is probably not adv., but adj.
agreeing with δόρυ, cf. Polyb. 1. 23. 7,
ναῦς αὐτάνδρους. δόρυ νήιον in Il. 15. 410
is a ship's plank : here it is used for
'ship,' like δόρυ in tragedy.
ἀλεγεινήν. Homeric; neither Homer
nor Ap. uses ἀλεγινός. The superlative,
infr. 764, 1103, is un-Homeric.
583. ἀποφλύξωσιν. φλύω, or φλύζω,
which means 'bubble' or 'brag,' has
three compounds in Ap., all peculiar
to himself. Here it is literally to
'sputter forth'; ἐκφλῦξαι in 1. 275 is to
'spurt forth,' i.e. 'sob'; ἐπιφλύειν in 1.
481 c. dat. is to 'bluster at.'
ὑπέρβια, v. n. 15: note the typical
alteration of ἀτάσθαλα μηχανόωντες, Od.
18. 143.
584. μάλα περ χατέοντα, cf. Od. 2.
249, μάλα περ χατέουσα : Il. 9. 518,
χατέουσί περ ἔμπης : Il. 15. 399, χατέ-
οντί περ ἔμπης. For a possible instance
of χατέω c. acc., v. n. 84.
585. δέχθαι. For the omission of ἄν,
v. n. 377.
ἐφέστιον, 'as a guest in his palace,'
in the Homeric sense of 'at the hearth.'
In the post-Homeric ceremony of purification from murder, the first act of
the suppliant was to take sanctuary
at the hearth of his host : cf. Hdt. 1.
35 for Croesus' words to Adrastus,
τίς ἔων ἐπίστιός μοι ἐγένεο. It may
bear this later meaning 'suppliant'
infr. 1117.

ξείνων μειλιχίη τε θεουδείη τ᾽ ἐκέκαστο,
εἰ μή οἱ Ζεὺς αὐτὸς ἀπ᾽ οὐρανοῦ ἄγγελον ἧκεν
Ἑρμείαν, ὥς κεν προσκηδέος ἀντιάσειεν·
μὴ καὶ ληιστῆρας ἐὴν ἐς γαῖαν ἰόντας
ἔσσεσθαι δηναιὸν ἀπήμονας, οἷσι μέμηλεν   590
ὀθνείοις ἐπὶ χεῖρα ἐὴν κτεάτεσσιν ἀείρειν,
κρυπταδίους τε δόλους τεκταινέμεν, ἠδὲ βοτήρων
αὔλια δυσκελάδοισιν ἐπιδρομίῃσι δαΐξαι.
νόσφι δὲ οἷ αὐτῷ φάτ᾽ ἐοικότα μείλια τίσειν
υἷας Φρίξοιο, κακορρέκτῃσιν ὀπηδοὺς   595
ἀνδράσι νοστήσαντας ὁμιλαδόν, ὄφρα ἑ τιμῆς

594 νόσφι δέ οἱ Brunck : νόσφιν δ᾽ οἱ Paris. unus : νόσφιν δ᾽ οἱ vulg.

586. θεουδείη, 'fear of Heaven.' This noun of the Homeric θεοειδής is first here; for the plural, cf. Greg. Naz. in *Anth. Pal.* I. 96. 2, πιστὸς ἐών, Χριστὸν δὲ θεουδείῃσιν ἰαίνων.

ἐκέκαστο. This may be a mixture of two phrases, (*a*) περὶ πάντων ἔμμεναι ἄλλων, *Il.* I. 287: (*b*) τινός τινι κέκασθαι, as in *Il.* 24. 546, as opposed to the usual Homeric use of the accusative of the person and the dative of the thing. Possibly περί and ἐκέκαστο, as so often in Homer with verbs compounded with περί, are *in tmesi*; the cpd. is first definitely found in Nicander, *Th.* 38, c. acc. περί, too, might possibly be taken adverbially here. But on the whole it is best to take the phrases separately, 'who, beyond all other strangers, excelled in fear of Heaven.'

588. Ἑρμείαν. It was from Hermes, according to Apollodorus, that Nephele, the mother of Phrixus, obtained the ram. Here, however, Hermes is probably acting as his father's herald, serving Zeus particularly in his capacity as Φύξιος; cf. Aesch. *Ch.* I of Hermes, πατρῷ᾽ ἐποπτεύων κράτη.

προσκηδέος, 'that in him he might meet a kindly host.' In 4. 717, εἴτε καὶ ἐμφύλῳ προσκηδέες ἀντιόωσιν, Ap. seems to follow the derivation from κῆδος, 'affinitas,' *i.e.* 'as kinsmen stained with a kinsman's blood.' Mooney there translates 'careworn': but Ap. is probably reproducing the two possible meanings of *Od.* 21. 35, ξεινοσύνης προσκηδέος, 'kindly,' or 'connected with kinship.'

ἀντιάσειεν, 'meet,' v. n. 35.

589. ληιστῆρας, 'pirates.' Homer has also ληϊστορες, which is not in Ap. This use of μὴ καί, 'much less,' is peculiar to Ap., cf. 2. 192.

590. δηναιόν, 'for long,' v. n. 53.

591. ὀθνείοις, 'of a stranger,' v. nn. 389, 403; for ἐήν v. n. 26.

593. δυσκελάδοισιν, 'evil-sounding,' cf. 96 δυσηχής. It is used once of φόβος in *Il.* 16. 357, and once in Ap.; Δυσκέλαδος is a proper name in *Arg.* 4. 565. Hes. *Op.* 196 uses it of ζῆλος.

ἐπιδρομίῃσι, 'incursions,' form of ἐπιδρομή peculiar to Ap., v. n. 144.

δαΐξαι, 'destroy,' a departure from the Homeric meaning 'cleave,' 'pierce': cf. Aesch. *Supp.* 680, πόλιν δαΐζων, 'utterly destroying.'

594. νόσφι, *i.e.* apart altogether from Jason and his company.

ἐοικότα, 'proper,' as often in Homer.

μείλια, 'recompense,' the Homeric use; for others, v. n. 135.

595. υἷας, v. n. 196 for the form.

κακορρέκτῃσιν, 'evil doers,' here only.

ὀπηδούς, 'companions to,' un-Homeric. For the dative, cf. H. Hom. *Herm.* 450, μούσῃσιν ὀπηδός.

596. ὁμιλαδόν, 'in a crowd,' thrice in the *Iliad*, cf. ὁμιληδόν in Hes. *Sc.* 170. L. and S. take it wrongly c. dat.

τιμῆς. For the gen., cf. Eur. *Med.* 70, παῖδας γῆς ἐλᾶν, and *Arg.* 4. 386 for the ordinary Homeric use with ἐκ. Similarly ἐσάωθεν is used c. gen. infr. 1127, and with ἐκ in 2. 610. Aeetes is very sensitive about his σκῆπτρα καὶ τιμή, cf. 376. Perhaps behind this scene

καὶ σκήπτρων ἐλάσειαν ἀκηδέες· ὥς ποτε βάξιν
λευγαλέην οὗ πατρὸς ἐπέκλυεν Ἡελίοιο,
χρειώ μιν πυκινόν τε δόλον βουλάς τε γενέθλης
σφωιτέρης ἀπάτην τε πολύτροπον ἐξαλέασθαι·　　　　600
τῶ καὶ ἐελδομένους πέμπειν ἐς Ἀχαιίδα γαῖαν
πατρὸς ἐφημοσύνῃ, δολιχὴν ὁδόν. οὐδὲ θυγατρῶν
εἶναί οἱ τυτθόν γε δέος, μή πού τινα μῆτιν
φράσσωνται στυγερήν, οὐδ' υἱέος Ἀψύρτοιο·
ἀλλ' ἐνὶ Χαλκιόπης γενεῇ τάδε λυγρὰ τετύχθαι.　　　　605
καί ῥ' ὁ μὲν ἄσχετα ἔργα πιφαύσκετο δημοτέροισιν
χωόμενος· μέγα δέ σφιν ἀπείλεε νῆά τ' ἔρυσθαι

599 χρειώ Vatt. tres, L. man. sec., v. l. in schol. Flor.: χρῆναι vulg.
600 ἀπάτην Platt: ἄτην vulg.　　　601 καὶ ἐελδομένους L 16, Pariss.:
κε ἐλδομένους L: κε καὶ ἐελδομένους G.　　　πέμπεν LG.　　　606 δημογέρουσι
Spitzner.

and the other may lie a *Märchen* of the type in which the suitor roughly treats, or even murders, his father-in-law, takes possession of the castle and treasure, and marries the daughter; *e.g.* the legend of Kilhweh and Olwen. In such a case, the anxiety of Aeetes is well understandable.

597. ἀκηδέες, 'without sorrow,' *i.e.* 'reckless,' as in *Il.* 21. 123. For the other meaning in Homer, v. n. 260.

βάξιν. The story of the oracle given to Aeetes is apparently borrowed from Herodorus, ap. schol. *Arg.* 3. 594. Elsewhere, as in Pind. *Pyth.* 4. 72, *Or. Arg.* 56, it is Pelias who is fated to be slain by an Aeolid. In *Arg.* 1. 5, the warning given to Pelias is directed not against his kin, but vaguely against a one-sandalled man.

598. ἐπέκλυεν, 'heard.' For the acc. of thing and gen. of person, cf. *Il.* 23. 652, αἶνον ἐπέκλυε Νηλεΐδαο; for the gen. cf. *Od.* 5. 150, Ζηνὸς ἐπέκλυεν ἀγγελιάων.

599. χρειώ, v. n. 12. Homer does not use χρειώ elliptically for χρή, but always χρεώ; nor does he, like Ap., use χρεώ for the inf. χρῆναι.

600. σφωιτέρης, 'his,' v. n. 26.
ἀπάτην. Read this with Platt for MSS. ἄτην. 'Wily doom' is an odd expression at the best of times, and Aeetes has all along been accusing the Argonauts of duplicity.

πολύτροπον, 'shifty.' Ap. probably took this sense in *Od.* 1. 1 of Odysseus, ἄνδρα μοι, ἔννεπε, Μοῦσα, πολύτροπον, which was taken by others in the sense of 'much wandered,' anticipating the next words ὃς μάλα πολλὰ Πλάγχθη.

ἐξαλέασθαι, 'avoid,' v. n. 466. For the rhythm, cf. Hes. *Op.* 105, etc., Διὸς νόον ἐξαλέασθαι.

601. ἐελδομένους, 'at their own desire': for the form, v. n. 383. Aeetes, like Chalciope, 267 supr., is at pains to stress the fact that the sons of Phrixus need never have left Colchis except of their own volition.

602. πατρός, v. n. 263. Phrixus had bidden them return to Orchomenos to take possession of his inheritance.

603. τυτθόν γε δέος, 'not the slightest fear': cf. *Arg.* 2. 873, τῷ μή μοι τυτθόν γε δέος περὶ νηὶ πελέσθω.

606. ἄσχετα κ.τ.λ. A variant of *Il.* 15. 97, οἷα Ζεὺς κακὰ ἔργα πιφαύσκεται, cf. 1322 infr.

δημοτέροισιν. Alexandrine, cf. *Arg.* 1. 783: 'the people of the land.'

607. ἀπείλεε, 'ordered them with threats,' here only in this sense.
ἔρυσθαι, 'to watch the ship and the crew as well,' cf. 713 infr. Homer has this both with and without hiatus: *Od.* 9. 194, καὶ νῆα ἔρυσθαι: *Od.* 14. 260, καὶ νῆας ἔρυσθαι. Ap. has it without hiatus, and with a typical variant in τε for the Homeric καί.

ἠδ' αὐτούς, ἵνα μήτις ὑπὲκ κακότητος ἀλύξῃ.

Τόφρα δὲ μητέρ' ἐήν, μετιὼν δόμον Αἰήταο,
"Αργος παντοίοισι παρηγορέεσκ' ἐπέεσσιν,   610
Μήδειαν λίσσεσθαι ἀμυνέμεν· ἡ δὲ καὶ αὐτὴ
πρόσθεν μητιάασκε· δέος δέ μιν ἴσχανε θυμόν,
μή πως ἠὲ παρ' αἶσαν ἐτώσια μειλίσσοιτο
πατρὸς ἀτυζομένην ὀλοὸν χόλον, ἠὲ λιτῇσιν
ἐσπομένης ἀρίδηλα καὶ ἀμφαδὰ ἔργα πέλοιτο.   615
Κούρην δ' ἐξ ἀχέων ἀδινὸς κατελώφεεν ὕπνος

608 ὑπ' ἐκ Pariss. quatt.: ὑπὲκ Wellauer: ὑπὲρ LG. vulg.   613 μειλίσσοιτο
Platt: μειλίσσετο supr. ε scr. αι L: μειλίσσετο G: μειλίσαιτο vulg.: μιν λίσσοιτο
Herwerden.   615 ἀμφαδὸν G.

608. κακότητος, 'misfortune,' v. n. 95. For the genitive, cf. *Il.* 13. 89, φεύξεσθαι ὑπὲκ κακοῦ.

ἀλύξῃ, 'escape.' ἀλύσκω in Homer takes an accusative, like the compound ὑπεξαλύσκω 551 supr. This is a typical variant of *Od.* 3. 175, ὄφρα τάχιστα ὑπὲκ κακότητα φύγοιμεν, and *Od.* 10. 129, ἵν' ὑπὲκ κακότητα φύγοιμεν.

611. ἡ δέ, *i.e.* Chalciope; 'she too had been thinking of this.'

612. θυμόν, 'fear restrained her eager desire,' adapted from *Il.* 14. 387, ἀλλὰ δέος ἰσχάνει ἄνδρας.

613. παρ' αἶσαν, either 'beyond all measure,' as in Pind. *Pyth.* 8. 13, παρ' αἶσαν ἐξερεθίζων, or, with Seaton, 'lest fate should withstand.' The latter is perhaps more probable in view of the Homeric ὑπὲρ αἶσαν, *Il.* 6. 487, cf. *ib.* 17. 321, ὑπὲρ Διὸς αἶσαν.

μειλίσσοιτο. L. and G. (v. crit. note) seem to suggest the present rather than the aorist; Brunck, however, proposes the latter, and censures the vulgate for having -σ- and not -ξ- in the aorist.

614. ἀτυζομένην, 'in terror of her father's awful anger': for the accusative, cf. *Il.* 6. 468, ὄψιν ἀτυχθείς. Homer uses the verb mostly abs., in the sense of 'bewildered.' Ap. has also the late ἀτύζω, 'strike with terror,' 1. 465: cf. Theoc. 1. 56.

615. ἀρίδηλα, 'clear.' This is first in Simonides, but the Homeric ἀρίζηλος is used infr. 958. πέλοιτο here is an obvious variant of *Od.* 19. 391, ἀμφαδὰ ἔργα γένοιτο; for ἀμφαδά, v. n. 97.

616-824. The symmetry and balance

of these lines should be observed. They fall into three definite sections, and in each section an analysis reveals a deliberate and effective scheme.

SECTION 1. Medea alone.

Introduction and Dream	616–632	17 lines
Indecision of Medea	633–640	8 ,,
Decision	641–647	7 ,,
Indecision again	648–655	8 ,,
Simile ; entrance of Chalciope	656–672	17 ,,

SECTION 2. Medea and Chalciope.

Entrance of Chalciope	673–680	8 ,,
Confusion and speech of M.	681–694	14 ,,
Effect on Chalciope	695–696	2 ,,
Speech and tears of C.	697–710	14 ,,
Medea's speech	711–717	7 ,,
Chalciope's reply	718–724	7 ,,
Medea's reply	725–738	14 ,,

SECTION 3. Medea alone again.

Indecision	740–770	31 ,,
Lament	771–801	31 ,,
Decision	802–808½	7½ ,,
Indecision	808½–816	7½ ,,
Final Decision	817–824	8 ,,

There is a still more subtle balance in 740–801 which can be traced out. One must not insist too closely on purely numerical correspondence, but Ap. is clearly following out a definite scheme, and even his greatest detractors must admit that he has hidden the seams well: v. further in *Class. Rev.* 39 (1925), pp. 115–6.

616–664. Medea is visited by dreadful dreams, and resolves to take counsel with her sister.

616. ἀδινός. In Homer, this means 'loud, thronging.' Ap. uses it freely in three senses: (1) 'deep,' as here, of sleep, cf. 748; (2) 'miserable,' 635, 1104; (3) 'frequent,' of εὐνή 1206, which

λέκτρῳ ἀνακλινθεῖσαν. ἄφαρ δέ μιν ἠπεροπῆες,
οἷά τ᾽ ἀκηχεμένην, ὀλοοὶ ἐρέθεσκον ὄνειροι.
τὸν ξεῖνον δ᾽ ἐδόκησεν ὑφεστάμεναι τὸν ἄεθλον,
οὔτι μάλ᾽ ὁρμαίνοντα δέρος κριοῖο κομίσσαι,   620
οὐδέ τι τοῖο ἕκητι μετὰ πτόλιν Αἰήταο
ἐλθέμεν, ὄφρα δέ μιν σφέτερον δόμον εἰσαγάγοιτο
κουριδίην παράκοιτιν· ὀίετο δ᾽ ἀμφὶ βόεσσιν
αὐτὴ ἀεθλεύουσα μάλ᾽ εὐμαρέως πονέεσθαι·
σφωιτέρους δὲ τοκῆας ὑποσχεσίης ἀθερίζειν,   625
οὕνεκεν οὐ κούρῃ ζεῦξαι βόας, ἀλλά οἱ αὐτῷ
προύθεσαν· ἐκ δ᾽ ἄρα τοῦ νεῖκος πέλεν ἀμφήριστον
πατρί τε καὶ ξείνοις· αὐτῇ δ᾽ ἐπιέτρεπον ἄμφω
τὼς ἔμεν, ὥς κεν ἐῇσι μετὰ φρεσὶν ἰθύσειεν.

the schol. *ad loc.* takes in the preceding sense. It is probably connected with ἄδην, ἀδρός, 'great.'

κατελώφεεν, 'relieved.' Transitive here, but intr. in *Od.* 9. 460, 'cease,' κὰδ δέ κ᾽ ἐμὸν κῆρ Λωφήσειε κακῶν. Ap. uses in an intransitive sense λωφάω, λωφέω, the latter c. gen. in 784, and a new compound in 1. 1161, μετελώφεον 'ceased.' ἀπό...λωφήσομεν δίψαν is trans., 4. 1417.

ὕπνος, cf. Soph. *Ph.* 766, λαμβάνει γὰρ οὖν ὕπνος μ᾽, ὅταν περ τὸ κακὸν ἐξίῃ τόδε. The motif of this dream is imitated in *Aen.* 4. 465, where Dido is afflicted with evil visions before she has made up her mind to die. In both cases, the dream strengthens the purpose, a favourite literary device; but it must be remembered that the ancients attached deeper meaning to dreams than we do in ordinary life, and not merely in literature.

617. **ἀνακλινθεῖσαν**, 'as she lay on her bed': this recalls *Od.* 18. 189, εὗδε δ᾽ ἀνακλινθεῖσα.

ἠπεροπῆες, 'deceitful': here and in the *Odyssey* only, v. n. 563. There is a fem. form ἠπεροπηίς in a fragment of an unknown poet ap. Strabo 1. 17, βουλῇ καὶ μύθοισι καὶ ἠπεροπηίδι τέχνῃ.

618. **ἐρέθεσκον**. For the Ionic imperfect, cf. infr. 1103. This word in the *Iliad* is used always of provoking a person to anger; in the *Odyssey*, as here, it is used of mental sources of trouble, *e.g. Od.* 4. 813, ὀδυνάων Πολλέων, αἵ μ᾽ ἐρέθουσι κατὰ φρένα καὶ κατὰ θυμόν.

619. **ἐδόκησεν**, 'she thought': this transitive use is Homeric.

ὑφεστάμεναι, 'undertake': here only with rough breathing, v. n. 501 supr.

620. **κομίσσαι**. The usual epic reduplication of the -σ-; here it is rather in the sense 'win,' as in *Il.* 2. 875, χρυσὸν δ᾽ Ἀχιλεὺς ἐκόμισσε, rather than 'recover,' as in Pind. *Ol.* 13. 59 (82), Ἑλέναν κομίζοντες.

622. **σφέτερον**, 'his,' v. nn. 26, 186.

623. **κουριδίην**. Common in Homer, properly of a 'lawful' wife as opposed to a concubine. The contrast is brought out in *Arg.* 1. 611, with regard to the men of Lemnos; δὴ γὰρ κουριδίας μὲν ἀπηνήναντο γυναῖκας Ἄνερες ἐχθήραντες, ἔχον δ᾽ ἐπὶ ληιάδεσσιν Τρηχὺν ἔρον.

ἀμφί, v. n. 117.

βόεσσιν. This form is here only in the poem, elsewhere Ap. uses βουσίν: both are Homeric.

625. **σφωιτέρους**, 'her,' v. nn. 26, 186.

ἀθερίζειν, 'make light of,' v. n. 80; Homer uses only c. acc.

626. **οἱ αὐτῷ**, *sc.* Ἰήσονι.

627. **ἀμφήριστον**, 'disputed': cf. Arat. 712, ἀμφήριστα πέλοιτο, 'it might be disputed.' It is used of a dead heat in a chariot race in *Il.* 23. 382, καί νύ κεν ἢ παρέλασσ᾽ ἢ ἀμφήριστον ἔθηκεν.

628. **ἐπιέτρεπον**, 'they both laid the decision on her, as she in her own mind should direct.' For the hiatus, v. n. 501, contr. *Arg.* 1. 642, ἐπέτρεπον.

629. **ἰθύσειεν**. In Homer, the use of this word with the genitive belongs to

ἡ δ' ἄφνω τὸν ξεῖνον, ἀφειδήσασα τοκήων,   630
εἵλετο· τοὺς δ' ἀμέγαρτον ἄχος λάβεν, ἐκ δ' ἐβόησαν
χωόμενοι· τὴν δ' ὕπνος ἅμα κλαγγῇ μεθέηκεν.
παλλομένη δ' ἀνόρουσε φόβῳ, περί τ' ἀμφί τε τοίχους
πάπτηνεν θαλάμοιο· μόλις δ' ἐσαγείρατο θυμὸν
ὡς πάρος ἐν στέρνοις, ἀδινὴν δ' ἀνενείκατο φωνήν·   635
'Δειλὴ ἐγών, οἷόν με βαρεῖς ἐφόβησαν ὄνειροι.
δείδια, μὴ μέγα δή τι φέρει κακὸν ἥδε κέλευθος
ἡρώων. περί μοι ξείνῳ φρένες ἠερέθονται.
μνάσθω ἐὸν κατὰ δῆμον Ἀχαιίδα τηλόθι κούρην·
ἄμμι δὲ παρθενίη τε μέλοι καὶ δῶμα τοκήων.   640

634 μόγις G.   637 φέρει L, vulg., Platt: φέρῃ Paris. unus, Vind. G.
a man. sec.

the *Iliad*, that with infinitive to the *Odyssey*; for the former, cf. infr. 1060, for the latter *Arg.* 4. 1008. The accusative in 2. 950 is unique, ὅ κεν ᾗσι μετὰ φρεσὶν ἰθύσειεν.

630. ἀφειδήσασα, 'neglecting,' v. n. 527.

631. ἀμέγαρτον, 'unenviable,' *i.e.* 'miserable.' This may refer to *Il.* 2. 420, πόνον δ' ἀμέγαρτον ὄφελλεν, where Aristarchus read ἀλίαστον against the MSS.: cf. also *Od.* 11. 400, ἀνέμων ἀμέγαρτον ἀυτμήν. The account of this dream is imitated by Val. Flacc. 7. 141 f. ; 'Dixerat haec, stratoque graves proiecerat artus, Si veniat miserata quies, cum saevior ipse Turbat agitque sopor; supplex hinc sternitur hospes Hinc pater. Illa nova rumpit formidine somnos Erigiturque toro.'

632. ἅμα κλαγγῇ, 'and with the cry, sleep left her.' Platt compares Tennyson, *Last Tournament*: 'Then out of Tristram waking, the red dream Fled with a shout,' of which this may be the original, though in a slightly different sense.

633. παλλομένη, cf. Moschus, *Europa* 16, ἡ μὲν ἀπὸ στρωτῶν λεχέων θόρε δειμαίνουσα Παλλομένη κραδίην.

περί τ' ἀμφί τε, cf. *Il.* 17. 760, περὶ τ' ἀμφί τε τάφρον. Homer has also ἀμφὶ περί, without case in *Il.* 21. 10, with accusative in *Il.* 23. 191, and with dative in *Od.* 11. 609.

634. ἐσαγείρατο, adapted with slight alteration from *Il.* 21. 417, μόγις δ' ἐσαγείρατο θυμόν: v. also n. 288, ἄηντο.

635. ἀδινήν, 'miserable,' v. n. 616. For the Homeric adaptation v. n. 463: cf. Moschus, *Europa* 20, ὄψε δὲ δειμαλέην ἀνενείκατο παρθένον αὐδήν: *ib.* 134, ἀμφὶ ἑ παπτήνασα τόσην ἀνενείκατο φωνήν.

636. For the belief in visions seen in dreams, cf. Soph. *Ph.* 847, πάντων ἐν νόσῳ εὐδρακὴς Ὕπνος ἄυπνος λεύσσειν: Aesch. *Eum.* 104, εὕδουσα γὰρ φρὴν ὄμμασιν λαμπρύνεται. With the sentiment, cf. *Aen.* 4. 9, 'quam me suspensam insomnia terrent'; and Moschus, *Europa* 21, τίς μοι τοιάδε φάσματ' ἐπουρανίων προίηλεν; Ποῖοί με στρωτῶν λεχέων ὕπερ ἐν θαλάμοισιν Ἡδὺ μάλα κνώσσουσαν ἀνεπτοίησαν ὄνειροι...;

637. φέρει. This is retained by Platt against φέρῃ of the inferior MSS. The indicative makes the fear more vivid, and Ap. was under no obligation to follow the Homeric use with the subjunctive.

κέλευθος, lit. 'voyage,' *i.e.* 'visit.'

638. ἠερέθονται, v. n. 368: 'my heart trembles with fear for the stranger.' This and 368 recall *Il.* 3. 108, αἰεὶ δ' ὁπλοτέρων ἀνδρῶν φρένες ἠερέθονται, and may be meant to support the passage against its rejection by Aristarchus.

639. μνάσθω, 'let him woo.' Homer uses this sense with the genitive in the *Odyssey*; in the *Iliad*, it is to 'remember,' as infr. 1110. Ap. has also the accusative infr. 1069, in the latter sense.

Ἀχαιίδα, v. n. 347.

640. ἄμμι. It is a mistake to regard this as a mere confusion of singular and

ἔμπα γε μὴν θεμένη κύνεον κέαρ, οὐκέτ᾽ ἄνευθεν
αὐτοκασιγνήτης πειρήσομαι, εἴ κέ μ᾽ ἀέθλῳ
χραισμεῖν ἀντιάσῃσιν, ἐπὶ σφετέροις ἀχέουσα
παισί· τό κέν μοι λυγρὸν ἐνὶ κραδίῃ σβέσαι ἄλγος.᾽
    Ἦ ῥα, καὶ ὀρθωθεῖσα θύρας ὤιξε δόμοιο,   645
νήλιπος, οἰέανος· καὶ δὴ λελίητο νέεσθαι

644 σβέσαι Madvig : σβέσοι codd.

plural due to emotion, as in Eur. *Hipp.*
244, αἰδούμεθα γὰρ τὰ λελεγμένα μοι.
Brunck rightly observes with regard to
παρθενίη that 'Medeae servanda erat
virginitas, quia Hecates sacerdotio fun-
gebatur,' and de Mirmont can scarcely
be right in assuming that in her troubled
condition, Medea would hardly consider
this. Surely she is trying to imagine
herself, not as Medea, but as a virgin
priestess and good daughter. The plural
is very subtle and is properly in place
here; similarly in English the 'editorial
we' is much less subjective than the
first person singular. For the virginity
of priestesses, cf. Theonoe's prayer in
Eur. *Hel.* 1006-8, ἡ Κύπρις δέ μοι Ἵλεως
μὲν εἴη, συμβέβηκε δ᾽ οὐδαμοῦ· Πειράσομαι δὲ παρθένος μένειν ἀεί: and for this
passage Seneca, *Medea* 238-9, 'Virgini
placeat pudor Paterque placeat.'
    641. ἔμπα. Homer has ἔμπης, as in
16 supr. This form is first in Pindar and
Sophocles.
    θεμένη, 'forcing my heart to reckless-
ness.' Cf. *Il.* 9. 629, ἄγριον ἐν στήθεσσι
θέτο μεγαλήτορα θυμόν: *Arg.* 4. 1669,
θεμένη δὲ κακὸν νόον 'steeling her heart
to evil': and Tyrtaeus, line 5, ap. Stob.
4. 9, of a warrior, ἐχθρὰν μὲν ψυχὴν
θέμενος.
    ἄνευθεν. Take αὐτοκασιγνήτης with
both ἄνευθεν and πειράσομαι: 'I will
no longer keep aloof from my sister,
but will make trial of her....' Seaton
(*Class. Rev.* 1914, 18 A) objects to
Mooney's rendering 'I will not essay
anything without my sister, if haply...,'
as involving the translation of οὐκέτι as
οὔπω, the taking as concessive of the
causal θεμένη, and as conditional of εἰ,
which depends directly on πειράσομαι.
    643. χραισμεῖν, 'to help in the task.'
Ap. is the first to use this verb posi-
tively; Homer uses it in the *Iliad* only,
always with a negative implied or expressed.

ἐπί. This use is common after Homer
with verbs of mental affliction; cf. *Il.*
9. 492, ἐπὶ σοὶ (*i.e.* 'for thee') μάλα
πόλλ᾽ ἔπαθον.
    σφετέροις, 'her,' v. nn. 26, 186.
    645. ὤιξε, 'opened': Homer has also
ᾤξε in *Il.* 24. 457. This may be modelled
on *Od.* 10. 230, etc., ἡ δ᾽ αἶψ᾽ ἐξελθοῦσα
θύρας ὤιξε φαεινάς.
    646. νήλιπος, 'barefoot.' This word
is first in Alexandrine writers: cf. Lyc.
635, ἄχλαινον ἀμπρεύσουσι νήλιπον
βίον, which is very close to νήλιπος,
οἰέανος. νηλίπους is in Soph. *O. C.* 349,
ἀνάλιπος in Theoc. 4. 56. The scholiast
on Theocritus derives it from ἤλιψ,
'shoe,' Eustathius from νη-λίπος, 'not
fat,' *i.e.* 'unkempt.' Like Medea in her
haste, so too the chorus of women in
Aesch. *Prom.* have no shoes; cf. 135,
σύθην δ᾽ ἀπέδιλος ὄχῳ πτερωτῷ. Medea
as a heroic figure naturally wore no
shoes in the palace; the Greeks seem
to have gone barefoot in their houses,
especially in summer, and to have worn
σανδάλια or ὑποδήματα out of doors. It
was not till Attic times that women
adopted Περσικαί, 'house-slippers.'
    οἰέανος, here only, 'clad in a single
garment.' Homer uses ἑανός in the *Iliad*
only, with a short -α- as noun, with
long -α- as adjective: Ap. uses it always
as adjective with the short vowel.
Primarily this word is a gloss on the
Homeric οἰοχίτων, *Od.* 14. 489, 'wearing
only a chiton or undergarment,' adapted
to women's dress. Whether this garment
was Medea's customary night attire, or
merely put on to move from room to
room, is an open question. The Greeks
seem to have slept usually 'in puris
naturalibus'; but that too is an open
question, the more so as γυμνός in this
connection may mean either 'naked,'
or as here, 'lightly clad.'
    λελίητο, 'she was anxious to': late
epic pluperfect, v. n. 80.

αὐτοκασιγνήτηνδε, καὶ ἕρκεος οὐδὸν ἄμειψεν.
δὴν δὲ καταυτόθι μίμνεν ἐνὶ προδόμῳ θαλάμοιο,
αἰδοῖ ἐεργομένη· μετὰ δ' ἐτράπετ' αὖτις ὀπίσσω
στρεφθεῖσ'· ἐκ δὲ πάλιν κίεν ἔνδοθεν, ἄψ τ' ἀλέεινεν   650
εἴσω· τηΰσιοι δὲ πόδες φέρον ἔνθα καὶ ἔνθα·
ἤτοι ὅτ' ἰθύσειεν, ἔρυκέ μιν ἔνδοθεν αἰδώς·
αἰδοῖ δ' ἐργομένην θρασὺς ἵμερος ὀτρύνεσκεν.
τρὶς μὲν ἐπειρήθη, τρὶς δ' ἔσχετο, τέτρατον αὖτις
λέκτροισιν πρηνὴς ἐνικάππεσεν εἰλιχθεῖσα.   655
ὡς δ' ὅτε τις νύμφη θαλερὸν πόσιν ἐν θαλάμοισιν

648 ἐνὶ LG: ἐπὶ vulg.   651 τηΰσιοι Vat. unus, Pariss. duo: τῆσιοι L:
τηυσίην G: κηδόσυνοι Pariss. tres: κηδόμενοι Vat. unus.   655 λέκτροισιν G:
λέκτροισι L.

647. -δε. Apollonius is the first to use the locative -δε of persons. Homer uses it only of nouns denoting place; even Il. 24. 338, Πηλεΐωνάδε, is not εἰς Ἀχιλλέα but εἰς Ἀχιλλέως. Aristophanes read κεφαλήνδε for κεφαλῇ δέ in Od. 14. 349; and Apollonius, probably Rhodius, read ἐγκέφαλόνδε for ἐγκέφαλος δέ in Il. 11. 97, discarding the following line. This may be reflected in λευκανίηνδε in Arg. 2. 192.

ἕρκεος οὐδόν, 'crossed the threshold of the court,' cf. 280. Like the Homeric house, and unlike that of Cypris in 39 supr., the palace of Aeetes has a πρόδομος between the courtyard and the μέγαρον.

648. καταυτόθι. Ap. uses this word frequently, entire or in tmesi. κατ' αὐτόθι λείπειν in Il. 21. 201, Od. 21. 90, seem to be in tmesi with the verb; but it may not be so in Il. 10. 273 λιπέτην δὲ κατ' αὐτόθι. Homer has, at any rate, παραυτόθι or παρ' αὐτόθι, not in tmesi with the verb, in Il. 23. 147.

650. ἀλέεινεν, 'shrank back,' here only intransitive. For the accusative, δίσσοντ' ἀλέεινε, in 2. 76, cf. Od. 1. 433, χόλον δ' ἀλέεινε γυναικός. It is c. inf. in Il. 6. 167, κτεῖναι μέν ῥ' ἀλέεινε, and without case in Homer only in Od. 4. 251, κερδοσύνῃ ἀλέεινεν, 'evaded the question.'

651. τηΰσιοι, 'vainly her feet bore her hither and thither.' Homer has this adj. only in the phrase τηϋσίην ὁδόν, Od. 3. 316, 15. 13: cf. H. Hom. Ap. 540, τηῦσιον ἔπος.

652. ἰθύσειεν, 'whenever she darted forth,' v. n. 629.

653. ἐργομένην, 'restrained by shame.' Also resolved form ἐεργομένη 649 supr.; both are Homeric.

654. τρίς. Three is a conventional symbol in folklore for an indefinite number; four carries the idea a little further, like 'N + 1,' 'thousand and one nights.' This formula 3—3—4 occurs in Homer passim; in all essentials it is that of Il. 22. 194, ὁσσάκι...τοσσάκι... πύματόν τε καὶ ὕστατον. It simply means that Medea tried 'again and again.' See Archiv für Religionswissenschaft, 21 (1922), pp. 47 f.

655. λέκτροισιν. Read this with G. and Mooney against λέκτροισι of L.: v. n. 290.

ἐνικάππεσεν, 'fell down upon,' or rather, with the common force of πίπτω, 'threw herself down upon.' For the compound, cf. Od. 5. 374, ἁλὶ κάππεσε: the double compound is un-Homeric, cf. Anth. Pal. 9. 82. 3, Ἴων ὅρμῳ ἐνικάππεσεν.

εἰλιχθεῖσα, 'threw herself in a heap,' used of sudden rapid motion; cf. Od. 20. 24, where Odysseus on his bed ἑλίσσετο ἔνθα καὶ ἔνθα, and Il. 12. 74, ἑλιχθέντων ὑπ' Ἀχαιῶν, 'as they rallied' (Leaf). This passage is imitated in Aen. 4. 690, 'ter sese attollens subitoque adnixa levavit, Ter revoluta toro est, oculisque errantibus alto Quaesivit coelo lucem ingemuitque reperta.' Ruhnken considers it also to be the original of Ovid, Her. 4. 7-8, 'Ter tecum conata loqui

μύρεται, ᾇ μιν ὅπασσαν ἀδελφεοὶ ἠδὲ τοκῆες,
οὐδέ τί πω πάσαις ἐπιμίσγεται ἀμφιπόλοισιν
αἰδοῖ ἐπιφροσύνῃ τε· μυχῷ δ' ἀχέουσα θαάσσει·
τὸν δέ τις ὤλεσε μοῖρα, πάρος ταρπήμεναι ἄμφω   660
δήνεσιν ἀλλήλων· ἡ δ' ἔνδοθι δαιομένη περ
σῖγα μάλα κλαίει χῆρον λέχος εἰσορόωσα,
μή μιν κερτομέουσαι ἐπιστοβέωσι γυναῖκες·
τῇ ἰκέλη Μήδεια κινύρετο. τὴν δέ τις ἄφνω
μυρομένην μεσσηγὺς ἐπιπρομολοῦσ' ἐνόησεν   665
δμωάων, ἥ οἱ ἐπέτις πέλε κουρίζουσα·

659 ἀκέουσα G, Pariss. duo, Brunck, Wellauer.   661 γήθεσιν Damste.
666 κουριζούσῃ Meineke.

ter inutilis haesit Lingua, ter in primo destitit ore sonus.'

657. μύρεται, 'weeps,' v. n. 463.

ἀδελφεοί, cf. 731 ἀδελφειοί: both forms are Homeric, but neither Homer nor Apollonius uses ἀδελφός.

658. ἐπιμίσγεται, 'associates with,' reminiscent of *Od.* 6. 241, ἐπιμίσγεται ἀντιθέοισιν. In the *Odyssey* it is always of peaceful relations, in the *Iliad*, of hostile relations, 'clash.'

659. ἐπιφροσύνῃ, cf. 4. 1115, ἐπιφροσύνῃσι, Or. *Arg.* 238, ἐπιφροσύνῃσι νόοιο, 'wise reserve,' 'thoughtfulness.' Homer uses it only in the *Odyssey*, sing. in 5. 437, plural in 19. 22.

ἀχέουσα, 'silent.' Read this with L., rather than ἀκέουσα of G. etc., for which v. n. 85: cf. *Od.* 11. 142, ἡ δ' ἀκέουσ' ἧσται.

θαάσσει, 'sits,' epic word, used by Ap. only in forms of the present; Homer has also the imperfect.

661. δήνεσιν. This in Homer means 'cunning wiles,' cf. infr. 1168: here Ap. has apparently extended its meaning to 'blandishments.' It is unnecessary to alter to γήθεσιν or ἥδεσιν, still less to resort to crude 'restorations' like ἤβης, εὐνῆς, etc. What Ap. meant is the same as Catullus meant by 'ludite' in 61. 207, 'Ludite ut lubet, et brevi Liberos date'; but precise definition is avoided by the delicate vagueness of δήνεσιν. Apollonius is trying to lift romantic love to a high level, and, considering the very crude way in which this aspect was treated by the earlier writers, we can hardly deem him to have failed here,

however we might have preferred to express it ourselves.

δαιομένη, 'with her heart on fire,' cf. 286 ἐνεδαίετο.

662. χῆρον, 'her widowed couch.' Homer uses only χήρη, or χῆραι γυναῖκες, *Il.* 2. 289, as substantives. This use as adj. is first in Eur. *Alc.* 862, χήρων μελάθρων.

663. ἐπιστοβέωσι, 'scold, mock': this verb occurs only here and in *Arg.* 4. 1725. In this sense we find στοβάζω in Hesychius, and στοβέω in the *Et. Mag.* στόβος is either 'abuse,' as in Hesychius, or 'boasting' as in Lyc. 395.

664. κινύρετο, 'wept,' v. n. 259.

664–680. A servant reports Medea's plight to Chalciope, and she comes in alarm to her sister's chamber.

665. μυρομένην, 'as she wept,' v. n. 463.

μεσσηγύς, 'in the midst of' her tears, v. n. 307.

ἐπιπρομολοῦσα, 'coming forth.' This compound, like ἐπιπροφανέντας infr. 917, is peculiar to Ap. ἐπιπρό is frequent in Ap., though first used by him; ἐπιπροΐημι of 124, 379 is Homeric.

666. ἐπέτις. This fem. form is here only.

κουρίζουσα, 'youthful': cf. *Od.* 22. 185, κουρίζων. It is transitive in Hes. *Th.* 347, where κουρίζουσι means κούρους τρέφουσι, 'have in their charge.' Medea, being a maiden, has youthful attendants; Polyxo, on the other hand, in *Arg.* 1. 671, being old, has 'grizzled damsels' in attendance. Compare κουροτρόφον, n. 861.

Χαλκιόπη δ' ἤγγειλε παρασχεδόν· ἡ δ' ἐνὶ παισὶν
ἧστ' ἐπιμητιόωσα κασιγνήτην ἀρέσασθαι.
ἀλλ' οὐδ' ὡς ἀπίθησεν, ὅτ' ἔκλυεν ἀμφιπόλοιο
μῦθον ἀνώιστον· διὰ δ' ἔσσυτο θαμβήσασα   670
ἐκ θαλάμου θάλαμόνδε διαμπερές, ᾗ ἔνι κούρη
κέκλιτ' ἀκηχεμένη, δρύπτεν δ' ἑκάτερθε παρειάς·
ὡς δ' ἴδε δάκρυσιν ὄσσε πεφυρμένα, φώνησέν μιν·
'Ὢ μοι ἐγώ, Μήδεια, τί δὴ τάδε δάκρυα λείβεις;
τίπτ' ἔπαθες; τί τοι αἰνὸν ὑπὸ φρένας ἵκετο πένθος;   675

672 δρύπτεν Platt : δρύψεν codd.

667. **παρασχεδόν**, 'forthwith,' v. n. 440. Apollonius did well thus to transfer the initiative from the servant to the sister. This messenger girl is the counterpart of the nurse-confidante of the simile in *Arg.* 1. 270, of Euripides, and above all of the New Comedy, and Ap. has not been able to dispense with her entirely. But it was he first, as far as we can see, who took the decisive step of abolishing her function as a 'go-between,' and of giving romantic love an opportunity of finding its higher level; v. Introd., p. xlii.

668. **ἐπιμητιόωσα**, 'devising.' This compound is here only; but the simple verb is common in both Homer and Ap., *e.g.* 743 infr.

ἀρέσασθαι, 'to win over,' cf. 301 supr.

669. **οὐδ' ὡς**. This refers forward, *i.e.* 'even though the message was from a casual slave girl.' Contrast *Od.* 1. 6, οὐδ' ὡς ἑτάρους ἐρρύσατο, etc., where it refers to what has gone before.

ἀπίθησεν, 'did not disregard,' v. n. 105.

670. **ἀνώιστον**, 'unexpected,' v. n. 6.

διὰ...ἔσσυτο, 'hastened through.' Homer uses only διέσσυτο of this verb, usually with genitive, but once without case, *Il.* 5. 661, αἰχμὴ δὲ διέσσυτο μαιμώωσα.

671. **ἐκ θαλάμου θάλαμόνδε**, cf. 249. Much less effectively in Val. Flacc. 6. 477 f., Juno enters Medea's bedchamber in the disguise of her sister Chalciope. Similarly *ib.* 7. 210, Venus enters disguised as Circe.

διαμπερές, 'right through,' *i.e.* to the chamber. Here and in 4. 1203 without case; in 2. 319, 4. 1253 with genitive, cf. Soph. *Ph.* 791, εἴθε σοῦ διαμπερὲς Στέρνων ἔχοιτ' ἄλγησις ἥδε. Homer has

also the accusative, *Il.* 5. 284, κενεῶνα διαμπερές, 'through the flank,' which may, however, depend on βέβλημαι preceding.

672. **δρύπτεν**. This imperfect is rightly restored by Platt for δρύψεν of the MSS.; Medea did not make one big scratch and have done with it! There are similar confusions of προτιάπτω and καλύπτω in *Il.* 24. 110, 20, *Il.* 14. 114. Cf. *Il.* 2. 700, ἀμφιδρυφὴς ἄλοχος: 11. 393, ἀμφίδρυφοι παρειαί: Eur. *Hec.* 655, δρύπτεται δὲ παρειάν: Or. *Arg.* 596, στήθεα δρυπτομένη.

673. **ὄσσε**. Homer uses both plural and dual adjectives with this noun, cf. *Il.* 13. 435, 14. 236, ὄσσε φαεινά, ὄσσε φαεινώ.

πεφυρμένα, 'all dimmed with tears,' Homeric and tragic word.

φώνησέν μιν, 'addressed her.' The acc. μιν looks like a piece of Homeric criticism; Ap. may be following Zenodotus in reading the accusative rather than dative in *Il.* 14. 469, ἐγέγωνεν ἀμύμονα Πουλυδάμαντα. The μιν in such phrases as *Il.* 1. 201, καί μιν φωνήσας ἔπεα πτερόεντα προσηύδα, depends probably on προσηύδα; cf. Soph. *Aj.* 73, Αἴαντα φωνῶ, 'call by name.'

674. **ᾧ μοι**. Homer has ὤ and ὤ μοι without the iota subscript; οἵ, οἵ ἐγώ, and αἴμοι are common in tragedy. Apollonius, *de adv.* ap. Bekker, *Anecdota*, 536. 28, considers ᾧ μοι and ὤ μοι to be false forms, and cites other forms, viz. ὠοιοί, ὠαιαί, ὤαι.

675. **τίπτε**, *i.e.* τί ποτε, either 'what,' as here, or 'why' as in 129. Both are Homeric.

ὑπὸ φρένας, 'over thy heart,' un-Homeric use, v. n. 288, cf. 1404.

ἢ νύ σε θευμορίη περιδέδρομεν ἄψεα νοῦσος,
ἠέ τιν᾽ οὐλομένην ἐδάης ἐκ πατρὸς ἐνιπὴν
ἀμφί τ᾽ ἐμοὶ καὶ παισίν; ὄφελλέ με μήτε τοκήων
δῶμα τόδ᾽ εἰσοράαν, μηδὲ πτόλιν, ἀλλ᾽ ἐπὶ γαίης
πείρασι ναιετάειν, ἵνα μηδέ περ οὔνομα Κόλχων.᾽   680
    ῝Ως φάτο· τῆς δ᾽ ἐρύθηνε παρήια· δὴν δέ μιν αἰδὼς
παρθενίη κατέρυκεν ἀμείψασθαι μεμαυῖαν.
μῦθος δ᾽ ἄλλοτε μέν οἱ ἐπ᾽ ἀκροτάτης ἀνέτελλεν
γλώσσης, ἄλλοτ᾽ ἔνερθε κατὰ στῆθος πεπότητο.
πολλάκι δ᾽ ἱμερόεν μὲν ἀνὰ στόμα θῦεν ἐνισπεῖν·   685

676 θευμορίη Stephanus, H. J. Rose: θευμορίη codd.   679 δώμαθ᾽ ὅγ᾽
(*i.e.* Phrixus) Brunck.   685 θῦεν Merkel.   686 φθογγὴ Brunck.   περαι-

676. **θευμορίη**, 'sent by Heaven,'
v. n. 144. If this is adj., it is a Doric
form of the Pindaric θεόμορος peculiar
to Ap. Probably it should be taken
here, with Stephanus, as a substantive,
corresponding to the Homeric θεσπεσίη,
Il. 2. 367: cf. Call. ap. *Anth. Pal.* 12.
71. 4, χαλεπῇ δ᾽ ἥντεο θευμορίῃ. It may
be also a noun in 974 infr., rather than
adjective agreeing with ἄτη. In *Anth.
Pal.* 7. 367 it means 'divine fate.'
περιδέδρομεν. Ap. uses περιτέτροφεν
as transitive in 2. 738, ἀργινόεσσαν ἀεὶ
περιτέτροφε πάχνην, and here he may
be referring to the unique intransitive
use in *Od.* 23. 237, πολλὴ δὲ περὶ χροὶ
τέτροφεν ἅλμη, and supporting the var.
lect. of the scholia and two MSS., περὶ...
δέδρομε.
677. **ἐνιπήν**, 'threat.' Homer uses the
plural in this sense, and the singular
for 'reproach': cf. infr. 931, ἠνίπαπε
'declared,' with the usual Homeric idea
of censure, Pind. *Pyth.* 4. 201 (358),
ἐνίπτων ἐλπίδας.
678. **ὄφελλε,** cf. 466. This impersonal
use in a wish is unique; the scholiast is
curiously silent on the point. Call. ap.
Anth. Pal. 7. 271 uses ὤφελε like εἴθε
as an adverb in a wish, ὤφελε μηδ᾽
ἐγένοντο θοαὶ νέες: Pind. *Nem.* 2. 6
has ὀφείλει in the sense of 'oportet':
cf. *Or. Arg.* 1159 ὄφελόν με ὀλέσθαι.
680. **πείρασι,** 'at the end of the
world': cf. *Il.* 8. 478, Hes. *Op.* 168,
πείρατα γαίης.
ἵνα κ.τ.λ., cf. infr. 1092.
681–743. Medea so works upon
Chalciope's fear for her sons that she

asks for assistance on their behalf;
Medea promises her aid.
681. **ἐρύθηνε.** This is probably intransitive, 'blushed,' though it *may* be
trans., 'made her cheeks blush.' It is
trans. in 4. 474, *Or. Arg.* 228; and
either trans. or intrans. with accusative
of respect in *Arg.* 1. 791, παρθενικὰς
ἐρύθηνε παρηίδας. Homer uses ἐρυθαίνω
only in middle, using for active ἐρεύθω,
e.g. *Il.* 11. 394, αἵματι γαῖαν ἐρεύθων,
though Wilamowitz reads in *Bacchylides*
12. 152, (ἐρ)ευθε αἵματι γαῖα: contrast
Arg. 1. 778, καλὸν ἐρευθόμενος, and
v. n. 163.
682. **παρθενίη.** Homer has this word
only in *Od.* 11. 245 as adj., λῦσε δὲ
παρθενίην ζώνην: the line was unknown
to Zenodotus and rejected by Aristarchus,
and Pollux (7. 68) read παρθενικήν,
which as adj. is a definitely un-Homeric
use, v. n. 4 supr. Elsewhere Ap. uses
παρθενίη as substantive, 'maidenhood,'
and this passage may be meant to
indicate his acceptance of the Homeric
line.
683. **ἀνέτελλεν,** 'rose to the tip of her
tongue,' cf. infr. 959 of a star rising; for
transitive use, v. n. 520.
685. **ἀνὰ στόμα. ἀνά** conveys the idea
of upward motion, 'rushed up to the
lips.' Mooney's citation of *Il.* 2. 250 is
not quite parallel: ἀνὰ στόμ᾽ ἔχειν is
simply to 'have *on* the lips.'
θῦεν, sc. μῦθος, 'often to her lovely
lips it rushed, struggling for utterance.'
It is unnecessary to alter with editors
to θῦ‍εν, for which cf. 755. θύω is the
Homeric form, θυίω is first in H. Hom.

φθογγῇ δ' οὐ προύβαινε παροιτέρω· ὀψὲ δ' ἔειπεν
τοῖα δόλῳ· θρασέες γὰρ ἐπεκλονέεσκον Ἔρωτες·
'Χαλκιόπη, περί μοι παίδων σέο θυμὸς ἄηται,
μή σφε πατὴρ ξείνοισι σὺν ἀνδράσιν αὐτίκ' ὀλέσσῃ.
τοῖα κατακνώσσουσα μινυνθαδίῳ νέον ὕπνῳ   690
λεῦσσον ὀνείρατα λυγρά, τά τις θεὸς ἀκράαντα
θείη, μηδ' ἀλεγεινὸν ἐφ' υἱάσι κῆδος ἕλοιο.'
  Φῆ ῥα, κασιγνήτης πειρωμένη, εἴ κέ μιν αὐτὴ
ἀντιάσειε πάροιθεν ἑοῖς τεκέεσσιν ἀμύνειν.
τὴν δ' αἰνῶς ἄτλητος ἐπέκλυσε θυμὸν ἀνίη   695
δείματι, τοῖ' ἐσάκουσεν· ἀμείβετο δ' ὧδ' ἐπέεσσιν·
'Καὶ δ' αὐτὴ τάδε πάντα μετήλυθον ὁρμαίνουσα,
εἴ τινα συμφράσσαιο καὶ ἀρτύνειας ἀρωγήν.

τέρω Brunck.   687 ἐπικλονέεσκον Paris. unus, Brunck.   690 κατακνώσασα Vatt.
tres, Vind., Brunck.   691 λεῦσσον Brunck, Platt: λεύσσω codd.   692 υἱέσι vulg.

Herm. 560 of the Thriae 'being in-
spired': cf. Hesych. θυίω· ὁρμῶ: ἔθυιεν·
ἐνεμαίνετο, ἔτρεχεν.
ἐνισπεῖν. The force of the aorist may
be 'strove to utter and have done with
it.' There is no special force in 917 infr.
686. **παροιτέρω.** This adv. is first
here, though the adj. is Homeric, cf.
24 supr.
ἔειπεν, i.e., of course, Medea.
687. **ἐπεκλονέεσκον.** Iterative forms
with augment are unusual, but cf. 4.
1725, ἐπεστοβέεσκον: Od. 20. 7, ἐμισγέσ-
κοντο. This word is first in Ap., 'were
pressing her hard,' though Homer has
νηυσὶν ἐπὶ κλονέονται, Il. 18. 7. In Arg.
1. 783, ἐπεκλονέοντο γυναῖκες Γηθόσυναι,
the scholiast objects to the use in connection with joy of κλόνος, which is
properly ταραχή: cf. also Qu. Sm. 8.
426, δῆριν ἐπικλονέουσα, 'shouting over
the strife.'
Ἔρωτες, v. n. 452.
688. **ἄηται,** 'is in a flutter,' v. n. 288.
Contrast with this motif of Medea
pleading the children as an excuse for
helping Jason, that of Eur. Med. 343,
where she pleads them as excuse to
Creon for taking vengeance on Jason,
esp. 348, κείνους δὲ κλαίω συμφορᾷ
κεχρημένους: cf. also the suggestions of
the nurse to Phaedra in Eur. Hipp.
305 f. for the more ignoble purpose of
furthering a married woman's amour.

690. **κατακνώσσουσα,** 'in my sleep':
here only and in Or. Lithica 316. Homer
has the simple κνώσσω, which is in
lyric poetry but never in Attic.
μινυνθαδίῳ, 'short.' In Homer, this
is usually of persons, 'short-lived': but
cf. of αἰών, ἄλγος in Il. 4. 478, 22. 54.
691. **λεῦσσον.** Platt's restoration of
MSS. λεύσσω, which can only mean 'I
saw, and still see.' Brunck read it also,
but on wrong grounds; he read κατακνώσασα with the inferior MSS., and
altered the text to accord, 'quod cum
participio aoristi congruit.'
ἀκράαντα, 'may some god forbid its
fulfilment': cf. Od. 2. 202, μυθέαι
ἀκράαντον, 'which will not come to pass.'
692. **κῆδος,** 'sorrow.' Homer uses the
singular in this sense, but the plural is
commoner both in Homer and Ap. In
Arg. 1. 48, it is in the post-Homeric
sense of 'affinitas,' τῆς μιν ἀνώγει
Πηοσύνη καὶ κῆδος.
695. **ἐπέκλυσε,** 'came over her soul
like a flood': cf. Il. 23. 61, ὅθι κύματ'
ἐπ' ἠιόνας κλύζεσκον. In Arg. 1. 257, it
is 'to sweep away,' ὡς ὄφελεν καὶ Φρίξον
...Κῦμα μέλαν κριῷ ἅμ' ἐπικλύσαι.
696. **δείματι.** Common in trag. and
Ap., both sing. and plural: Homer has
it only in Il. 5. 682, δεῖμα φέρων
Δαναοῖσι.
698. **συμφράσσαιο,** 'join with me in
devising,' v. n. 87.

ἀλλ' ὄμοσον Γαῖάν τε καὶ Οὐρανόν, ὅττι τοι εἴπω
σχήσειν ἐν θυμῷ, σύν τε δρήστειρα πελέσθαι.   700
λίσσομ' ὑπὲρ μακάρων σέο τ' αὐτῆς ἠδὲ τοκήων,
μή σφε κακῇ ὑπὸ κηρὶ διαρραισθέντας ἰδέσθαι
λευγαλέως· ἢ σοίγε φίλοις σὺν παισὶ θανοῦσα
εἴην ἐξ Ἀίδεω στυγερὴ μετόπισθεν Ἐρινύς.'
   Ὣς ἄρ' ἔφη, τὸ δὲ πολλὸν ὑπεξέχυτ' αὐτίκα δάκρυ·   705
νειόθι θ' ἀμφοτέρῃσι περίσχετο γούνατα χερσίν,
σὺν δὲ κάρη κόλποις περικάββαλεν. ἔνθ' ἐλεεινὸν

700 σχησέμεν Rzach.   πελέσθαι Platt : πέλεσθαι codd.

699. Γαῖάν τε καὶ Οὐρανόν, cf. 714.
Apollonius probably knew nothing whatever about Colchian religion, and chose
these simply as the primal gods likely to
be worshipped by barbarians. Compare
Varro, de ling. lat. 5. 58, 'terra enim et
caelum, ut Samothracum initia docent,
sunt dei magni': Caesar, Bell. Gall. 6. 21
of the Germans, 'deorum numero eos
solos ducunt quos cernunt et quorum
aperte opibus iuvantur, Solem et Vul-
canum et Lunam; reliquos ne fama
quidem acceperunt.' So too Here in Il.
15. 36 begins her oath to Zeus by Earth
and Heaven, ἴστω νῦν τόδε Γαῖα καὶ
Οὐρανὸς εὐρὺς ὕπερθε....
   700. σύν, 'and also,' cf. 707, 1175;
it is unnecessary with L. and S. to regard
it as a new compound συνδρήστειρα in
tmesi. δρήστειρα πελέσθαι is a typical
variant of the Homeric δρήστειραι ἔασιν,
Od. 10. 349, 19. 345.
   πελέσθαι. Accentuate this with Platt
as aorist, cf. the gnomic aorist πέλε in
Qu. Sm. 10. 66. Ap. uses the aorist
freely after verbs of swearing, and also
mixes up the future and aorist as in
767 infr. It is unnecessary to take it
as an 'imperative' infinitive, for which v.
infr. 1032. For the contrast between the
continuous present and the momentary
aorist, cf. Soph. Ph. 1397, ἔα με πάσχειν
ταῦθ' ἅπερ παθεῖν με δεῖ.
   701. ὑπέρ, 'for the sake of': cf. Il.
15. 660, λίσσεθ' ὑπὲρ τοκέων γουνούμενος
ἄνδρα ἔκαστον : ib. 665, τῶν ὑπερ ἐνθάδ'
ἐγὼ γουνάζομαι οὐ παρεόντων.
   702. σφε, i.e. the sons of Chalciope.
   διαρραισθέντας, 'destroyed.' Both
Homer and Ap. use this verb active

and passive; cf. Aesch. Prom. 238,
διαρραισθέντας εἰς Ἅιδου μολεῖν.
   ἰδέσθαι. The active and middle of this
verb appear to be used indiscriminately,
v. Leaf on Il. 1. 203.
   703. λευγαλέως, 'in sorry plight,'
v. n. 263.
   704. Ἐρινύς. Compare the words of
Dido to Aeneas, Aen. 4. 385, 'Et cum
frigida mors anima seduxerit artus,
Omnibus umbra locis adero.' The
Erinyes of Homer are the agents of the
gods below, in particular of Zeus κατα-
χθόνιος and Persephone: Aeschylus in
the Eumenides introduced them on the
stage as the representatives of the
murdered Clytemnaestra. Apollonius
speaks of the Erinys of a personal
avenging spirit, in general infr. 776 and
2. 220, in particular here and 4. 476;
on the other hand Medea speaks in the
plural of her own Erinyes, 4. 386, and
Circe, ib. 714, prays to stop the Erinyes
from their pursuit. Ap. follows the
Aeschylean rather than the Homeric
conception; but the idea of the Erinys
as a personal avenger of the individual
belongs more to folklore than to literature.
   705. ὑπεξέχυτο, lit. 'flowed out
gently.' The double compound is first
here; both Homer and Ap. have the
single compound.
   706. νειόθι, v. n. 164.
   707. περικάββαλεν, 'let her head fall
on Medea's bosom.' The double compound is first here, and reappears in
Quintus Smyrnaeus and Nonnus; the
simple compound is Homeric and common, cf. 1308 infr.

ἄμφω ἐπ' ἀλλήλῃσι θέσαν γόον· ὦρτο δ' ἰωὴ
λεπταλέη διὰ δώματ' ὀδυρομένων ἀχέεσσιν.
τὴν δὲ πάρος Μήδεια προσέννεπεν ἀσχαλόωσα·   710
'Δαιμονίη, τί νύ τοι ῥέξω ἄκος, οἷ' ἀγορεύεις,
ἀράς τε στυγερὰς καὶ Ἐρινύας; αἱ γὰρ ὄφελλεν
ἔμπεδον εἶναι ἐπ' ἄμμι τεοὺς υἷας ἔρυσθαι.
ἴστω Κόλχων ὅρκος ὑπέρβιος ὅντιν' ὀμόσσαι
αὐτὴ ἐποτρύνεις, μέγας Οὐρανός, ἥ θ' ὑπένερθεν   715
Γαῖα, θεῶν μήτηρ, ὅσσον σθένος ἐστὶν ἐμεῖο,
μή σ' ἐπιδευήσεσθαι, ἀνυστά περ ἀντιόωσαν.'

715 ἥ θ' Valckenaer: ἠδ' LG: ἡ δὲ vulg.

708. **θέσαν γόον**, i.e. ἔκλαιον, cf. Od.
1. 116, σκέδασιν θεῖναι for σκεδάσαι, etc.
With these lines, cf. Ach. Tat. 1. 14. 1:
ταῦτα μὲν οὖν οὕτως ἐκώκυεν ὁ πατήρ·
ἑτέρωθεν δὲ καθ' αὑτὸν ὁ Κλεινίας· καὶ
ἦν θρήνων ἅμιλλα, ἐραστοῦ καὶ πατρός.
ἰωή. Properly this is of a loud sound,
such as a blast of wind or a shout. But
from such a use as Od. 17. 261, ἰωὴ
φόρμιγγος, it comes to be associated
with gentler sounds, hence the adj. here
λεπταλέη.
709. **λεπταλέη**, 'soft.' This reproduces, with typical alteration, the only
Homeric use of the word, Il. 18. 571,
λεπταλέη φωνῇ. In 875 infr., cf. 4. 169,
it is used of garments.
710. **ἀσχαλόωσα**, 'in her distress,'
v. n. 433, cf. 448.
711. **δαιμονίη**, cf. 1120. Here, as in
Homer, the word is applied quite
generally, and without any concrete
conception of a definite δαίμων, to one
whose actions are ill-omened or irrational,
as opposed to ἔνθεος, one whose actions
are directed by a particular god: v.
Nilson, Archiv für Religionswissenschaft,
22 (1923), pp. 378–9. The later spiritual
conception of δαίμονες gave the adjective
the connotation of 'demoniacal possession,' and strong mental obsession considered in this light accounts for the
personification of Αἰδώς, Ἔλεος, Φόβος,
Γέλως, etc., for which v. Farnell, Cults,
5. 444.
ἄκος, 'remedy': cf. Il. 9. 250, Od.
22. 481, κακοῦ, κακῶν, ἄκος.
οἷ' ἀγορεύεις, i.e. ὅτι τοῖα ἀγορεύεις,
a tag from Homer, Il. 18. 95, etc.

712. **Ἐρινύας**, v. n. 704: 'such things
as curses and Furies.'
713. **υἷας**, for the form, v. n.
196.
ἔρυσθαι, v. n. 607: 'would that it
were firmly in my power to protect....'
714. **ὑπέρβιος**, v. n. 15, 'mighty,'
contrast 583. This is modelled on the
oath in Od. 5. 184, ἴστω νῦν τόδε Γαῖα
καὶ Οὐρανὸς εὐρὺς ὕπερθε, Καὶ τὸ κατειβό-
μενον Στυγὸς ὕδωρ, ὅς τε μέγιστος Ὅρκος
δεινότατός τε πέλει μακάρεσσι θεοῖσι.
715. **ὑπένερθεν**, 'below,' always abs.
in Ap.; Homer has it also c. gen.
716. **θεῶν μήτηρ**. In Arg. 1. 1094,
Rhea is referred to as μητέρα συμπάντων
μακάρων: the identification of Cybele
with earth is sound.
ὅσσον κ.τ.λ. This is modelled on Od.
23. 127, οὐδέ τί φημι Ἀλκῆς δευήσεσθαι,
ὅση δύναμίς γε πάρεστι: cf. Il. 22. 20,
εἴ μοι δύναμίς γε παρείη.
717. **ἐπιδευήσεσθαι**, 'thou shalt not
be in want.' In this sense, and in that
of 'falling short of,' Homer uses the
genitive; in the latter, Ap. uses the
accusative of the thing, Arg. 2. 1220,
οὔτε γὰρ ὧδ' ἀλκὴν ἐπιδευόμεθα. Both
use the adj. ἐπιδευής, either alone or
c. gen.
ἀνυστά, 'if only what you ask can
be accomplished.' This adj. is first in
Eur. Her. 961, οὐκ ἔστ' ἀνυστὸν τόνδε
σοι κατακτανεῖν.
περ. This can intensify as well as
modify; v. Munro, Hom. Gr. 353, cf.
Od. 1. 315, μή μ' ἔτι νῦν κατέρυκε
λιλαιόμενόν περ ὁδοῖο, 'eager as I am.'
ἀντιόωσαν, 'requesting,' v. n. 35.

Φῆ ἄρα· Χαλκιόπη δ' ἠμείβετο τοῖσδ' ἐπέεσσιν·
'Οὐκ ἂν δὴ ξείνῳ τλαίης χατέοντι καὶ αὐτῷ
ἠ δόλον, ἤ τινα μῆτιν ἐπιφράσσασθαι ἀέθλου,   720
παίδων εἴνεκ' ἐμεῖο; καὶ ἐκ κείνοιο δ' ἱκάνει
Ἄργος, ἐποτρύνων με τεῆς πειρῆσαι ἀρωγῆς·
μεσσηγὺς μὲν τόνγε δόμῳ λίπον ἐνθάδ' ἰοῦσα.'
Ὡς φάτο· τῇ δ' ἔντοσθεν ἀνέπτατο χάρματι θυμός,
φοινίχθη δ' ἄμυδις καλὸν χρόα, κὰδ δέ μιν ἀχλὺς   725
εἷλεν ἰαινομένην, τοῖον δ' ἐπὶ μῦθον ἔειπεν·
'Χαλκιόπη, ὡς ὕμμι φίλον τερπνόν τε τέτυκται,
ὣς ἔρξω. μὴ γάρ μοι ἐν ὀφθαλμοῖσι φαείνοι
ἠώς, μηδέ με δηρὸν ἔτι ζώουσαν ἴδοιο,
εἴ γέ τι σῆς ψυχῆς προφερέστερον, ἠέ τι παίδων   730
σῶν θείην, οἳ δή μοι ἀδελφειοὶ γεγάασιν,
κηδεμόνες τε φίλοι καὶ ὁμήλικες. ὣς δὲ καὶ αὐτὴ
φημὶ κασιγνήτη τε σέθεν κούρη τε πέλεσθαι,

---

721 ἐκ κείνου ὅδ' Pariss., Brunck.   723 δόμῳ Paris. unus: δόμων G, L 16,
Paris. unus: δόμον vulg.   730 εἴ γέ τι Merkel: εἴ κέ τι Wellauer:
εἰ ἔτι vulg.

719. τλαίης, 'couldst thou not bring thyself to...?' For the form of the question, cf. Od. 6. 57, Πάππα φίλ', οὐκ ἂν δή μοι ἐφοπλίσσειας ἀπήνην; and Od. 7. 22.

720. ἐπιφράσασθαι, 'devise': cf. 2. 1058, Il. 2. 282, μῆτιν, βουλήν, ἐπιφ., and n. 83 ἐπιφραδέως.

721. ἐκ, stronger than ἀπό, implying that he was sent, rather than came of his own accord.

722. πειρῆσαι, the normal use with genitive, v. n. 10.

723. μεσσηγύς, 'meanwhile,' v. n. 307.

724. ἀνέπτατο, 'leapt with joy,' literally, 'fluttered.' First in Hdt. and tragedy; cf. Soph. Ant. 1307, φόβῳ ἀνέπταν, etc.

725. φοινίχθη, 'all at once her fair face flushed': cf. Theoc. 20. 16, χρόα φοινίχθην ὑπὸ τὠλγεος. This verb is first in tragedy.
ἄμυδις. Homeric; 'at the same time' as when her heart was jumping for joy.
κάδ. This may be modelled on Od. 9. 372, κὰδ δέ μιν ὕπνος ᾕρει πανδαμάτωρ.

ἀχλύς, 'mist': often in Homer in this sense of a mist coming over the eyes.

726. ἰαινομένην. In Homer, to 'melt,' as in Od. 12. 175, αἶψα δ' ἰαίνετο κηρός: hence to 'gladden,' Il. 24. 119, δῶρά τ' Ἀχιλλῆϊ φέρεμεν τά τε θυμὸν ἰήνῃ, v. n. 1019 infr.

730. προφερέστερον. Homeric, 'superior to,' v. n. 465.

731. ἀδελφειοί. For the form, v. n. 657. Chalciope was the elder sister of Medea, so much so that she regarded the sons of Chalciope as her brothers.

732. κηδεμόνες, 'kinsmen.' This is first found in the sense of κηδεστής, 'kinsman,' in Eur. Med. 991; it is in Homer only in Il. 23. 163, 674, in connection with mourning rather than kinship, for which v. Leaf ad loc. Ap. is closer to the Homeric sense of 'kindred mourners' in 1274 infr.

733. κασιγνήτη κούρη τε. Compare Electra's lament for her brother in Soph. El. 1147, ἀλλ' ἐγὼ τρόφος, Ἐγὼ δ' ἀδελφή σοι προσηυδώμην ἀεί.

ἶσον ἐπεὶ κείνοις με τεᾷ ἐπαείραο μαζῷ
νηπυτίην, ὡς αἰὲν ἐγώ ποτε μητρὸς ἄκουον.   735
ἀλλ' ἴθι, κεῦθε δ' ἐμὴν σιγῇ χάριν, ὄφρα τοκῆας
λήσομαι ἐντύνουσα ὑπόσχεσιν· ἦρι δὲ νηὸν
οἴσομαι εἰς Ἑκάτης θελκτήρια φάρμακα ταύρων.'   738
  Ὣς ἥγ' ἐκ θαλάμοιο πάλιν κίε, παισί τ' ἀρωγὴν   740
αὐτοκασιγνήτης διεπέφραδε. τήν γε μὲν αὖτις
αἰδώς τε στυγερόν τε δέος λάβε μουνωθεῖσαν,
τοῖα παρὲξ οὗ πατρὸς ἐπ' ἀνέρι μητιάασθαι.
  Νὺξ μὲν ἔπειτ' ἐπὶ γαῖαν ἄγεν κνέφας· οἱ δ' ἐνὶ πόντῳ
ναυτίλοι εἰς Ἑλίκην τε καὶ ἀστέρας Ὠρίωνος   745

737 λήσομεν ἐντύνουσαι Hermann.   738 οἴσομαι supr. οἵ scr. ἐι L: οἴχομαι
Ruhnken: εἴσομαι Brunck.   Schol. Flor. monet in quibusdam exemplaribus post
hunc versum legi οἰσομένη ξείνῳ, ὑπὲρ οὗ τόδε νεῖκος ὄρωρε. Hunc in textum
receperunt Ruhnken, Brunck, Wellauer.   741 μιν αὖθις codd.: μὲν αὖτις
Brunck: μεταῦτις Koechly: μάλ' αὖτις coni. anon. ap. Merkel: τήν γε μὲν αὖτις
Platt: κὰδ δέ μιν Damste: τὴν δέ τοι Brunck.   744 ἄγεν L: ἄγε G.
745 ναυτίλοι Ox. Pap. 4. p. 187, et coniecerat Porson: ναῦται codd.

735. νηπυτίην, 'when I was an infant.' Here only as fem. of adjective νηπύτιος; the latter is always masculine in Homer. It is unique in *Arg.* 4. 791 as substantive, ἐξέτι νηπυτίης, 'from childhood.' It is interesting to see how, in spite of all endeavours, the τρόφος insists on intruding herself into the romance; Medea is for the moment regarding her sister as a combination of τρόφος and ἀδελφή, and can be confidential with her in either capacity: cf. n. 667 supr., Introd., p. xlii.

737. ἐντύνουσα, 'carrying out my promise,' an extension of the Homeric idea of 'preparing' something; for the middle, v. n. 510, for the hiatus in the weak caesura, v. n. 263.

738. θελκτήρια, repeated 766 infr. Homer uses θελκτήριον, θελκτήρια, as substantives: the adj. is first found in tragedy c. gen., cf. 33 supr. For the line omitted in the text but quoted in the scholia, v. crit. note. It may belong to an earlier recension; with it, cf. *Il.* 7. 374, etc., τοῦ εἵνεκα νεῖκος ὄρωρε. With this scene, in which Medea dreams that she performs the task herself, wakes, and then decides to use drugs, compare that in Eur. *Med.* 376 f., where she decides not to commit direct murder,

but to use her magic drugs, esp. 384–5, κράτιστα τὴν εὐθεῖαν, ᾗ πεφύκαμεν Σοφαὶ μάλιστα, φαρμάκοις αὐτοὺς ἑλεῖν.

740. ἥγε, *i.e.* Chalciope.

741. διεπέφραδε. Homeric, 'told in detail to her sons.'

τήν γε μὲν αὖτις. Read this with Platt for the amazing τὴν δέ μιν αὖθις of the mss., for which v. crit. appendix, p. 140.

743. παρέξ, 'in defiance of her father.' Homer normally uses the genitive with this word, but in this sense he has the accusative, as in *Il.* 10. 391, 24. 434: cf. *Arg.* 1. 130, παρὲκ νόον. For its use as adverb, v. n. 195.

744–801. Medea, left alone again, is a prey to shame and fear.

744. ἄγεν, for the final -ν, v. note on 290, and crit. appendix, p. 139.

745. ναῦται εἰς. When a hiatus of this character occurs in Homer, there is always a pause before the next word, as in *Od.* 11. 188, *Il.* 1. 39, 2. 209; moreover, -αι in hiatus is rare, v. Munro, *Hom. Gr.* 1, par. 380. It is satisfactory that Porson's conjecture ναυτίλοι has been confirmed by *Ox. Pap.* 1904, Vol. 4, p. 137.

Ἑλίκην, cf. 1195. This is the Great Bear, which derives this name from the

ἔδρακον ἐκ νηῶν· ὕπνοιο δὲ καί τις ὁδίτης
ἤδη καὶ πυλαωρὸς ἐέλδετο· καί τινα παίδων
μητέρα τεθνεώτων ἀδινὸν περὶ κῶμ' ἐκάλυπτεν·
οὐδὲ κυνῶν ὑλακὴ ἔτ' ἀνὰ πτόλιν, οὐ θρόος ἦεν
ἠχήεις· σιγὴ δὲ μελαινομένην ἔχεν ὄρφνην.   750
ἀλλὰ μάλ' οὐ Μήδειαν ἐπὶ γλυκερὸς λάβεν ὕπνος.

748 τεθνεώτων Stephanus : τεθνειώτων LG : τεθναότων Rzach.

fact that it revolves round the Pole.
For its importance as a sign for sailors,
v. Arat. 37, Ἑλίκῃ γε μὲν ἄνδρες Ἀχαιοὶ
Εἰν|ἀλὶ τεκμαίρονται ἵνα χρὴ νῆας ἀγίνειν.
Ὠρίωνος. Orion was killed by a
scorpion, and put by Zeus along with
it among the stars. His setting was
generally followed by storms, Hes. Op.
621, δὴ τότε παντοίων ἀνέμων θυίουσιν
ἀῆται: Arg. I. 1201, εὖτε μάλιστα
Χειμερίη ὀλοοῖο δύσις πέλει Ὠρίωνος.
747. πυλαωρός, 'warder,' as in Homer.
ἐέλδετο, 'longed for,' v. n. 383, cf.
1259.
748. τεθνεώτων. This is the sole
exception in the poem to the rule that
synizesis in thesi must be in the first or
sixth foot. On the analogy of ἐφεσταότας
in 1276, Rzach reads τεθναότων, which
is in Quintus Smyrnaeus, and which
he suggests was borrowed from Ap.,
Gramm. Studien zu Ap. Rh., pp. 44-6.
ἀδινόν, 'deep,' v. n. 616. Note the
typical adaptations of Il. 14. 359,
μαλακὸν περὶ κῶμα κάλυψα: Od. 18. 201,
μαλακὸν περὶ κῶμα κάλυψα.
749. ὑλακή, 'barking.' Homer uses
ὑλαγμός, Aesch. and Eur. have ὕλαγμα:
this is first in a quotation ap. Plat.
Legg. 967 D, cf. infr. 1040, 1217.
θρόος. Homeric, used especially of
voices.
750. ἠχήεις. Homeric, 'the sound of
human voices.'
μελαινομένην, 'silence held the
blackening gloom.' Aratus, Phaen. 804,
uses this word of the moon: Homer
has it of a blood stain, and of newly
ploughed earth, Il. 5. 354, 18. 548.
ὄρφνην, 'darkness.' The adjective
ὀρφναῖος is Homeric, but the noun is
first in Theognis and tragedy.
744-751. This has been rightly called
by Mooney 'one of the intensely human
passages in Greek literature'; Prescott,
however (Class. Phil. 1913, p. 372),

maintains that it has a touch of sensa-
tionalism that is truly Hellenistic. Its
original ancestor is probably Il. 2. 1 f.:
ἄλλοι μέν ῥα θεοί τε καὶ ἀνέρες ἱπποκορυσ-
ταὶ Εὖδον παννύχιοι, Δία δ' οὐκ ἔχε
νήδυμος ὕπνος, κ.τ.λ. It is not until the
lyric poets that sleep is applied to
inanimate objects; Alcman, frag. 60,
εὕδουσιν δ' ὀρέων κορυφαί τε καὶ φάραγγες,
Πρώονές τε καὶ χαράδραι, Φῦλά τε ἕρπεθ'
ὅσα τρέφει μέλαινα γαῖα, Θῆρές τ' ὀρεσ-
κῴοι καὶ γένος μελισσᾶν, Καὶ κνώδαλ' ἐν
βένθεσι πορφυρέας ἁλός, Εὕδουσιν δ'
οἰωνῶν Φῦλα τανυπτερύγων: Simonides,
Hymn of Danae ap. Dion. Hal. Comp.
26. 15, εὗδε βρέφος, εὐδέτω δὲ πόντος,
(Ἀμέτερον δ') ἄμετρον Εὐδέτω κακόν: it
is similarly used of the sea in Aesch.
Ag. 565, εὖτε πόντος ἐν μεσημβριναῖς
Κοίταις ἀκύμων νηνέμοις εὕδοι πεσών.
There is a further extension of the
idea in the New Comedy; Antiphanes (?)
ap. Ath. 10. 449 D (Didot, Comici Graeci,
p. 570), ὕπνος βροτείων, ὦ κόρη, παυστὴρ
κακῶν: anon. ap. Plut. de Superstitione
166 B (p. 749), ὅ τι προῖκα μόνον ἔδωκαν
ἥμιν οἱ θεοί: anon. ap. schol. Il. 14.
232 (p. 607), ὕπνος, τὰ μικρὰ τοῦ θανάτου
μυστήρια: and Diphylus' comparison of
sleep with death (p. 647), frag. incert. 5,
τούτων ὁ θάνατος ὥσπερ ἰατρὸς φανεὶς
Ἀπέπαυσε τοὺς ἔχοντας ἀναπλήσας ὕπνου.
This actual passage recalls Theoc. 2.
38, ἠνίδε σιγᾷ μὲν πόντος, σιγῶσι δ'
ἀῆται, Ἁ δ' ἐμὰ οὐ σιγᾷ στέρνων ἔντοσθεν
ἀνία. It has three imitations in Latin
literature ; Verg. Aen. 4. 522, 'nox erat,
et placidum carpebant fessa soporem
Corpora per terras, silvaeque et saeva
quierant Aequora, cum medio volvuntur
sidera lapsu, Cum tacet omnis ager,
pecudes pictaeque volucres Quaeque
lacus late liquidos, quaeque aspera
dumis Rura tenent, somno positae sub
nocte silenti. At non infelix animi
Phoenissa...': Varro Atacinus ap.

πολλὰ γὰρ Αἰσονίδαο πόθῳ μελεδήματ' ἔγειρεν
δειδυῖαν ταύρων κρατερὸν μένος, οἷσιν ἔμελλεν
φθίσθαι ἀεικελίῃ μοίρῃ κατὰ νειὸν Ἄρηος.
πυκνὰ δέ οἱ κραδίη στηθέων ἔντοσθεν ἔθυιεν,   755
ἠελίου ὥς τίς τε δόκοις ἐνιπάλλεται αἴγλη
ὕδατος ἐξανιοῦσα, τὸ δὴ νέον ἠὲ λέβητι
ἠέ που ἐν γαυλῷ κέχυται· ἡ δ' ἔνθα καὶ ἔνθα
ὠκείῃ στροφάλιγγι τινάσσεται ἀίσσουσα·

753 εἰδυῖαν Lobeck: δειδιυῖαν coni. Monro.   755 ἔθυεν G.   756 δοκοῖς
Knaack, e Verg. Aen. 8. 23: δόμοις codd.

Seneca Controv. 7. 1. 27, 'desierant latrare canes, urbesque silebant, Omnia noctis erant, placida composta quiete,' to which Ovid made the famous objection that the last three words are superfluous: and Val. Flacc. 3. 417, 'iamque sopor mediis tellurem presserat horis, Et circum tacito volitabant somnia mundo,' cf. 7. 3, 'noxque ruit soli veniens non mitis amanti.' But none of these imitations have really improved on the original; there every word adds something to its phrase, every phrase and every separate idea adds something of beauty and value to the whole. We could cheerfully have sacrificed much of Apollonius for more in this strain.

752. μελεδήματα. This is a slight adaptation of Od. 15. 7, Τηλέμαχον δ' οὐχ ὕπνος ἔχε γλυκύς, ἀλλ' ἐνὶ θυμῷ Νύκτα δι' ἀμβροσίην μελεδήματα πατρὸς ἔγειρεν: cf. Od. 19. 516 of Penelope, and Vergil, supr. cit. This theme is treated at length in Ach. Tat. 1. 6. 2–3; οὐδὲ ὕπνου τυχεῖν ἠδυνάμην. ἔστι μὲν γὰρ φύσει καὶ τἆλλα νοσήματα καὶ τὰ τοῦ σώματος τραύματα ἐν νυκτὶ χαλεπώτερα, καὶ ἐπανίσταται μᾶλλον ἡμῖν ἡσυχάζουσι καὶ ἐρεθίζει τὰς ἀλγηδόνας· ὅταν γὰρ ἀναπαύηται τὸ σῶμα, τότε σχολάζει τὸ ἕλκος νοσεῖν. τὰ δὲ τῆς ψυχῆς τραύματα, μὴ κινουμένου τοῦ σώματος, πολὺ μᾶλλον ὀδυνᾷ.

753. δειδυῖαν. This is a new form; Lobeck reads εἰδυῖαν, Monro δειδιυῖαν. δειδιότες in 1329 is Homeric.

754. φθίσθαι, 'to die by a shameful death.' Homer does not use the plain dative of agent with this word, cf. Il. 8. 359, ὑπ' Ἀργείων φθίμενος: 13. 667,

νούσῳ ὑπ' ἀργαλέῃ φθίσθαι. Compare Aesch. Th. 971, πρὸς φίλου γ' ἔφθισο, contrast Soph. O. T. 962, νόσοις ἐφθιτο.

ἀεικελίῃ. Homeric; in Od. 19. 341, it is of two terminations, but to this Ap. has no parallel.

755. πυκνά, 'often,' cf. 822, and Od. 13. 438, πυκνὰ ῥωγαλέην, 'much torn.' ἔθυιεν, 'danced madly,' v. n. 685.

756. ἠελίου κ.τ.λ. This simile is an amplification of Od. 7. 84, ὥς τε γὰρ ἠελίου αἴγλη πέλεν ἠὲ σελήνης καθ' ὑψερεφὲς μεγαλήτορος Ἀλκινόοιο. It is imitated by Dio Chrysostom and Aristaenetus, and in particular by Vergil, Aen. 8. 22: 'sicut aquae tremulum labris ubi lumen aenis Sole repercussum aut radiantis imagine lunae Omnia pervolitat late loca iamque sub auras Erigitur summique ferit laquearia tecti.' From the last line, Knaack (Hermes, 1883 (18), 29) restored δοκοῖς for MSS. δόμοις, 'roof-beams,' which should be incorporated in the text: for a similar restoration, cf. Eur. Hipp. 468, οὐδὲ στέγην γάρ, ἧς κατηρεφεῖς δοκοί, Κανὼν ἀκριβώσει' ἄν.

757. ἐξανιοῦσα, 'reflected from,' lit. 'coming out of.' This compound of the Homeric ἀνέρχομαι is first in Eur. Tro. 753, γῆς ἐξανελθών: cf. H. Hom. Pan 15, ἄγρης ἐξανίων, and 69 supr.

νέον, 'lately,' i.e. freshly poured, and not yet settled.

758. γαυλῷ, 'milking pail,' once in Homer, Od. 9. 223.

759. στροφάλιγγι, 'quickly twisting now here, now there': cf. Il. 16. 775, ἐν στροφάλιγγι κονίης, 'in the whirl of dust.'

GA   6

ὡς δὲ καὶ ἐν στήθεσσι κέαρ ἐλελίζετο κούρης.　760
δάκρυ δ' ἀπ' ὀφθαλμῶν ἐλέῳ ῥέεν· ἔνδοθι δ' αἰεὶ
τεῖρ' ὀδύνη σμύχουσα διὰ χροός, ἀμφί τ' ἀραιὰς
ἶνας καὶ κεφαλῆς ὑπὸ νείατον ἰνίον ἄχρις,
ἔνθ' ἀλεγεινότατον δύνει ἄχος, ὁππότ' ἀνίας
ἀκάματοι πραπίδεσσιν ἐνισκίμψωσιν Ἔρωτες.　765
φῆ δέ οἱ ἄλλοτε μὲν θελκτήρια φάρμακα ταύρων
δωσέμεν, ἄλλοτε δ' οὔτι· καταφθίσθαι δὲ καὶ αὐτή·
αὐτίκα δ' οὔτ' αὐτὴ θανέειν, οὐ φάρμακα δώσειν,
ἀλλ' αὔτως εὔκηλος ἐὴν ὀλησέμεν ἄτην.

762 θ' ἀραιάς G.　　765 ἐνιχρίμψωσιν G.

760. **ἐλελίζετο**, 'trembled,' as in *Il.*
22. 448, γυῖ' ἐλελίχθη. It is used in
Arg. 4. 143 of a serpent 'unrolling' his
coils, ἀπειρεσίας ἐλέλιξεν Ῥυμβόνας, as
in *Il.* 2. 316, 11. 39.
761. **ἐλέῳ**, 'through pity': causal dat.,
v. n. 462.
762. **τεῖρε**, 'tortured her': cf. *Il.* 22.
242, ἔνδοθι θυμὸς ἐτείρετο πένθεϊ. This
may be an adaptation of *Il.* 11. 398,
ὀδύνη δὲ διὰ χροὸς ἦλθ' ἀλεγεινή.
σμύχουσα, 'smouldering': Homer
does not use this metaphorical sense,
v. n. 446.
ἀραιάς, 'fine,' 'thin,' as in Homer.
The etymology is uncertain, though it
seems to have had a digamma at one
time, v. Leaf on *Il.* 5. 425; G. gives a
rough breathing, v. crit. n.
763. **ἶνας**, *lit.* 'muscles,' translate
'nerves.' Homer uses it in the sing.,
meaning 'strength,' *e.g. Il.* 23. 720,
κρατερὴ...ἶς Ὀδυσῆος, and once in the
sense of ἰνίον, *Il.* 17. 522. In the present
sense, cf. *Od.* 11. 219, οὐ γὰρ ἔτι σάρκας
τε καὶ ὀστέα ἶνες ἔχουσιν.
νείατον, 'deep down,' adj. The form
νέατος, infr. 1193, etc., is in Homer
only in *Il.* 11. 712.
ἰνίον. In *Il.* 5. 73, κεφαλῆς κατὰ ἰνίον,
14. 495, διὰ ἰνίον ἦλθε, this has the
digamma, but not in Apollonius' nor
Theocritus, *Id.* 25. 264. Didymus, on
Il. 5. 73, describes it as τὸ πλατὺ καὶ
παχὺ νεῦρον τὸ καθῆκον ἀπὸ τῆς κεφαλῆς
ἐπὶ τὸν αὐχένα.
ἄχρις, either adverb, 'to the very
bottom,' as in *Il.* 16. 324, ἀπὸ δ' ὀστέον
ἄχρις ἄραξε, or as adverb with preposition, though in such a case Homer

puts it before, and not after, the preposition. Following the noun in this
sense, it is rarer, *e.g.* Nonn. *Dion.* 5.
153, ἐς ὄμφαλον ἄχρις; as preposition
c. gen., cf. 875 infr., *Od.* 18. 370,
νήστιες ἄχρι μάλα κνέφαος.
764. **ἀλεγεινότατον**. Homer does not
use the comparative or superlative of
this adjective, cf. 1103, v. n. 582.
δύνει, 'sinks in': cf. *Il.* 17. 392,
δύνει δέ τ' ἀλοιφή.
765. **ἐνισκίμψωσιν**, scholiast ἐμπέσω-
σιν, wrongly: it is transitive here, as in
153, v. n. *ad loc.* Translate, 'whenever
the unwearying Loves implant their
pangs within the heart.'
Ἔρωτες, v. n. 452, cf. 687, 937.
These physical details, which to our
idea spoil the beauty of the passage, are
expressive of the new science of anatomy,
which was first properly studied at this
time in Alexandria, and of which a
knowledge is revealed by such works
as the *Apoxyomenos*, which is probably
by a third-century imitator of Lysippus.
Previously the Greeks had refrained
from dissecting dead bodies, from
motives of piety. See also schol. *Il.* 14.
216, 2. 20, and Mackail's note to the
Nature section of his *Selections from
the Greek Anthology.*
766. **θελκτήρια**, v. n. 33, cf. 738.
767. **καταφθίσθαι...δώσειν**. Apollonius is prone to mix up the future and
aorist as here, v. n. 700. For the aorist
used vividly as future, v. Goodwin,
Moods and Tenses, 61: cf. Eur. *Alc.* 386,
ἀπωλόμην ἄρ', εἴ με δὴ λείψεις.
769. **ὀλησέμεν**, 'endure her fate in
silence.' The verb is Alexandrine, though

ἑζομένη δήπειτα δοάσσατο, φώνησέν τε·   770
'Δειλὴ ἐγώ, νῦν ἔνθα κακῶν ἢ ἔνθα γένωμαι;
πάντῃ μοι φρένες εἰσὶν ἀμήχανοι· οὐδέ τις ἀλκὴ
πήματος· ἀλλ' αὔτως φλέγει ἔμπεδον. ὡς ὄφελόν γε
Ἀρτέμιδος κραιπνοῖσι πάρος βελέεσσι δαμῆναι,
πρὶν τόνγ' εἰσιδέειν, πρὶν Ἀχαιίδα γαῖαν ἱκέσθαι   775
Χαλκιόπης υἷας. τοὺς μὲν θεὸς ἤ τις Ἐρινὺς
ἄμμι πολυκλαύτους δεῦρ' ἤγαγε κεῖθεν ἀνίας.
φθίσθω ἀεθλεύων, εἴ οἱ κατὰ νειὸν ὀλέσθαι
μοῖρα πέλει. πῶς γάρ κεν ἐμοὺς λελάθοιμι τοκῆας
φάρμακα μησαμένη; ποῖον δ' ἐπὶ μῦθον ἐνίψω;   780
τίς δὲ δόλος, τίς μῆτις ἐπίκλοπος ἔσσετ' ἀρωγῆς;
ἢ μιν ἄνευθ' ἑτάρων προσπτύξομαι οἷον ἰοῦσα;

775 ἱεσθαι Herwerden.   782 ἑτάρων scripsi: ἑτάρων codd.   ἰοῦσα Platt: ἰδοῦσα codd.

ὄτλος is tragic: ὀτλεύω is ἅπ. λεγ. in *Arg.* 2. 1008.

770. **δοάσσατο**, 'sat in indecision': v. n. 21, cf. 819 infr.

771. **ἔνθα κακῶν**, 'in this extreme of misery or that': cf. Val. Flacc. 7. 9-10, 'nunc ego quo casu vel quo sic pervigil usque Ipsa volens errore trahor?' Homer does not use ἔνθα with the local genitive; cf. Soph. *Aj.* 659, γαίας ἔνθα; Eur. *Tro.* 685, ἔνθα πημάτων κυρῶ, etc.

772: **ἀλκή**, 'there is no help for my pain': cf. *Il.* 21. 528, οὐδέ τις ἀλκὴ γίγνεται: Hes. *Op.* 201, κακοῦ δ' οὐκ ἔσσεται ἀλκή.

773. **φλέγει**, 'it burns.' Elsewhere in Ap. and always in Homer φλέγω is transitive; this intr. use is first in tragedy.
ἔμπεδον, 'continually': common in Homer, *e.g. Il.* 17. 434, ἀλλ' ὥς τε στήλη μένει ἔμπεδον.

774. **κραιπνοῖσι**, 'swift': common in Homer, cf. Pind. *Pyth.* 4. 90 (160), βέλος Ἀρτέμιδος...κραιπνόν. For Artemis as the bringer of sudden death to women, as Apollo to men, cf. *Il.* 19. 59, *Od.* 11. 172, etc.

775. **ἱκέσθαι**, cf. *Od.* 15. 30, πρὶν πατρίδα γαῖαν ἱκέσθαι. Like Aeetes supr. 374, Medea imagines that the sons of Phrixus actually reached Greece. Herwerden tries to remove the incon-

sistency by reading ἱεσθαι, but in epic this -ι- is always long.

776. **Ἐρινύς**, v. n. 704.

777. **πολυκλαύτους**, 'for our grief, a source of many tears.' First in this sense in Empedocles 318, πολυκλαύτων τε γυναίκων, cf. of the Eridanus in Arat. 360, Ἡριδάνοιο, πολυκλαύτου ποταμοῖο: in tragedy, it means also 'much lamented,' *e.g.* Eur. *Ion* 869. Here probably it is in the former and bolder sense.
κεῖθεν, *i.e.* from Greece.

780. **μησαμένη**, in Homer, this is to 'contrive,' 'plan.' Here it is rather 'compose,' as in Simon. ap. Plut. 79 c, of the bee μέλι μηδομέναν, which is 'making honey,' rather than 'with thoughts of honey in her mind.'
ἐπί, adverbial: cf. Soph. *O. T.* 181, ἄλοχοι πολιαί τ' ἐπὶ ματέρες.

781. **ἐπίκλοπος**, 'crafty,' cf. 912. Homer uses this of persons only: Hesiod first applies it to things *Op.* 67, ἐπίκλοπον ἦθος.

782. **ἑτάρων**, accentuate against the MSS. as fem., for these are Medea's companions, and they were maidens: contrast infr. 908, 913, of Jason's companions, ἑτάρων ἄπο μοῦνον. ἑτάρη is in *Il.* 4. 441, and its single occurrence in Homer adds to the likelihood of its single occurrence in Ap. also: cf. also Call. *H. Zeus* 45, Κυρβάντων ἑτάραι.

δύσμορος· οὐ μὲν ἔολπα καταφθιμένοιό περ ἔμπης
λωφήσειν ἀχέων· τότε δ᾽ ἂν κακὸν ἄμμι πέλοιτο,
κεῖνος ὅτε ζωῆς ἀπαμείρεται. ἐρρέτω αἰδώς,   785
ἐρρέτω ἀγλαΐη· ὁ δ᾽ ἐμῇ ἰότητι σαωθεὶς
ἀσκηθής, ἵνα οἱ θυμῷ φίλον, ἔνθα νέοιτο.
αὐτὰρ ἐγὼν αὐτῆμαρ, ὅτ᾽ ἐξανύσειεν ἄεθλον,
τεθναίην, ἢ λαιμὸν ἀναρτήσασα μελάθρῳ,
ἢ καὶ πασσαμένη ῥαιστήρια φάρμακα θυμοῦ.   790
ἀλλὰ καὶ ὣς φθιμένη μοι ἐπιλλίξουσιν ὀπίσσω
κερτομίας· τηλοῦ δὲ πόλις περὶ πᾶσα βοήσει

789 μελάθρων vulg.: μελάθρου Vrat., Vind., Brunck.   791 ἐπιλλίξουσιν
O. Schneider: ἐπιλλίζουσιν codd.

προσπτύξομαι, 'greet': cf. *Od.* 17.
509, ὄφρα τί μιν προσπτύξομαι ἠδ᾽
ἐρέωμαι. It is properly of a garment, to
'fold close,' hence to 'embrace.' 1025
infr., τοίοισι προσπτύξατο, is simply to
'address': but μύθῳ π., in *Od.* 2. 77, is
stronger, to 'importune.'
ἰοῦσα. Read this with Platt for MSS.
ἰδοῦσα, a common confusion. It should
be noticed, however, that ἰδοῦσα gives
the neat but very artificial arrangement
ἄνευθ᾽ ἑτάρων (μόνη), προσπτύξομαι (συμ-
βλήσομαι), οἷον ἰδοῦσα (μόνῳ).
783. **δύσμορος**, cf. 809 δυσάμμορος.
This refers, of course, to Medea; this adj.,
as it happens, is always masc. in Homer.
καταφθιμένοιο, sc. Ἰήσονος.
784. **λωφήσειν**, 'cease from,' v. n. 616.
785. **ἀπαμείρεται**, v. n. 186.
ἐρρέτω, contrast 466, where it was
Jason of whom this word was used.
But it is now Jason who is to be saved,
and honour and modesty are to be
thrown to the winds.
786. **ἀγλαΐη**, 'honour': cf. the description in *Od.* 15. 78 of a feast, as
κῦδός τε καὶ ἀγλαΐη.
ἰότητι, cf. *Il.* 15. 41, δι᾽ ἐμὴν ἰότητα,
1116 infr., and v. n. 545.
787. **ἀσκηθής**, 'unharmed,' cf. 1081:
Homer uses this adj. only of persons,
Ap. of things also, as 2. 690 νόστος.
νέοιτο. Homeric, 'let him go': cf.
Val. Flacc. 6. 599, 'eat atque utinam
superetque labores.' In Call. *H. Ap.*
113, ὁ δὲ μῶμος, ἵν᾽ ὁ φθόνος, ἔνθα νέοιτο,
some personify Φθόνος, and make it refer
to Apollonius in his self-imposed exile
in Rhodes.

788. **ἐξανύσειεν**, v. n. 188: for the
attraction of the mood, cf. 1112, ἐκλελάθοιο.
789. **ἀναρτήσασα.** This verb is not
in epic before Ap., but Plato uses the
passive, 'to be hung up,' and Euripides
the active metaphorically, 'to make dependent on.' With this use, cf. Plut. 2.
841, ἑαυτὸν ἀναρτᾶν. Hanging is the
orthodox form of suicide for women in
antiquity; cf. of Jocasta in *Od.* 11. 278,
ἁψαμένη βρόχον αἰπὺν ἀφ᾽ ὑψηλοῖο μελάθρου. With this resolve to die, cf. Phaedra
in Eur. *Hipp.* 400–2, ἐπειδὴ τοισίδ᾽ οὐκ
ἐξήνυτον Κύπριν κρατῆσαι, κατθανεῖν ἔδοξέ
μοι Κράτιστον, οὐδεὶς ἀντερεῖ, βουλευμάτων.
μελάθρῳ. Here in the original sense
of 'roof-beam,' cf. *Od.* supr. cit.: the
idea of 'hall,' as in *Arg.* 2. 1087, is
secondary.
790. **ῥαιστήρια**, 'destructive of life':
for the gen. cf. 738, 766. The word is
Alexandrine, cf. Lyc. 525, βαρεῖαν
ἐμβολὴν ῥαιστηρίαν: for the meaning,
cf. schol. *ib.* φθαρτικήν, ἀφανιστικήν.
Oppian, *Hal.* 2. 28, Ἡφαίστῳ δὲ μέλει
ῥαιστήριος ἱδρώς, derives it from the
Homeric ῥαιστήρ, 'hammer,' *Il.* 18.
477, cf. infr. 1254.
791. **ἐπιλλίξουσιν**, 'leering,' 'mock-
ing,' as in *Arg.* 4. 389: cf. *Od.* 18. 11,
οὐκ ἀίεις ὅτι δή μοι ἐπιλλίζουσιν ἅπαντες,
and *Arg.* 1. 486, of the drunken leer of
Idas, καί μιν ἐπιλλίζων ἠμείβετο κερ-
τομίοισιν.
792. **κερτομίας**, a rather bold use of
the cognate accusative, 'to leer taunts at
a person.' It is an extension, typically

πότμον ἐμόν· καί κέν με διὰ στόματος φορέουσαι
Κολχίδες ἄλλυδις ἄλλαι ἀεικέα μωμήσονται·
ἥτις κηδομένη τόσον ἀνέρος ἀλλοδαποῖο 795
κάτθανεν, ἥτις δῶμα καὶ οὓς ἤσχυνε τοκῆας,
μαργοσύνῃ εἴξασα. τί δ' οὐκ ἐμὸν ἔσσεται αἶσχος;
ὤ μοι ἐμῆς ἄτης. ἦ τ' ἂν πολὺ κέρδιον εἴη
τῇδ' αὐτῇ ἐν νυκτὶ λιπεῖν βίον ἐν θαλάμοισιν
πότμῳ ἀνωίστῳ, κάκ' ἐλέγχεα πάντα φυγοῦσαν, 800
πρὶν τάδε λωβήεντα καὶ οὐκ ὀνομαστὰ τελέσσαι.'
Ἦ, καὶ φωριαμὸν μετεκίαθεν, ᾗ ἔνι πολλὰ
φάρμακά οἱ, τὰ μὲν ἐσθλά, τὰ δὲ ῥαιστήρι', ἔκειτο.
ἐνθεμένη δ' ἐπὶ γούνατ' ὀδύρετο. δεῦε δὲ κόλπους
ἄλληκτον δακρύοισι, τὰ δ' ἔρρεεν ἀσταγὲς αὔτως, 805

794 ἄλλη vulg.   805 ἀστεγὲς vulg.

Alexandrine, of e.g. κερτομίας μυθήσασθαι in Il. 20. 202.

περὶ...βοήσει. If this is a compound verb, it is first here: the adj. περιβόητος is Attic.

793. διὰ στόματος φορέουσαι, cf. Eur. Andr. 95, διὰ γλώσσης ἔχειν: Xen. Cyr. 1. 4. 25, τὸν Κῦρον διὰ στόματος εἶχον : Theoc. 12. 21, πᾶσι διὰ στόματος.

794. μωμήσονται. This is modelled on Il. 3. 411, Τρωαὶ δέ μ' ὀπίσσω Πᾶσαι μωμήσονται: ἀεικέα is cognate accusative.

795. ἥτις...κάτθανεν. This construction may be due to semi-quotation as in Od. 6. 276 f., or it may be modelled on Zenodotus, who read ἤγειρε for ἤγειρα in Od. 2. 41, οὐχ ἑκὰς οὗτος ἀνήρ...ὃς λαὸν ἤγειρα. With ἀλλοδαποῖο, cf. Thuc. 3. 13. 5, ἀλλοτρίας γῆς πέρι οἰκεῖον κίνδυνον ἕξειν.

797. μαργοσύνη, 'lust,' post-Homeric form of Attic μαργότης: Homer has μάργος, μαργαίνειν, for which v. n. 120.

798. ὤ μοι, v. n. 674.

πολύ, πολλόν is more frequent in Ap., but both are Homeric; v. n. 313.

κέρδιον, 'nobler,' v. n. 426. This is a variant of Il. 1. 169, ἐπεὶ ἦ πολὺ φέρτερόν ἐστιν, and still more of Il. 5. 201, ἦ τ' ἂν πολὺ κέρδιον ἦεν.

799. λιπεῖν βίον, a common tragic phrase, cf. Eur. Or. 948, ὑπέσχετ' ἐν τῇδ' ἡμέρᾳ λείψειν βίον.

θαλάμοισιν. For this plural as applied to the women's quarters, cf. Hdt. 1. 34. 5,

ἐκ τῶν ἀνδρεώνων...ἐς τοὺς θαλάμους, and 656 supr. : in a general sense, cf. 236 supr.: for a bridal chamber, cf. 1128 infr.

800. ἀνωίστῳ, 'mysterious,' v. n. 6.

κάκ' ἐλέγχεα. Homer uses this phrase as a term of abuse, Il. 2. 235, etc.

801. λωβήεντα, 'dishonourable,' late word, also in Tryphiodorus, v. n. 74.

802-824. She brings her casket of drugs, and at last resolves to give Jason every aid.

802. φωριαμόν, 'casket.' Used in Homer for chests for clothes, but of uncertain gender, in Od. 15. 104, Il. 24. 228. Schol. Ar. Clouds 749 tells how the magic drugs of Thessaly grew when Medea dropped her casket in her flight over Thessaly.

803. ῥαιστήρια, 'destructive of life,' v. n. 790: cf. Od. 4. 229, πλεῖστα φέρει ζείδωρος ἄρουρα Φάρμακα, πολλὰ μὲν ἐσθλὰ μεμιγμένα πολλὰ δὲ λυγρά.

804. ἐνθεμένη, 'placing it on her knees, she wept': cf. Od. 21. 56, φίλοις ἐπὶ γούνασι θεῖσα Κλαῖε μάλα λιγέως, and Aen. 4. 30, 'sic effata sinum lacrimis opplevit obortis.'

δεῦε, cf. Il. 9. 570, δεύοντο δὲ δάκρυσι κόλποι.

805. ἄλληκτον, 'unceasingly,' v. n. 74.

ἀσταγές, not in drops, i.e. 'in floods,' corresponding to the tragic ἄστακτος, ἀστακτί, cf. Eur. I. T. 1242, Soph. O.C. 1251, 1646. It may be adj. in Nic. Ther. 307, ὀνύχων δὲ κατείβεται ἀσταγὲς αἷμα.

αἶν' ὀλοφυρομένης τὸν ἐὸν μόρον. ἵετο δ' ἥγε
φάρμακα λέξασθαι θυμοφθόρα, τόφρα πάσαιτο.
ἤδη καὶ δεσμοὺς ἀνελύετο φωριαμοῖο,
ἐξελέειν μεμαυῖα, δυσάμμορος. ἀλλά οἱ ἄφνω
δεῖμ' ὀλοὸν στυγεροῖο κατὰ φρένας ἦλθ' Ἀΐδαο.   810
ἔσχετο δ' ἀμφασίῃ δηρὸν χρόνον, ἀμφὶ δὲ πᾶσαι
θυμηδεῖς βιότοιο μεληδόνες ἰνδάλλοντο.
μνήσατο μὲν τερπνῶν, ὅσ' ἐνὶ ζωοῖσι πέλονται,
μνήσαθ' ὁμηλικίης περιγηθέος, οἷά τε κούρη·
καί τέ οἱ ἠέλιος γλυκίων γένετ' εἰσοράασθαι,   815
ἢ πάρος, εἰ ἐτεόν γε νόῳ ἐπεμαίεθ' ἕκαστα.
καὶ τὴν μέν ῥα πάλιν σφετέρων ἀποκάτθετο γούνων,
Ἥρης ἐννεσίῃσι μετάτροπος, οὐδ' ἔτι βουλὰς

807 δέξασθαι O. Schneider.   816 εἰ Pariss. tres: ἦ vulg.   818 οὐδ' ἔτι
Valckenaer: οὐδέ τι codd., cf. 325.

806. αἶν', cf. *Od.* 22. 447, 10. 409,
Il. 24. 328, αἶν', οἰκτρ, πόλλ' ὀλοφυρό-
μεναι.
ἥγε, for the emphatic use, cf. 248.
807. θυμοφθόρα, 'destructive,' probably meant to recall the θυμοφθόρα
φάρμακα of Ephyre in *Od.* 2. 329.
τόφρα. This use as a conjunction is
Alexandrine; for the Homeric use, cf.
609, etc. Homer has ὄφρα in the temporal sense of τόφρα in *Il.* 15. 547,
which some editors alter needlessly to
τόφρα.
809. δυσάμμορος, 'ill-fated one.'
Homer uses always like this in parenthesis; probably *Arg.* 1. 253 should be
punctuated accordingly, Αἴσων αὖ,—
μέγα δή τι δυσάμμορος.
811. ἀμφασίῃ, v. n. 76: 'For a long
time she held back in speechless horror.'
δηρὸν χρόνον, cf. *Il.* 14. 206, etc.: it
is more usual as adverb, 729, 1049, etc.
812. θυμηδεῖς, 'pleasing': cf. *Od.* 16.
389, χρήματα...θυμηδέα.
μεληδόνες, compare Simonides 14. 2,
ἀνθρώπων ἄπρακτοι μεληδόνες: Ap. has
the Homeric μελεδῶναι in 2. 627.
ἰνδάλλοντο, 'flashed across her mind,'
v. n. 453.
814. ὁμηλικίης, *lit.* 'friends of her
own age,' an adaptation of *Il.* 3. 175,
ὁμηλικίην ἐρατεινήν. Equivalent to ὁμῆλιξ
of 732 supr.; cf. *Od.* 22. 209, ὁμηλικίη
δέ μοι ἔσσι.

περιγηθέος, 'very joyful': first in
Apollonius, cf. 4. 572, 888.
οἷά τε, 'as a maiden does,' cf. *Od.* 3.
73, Arat. 371.
815. γλυκίων. This line recalls *Il.* 2.
453, τοῖσι δ' ἄφαρ πόλεμος γλυκίων γένετ'
ἠὲ νέεσθαι.
816. εἰ ἐτεόν γε. Mooney explains
this as a protasis, 'if she truly weighed
each prospect in her mind'; but Fitch
rightly observes that Ap. presses it
rather to mean 'in proportion as,' *i.e.*
'in proportion as she weighed each
prospect in her mind, the sun grew
sweeter than ever to behold.'
ἐπεμαίετο, *lit.* 'was laying hold of
with her mind,' v. n. 106.
817. σφετέρων, 'her,' v. n. 26.
ἀποκάτθετο, 'put away from off her
knees,' cf. 1287: this compound of
the Homeric κατατίθημι is peculiar to
Ap.
818. ἐννεσίῃσι, 'through the promptings of Here': cf. Call. *H. Art.* 108,
Ἥρης ἐννεσίῃσι, and n. 29 supr.
μετάτροπος, 'all changed in purpose.'
The force of μετά is 'reverting to her
original idea,' *i.e.* of helping Jason.
Cf. Call. *H. Del.* 99, μετάτροπος αὖτις
ἐχώρει, 'turned and went back': Hes.
Th. 89, μετάτροπα ἔργα τελεῦσι, 'put
the situation back where it was.'
Homer has μετατρέπω, but not this
adjective.

ἄλλῃ διάζεσκεν· ἐέλδετο δ' αἶψα φανῆναι
ἠῶ τελλομένην, ἵνα οἱ θελκτήρια δοίη   820
φάρμακα συνθεσίῃσι, καὶ ἀντήσειεν ἐς ὠπήν.
πυκνὰ δ' ἀνὰ κληῖδας ἑῶν λύεσκε θυράων,
αἴγλην σκεπτομένη· τῇ δ' ἀσπάσιον βάλε φέγγος
Ἠριγενής, κίνυντο δ' ἀνὰ πτολίεθρον ἕκαστοι.

Ἔνθα κασιγνήτους μὲν ἔτ' αὐτόθι μεῖναι ἀνώγει   825
Ἄργος, ἵνα φράζοιντο νόον καὶ μήδεα κούρης·
αὐτὸς δ' αὖτ' ἐπὶ νῆα κίεν προπάροιθε λιασθείς.

Ἡ δ' ἐπεὶ οὖν τὰ πρῶτα φαεινομένην ἴδεν ἠῶ
παρθενική, ξανθὰς μὲν ἀνήψατο χερσὶν ἐθείρας,
αἵ οἱ ἀτημελίῃ καταειμέναι ἠερέθοντο,   830

819 ἄλλῃ G. vulg.   826 δήνεα vulg.   827 κίεν L: κίε G.

819. ἄλλῃ, 'in any other way': cf.
Il. 15. 51, καὶ εἰ μάλα βούλεται ἄλλῃ.
The local use in *Arg.* 1. 822 is also
Homeric, ἠέ πῃ ἄλλῃ...ἵκοιντο.
δοιάζεσκεν, 'was in doubt about,' v. n.
21. This corresponds to the Homeric
διάνδιχα μερμήριξε, *Il.* 1. 189, and not
to the Homeric δοάσσατο, which seems
to be from a different root, v. n. 21 supr.
ἐέλδετο, 'wished,' v. n. 383.
820. τελλομένην, 'rising dawn,' cf. 1.
688, 1360. The simple verb is first in
Pindar and tragedy; Homer has only
compounds, cf. 276 supr., ἐπιτέλλεται.
821. ἐς ὠπήν. Alexandrine, cf. 908,
'meet him face to face.'
822. πυκνά, 'often,' v. n. 755.
ἀνά ... λύεσκε, 'was continually
loosening.' Homer has ἀλλύουσαν,
ἀλλύεσκον, ἀλλύεσκεν, ἀνέλυσαν in the
Odyssey only.
823. αἴγλην, 'gleam,' common in
Homer, especially of the sun. Hence
Αἴγλη is personified as a mythological
figure, *Arg.* 4. 1428, etc.
ἀσπάσιον, modelled perhaps on *Il.*
10. 35, τῷ δ' ἀσπάσιος γένετ' ἐλθών: cf.
also Val. Flacc. 7. 21, 'tum iactata
toro totumque experta cubile Ecce videt
tenui candescere lumen eoo.'
824. Ἠριγενής. Peculiar to Ap.,
here and in 2. 450 as proper name,
infr. 1224 as epithet: Homer uses
ἠριγένεια for both purposes.
κίνυντο, 'moved': cf. *Il.* 4. 332,
κίνυντο φάλαγγες.

ἀνὰ πτολίεθρον, cf. *Arg.* 1. 812, 825;
the noun is Homeric, but not this actual
phrase.
ἕκαστοι. For the plural, cf. 493 supr.,
Il. 1. 550, *Od.* 9. 164, etc.
825–827. Argos goes to report to
Jason; his companions wait at the
palace to watch the course of events.
826. φράζοιντο, 'observe'; cf. *Od.*
17. 161, οἰωνὸν...ἐφρασάμην. For the
form, v. n. 13.
827. κίεν, v. crit. app. on 290, p. 139.
λιασθείς, 'withdrawing,' cf. 1164,
Homeric. De Mirmont takes it with
προπάροιθε, of the ship, 'from which he
had been absent till now.'
828–886. Medea takes from her casket
the Promethean Charm, and drives with
her companions to the temple of Hecate.
829. ἀνήψατο, 'gathered up,' cf. 50.
This passage is clearly based on the
description of Here's toilet in *Il.* 14.
170. Contrast with it *Aen.* 4. 590, where
Dido disorders her hair in grief at the
departure of the fleet.
830. ἀτημελίῃ, 'neglect,' v. n. 144
for the form. The noun is here only;
the adj. in 1. 812 is used by Plut. *Ant.*
18 of disordered hair.
καταειμέναι, from καθίημι, 'let down.'
In Homer it is always from κατὰ-ἕννυμι,
'covered with.' Compare διαειμένος in
Arg. 2. 372, which is from δίημι,
though the schol. may be right in finding the Homeric meaning in 1. 939,
ἰσθμὸς καταειμένος, either 'sloping away

αὐσταλέας δ' ἔψησε παρηίδας· αὐτὰρ ἀλοιφῇ
νεκταρέῃ φαιδρύνετ' ἔπι χρόα· δῦνε δὲ πέπλον
καλόν, ἐυγνάμπτοισιν ἀρηρέμενον περόνῃσιν·
ἀμβροσίῳ δ' ἐφύπερθε καρήατι βάλλε καλύπτρην
ἀργυφέην. αὐτοῦ δὲ δόμοις ἔνι δινεύουσα   835
στεῖβε πέδον λήθῃ ἀχέων, τά οἱ ἐν ποσὶν ἦεν
θεσπέσι', ἄλλα τ' ἔμελλεν ἀεξήσεσθαι ὀπίσσω.
κέκλετο δ' ἀμφιπόλοις, αἵ οἱ δυοκαίδεκα πᾶσαι
ἐν προδόμῳ θαλάμοιο θυώδεος ηὐλίζοντο
ἥλικες, οὔπω λέκτρα σὺν ἀνδράσι πορσύνουσαι,   840
ἐσσυμένως οὐρῆας ὑποζεύξασθαι ἀπήνῃ,

832 ἐπὶ codd.   833 ἀρηρεμένον G: ἀρηρημένον Pariss. tres: ἀρηράμενον Brunck.
835 ἀργυρέην vulg.   838 ἀμφιπόλοις Koechly: ἀμφιπόλοισιν codd.
840 πορσαίνουσαι Brunck.

from the land,' *demissus*, or, 'covered
with the waves.' For the hiatus, v. n.
501.

ἠερέθοντο, v. n. 368.

831. αὐσταλέας, 'dry,' an Alexandrine form: Homer uses it only in
Od. 19.327, with the diphthong resolved,
as do also Hesiod and Theocritus.

ἔψησε, 'wiped,' tragic and un-Homeric: Hdt. 6. 61 has καταψάω. It is
intransitive in Soph. *Tr.* 678, 'crumbled
away.'

832. νεκταρέῃ, 'fragrant,' as in
Homer: the adv. νεκτάρεον, infr. 1009,
is peculiar to Ap.

φαιδρύνετ' ἔπι, rather than ἐπί,
cf. 1136, 1193. The compound is
peculiar to Ap., cf. 4. 663. For the
simple verb, cf. 1043, and n. 300: for
χρόα, cf. Hes. *Op.* 753, χρόα φαιδρύνεσθαι.

833. ἐυγνάμπτοισιν, 'well-bent':
modelled on *Od.* 18. 294, περόναι...
κληῖσιν ἐυγνάμπτοις ἀραρυῖαι, and *Il.* 3.
331, καλάς, ἀργυρίοισιν ἐπισφυρίοις ἀρα-
ρυίας.

ἀρηρέμενον, 'fitted with': this perfect
participle of ἀραρίσκω is peculiar to
Apollonius, and accented in the Aeolic
manner.

834. ἐφύπερθε, abs., v. n. 217; the
datives depend on βάλλε. Cf. *Od.* 5.
232, (βάλετο) κεφαλῇ δ' ἐφύπερθε καλύπτρην. For καλύπτρην, v. n. 445.

835. ἀργυφέην, 'silver-white,' used of
φᾶρος in *Od.* 5. 230. It is a typical

adaptation of the conventional Homeric
epithets λαμπρός, λιπαρός, v. n. 445.

δινεύουσα, 'moving quickly to and
fro': adapted from *Od.* 19. 67, δινεύων
κατὰ οἶκον, v. n. 310.

836. στεῖβε, 'trod the ground': cf.
Eur. *Hel.* 869, κέλευθον...ποδὶ Στείβων
ἀνοσίῳ. It is used in Homer of 'tramp-
ling under foot,' of clothes in the
washing pit, *Od.* 6. 92, στεῖβον δ' ἐν
βόθροισι.

ἐν ποσίν, 'at her feet,' cf. 314.

837. θεσπέσια, either ' heaven-sent,'
or 'immense,' v. n. 392. For use as
adverb, v. n. 443, cf. 1064.

838. κέκλετο, 'ordered,' cf. 85, 908,
and *Il.* 6. 286, ἀμφιπόλοισιν Κέκλετο.
The description of Medea's setting forth,
here and infr. 869 f., should be compared
with that of Nausicaa in *Od.* 6. 71–84.

839. ηὐλίζοντο, 'used to pass the
night,' v. n. 325. So too outside the
bedchamber of Nausicaa in *Od.* 6. 18
there slept two ἀμφίπολοι, one on either
side of the door-posts.

840. ἥλικες, 'of like age.' Once in
Homer of oxen, *Od.* 18. 373; compare
Moschus, *Europa* 28, where Europa
on waking φίλας δ' ἐπεδίζεθ' ἑταίρας
Ἥλικας...Τῇσιν ἀεὶ συνάθυρεν.

πορσύνουσαι, 'making ready,' hence
'sharing,' v. n. 40.

841. ἐσσυμένως, 'speedily': Homeric,
and common in Ap.

οὐρῆας. Homeric, 'mules.' In *Il.* 10.
83, ἠέ τιν' οὐρήων διζήμενος, ἢ τιν'

οἵ κέ μιν εἰς Ἑκάτης περικαλλέα νηὸν ἄγοιεν.
ἔνθ᾽ αὖτ᾽ ἀμφίπολοι μὲν ἐφοπλίζεσκον ἀπήνην·
ἡ δὲ τέως γλαφυρῆς ἐξείλετο φωριαμοῖο
φάρμακον, ὅ ῥά τέ φασι Προμήθειον καλέεσθαι.   845
τῷ εἴ κ᾽ ἐννυχίοισιν ἀρεσσάμενος θυέεσσιν
κούρην μουνογένειαν ἑὸν δέμας ἰκμαίνοιτο,
ἦ τ᾽ ἂν ὅγ᾽ οὔτε ῥηκτὸς ἔοι χαλκοῖο τυπῆσιν,
οὔτε κεν αἰθομένῳ πυρὶ εἰκάθοι· ἀλλὰ καὶ ἀλκῇ
λωίτερος κεῖν᾽ ἦμαρ ὁμῶς κάρτει τε πέλοιτο.   850
πρωτοφυὲς τόγ᾽ ἀνέσχε καταστάξαντος ἔραζε

846 ἐννυχίοις τις Brunck.   847 κούρην de Mirmont: Κούρην L: Δαῖραν
G. schol.

ἑταίρων, Aristarchus took it to be a longer form of οὖρος, 'warder,' and athetised the line.

842. **περικαλλέα**, cf. H. Hom. *Ap.* 80, περικαλλέα νηόν.

843. **ἐφοπλίζεσκον**, 'were making ready as usual.' Medea went every day to the temple, v. 251 supr.: ἐφοπλίζειν ἄμαξαν, ἀπήνην, is Homeric.

844. **φωριαμοῖο**, v. n. 802.

845. **Προμήθειον.** There is a pompous description of this charm in Val. Flacc. 7. 356 f. There is a striking parallel to the description which follows here, in that of the μῶλυ which grew from the blood of Picoloos when he was slain by Helios, Alex. Paph. ap. Eustath. in *Od.* 1658. 45 f., εἶναι δ᾽ αὐτῷ ἄνθος ἴκελον γάλακτι διὰ τὸν ἀνελόντα λευκὸν Ἥλιον, ῥίζαν δὲ μέλαιναν διὰ τὸ τοῦ γίγαντος μέλαν αἷμα. Similar magic plants are the cithara, which grew from the blood of Orpheus, and gave out the sound of the lyre at the celebration of the Dionysia (*F.H.G.* 4. 367); the anemone from the blood of the dying Adonis (Ovid. *Met.* 10. 375); the hyacinth from Telamonian Ajax (Euphorion ed. Meineke, *frag.* 36) or from Oebalus (Ovid. *Met.* 13. 395); the violets from Attis (Firmicus Mat. *de err.* 3); and the pomegranate from Adgistis (Arnobius 5. 5). Likewise the Phaeacians (*Arg.* 4. 992), Telchines and Sirens were born from the blood of Ouranos, blind moles from that of the blind Phineus (Oppian, *Cyneg.* 2. 628), serpents from that of the Gorgon (*Arg.* 4. 1515), etc. The earthquake is caused directly by the

pulling of the root, because it would be connected directly with Tartarus, the home of the Titans (cf. 865); the pulling of the root hurts Prometheus, by sympathetic magic, because it, being of his blood, is 'en rapport' with him. Compare 'Sweetheart Roland' (Grimm, *Kinder- und Hausmärchen* 56), where three drops of blood left in a house can speak with the voice of their dead owner.

846. **ἀρεσσάμενος**, 'after appeasing,' v. n. 301.

847. **κούρην.** Follow de Mirmont and Seaton in reading κούρην, *i.e.* Hecate; it is she, and not Persephone, who is the patroness of magic. For MSS. Κούρην and Δαῖραν, v. crit. appendix, p. 140.

ἰκμαίνοιτο, 'make wet': first in Ap., cf. *Arg.* 4. 1066, ὡς τῆς ἰκμαίνοντο παρηίδες. The active is in Nicander and Plutarch.

848. **ῥηκτός**, 'wounded': cf. *Il.* 13. 323, χαλκῷ τε ῥηκτὸς μεγάλοισί τε χερμαδίοισιν.

τυπῆσιν, 'by the stroke of bronze,' adapted from *Il.* 5. 887, ἕα χαλκοῖο τυπῆσιν: the singular is in Nic. *Th.* 129.

849. **εἰκάθοι**, 'would not flinch from': this form of εἴκω is first found in tragedy.

850. **λωίτερος**, 'superior,' v. n. 187: the masculine is here only.

κεῖν᾽ ἦμαρ, 'for that one day,' cf. αὐτῆμαρ in this sense infr. 1050: Homer uses it in the sense 'on the same day,' cf. αὐτῆμαρ in *Il.* 1. 81.

851. **πρωτοφυές**, *lit.* 'first grown,' peculiar to Ap. For Alexandrine compounds with πρωτο-, cf. Call. *H. Art.* 104 πρωτάγριον, *ib.* 228 πρωτόθρονε.

αἰετοῦ ὠμηστέω κνημοῖς ἔνι Καυκασίοισιν
αἱματόεντ' ἰχῶρα Προμηθῆος μογεροῖο.
τοῦ δ' ἤτοι ἄνθος μὲν ὅσον πήχυιον ὕπερθεν
χροιῇ Κωρυκίῳ ἴκελον κρόκῳ ἐξεφαάνθη,   855
καυλοῖσιν διδύμοισιν ἐπήορον· ἡ δ' ἐνὶ γαίῃ
σαρκὶ νεοτμήτῳ ἐναλιγκίη ἔπλετο ῥίζα.
τῆς οἵην τ' ἐν ὄρεσσι κελαινὴν ἰκμάδα φηγοῦ
Κασπίῃ ἐνὶ κόχλῳ ἀμήσατο φαρμάσσεσθαι,
ἑπτὰ μὲν ἀενάοισι λοεσσαμένη ὑδάτεσσιν,   860

853 Προμηθεῖος L.   854 δή τοι Vrat., Vind.: δήτοι LG.   πηχύϊον LG.
856 διδύμοισι μετήορον Et. Mag. 551. 48.   859 ἐνὶ Pariss. duo, Rzach, Gerhard.

Homer has πρωτό-γονος, -παγής, -πλοος, and -τόκος.

ἀνέσχε, intr. 'grew up': cf. 1383, and v. n. 161.

καταστάξαντος, 'when the eagle lets fall in drops,' first in tragedy. Cf. Aesch. frag. 327 (Sidgwick) of the ritual of purification, καταστάξας χεροῖν (αἷμα).

852. ὠμηστέω, 'cruel,' lit. 'eating raw flesh.' Homer uses in the Iliad only, but it is common in tragedy. There was a description in Arg. 2. 1259 of this eagle, as seen by the Argonauts on its way to the rock of Prometheus. Καυκασίοισιν, as in Aesch. Prom. passim.

853. ἰχῶρα, 'divine blood': cf. Il. 5. 340, ἄμβροτον αἷμα θεοῖο, ἰχώρ. In Aesch. Ag. 1480, νέος ἰχώρ, probably ἵχαρ, 'desire' should be read, cf. the corrupted passage ib. Supp. 850; the contemporary meaning of ἰχώρ was 'pus.'

854. πήχυιον, cf. 1207, 'a cubit high,' first in Mimnermus. L. & S. wrongly make it substantive in Arg. 1. 379, meaning τροπωτήρ, following the unintelligible meaning in Et. Mag. 671. 8 on the passage.

855. χροιῇ. For the dative of respect, cf. Xen. Mem. 2. 1. 31, τοῖς σώμασιν ἀδύνατοι...ταῖς ψυχαῖς ἀνόητοι: for the acc., which is usual, v. Goodwin, Gk. Gr. 1182.

Κωρυκίῳ, from the Corycian cave in Cilicia, which was famous in antiquity for its saffron: it is to be distinguished from the cave of the same name on Parnassus, in Arg. 2. 711.

ἐξεφαάνθη. Both this, and 2. 676 ἐξεφάνη, are Homeric.

856. καυλοῖσιν. This meaning 'stalk' is first found in comedy. Homer uses it in the Iliad only, of a spear-shaft; the specific use 'cauliflower' is in Alexis.

ἐπήορον, 'supported on twin stalks,' peculiar to Ap.; cf. 2. 1065, ἐπήορα δούραθ' ὕπερθεν: 4. 142, ἐπήορος ἐξανιοῦσα. διδύμοισι μετήορον of the Et. Mag. may belong to the earlier recension, but is possibly a mere misquotation; cf. μετήοροι Arat. 406, etc., and contrast ib. 396, 895 ἀπήοροι, 'distant.'

857. νεοτμήτῳ, 'freshly cut,' first in Plato: cf. Theoc. 7. 134, ἔν τε νεοτμάτοισι γεγαθότες οἰναρέαισι.

ἔπλετο, 'was': syncope of this verb is permissible in Homer with the augment.

858. ἰκμάδα, 'like the dark sap of a mountain oak.' This is used in Il. 17. 392, ἄφαρ δέ τε ἰκμὰς ἔβη, of the moisture which comes from a hide during tanning; cf. Hdt. 3. 125, of the moisture from a corpse exposed to the sun, ἀνιεὶς αὐτὸς ἐκ τοῦ σώματος ἰκμάδα.

859. Κασπίῃ, for the text and metre of this line, v. crit. appendix, p. 140. The Caspian sea was supposed to be connected with Ocean, where, as the scholiast explains, the greatest shells were to be found.

φαρμάσσεσθαι, for the active in the same sense, v. n. 478.

860. ἑπτά, i.e. ἑπτάκις, contrast 2. 974 τετράκις for τέσσαρες: seven is a conventional number in ritual and folklore.

ἀενάοισι, v. n. 222: cf. Od. 13. 109, ὕδατ' ἀενάοντα.

ἑπτάκι δὲ Βριμὼ κουροτρόφον ἀγκαλέσασα,
Βριμὼ νυκτιπόλον, χθονίην, ἐνέροισιν ἄνασσαν,
λυγαίῃ ἐνὶ νυκτί, σὺν ὀρφναίοις φαρέεσσιν.
μυκηθμῷ δ᾽ ὑπένερθεν ἐρεμνὴ σείετο γαῖα,
ῥίζης τεμνομένης Τιτηνίδος· ἔστενε δ᾽ αὐτὸς   865
Ἰαπετοῖο πάις ὀδύνῃ πέρι θυμὸν ἀλύων.
τό ῥ᾽ ἥγ᾽ ἐξανελοῦσα θυώδεϊ κάτθετο μίτρῃ,
ἥ τέ οἱ ἀμβροσίοισι περὶ στήθεσσιν ἔερτο.

863 ὀρφναίοισι φάρεσσι Paris. unus, Brunck.   865 αὔτως prop. Mooney.
867 τό ῥ᾽ Brunck: τόν ῥ᾽ LG, vulg.: τορρ᾽ Pariss. tres.

861. **Βριμώ**, cf. Lyc. 1180, θύσθλοις Φεραίαν ἐξακεύμενοι θεάν. She was a goddess worshipped at Pherae in Thessaly, identified sometimes with Artemis-Hecate, sometimes with Demeter, and, according to Prop. 2. 2. 11, beloved of Hermes. She was connected in consequence with Eleusis, where the birth of Inachos-Brimos from Persephone-Brimo was announced by the hierophant in these words; ἱερὸν ἔτεκε πότνια κοῦρον Βριμὼ Βριμόν (— Hippolyt. (?) omn. haer. ref. p. 115 Miller).
κουροτρόφον. Hecate is first mentioned in this capacity in Hes. *Th.* 450, θῆκε δέ μιν Κρονίδης κουροτρόφον, cf. κουρίζουσα, 666 supr. Odysseus uses it of his native land, *Od.* 9. 27, τρηχεῖ, ἀλλ᾽ ἀγαθὴ κουροτρόφος; it is in Hes. *Op.* 228 and Eur. *Bacc.* 420, of Eirene; in Theoc. 18. 50, of Latona the mother of Artemis.
862. **νυκτιπόλον**, 'the wanderer by night,' cf. *Arg.* 4. 1020, ἴστω νυκτιπόλου Περσηΐδος ὄργια κούρης: the adj. is first in Eur. *Ion* 718, νυκτιπόλοις ἅμα σὺν Βάκχαις. For the ritual accumulation of epithets, see the Orphic hymns *passim*.
ἐνέροισιν, 'the dead': cf. *Il.* 15. 188, Ἀΐδης ἐνέροισιν ἀνάσσων. For the dative, cf. also *Il.* 5. 546, ἄνδρεσσιν ἄνακτα.
863. **λυγαίη**, 'dark,' cf. v. 1361, v. n. 323: cf. *Aen.* 4. 513, 'Falcibus et messae ad lunam quaeruntur aenis Pubentes herbae nigri cum lacte veneni.'
ὀρφναίοις, 'dark.' In Homer, always as epithet of night; Ap. uses ὀρφναίη as noun for 'night' in 2. 670.
864. **μυκηθμῷ.** Frequent in Homer of the lowing of oxen, cf. infr. 1297 and Arat. 1118. μυκηθμοῖο περιπλειοι. This

sense of 'earthquake' is in Lucian, *Per.* 39, μυκηθμὸς γῆς, cf. Dio Cass. 68. 24, μύκημα of the earth.
ὑπένερθεν, cf. *Od.* 12. 242, ὑπένερθε δὲ γαῖα φάνεσκεν.
ἐρεμνή, 'dark': used of γαῖα in *Od.* 24. 106, cf. H. Hom. *Herm.* 427, infr. 1191.
865. **Τιτηνίδος.** Strictly speaking, Prometheus was only the son of a Titan, Iapetus 1087 infr.
866. **πέρι.** Take this, not as adverb meaning περισσῶς, but with ὀδύνῃ: cf. H. Hom. *Dem.* 429, περὶ χάρματι: Aesch. *Pers.* 696, περὶ τάρβει: *id. Cho.* 35, περὶ φόβῳ.
ἀλύων, 'his soul distraught with pain': cf. Soph. *Ph.* 1194, ἀλύοντα χειμερίῳ λύπᾳ. The long -υ- is only here in Ap. and in *Od.* 9. 398, on both occasions ending a line: elsewhere in Homer and Ap. it is short. θυμόν is cognate accusative.
867. **ἐξανελοῦσα**, 'taking it out of the casket': Homer has the single, but not the double, compound. Compare H. Hom. *Dem.* 254, ἐξανελοῦσα πυρός: Eur. *Ion* 269, γῆθεν ἐξανείλετο.
μίτρῃ. The following line is required, as μίτρη can also mean a headband, *e.g.* Eur. *Bacc.* 833, ἐπὶ κάρᾳ δ᾽ ἔσται μίτρα, cf. of a 'boudoir-cap,' Eur. *Hec.* 924. Ap., however, uses it only of a waistband, 156, 1013.
868. **ἔερτο**, from εἴρω: cf. of a necklace 'strung together,' *Od.* 15. 460, χρύσεον ὅρμον ἔχων, μετὰ δ᾽ ἠλέκτροισιν ἔερτο, 18. 296, ὅρμον ... ἠλέκτροισιν ἐερμένον. περὶ...ἔερτο is a typical adaptation of a Homeric phrase to a new sense, 'was fastened together round her waist,' *i.e.* 'ran.' cf. λέξις εἰρομένη.

ἐκ δὲ θύραζε κιοῦσα θοῆς ἐπεβήσατ' ἀπήνης·
σὺν δέ οἱ ἀμφίπολοι δοιαὶ ἑκάτερθεν ἔβησαν. 870
αὐτὴ δ' ἡνί' ἔδεκτο καὶ εὐποίητον ἱμάσθλην
δεξιτερῇ, ἔλαεν δὲ δι' ἄστεος· αἱ δὲ δὴ ἄλλαι
ἀμφίπολοι, πείρινθος ἐφαπτόμεναι μετόπισθεν,
τρώχων εὐρεῖαν κατ' ἀμαξιτόν· ἂν δὲ χιτῶνας
λεπταλέους λευκῆς ἐπιγουνίδος ἄχρις ἄειρον. 875
οἵη δὲ λιαροῖσιν ἐφ' ὕδασι Παρθενίοιο,
ἠὲ καὶ Ἀμνισοῖο λοεσσαμένη ποταμοῖο

871 ἡνία δέδεκτο Vrat., Vind. : ἡνία δέκτο coni. Wellauer.

869. ἐπεβήσατο, cf. 1152, 4. 458.
This is clearly modelled on *Il.* 8. 44,
ἑοῦ δ' ἐπεβήσετο δίφρου, cf. 13. 26, 24.
322, Call. *Lout. Pall.* 65. The greatest
uncertainty exists as to the form of the
aorist in Homer, v. Merry and Riddell
on *Od.* 1. 330. Venetus A. almost always
gives -ετο, presumably the reading of
Aristophanes and Zenodotus; to Aristarchus both views are attributed, -ατο
by schol. A. *Il.* 3. 262, -ετο by schol.
A. *Il.* 10. 513. Probably the former is
correct, and it seems to have been
favoured by Apollonius; our mss. give
-ατο consistently.
870. σύν, 'with her,' preposition, not
in tmesi with ἔβησαν.
δοιαὶ ἑκάτερθεν, two on each side, *i.e.*
four in all.
ἔβησαν, 'mounted,' sc. ἀπήνην.
Homer uses only the middle with the
accusative ; the active is to 'make to
mount or dismount.' Ap. has ἂν...βήσατο
in this sense, infr. 1236.
871. ἱμάσθλην, cf. *Il.* 13. 25–6, γέντο
δ' ἱμάσθλην Χρυσείην εὔτυκτον.
872. ἔλαεν, cf. *Arg.* 1. 755, where
Platt restores ἤλασεν for ἤλασεν. There
is a similar corruption of ἐτόλμαεν into
ἐτόλμασεν twice in Quintus Smyrnaeus.
Homer uses ἐλάειν as future, *Il.* 13. 315,
Od. 7. 319, etc.: as present, *Il.* 23. 334;
cf. H. Hom. *Herm.* 342, 355: as imperfect, *Il.* 24. 696, *Od.* 4. 2. Ap. has
the usual Homeric ἤλασεν in 1238 infr.
873. πείρινθος, 'the wicker body of
the car': cf. *Il.* 24. 190, πείρινθα δὲ
δῆσαι ἐπ' αὐτῆς.
874. τρώχων, 'ran,' Homeric. In
many details, this recalls the return of
Nausicaa in *Od.* 6. 316f.

875. λεπταλέους, v. n. 709.
ἐπιγουνίδος. Here, merely the knee ;
but in Homer properly the muscle above
the knee, a sign of vigour, *Od.* 17.
225, μεγάλην ἐπιγουνίδα θεῖτο ; for this
phrase, cf. Arat. 614, ἐπιγουνίδος ἄχρις.
ἄχρις, v. n. 763. The simile that
follows is based on *Od.* 6. 102 f., οἵη δ'
Ἄρτεμις εἶσι κατ' οὔρεα ἰοχέαιρα, Ἤ κατὰ
Τηΰγετον περιμήκετον ἢ Ἐρύμανθον,
Τερπομένη κάπροισι καὶ ὠκείῃς ἐλάφοισι,
Τῇ δέ θ' ἅμα νύμφαι, κοῦραι Διὸς αἰγιόχοιο,
Ἀγρονόμοι παίζουσι, γέγηθε δέ τε
φρένα Λητώ, Πασάων δ' ὑπὲρ ἥ γε κάρη
ἔχει ἠδὲ μέτωπα, Ῥεῖα δ' ἀριγνώτη
πέλεται, καλαὶ δέ τε πᾶσαι, Ὣς ἥ γ'
ἀμφιπόλοισι μετέπρεπε παρθένος ἀδμής.
It is imitated in *Aen.* 1. 498 f.; cf. also
the comparison in Qu. Sm. 1. 663, of the
slain Penthesileia with Artemis sleeping
after the chase. It is further imitated,
with no great success, by Val. Flacc.,
5. 343 f. ; it should be noticed that there
Medea is accompanied by her 'nutrix,'
v. n. 667.
876. λιαροῖσιν, v. n. 300.
Παρθενίοιο, a river in Paphlagonia,
mentioned in *Arg.* 2. 936; ᾧ ἔνι κούρη
Λητωΐς, ἀγρηθεν ὅτ' οὐρανὸν εἰσαναβαίνῃ,
Ὃν δέμας ἱμερτοῖσιν ἀναψύχει ὑδάτεσσιν.
877. Ἀμνισοῖο, a river of Crete,
with a shrine sacred to Eileithyia, *Od.*
19. 188, to whom the nymphs belonged.
For the nymphs, cf. the request of
Artemis to Zeus in Call. *H. Art.* 15,
δὸς δέ μοι ἀμφιπόλους Ἀμνισίδας εἴκοσι
νύμφας.
λοεσσαμένη, 'after bathing in.' For
the genitive, cf. *Il.* 6. 508, εἰωθὼς
λούεσθαι ἐϋρρεῖος ποταμοῖο : for the dative
with this verb, cf. 860 supr.

χρυσείοις Λητωὶς ἐφ' ἅρμασιν ἑστηυῖα
ὠκείαις κεμάδεσσι διεξελάσῃσι κολώνας,
τηλόθεν ἀντιόωσα πολυκνίσου ἑκατόμβης·   880
τῇ δ' ἅμα νύμφαι ἕπονται ἀμορβάδες, αἱ μὲν ἐπ' αὐτῆς
ἀγρόμεναι πηγῆς Ἀμνισίδος, αἱ δὲ δὴ ἄλλαι
ἄλσεα καὶ σκοπιὰς πολυπίδακας· ἀμφὶ δὲ θῆρες
κνυζηθμῷ σαίνουσιν ὑποτρομέοντες ἰοῦσαν·
ὡς αἵγ' ἐσσεύοντο δι' ἄστεος· ἀμφὶ δὲ λαοὶ   885
εἶκον, ἀλευάμενοι βασιληίδος ὄμματα κούρης.
αὐτὰρ ἐπεὶ πόλιος μὲν ἐυδμήτους λίπ' ἀγυιάς,

882 Ἀμνησίδος L, vulg.   αἱ coni. Prescott: ἀν O. Schneider, edd. plerique.
αἱ δὲ δὴ ἀμφὶ coni. Merkel: αἱ δὲ λιποῦσαι Koechly.   886 ἀλευόμενοι Brunck.

879. **κεμάδεσσι**, 'roes,' as in Homer.
This passage, and Call. *H. Art.* 112,
ἐν δ' ἐβάλευ χρύσεια, θεή, κεμάδεσσι
χαλινά, make untenable the view of the
Et. Mag. that it is the animal still in
the cave, as opposed to νεβρός, which
can go out to pasture.

διεξελάσῃσι, 'courses over the hills':
un-Homeric, but common in Hdt. of
an army on the march.

880. **ἀντιόωσα**, v. n. 35.

πολυκνίσου, 'richly-steaming,' compound first found here.

881. **ἅμα ἕπονται**, cf. 365 supr.,
συνέπονται, and *Od.* 6. 32, συνέριθος ἅμ'
ἕψομαι.

ἀμορβάδες. Here only: cf. Call. *H.
Art.* 45, θυγατέρας Λητωίδι πέμπον
ἀμορβούς, and for the latter in the sense
of 'herdsmen,' Call. *Hec. frag.* 6,
βουσσόον, ὅν τε μυῶπα βοῶν καλέουσιν
ἀμορβοί. Nicander has ἀμορβεύειν in the
sense of ἀκολουθεῖν.

882. **αἱ δὲ δὴ ἄλλαι**. Read this with
Prescott and the MSS., and reject the
ἀν of Schneider and editors. The accusative ἄλσεα depends on the idea of
motion in ἀγρόμεναι, 'gathering at the
springs or through the woods.' For the
same ending of a line, cf. 872, 1170,
4. 334 and Arat. 336.

883. **πολυπίδακας**, 'many-fountained
peaks,' epithet in the *Iliad* especially of
Ida, never in the *Odyssey*; cf. 70 supr.,
σκοπιαὶ περιμηκέες. The nymphs of
Artemis were classified in *Arg.* 1. 1226,
as nymphs of the peaks, of the glens,
of the water, and of the groves.

884. **κνυζηθμῷ**, 'whimper': cf. of the

dogs recognising the presence of the
invisible Athene in *Od.* 16. 163, κνυζηθμῷ
δ' ἑτέρωσε διὰ σταθμοῖο φόβηθεν.

σαίνουσιν, 'fawn.' Similarly, as the
result of a portent wrought by Rhea in
Arg. 1. 1145, the wild animals came
οὐρῇσιν σαίνοντες.

ὑποτρομέοντες, 'cowering before her
as she moves along.' Used in the *Iliad*,
both trans. and intransitive.

886. **βασιληίδος**. This feminine adjective is used by Homer of τιμή in *Il.*
6. 193; cf. 376 supr.

ὄμματα, 'shunning the eyes of the
royal maiden.' The family of the sun
were conspicuous for the radiance of
their eyes, cf. *Arg.* 4. 727: πᾶσα γὰρ
Ἠελίου γενεὴ ἀρίδηλος ἰδέσθαι ἦεν, ἐπεὶ
βλεφάρων ἀποτηλόθι μαρμαρυγῇσιν Οἷον
τε χρυσέην ἀντώπιον ἵεσαν αἴγλην. This,
however, is probably more than mere
Alexandrine deference to royalty; Medea
has the evil eye, cf. 4. 1670. Likewise
Dipaea had a 'double eye,' Eriphyle
could kill with a look any animal that
crossed her path, and there was power
in the eyes of the gods, Athene, Zeus,
and above all Nemesis and the Erinyes;
v. Seligmann, *Die Zauberkraft des Auges*,
p. 101. Compare Agar's emendation to
the dative in *Il.* 8. 164, ἔρρε κακῇ γλήνῃ,
'be off, and the evil eye be on you.'
The Greeks do not appear to have had
a scientific knowledge of hypnosis, but
they were well aware of the pheno-
menon.

887–911. Medea explains her plan
to her companions, and asks them to
withdraw when Jason appears.

νηὸν δ' εἰσαφίκανε διὲκ πεδίων ἐλάουσα,
δὴ τότ' ἐυτροχάλοιο κατ' αὐτόθι βῆσατ' ἀπήνης
ἰεμένη, καὶ τοῖα μετὰ δμωῇσιν ἔειπεν ·   890
''Ω φίλαι, ἦ μέγα δή τι παρήλιτον, οὐδ' ἐνόησα.
βῆν ἴμεν ἀλλοδαποῖσι μετ' ἀνδράσιν, οἵ τ' ἐπὶ γαῖαν
ἡμετέρην στρωφῶσιν. ἀμηχανίη βεβόληται
πᾶσα πόλις· τὸ καὶ οὔτις ἀνήλυθε δεῦρο γυναικῶν
τάων, αἳ τὸ πάροιθεν ἐπημάτιαι ἀγέρονται.   895
ἀλλ' ἐπεὶ οὖν ἱκόμεσθα, καὶ οὔ νύ τις ἄλλος ἔπεισιν,
εἰ δ' ἄγε μολπῇ θυμὸν ἀφειδείως κορέσωμεν
μειλιχίῃ, τὰ δὲ καλὰ τερείνης ἄνθεα ποίης
λεξάμεναι τότ' ἔπειτ' αὐτὴν ἀπονισσόμεθ' ὥρην.
καὶ δέ κε σὺν πολέεσσιν ὀνείασιν οἴκαδ' ἵκοισθε   900
ἤματι τῷδ', εἴ μοι συναρέσσετε τήνδε μενοινήν.
''Αργος γάρ μ' ἐπέεσσι παρατρέπει, ὡς δὲ καὶ αὐτὴ
Χαλκιόπη· τὰ δὲ σῖγα νόῳ ἔχετ' εἰσαΐουσαι

---

891 ita post ἐνόησα interpunxit Platt.   892 βῆν Prescott: μῆνιμ' Merkel:
ἔμμεναι Samuelsson : δὴν ἔμεν Platt: μὴ ἴμεν codd., Mooney.   895 ἀγέροντο
Brunck.   901 τῷδ' Platt : τῷ codd.   903 τὰ δὲ G., Brunck : τάδε L, vulg.

888. εἰσαφίκανε. Homeric compound,
cf. Od. 22. 99, infr. 1179.
διὲκ...ἐλάουσα, cf. 879 supr.
889. κατ' αὐτόθι κ.τ.λ. κατεβήσατο
in tmesi: v. n. 648.
891. παρήλιτον, 'I have greatly
sinned.' This compound of the Homeric
ἀλιταίνω is first in Ap.; for the accusative of the person, cf. 2. 246, ἦ ῥα θεοὺς
ὀλοῇσι παρήλιτες ἀφραδίῃσιν.
Punctuate this line with a full stop
after ἐνόησα, and read βῆν ἴμεν in 892 ;
'I have done great wrong, and did not
stop to think. I have come to go among
the strangers....' For the text, v. crit.
appendix, p. 141.
892. μετά. For the dative after a
verb of motion, compare Arg. 1. 648,
ἐς αὐγὰς 'Ηελίου ζωοῖσι μετ' ἀνδράσιν
(ἀμειβόμενος).
893. ἐπὶ...στρωφῶσιν. Probably in
tmesi, cf. 424, and Od. 17. 486, ἐπιστρωφῶσι πολῆας.
ἀμηχανίῃ, v. n. 336.
895. ἐπημάτιαι, compound of the
Homeric ἠμάτιαι, Il. 9. 72, found here
only.
ἀγέρονται. Formed as a present from
ἀγέροντο, as though it were imperfect

and not aorist; cf. 908 infr., κέκλομαι
from κέκλετο.
896. ἔπεισιν, 'will come near.'
897. ἀφειδείως, 'ungrudgingly': here
only in this form, v. n. 527.
898. τερείνης, repeated from 1. 1143,
slightly altered from Od. 9. 449, τέρεν'
ἄνθεα ποίης.
899. λεξάμεναι, 'having gathered.'
ἀνακλινθεῖσαι of the schol. may point to
an earlier version of the preceding words,
κατὰ καλά, or something of the sort.
αὐτὴν ὥρην, 'when the usual hour
comes round': for the accusative,
v. n. 417.
901. τῷδ', 'to-day,' Platt's reading
for MSS. τῷ, which is 'on that day
when...,' as in Od. 5. 309, etc. For
ἤματι τῷδε, cf. Od. 20. 116, Il. 13.
234, etc., Arg. 2. 797 and 538 supr.
συναρέσσετε, 'agree with me in...,'
cf. 1100 infr., and Arg. 4. 373, θέμις ἦν
συναρέσσαμεν; for the form, v. n. 301.
902. παρατρέπει, stronger than in
L. & S., 'makes me change my mind';
it is rather 'turns me aside from the
path of duty.' In 946 infr., παρατροπέω
is 'beguile.'
903. εἰσαΐουσαι, v. n. 145.

ἐξ ἐμέθεν, μὴ πατρὸς ἐς οὔατα μῦθος ἵκηται.
τὸν ξεῖνόν με κέλονται, ὅτις περὶ βουσὶν ὑπέστη,   905
δῶρ' ἀποδεξαμένην ὀλοῶν ῥύσασθαι ἀέθλων.
αὐτὰρ ἐγὼ τὸν μῦθον ἐπήνεον, ἠδὲ καὶ αὐτὸν
κέκλομαι εἰς ὠπὴν ἑτάρων ἄπο μοῦνον ἱκέσθαι,
ὄφρα τὰ μὲν δασόμεσθα μετὰ σφίσιν, εἴ κεν ὀπάσσῃ
δῶρα φέρων, τῷ δ' αὖτε κακώτερον ἄλλο πόρωμεν   910
φάρμακον. ἀλλ' ἀπονόσφι πέλεσθέ μοι, εὖτ' ἂν ἵκηται.'
Ὣς ηὔδα· πάσῃσι δ' ἐπίκλοπος ἥνδανε μῆτις.
αὐτίκα δ' Αἰσονίδην ἑτάρων ἄπο μοῦνον ἐρύσσας
Ἄργος, ὅτ' ἤδη τήνδε κασιγνήτων ἐσάκουσεν
ἠερίην Ἑκάτης ἱερὸν μετὰ νηὸν ἰοῦσαν,   915
ἦγε διὲκ πεδίου· ἅμα δέ σφισιν εἵπετο Μόψος
Ἀμπυκίδης, ἐσθλὸς μὲν ἐπιπροφανέντας ἐνισπεῖν
οἰωνούς, ἐσθλὸς δὲ σὺν εὖ φράσσασθαι ἰοῦσιν.

906 ὑποδεξαμένην G.   909 μετὰ Stephanus, et fort. Ox. Pap. 4. 691: κατὰ codd.   ὀπάσσοι Paris. unus, Brunck.   913 ἀπὸ νόσφιν G.   914 ὃς ἤδη Koechly.   916 μετὰ vulg.   918 σὺν εὖ φράσσασθαι Vatt. tres, Paris. unus: συνευφράσσασθαι LG, vulg.

904. ἐξ ἐμέθεν, common phrase, repeated from Homer.

905. περὶ βουσίν. The genitive is more usual; but cf. Od. 2. 245, μαχήσεσθαι περὶ δαιτί.

ὑπέστη. The common Homeric form, as in Il. 21. 273; v. n. 501.

906. ῥύσασθαι, 'rescue from the trials.' Homer uses with preposition and genitive; for this, cf. Eur. Alc. 770, κακῶν γὰρ μυρίων ἐρρύσατο, Pindar, Herodotus, etc.

908. κέκλομαι, 'I summon': for the form, v. n. 895.

εἰς ὠπήν, cf. 821.

909. ὄφρα. Homer uses this occasionally with the future indicative, Il. 16. 243, Od. 17. 6, but more usually with the subjunctive. Ap. has the subjunctive after a past tense where Homer uses the optative; contrast Od. 1. 261 with 1307 infr.

μετά. So Stephanus, and perhaps also Ox. Pap. 4. 691, against MSS. κατά. It may be meant to reproduce the unique use of μετά in this sense in Il. 1. 368, καὶ τὰ μὲν εὖ δάσαντο μετὰ σφίσιν υἷες Ἀχαιῶν.

σφίσιν, 'ourselves,' v. n. 26.

ὀπάσσῃ, v. crit. note, and n. 26 supr. on αἴ κε.

911. μοι, ethic dative, of course, not governed by ἀπονόσφι, 'Retire, I beg of you.'

912–946. Jason sets forth with Mopsus and Argos; these two withdraw at the bidding of a crow, and he goes alone to meet Medea.

912. ἐπίκλοπος, v. n. 781.

914. ἐσάκουσεν. Here with genitive, as in Soph. El. 883; in 1. 766 with ἀπό; cf. 904 supr. with ἐκ.

915. ἠερίην, 'early in the morning,' v. n. 417.

916. διέκ, v. n. 73, cf. 888.

917. ἐπιπροφανέντας, 'appearing before him': here only, but the single compound is Homeric.

918. σὺν...φράσσασθαι, 'to give counsel to those going on a journey.' For the word, v. n. 87; for the tmesis, cf. H. Hom. Herm. 294, σὺν δ' ἄρα φρασσάμενος. Goodwin takes it as a compound συνευφράζομαι. The scholiast and the Latin translators take ἰοῦσιν of the birds; ἀγαθὸς μὲν καὶ ἐπιφανέντας

Ἔνθ' οὔπω τις τοῖος ἐπὶ προτέρων γένετ' ἀνδρῶν,
οὔθ' ὅσοι ἐξ αὐτοῖο Διὸς γένος, οὔθ' ὅσοι ἄλλων   920
ἀθανάτων ἥρωες ἀφ' αἵματος ἐβλάστησαν,
οἷον Ἰήσονα θῆκε Διὸς δάμαρ ἤματι κείνῳ
ἠμὲν ἐσάντα ἰδεῖν, ἠδὲ προτιμυθήσασθαι.
τὸν καὶ παπταίνοντες ἐθάμβεον αὐτοὶ ἑταῖροι
λαμπόμενον χαρίτεσσιν· ἐγήθησεν δὲ κελεύθῳ   925
Ἀμπυκίδης, ἤδη που ὀισσάμενος τὰ ἔκαστα.
    Ἔστι δέ τις πεδίοιο κατὰ στίβον ἐγγύθι νηοῦ
αἴγειρος φύλλοισιν ἀπειρεσίοις κομόωσα,
τῇ θαμὰ δὴ λακέρυζαι ἐπηυλίζοντο κορῶναι.
τάων τις μεσσηγὺς ἀνὰ πτερὰ κινήσασα   930
ὑψοῦ ἐπ' ἀκρεμόνων Ἥρης ἠνίπαπε βουλάς·

927 ἔσκε O. Schneider.   931 βουλαῖς O. Schneider.

καὶ ἀπιόντας εὖ σημειώσασθαι schol.; de Mirmont translates it 'habile à conseiller ceux avec qui il allait'; but it is best, with Lobeck, to take it as *iter facientibus.*

919. ἐπί. Typical alteration of *Il.* 5. 637, ἐπὶ προτέρων ἀνθρώπων.

921. ἀφ' αἵματος, cf. *Il.* 19. 105, οἵ θ' αἵματος ἐξ ἐμεῦ εἰσίν : ib. 111, οἳ σῆς ἐξ αἵματος εἰσὶ γενέθλης.

922. θῆκε. Imitated from *Il.* 2. 482, τοῖον ἄρ' Ἀτρείδην θῆκε Ζεὺς ἤματι κείνῳ.

923. ἐσάντα, imitated also from *Od.* 11. 143, ἔτλη ἐσάντα ἰδεῖν οὐδὲ προτιμυθήσασθαι.

925. λαμπόμενον, 'radiant with every grace': cf. *Od.* 6. 237, κάλλεϊ καὶ χάρισι στίλβων : *Il.* 3. 392, κάλλεΐ τε στίλβων καὶ εἵμασιν : and 443 supr., 1018 infr.

χαρίτεσσιν, v. n. 444.

ἐγήθησεν. This takes the accusative in Homer, *Il.* 9. 77, τίς ἂν τάδε γηθήσειε. For the dative, cf. *Arg.* 1. 449, 2. 707.

926. ὀισσάμενος. The -σσ- is faulty, v. n. 456. The description of the beautification of Jason is imitated in *Aen.* 1. 589, where Aeneas is beautified by his mother before he appears to Dido; 'namque ipsa decoram Caesariem nato genetrix lumenque iuventae Purpureum et laetos oculis adflarat honores.'

927. στίβον, 'along the path': contrast 1218, v. n. 534.

928. κομόωσα, cf. Theoc. 7. 7-9, ταὶ δὲ παρ' αὐτὰν Αἴγειροι πτελέαι τε εὔσκιον ἄλσος ὕφαινον Χλωροῖσιν πετάλοισι κατασταφέες κομόωσαι. With 927, cf. *Il.* 2. 811, ἔστι δέ τις προπάροιθε πόλιος αἰπεῖα κολώνη.

929. λακέρυζαι, 'chattering,' epithet of the crow in Hes. *Op.* 747, cf. Arat. 949, λακέρυζα...κορώνη.

ἐπηυλίζοντο, 'used to roost.' The simple verb is Homeric, the compound is first in Thucydides, v. n. 325; cf. *Od.* 5. 65, ἔνθα δέ τ' ὄρνιθες τανυσίπτεροι εὐνάζοντο Σκῶπές θ' ἵρηκές τε τανύγλωσσοί τε κορῶναι.

κορῶναι. The crow was a lucky omen in affairs of love; cf. Nonnus, *Dion.* 3. 119, ἐπαινήσεις δὲ κορώνην, Καὶ γαμίων καλέσεις με θεόπροπον ὄρνιν Ἐρώτων.

930. μεσσηγύς, 'as she clapped her wings,' cf. for the adv. 665 supr., n. 307. Compare the obvious imitation in Nonn. *Dion.* 3. 102, καὶ πτέρα σεισαμένη φιλοκέρτομον ἰαχε φωνήν.

931. ὑψοῦ, cf. *Il.* 13. 12, ὑψοῦ ἐπ' ἀκρεμόνων...

ἀκρεμόνων, 'branches.' First in Eur. *Cyc.* 455.

ἠνίπαπε, 'declared,' with some idea also of censure, v. n. 677.

This motif of the vocal bird is carried to extreme lengths in Ach. Tat. 1. 15. 8, where a lover passing through his lady's garden recognises grasshoppers and swallows, οἱ μὲν τὴν Ἠοῦς ᾄδοντες εὐνήν, αἱ δὲ τὴν τοῦ Τηρέως τράπεζαν.

'Ἀκλειὴς ὅδε μάντις, ὃς οὐδ' ὅσα παῖδες ἴσασιν
οἶδε νόῳ φράσσασθαι, ὁθούνεκεν οὔτε τι λαρὸν
οὔτ' ἐρατὸν κούρη κεν ἔπος προτιμυθήσαιτο
ἠιθέῳ, εὖτ' ἄν σφιν ἐπήλυδες ἄλλοι ἔπωνται.   935
ἔρροις, ὦ κακόμαντι, κακοφραδές· οὐδέ σε Κύπρις
οὔτ' ἀγανοὶ φιλέοντες ἐπιπνείουσιν Ἔρωτες.'
Ἴσκεν ἀτεμβομένη· μείδησε δὲ Μόψος ἀκούσας
ὀμφὴν οἰωνοῖο θεήλατον, ὧδέ τ' ἔειπεν·
'Τύνη μὲν νηόνδε θεᾶς ἴθι, τῷ ἔνι κούρην   940
δήεις, Αἰσονίδη· μάλα δ' ἠπίη ἀντιβολήσεις

936 οὐδὲ codd., Peile: οὔτε Seaton, Mooney.

932. ἀκλειής. An Alexandrine form of ἀκλεής first found here; it is in a poet ap. Plut. *de aud. poet.* 38 F, ἀκλειὴς ἀδηλος ὑπαὶ νεφέεσσι σκεδάσθη, and in Nonnus. Cf. Verg. *Aen.* 4. 65, 'heu vatum ignarae mentes.'

οὐδ' ὅσα. This is generally taken to refer to the quarrel between Callimachus and Apollonius, with particular reference to Call. *H. Ap.* 106, οὐκ ἄγαμαι τὸν ἀοιδὸν ὃς οὐδ' ὅσα πόντος ἀείδει; but there are difficulties. It cannot be that Callimachus is the crow, and Mopsus takes the part of Apollonius; for the advice offered is taken. Linde ingeniously suggests that the lines were added when the poem was revised at Rhodes, in response to an objection that the earlier edition made no reference to the withdrawal of Mopsus. But all the theories are sketchy; and there is much to be said for Platt's view that there is no allusion here at all. 'Cannot two poets,' he says, 'use the words οὐδ' ὅσα without being accused of imitating or parodying each other?'

933. νόῳ, cf. *Il.* 16. 646, φράζετο θυμῷ.

ὁθούνεκεν. Here Apollonius aspirates, though he has the Ionic τούνεκα in 1. 338; the former shows the influence of tragedy, cf. 4. 1087, ἔκητι, 'quantum attinet ad.'

λαρόν, 'sweet,' but in Homer only of actual taste, as in *Arg.* 1. 456, εἴδατα καὶ μέθυ λαρόν.

935. ἠιθέῳ. For this conjunction with κούρῃ, cf. *Il.* 22. 128, παρθένος ἠίθεός τ' ὀαρίζετον ἀλλήλοιιν.

ἐπήλυδες, 'strangers': first in tragedy.

936. κακόμαντι. This is reminiscent of Agamemnon's abuse of Calchas in *Il.* 1. 106, μάντι κακῶν, κ.τ.λ.

κακοφραδές, 'you and your evil thoughts.' This is similarly used in abuse by Homer, *Il.* 23. 483, νεῖκος ἄριστε, κακοφραδές.

οὐδέ. Read this with Peile and the MSS., against Seaton's οὔτε, which is neither necessary for the Greek, nor an improvement in sense.

937. ἀγανοί, 'friendly': for a possible instance in the sense of 'respectful,' v. n. 78.

ἐπιπνείουσιν, 'breathe on thee in their kindness'; cf. Nonn. *Dion.* 3. 121, ἥλιτον, ἀλλά με Κύπρις ἐπέπνεεν. Homer has it usually in the most literal meaning, of the breath of the wind as in 1327 infr.: but cf. *Od.* 19. 138, ἐπέπνευσε φρεσὶ δαίμων.

Ἔρωτες, v. n. 452.

938. ἴσκεν, 'she spake,' v. n. 396.

ἀτεμβομένη, 'in reproach,' v. n. 99.

939. ὀμφήν. In Homer only of the voice of the gods, and it is an equally supernatural voice here; the bird speaks in its own tongue, and only Mopsus can understand.

θεήλατον, 'sent by Heaven.' Tragic, especially of plagues, etc.; but in Aesch. *Ag.* 1297, θεηλάτου βοός, it is in the literal sense, 'driven on by a god.'

941. δήεις, 'thou shalt find': this present with future meaning is peculiar to epic, Homer, Aratus, etc.

ἀντιβολήσεις, 'thou shalt meet her'; in this sense, the dative is Homeric, v. n. 179.

Κύπριδος ἐννεσίης, ἥ τοι συνέριθος ἀέθλων
ἔσσεται, ὡς δὴ καὶ πρὶν Ἀγηνορίδης φάτο Φινεύς.
νῶι δ᾽, ἐγὼν Ἄργος τε, δεδεγμένοι, εὖτ᾽ ἂν ἵκηαι,
τῷδ᾽ αὐτῷ ἐνὶ χώρῳ ἀπεσσόμεθ᾽· οἰόθι δ᾽ αὐτὸς   945
λίσσεό μιν πυκινοῖσι παρατροπέων ἐπέεσσιν.᾽
Ἧ ῥα περιφραδέως, ἐπὶ δὲ σχεδὸν ἤνεον ἄμφω.
οὐδ᾽ ἄρα Μηδείης θυμὸς τράπετ᾽ ἄλλα νοῆσαι,
μελπομένης περ ὅμως· πᾶσαι δέ οἱ, ἥντιν᾽ ἀθύροι
μολπήν, οὐκ ἐπὶ δηρὸν ἐφήνδανεν ἐψιάασθαι.   950
ἀλλὰ μεταλλήγεσκεν ἀμήχανος, οὐδέ ποτ᾽ ὄσσε
ἀμφιπόλων μεθ᾽ ὅμιλον ἔχ᾽ ἀτρέμας· ἐς δὲ κελεύθους
τηλόσε παπταίνεσκε, παρακλίνουσα παρειάς.
ἦ θαμὰ δὴ στηθέων ἐάλη κέαρ, ὁππότε δοῦπον

942 ἐννεσίαις Merkel. συνάριθμος G.   944 ἔστ᾽ ἂν Ziegler.   948 ἄλλο Merkel.
949 ὅμως G, Pariss. quatt.: ὁμῶς vulg.   950 ἐφήνδανον Pariss. quatt., Brunck.
954 στήθεσφ᾽ Herwerden.   ἐάλη Platt: ἐάγη codd.: ἐκ...ἐάγη Damste.

942. ἐννεσίης, v. n. 29.
συνέριθος, 'helper.' Similarly Athene
in disguise offers to be συνέριθος to
Nausicaa, Od. 6. 32. The word is always
feminine, and the schol. there derives it
as ἡ συνεργοῦσα τὰ ἔρια. The root, however, is rather ἐρ-, ἀρ-, as in ἀρτύω.
943. Φινεύς. For Phineus and his
prophecies, v. n. 549.
944. δεδεγμένοι, 'waiting until': this
is an adaptation of Il. 10. 62, δεδεγμέ-
νος εἰσόκεν ἔλθῃς, etc.
945. οἰόθι, like the Homeric οἰόθεν.
This is first in Ap. and Aratus 376.
946. παρατροπέων, cf. 902.
947–1007. Jason and Medea meet
alone, and he implores her aid.
947. περιφραδέως,'prudently.' Homer
uses this only in the recurrent phrase
ὤπτησάν τε περιφραδέως. The adjective
is not in Ap., but occurs in the Hymns,
and in lyrics in Soph. Ant. 347, περι-
φραδὴς ἀνήρ.
σχεδόν, 'at once,' cf. 4. 1591. Elsewhere it is 'near,' either of time or
place, abs. in 1149, with genitive in
1073. Homer uses it of place only, except for the doubtful οὔτ᾽ ἄρ᾽ ὑπερθορέειν
σχεδὸν οὔτε περῆσαι 'Ρηιδίη, Il. 12. 53.
Compounds are used both of place
and of time. Homer has only αὐτοσχεδόν, cominus, which in Ap. means
'forthwith,' v. n. 148; cf. Arat. 901,

ἀστέρες ἀλλήλων αὐτοσχεδὸν ἰνδάλλονται, 'seem to draw nearer to each other.'
ἐπὶ...ἤνεον, in tmesi, 'agreed.'
949. μελπομένης, 'nor was her heart
turned to other thoughts, for all that
she was playing.' The word includes
both song and dance, from the time of
Homer, e.g. Od. 6. 101 of a game of
ball, Ναυσικάα...ἤρχετο μολπῆς.
950. ἐπὶ δηρόν, cf. Il. 9. 415. δηρόν
is common as adverb; as adjective, v. n.
811.
ἐφήνδανεν, v. n. 171 : for the singular
after a parenthesis, v. n. 193.
ἐψιάασθαι, 'play,' v. n. 118.
951. μεταλλήγεσκεν, 'kept continually ceasing,' v. n. 110.
952. μετά. The dative is more usual;
but cf. Il. 9. 54, μετὰ πάντας ἄριστος.
953. παρακλίνουσα, 'turning her
cheeks aside': cf. Od. 20. 301, ἦκα παρα-
κλίνας κεφαλήν, Arat. 738 of the moon,
αἰεὶ δ᾽ ἄλλοθεν ἄλλα παρακλίνουσα μέτωπα. παρακλιδόν in Arg. 1. 315, etc.,
is Homeric; cf. infr. 1008 ἐγκλιδόν.
954. θαμά, 'often,' Homeric: θαμινόν
infr. 1266 is un-Homeric.
στηθέων. For this genitive, the common αὐτοῦ is the nearest parallel. In
1056 the gen. is ablatival. Damste's ἐκ
for ἢ is presumably founded on some
such use as Il. 10. 94, κραδίη δέ μοι ἔξω
Στηθέων ἐκθρώσκει.

ἢ ποδὸς ἢ ἀνέμοιο παραθρέξαντα δοάσσαι.   955
αὐτὰρ ὅγ' οὐ μετὰ δηρὸν ἐελδομένῃ ἐφαάνθη
ὑψόσ' ἀναθρῴσκων ἅ τε Σείριος Ὠκεανοῖο,
ὃς δή τοι καλὸς μὲν ἀρίζηλός τ' ἐσιδέσθαι
ἀντέλλει, μήλοισι δ' ἐν ἄσπετον ἧκεν ὀιζύν·
ὣς ἄρα τῇ καλὸς μὲν ἐπήλυθεν εἰσοράασθαι   960
Αἰσονίδης, κάματον δὲ δυσίμερον ὦρσε φαανθείς.
ἐκ δ' ἄρα οἱ κραδίη στηθέων πέσεν, ὄμματα δ' αὔτως
ἤχλυσαν· θερμὸν δὲ παρηίδας εἷλεν ἔρευθος.
γούνατα δ' οὔτ' ὀπίσω οὔτε προπάροιθεν ἀεῖραι
ἔσθενεν, ἀλλ' ὑπένερθε πάγη πόδας. αἱ δ' ἄρα τείως   965

957 ἀναθρῴσκων L.   958 ὅς ῥ' ἤτοι Hermann.   960 ἐσήλυθεν Pariss.
963 ἤχλυσαν supr. a scr. ε L: ἤχλυσεν G.

ἐάλη, *lit.* 'was constricted,' Platt's convincing emendation of mss. ἐάγη: Medea's heart could hardly be 'broken' every time she heard a noise. The nearest expression to that metaphor in Greek is the Homeric κατεκλάσθη ἦτορ, *Od.* 4. 538.

955. παραθρέξαντα, 'whenever she thought that she heard the passing sound of a footfall, or of the wind.' The compound in this form is peculiar to Ap.; the Ionic aorist θρέξασκον is Homeric.

δοάσσαι, v. n. 21.

956. μετὰ δηρόν, cf. n. 950.

ἐελδομένῃ, 'to her longing eyes,' v. n. 383, and cf. *Il.* 7. 7, Τρώεσσιν ἐελδομένοισι φανήτην.

957. ἀναθρῴσκων, *i.e.* striding along with a springing step. Note the variant of *Il.* 13. 140, ὕψι δ' ἀναθρῴσκων: 13. 371, ὕψι βιβάντα: and *Il.* 3. 23, μακρὰ βιβάς; and v. n. 556.

Σείριος, cf. *Arg.* 2. 516 for the legend of the scorching of the Cyclades by Sirius, and the help of Aristaeus. The genitive is ablatival, v. n. 954.

958. ἀρίζηλος, 'clear,' Homeric; cf. Pind. *Ol.* 2. 55, ἀστὴρ ἀρίζηλος. There seems to be some confusion in *Arg.* 2. 250, with ἀρίδηλος, for which v. n. 615. This simile is founded on the comparison of Hector with an οὔλιος ἀστήρ in *Il.* 11. 62, rather than on *Il.* 5. 5, as Mooney suggests; cf. also *Il.* 22. 26–31.

959. ἀντέλλει, 'rises,' post-Homeric. It is used of the sun in Soph. *O. C.* 1246, Hdt. 1. 204; v. n. 520.

ἐν...ἧκεν, cf. *Il.* 20. 80, ἐνῆκε δέ οἱ μένος.

961. κάματον, v. n. 289.

δυσίμερον, 'tortured by love': cf. *Arg.* 4. 4, ἄτης πῆμα δυσίμερον, Nonn. *Dion.* 42. 191. This adj. is first in Ap. The description of the arrival of Jason in all his beauty is imitated in *Aen.* 8. 588, of Pallas riding forth to battle: 'chlamyde et pictis conspectus in armis, Qualis ubi Oceani perfusus Lucifer unda, Quem Venus ante alios astrorum diligit ignis, Extulit os sacrum caelo tenebrasque resolvit.'

962. ἐκ...πέσεν, cf. 289, and *Il.* 10. 94, κραδίη δέ μοι ἔξω Στηθέων ἐκθρῴσκει.

αὔτως, *i.e.* just as she was.

963. ἤχλυσαν, 'grew misty,' intransitive; L. and S. read ἤχλυσεν, transitive, cf. Qu. Sm. 1. 598, ἀμφὶ δέ οἱ νὺξ Ὀφθαλμοὺς ἤχλυσε. Compare Archil. 103, ἔρως ὑπὸ καρδίαν ἐλυσθεὶς Πολλὴν κατ' ἀχλὺν ὀμμάτων ἔχευεν.

ἔρευθος, post-Homeric, v. n. 163. Contrast Verg. (?) *Ciris* 180, 'nullus in ore rubor; ubi enim rubor, obstat amori.' Cf. Leo's suggested supplementary lines to the Chorus of Seneca, *Medea* 97–8, 'Talem dum iuvenis conspicit, en rubor Perfudit subito purpureus genas.'

964. προπάροιθεν, apparently adapted from *Il.* 3 218, σκῆπτρον δ' οὔτ' ὀπίσω οὔτε προπρηνὲς ἐνώμα.

ἀμφίπολοι μάλα πᾶσαι ἀπὸ σφείων ἐλίασθεν.
τὼ δ' ἄνεῳ καὶ ἄναυδοι ἐφέστασαν ἀλλήλοισιν,
ἢ δρυσίν, ἢ μακρῇσιν ἐειδόμενοι ἐλάτῃσιν,
αἵ τε παρᾶσσον ἔκηλοι ἐν οὔρεσιν ἐρρίζωνται,
νηνεμίῃ· μετὰ δ' αὖτις ὑπὸ ῥιπῆς ἀνέμοιο   970
κινύμεναι ὁμάδησαν ἀπείριτον· ὡς ἄρα τώγε
μέλλον ἅλις φθέγξασθαι ὑπὸ πνοιῇσιν Ἔρωτος.
γνῶ δέ μιν Αἰσονίδης ἄτῃ ἐνιπεπτηυῖαν
θευμορίῃ, καὶ τοῖον ὑποσσαίνων φάτο μῦθον·
   'Τίπτε με, παρθενική, τόσον ἅζεαι, οἶον ἐόντα;   975
οὔ τοι ἐγών, οἷοί τε δυσαυχέες ἄλλοι ἔασιν
ἀνέρες, οὐδ' ὅτε περ πάτρῃ ἔνι ναιετάασκον,
ἦα πάρος. τῶ μή με λίην ὑπεραίδεο, κούρη,
ἤ τι παρεξερέεσθαι, ὅ τοι φίλον, ἠέ τι φάσθαι.
ἀλλ' ἐπεὶ ἀλλήλοισιν ἱκάνομεν εὐμενέοντες,   980
χώρῳ ἐν ἠγαθέῳ, ἵνα τ' οὐ θέμις ἔστ' ἀλιτέσθαι,

---

968 ἐελδόμενοι G.   970 ὑπαὶ vulg.   973 ἐνιπεπτηυῖαν vulg.: ἐνὶ πεπτηυῖαν L:
περιπεριπεπτηυῖαν G.   977 ναιετάεσκον vulg.   980 ἀλλήλοισιν G, Pariss.
quatt., Vrat., Vind.: ἀλλήλοις L.

966. ἐλίασθεν, v. n. 827, cf. Medea's request in 911 supr.

967. ἄνεῳ, v. n. 503.

ἐφέστασαν ἀλλήλοισιν, taken from *Il.* 13. 133, etc.

968. ἐειδόμενοι, cf. 4. 221, 1616, 'like.' Homer uses this participle uncontracted, the aorist contracted also; the uncontracted present is first in Pindar. The words are a variant of *Il.* 5. 560, ἐλάτῃσιν ἐοικότες ὑψηλῇσιν; cf. Val. Flacc. 7. 405, 'abietibus tacitis aut inmotis cyparissis Adsimiles rapidus quas nondum miscuit auster.'

969. παρᾶσσον, 'side by side,' v. n. 125.

970. νηνεμίῃ. This adverb, formed from the Homeric νηνεμία, is here and in Arat. 1033 only.

ῥιπῆς, typical variant of *Il.* 15. 171, ὑπὸ ῥιπῆς βορέαο, etc.: cf. 1372 infr., and 43 supr.

971. ὁμάδησαν, 'rustle,' v. n. 564.

ἀπείριτον, adv. 'unceasingly'; the adjective is Homeric. This passage is based on the description of the warriors

in *Il.* 12. 131 f.: τὼ μὲν ἄρα προπάροιθε πυλάων ὑψηλάων Ἕστασαν ὡς ὅτε τε δρύες οὔρεσιν ὑψικάρηνοι, Αἵ τ' ἄνεμον μίμνουσι καὶ ὑετὸν ἤματα πάντα, Ῥίζῃσιν μεγάλῃσι διηνεκέεσσ' ἀραρυῖαι.

974. θευμορίῃ, 'by heaven's will,' here probably adverb corresponding to the Homeric θεσπεσίῃ, v. n. 676. This situation is much less effectively treated in Val. Flacc. 7. 407; 'ergo ut erat vultu defixus uterque silenti, Noxque suum peragebat iter, iam iam ora levare Aesonidem farique cupit Medea priorem.'

ὑποσσαίνων, v. n. 396.

976. δυσαυχέες, 'vain boasters,' here only.

978. ὑπεραίδεο, 'stand in too great shame,' compound of Homeric αἰδέομαι found here only.

979. παρεξερέεσθαι, here only, 'enquire.' παρὲξ ἐρέουσα are separate in *Od.* 23. 16.

981. ἠγαθέῳ, 'holy,' from ἄγαν· θεῖος, frequent in Homer of holy places. The metre recalls *Il.* 2. 722, Λήμνῳ ἐν ἠγαθέῃ.

ἀμφαδίην ἀγόρευε καὶ εἴρεο· μηδέ με τερπνοῖς
φηλώσῃς ἐπέεσσιν, ἐπεὶ τὸ πρῶτον ὑπέστης
αὐτοκασιγνήτῃ μενοεικέα φάρμακα δώσειν.
πρός σ' αὐτῆς Ἑκάτης μειλίσσομαι ἠδὲ τοκήων   985
καὶ Διός, ὃς ξείνοις ἱκέτῃσί τε χεῖρ' ὑπερίσχει·
ἀμφότερον δ', ἱκέτης ξεῖνός τέ τοι ἐνθάδ' ἱκάνω,
χρειοῖ ἀναγκαίῃ γουνούμενος. οὐ γὰρ ἄνευθεν
ὑμείων στονόεντος ὑπέρτερος ἔσσομ' ἀέθλου.
σοὶ δ' ἂν ἐγὼ τίσαιμι χάριν μετόπισθεν ἀρωγῆς,   990
ᾗ θέμις, ὡς ἐπέοικε διάνδιχα ναιετάοντας,
οὔνομα καὶ καλὸν τεύχων κλέος· ὡς δὲ καὶ ὧλλοι
ἥρωες κλήσουσιν ἐς Ἑλλάδα νοστήσαντες
ἡρώων τ' ἄλοχοι καὶ μητέρες, αἵ νύ που ἤδη
ἡμέας ἠιόνεσσιν ἐφεζόμεναι γοάουσιν·   995
τάων ἀργαλέας κεν ἀποσκεδάσειας ἀνίας.
δή ποτε καὶ Θησῆα κακῶν ὑπελύσατ' ἀέθλων

987 δ' om. Merkel.   ξεῖνός τ' ἔτι vulg.   991 ᾗ Platt: ἢ codd., edd.
992 ἄλλοι Vatt. duo, Pariss., Wellauer.   994 που G, L 16: ποτ' vulg.
997 ὑπέλυεν G: ὑπέλυσεν Pierson.

982. **ἀμφαδίην**, 'openly,' v. n. 97.
983. **φηλώσῃς**, 'beguile,' first in tragedy, Aesch. *Ag.* 492, etc.
ὑπέστης, 'thou didst promise,' v. n. 501; this is modelled on *Il.* 4. 267, ὡς τὸ πρῶτον ὑπέστην.
984. **μενοεικέα**, 'which my soul desires': a common epithet in Homer of meat and drink.
985. **μειλίσσομαι**, 'entreat,' v. n. 105.
986. **ξείνοις**, cf. 193, and *Od.* 6. 207, πὰρ γὰρ Διός εἰσιν ἅπαντες ξεῖνοι.
988. **χρειοῖ ἀναγκαίῃ**. Phrase repeated from *Il.* 8. 57.
γουνούμενος. Homeric, but used only in present and imperfect.
989. **στονόεντος**, 'grievous.' Homeric, and recalls the στονόεντα ἀέθλους of Jason in Hes. *Th.* 994; but it is a stock phrase, especially in Hesiod.
ὑπέρτερος. In Homer, this is 'nobler,' or of the parts of a victim, 'outer.' This sense, 'triumphant over,' is first in tragedy, as in Eur. *Med.* 921, ἐχθρῶν τῶν ἐμῶν ὑπερτέρους: it is *lit.* 'greater than,' *e.g. Arg.* 1. 682, μύρια δηιοτῆτος ὑπέρτερα πήματα μίμνει. **ὑμείων**

is 'you and the gods' (Mooney), rather than 'you and your sister' (Seaton).
991. **ᾗ**. For the form, v. crit. notes and appendix, p. 141.
ἐπέοικε. For this accusative and infinitive, cf. *Il.* 1. 126, λαοὺς δ' οὐκ ἐπέοικε παλίλλογα ταῦτ' ἐπαγείρειν : it takes dative in *Il.* 9. 392.
διάνδιχα, 'in widely separated places,' v. n. 23.
992. **κλέος**. Jason made a similar offer to Aeetes in 391 supr.
993. **κλήσουσιν**. This form is first in H. Hom. *Hel.* 31. 18. Of the uncontracted forms, Apollonius uses κληίζεται, κεκλήισται, and ἐκλήισται, 4. 1153, 618, 990.
995. **ἐφεζόμεναι**, common with dative in Homer; it is c. gen. in Pind. *Nem.* 4. 67, cf. 1001 infr.
996. **ἀποσκεδάσειας**. This compound is in *Il.* 19. 309, v. n. 214. It is Homeric also *in tmesi*, cf. 1360; but *Od.* 8. 149 is the simple verb, σκέδασον δ' ἀπὸ κήδεα θυμοῦ. This line recalls *Od.* 17. 244, τῷ κέ τοι ἀγλαίας γε διασκεδάσειεν ἁπάσας.
997. **ὑπέλυσατο**, slight alteration of *Il.* 1. 401, ὑπελύσαο δεσμῶν.

παρθενικὴ Μινωὶς ἐυφρονέουσ' 'Αριάδνη,
ἥν ῥά τε Πασιφάη κούρη τέκεν 'Ηελίοιο.
ἀλλ' ἡ μὲν καὶ νηός, ἐπεὶ χόλον εὔνασε Μίνως,   1000
σὺν τῷ ἐφεζομένη πάτρην λίπε· τὴν δὲ καὶ αὐτοὶ
ἀθάνατοι φίλαντο, μέσῳ δέ οἱ αἰθέρι τέκμαρ
ἀστερόεις στέφανος, τόν τε κλείουσ' 'Αριάδνης,
πάννυχος οὐρανίοισιν ἐλίσσεται εἰδώλοισιν.
ὣς καὶ σοὶ θεόθεν χάρις ἔσσεται, εἴ κε σαώσῃς   1005
τόσσον ἀριστήων ἀνδρῶν στόλον. ἦ γὰρ ἔοικας
ἐκ μορφῆς ἀγανῇσιν ἐπητείῃσι κεκάσθαι.'
     'Ὣς φάτο κυδαίνων· ἡ δ' ἐγκλιδὸν ὄσσε βαλοῦσα

1001 λίπε...οἱ δὲ corr. man. sec.: λίπε τὴν δὲ L: λίπεν· οἱ δὲ Merkel.
1004 οὐρανίοις ἐνελίσσεται Merkel.   1005 σαώσῃς G: σαώσεις L, vulg.:
σαώσαις Paris. unus, Brunck.

998. ἐυφρονέουσα, 'with gracious intent,' cf. 484 supr.

1000. χόλον εὔνασε, from εὐνάζω, 'lulled his anger to rest': cf. Od. 4. 758, εὔνησε γόον, from εὐνάω. There are various forms of this legend of Ariadne: in Od. 11. 324, when Theseus and Ariadne reached the island of Dia (Naxos), she was slain by Artemis, while according to other versions, she was deserted there, and rescued and taken to wife by Dionysus. This version occurs in Arg. 4. 432, but is suppressed here: similarly the account of the Lemnian massacre in Book 1 is suppressed at first, but told in detail at a later stage. Ap. is much too fond of this inartistic method of showing that he knows several forms of a legend.

1001. ἐφεζομένη, for the genitive, v. n. 995.

1002. φίλαντο, the Homeric use; contrast 66 supr.

τέκμαρ, 'her sign.' This sense is first in Pindar and tragedy; cf. Eur. Hec. 1273, κυνὸς ταλαίνης σῆμα, ναυτίλοις τέκμαρ, following the explanation of Eustathius σημεῖον. It means 'fixed place' of stars in Arg. 1. 499, ἔμπεδον αἰὲν ἐν αἰθέρι τέκμαρ ἔχουσιν.

1003. στέφανος, 'her crown of stars'; this may be based on Arat. 71 f., αὐτοῦ κἀκείνης στέφανος τὸν ἀγαυὸς ἔθηκεν Σῆμ' ἔμεναι Διόνυσος ἀποιχομένης 'Αριάδνης. V. n. 141 for another instance of the Alexandrine interest in astronomy.

κλείουσιν. This is reminiscent of Od. 1. 338, τά τε κλείουσιν ἀοιδοί, which is more closely imitated in Arg. 1. 18, νῆα μὲν οὖν οἱ πρόσθεν ἐπικλείουσιν ἀοιδοί, cf. Call. H. Ap. 18, and v. n. 277: cf. 357 supr.

1004. πάννυχος, 'all night.' This form is here only in Ap.; both it and παννύχιος, 2. 308, are Homeric.

εἰδώλοισιν, 'rolls among the constellations of Heaven.' The word is first in this technical sense here and in Arat. 383, ἐναρηρότες εἰδώλοισιν, etc., cf. Nonn. Dion. 1. 256, γούνατι δ' εἰδώλοιο κ.τ.λ.

1007. ἐκ, 'to judge from': cf. Il. 10. 68, πατρόθεν ἐκ γενεῆς ὀνομάζων ἄνδρα ἕκαστον, 'calling each man by his lineage and his father's name.'

ἐπητείῃσι, 'from thy lovely form thou art likely to excel in gentle courtesy' (Seaton). This is a form found here only for the Homeric ἐπητύς, Od. 21. 306, οὐ γάρ τευ ἐπητύος ἀντιβολήσεις. For the Homeric adj. ἐπητής, Od. 18. 128, ἐπητῇ δ' ἀνδρὶ ἔοικας, Ap. has a feminine ἐπήτιδες in 2. 987, as restored by Lobeck for MSS. ἐπητέες, ἐπητίες.

1008–1062. Medea gives Jason the charm, and explains how he must conduct himself in the trials.

1008. κυδαίνων. Homeric; lit. 'gladden with a mark of respect or honour.'

ἐγκλιδόν, cf. Arg. 1. 790, ἡ δ' ἐγκλιδὸν ὄσσε βαλοῦσα Παρθενικὰς ἐρύθηνε

νεκτάρεον μείδησ᾽· ἐχύθη δέ οἱ ἔνδοθι θυμὸς
αἴνῳ ἀειρομένης, καὶ ἀνέδρακεν ὄμμασιν ἄντην·   1010
οὐδ᾽ ἔχεν ὅττι πάροιθεν ἔπος προτιμυθήσαιτο,
ἀλλ᾽ ἄμυδις μενέαινεν ἀολλέα πάντ᾽ ἀγορεῦσαι.
προπρὸ δ᾽ ἀφειδήσασα θυώδεος ἔξελε μίτρης
φάρμακον· αὐτὰρ ὅγ᾽ αἶψα χεροῖν ὑπέδεκτο γεγηθώς.
καί νύ κέ οἱ καὶ πᾶσαν ἀπὸ στηθέων ἀρύσασα   1015
ψυχὴν ἐγγυάλιξεν ἀγαιομένη χατέοντι·
τοῖος ἀπὸ ξανθοῖο καρήατος Αἰσονίδαο
στράπτεν Ἔρως ἡδεῖαν ἀπὸ φλόγα· τῆς δ᾽ ἀμαρυγὰς
ὀφθαλμῶν ἥρπαζεν· ἰαίνετο δὲ φρένας εἴσω

1013 προπρὸ δὲ μειδήσασα v.l. in schol.   1016 ἀγαλλομένη Pariss., Brunck,
Wellauer.   1018 πέμπεν pro στράπτεν e glossemate Pariss. quatt.

παρηίδας, and n. 953. It is first in the
Homeric Hymns.
1009. νεκτάρεον, 'with a smile
divinely sweet.' The adv. is peculiar
to Ap., though the adj. is Homeric; v.n.
832. This is an adaptation of the
Homeric δακρυόεν γελάσασα, Il. 6. 484,
'smiling through her tears.'
1010. ἀειρομένης...οἱ. For the enal-
lage, cf. Arg. 1. 355, 4. 170, and H.
Hom. Dem. 37, τόφρα οἱ ἐλπὶς ἔθελγε
μέγαν νόον ἀχνυμένης περ.
ἀνέδρακεν, a clear adaptation of Il.
14. 436, ἀνέδρακεν ὀφθαλμοῖσιν, as in
100 supr., q.v.
1011. πάροιθεν, i.e. πρῶτον. Elsewhere of time it is 'formerly,' and here
it may rather be local, i.e. 'which word
to put in front of the next.' Cf. Dido's
dilemma in Aen. 4. 371, 'quae quibus
anteferam...' and Val. Flacc. 7. 433,
'nec quibus incipiat demens videt,
ordine nec quo Quove tenus, prima
cupiens effundere voce Omnia.'
1013. προπρό, v. n. 453.
ἀφειδήσασα, 'ungrudgingly,' v. n.
527.
θυώδεος, 'fragrant,' cf. 224: Homeric
word, and common in later poetry.
μίτρης, 'waistband,' v. n. 867.
1015. ἀρύσασα, 'drawing out.' First
in Hes. Sc. 301 of drawing of wine,
οἵ γε μὲν ἐτράπεον, τοὶ δ᾽ ἤρυον; for this
use cf. Emped. frag. 138 D, ap. Arist.
Poet. 21. 5, χαλκῷ ἀπὸ ψυχὴν ἀρύσας.
1016. ἐγγυάλιξεν, lit. 'put into the
hand,' i.e. 'give,' Homeric. χατέοντι is

better taken with this than with ἀγαιομένη, as in Seaton's translation: i.e. 'in her
loving admiration she would have given
her very soul to him, had he so desired
it,' rather than 'exulting in his desire.'
ἀγαιομένη, 'in loving admiration,'
v. n. 470.
1018. ἀπό...στράπτεν. This compound is not recognised by the lexicographers; contrast Arat.430, ἀπαστράψαντος
from ἀπ-ἀστράπτω. This passage recalls
the earlier comparison of Love with fire.
For the simple verb, cf. 1216; it is first
in Soph. O.C. 1515 in the sense of
ἀστράπτω. Compare also Soph. frag.
(Pearson), Vol. 2. 474, τοίαν Πέλοψ
ἴυγγα θηρατηρίαν Ἔρωτος, ἀστραπήν
τιν᾽ ὀμμάτων ἔχει: Moschus, Europa 86,
ἵμερον ἀστράπτεσκε: and for references
to the power of Love residing in the
eyes, Pearson in Class. Rev. 23 (1909),
256 B.
Ἔρως. This may be developed from
Eur. Med. 526 f., where Jason says that
Cypris, not Medea was his saviour, and
that Medea was unable to act otherwise
under the persuasion of Love, esp. 530,
ὡς Ἔρως σ᾽ ἠνάγκασε Τόξοις ἀφύκτοις
τοὐμὸν ἐκσῶσαι δέμας.
ἀμαρυγάς, 'captivated her flashing
eyes': cf. H. Hom. Her. 45, ἀπ᾽
ὀφθαλμῶν ἀμαρυγαί, and v. n. 288. Cf.
also Ov. Am. 2. 19. 19, 'tu quoque,
quae nostros rapuisti nuper ocellos.'
1019. ἰαίνετο, 'was warmed.' Modelled
probably on Il. 23. 597, τοῖο δὲ θυμὸς
Ἰάνθη, ὡς εἴ τε περὶ σταχύεσσιν ἐέρση

τηκομένη, οἷόν τε περὶ ῥοδέῃσιν ἐέρση 1020
τήκεται ἠῴοισιν ἰαινομένη φαέεσσιν.
ἄμφω δ' ἄλλοτε μέν τε κατ' οὔδεος ὄμματ' ἔρειδον
αἰδόμενοι, ὁτὲ δ' αὖτις ἐπὶ σφίσι βάλλον ὀπωπάς,
ἱμερόεν φαιδρῇσιν ὑπ' ὀφρύσι μειδιόωντες.
ὀψὲ δὲ δὴ τοίοισι μόλις προσπτύξατο κούρη· 1025
'Φράζεο νῦν, ὥς κέν τοι ἐγὼ μητίσομ' ἀρωγήν.
εὖτ' ἂν δὴ μετιόντι πατὴρ ἐμὸς ἐγγυαλίξῃ
ἐξ ὄφιος γενύων ὀλοοὺς σπείρασθαι ὀδόντας,
δὴ τότε μέσσην νύκτα διαμμοιρηδὰ φυλάξας,
ἀκαμάτοιο ῥοῇσι λοεσσάμενος ποταμοῖο, 1030
οἶος ἄνευθ' ἄλλων ἐνὶ φάρεσι κυανέοισιν
βόθρον ὀρύξασθαι περιηγέα· τῷ δ' ἔνι θῆλυν
ἀρνειὸν σφάζειν, καὶ ἀδαίετον ὠμοθετῆσαι,

1020 περὶ ῥοδέῃσιν Wellauer, Schaefer : περιρροδέοισιν L : περιρροδέεσσιν G : περὶ ῥοδέοισιν vulg.   ἐέρση L.   1023 τοτὲ δ' Pariss. quatt.

Λήϊου ἀλδήσκοντος, where Lange, followed by Leaf, reads dative, but considers that Apollonius must have had the nominative in his text; cf. Il. 24. 321, ἐνὶ φρεσὶ θυμὸς ἰάνθη, and v. n. 726.

1020. τηκομένη, 'melting': cf. Od. 19. 136, κατατήκομαι ἦτορ.

ῥοδέῃσιν. Archil. frag. 29 has ῥοδῆς; the uncontracted form is found here only. With this simile, cf. Aesch. Ag. 1391, χαίρουσαν οὐδὲν ἧσσον ἢ διοσδότῳ Γάνει σπορητὸς κάλυκος ἐν λοχεύμασιν.

1021. φαέεσσιν, 'in the light of day.' This dative is first in Hes. ap. Paus. 9. 40. 6: Homer, Od. 16. 15, etc., uses the plural in the sense of 'eyes.'

1022. ἔρειδον, cf. Eur. Iph. Aul. 1123, ἐς γῆν ἐρείσασ' ὄμμα, and 22 supr.

1023. σφίσι, i.e. ἀλλήλοις, v. n. 26.

ὀπωπάς, here and in 4. 1670, 'eyes'; in 2. 109, 445 'eyeballs.' Homer uses it of the power of sight, Od. 9. 512, ἀμαρτήσεσθαι ὀπωπῆς.

1024. ἱμερόεν, cf. 1009, and Il. 18. 570, ἱμερόεν κιθάριζε. The adverb is stronger here, more closely connected with ἵμερος, i.e. 'with the light of love beneath their radiant brows' (Seaton).

ὑπ' ὀφρύσι, cf. Il. 13. 88, ὑπ' ὀφρύσι δάκρυα λεῖβον.

1025. προσπτύξατο, 'addressed,' properly 'embraced': cf. 1104, v. n. 782.

1026. μητίσομαι, 'devise': cf. Il. 15. 349, θάνατον μητίσομαι, and the imitation in Val. Flacc. 7. 61, 'modo nostra prior tu perfice iussa.'

1027. ἐγγυαλίξῃ, 'give,' v. n. 1016.

1028. σπείρασθαι. Un-Homeric, but common in Hesiod; the inf. is epexegetic, 'so as to sow them.' The middle is unnecessary; cf. Eur. Bacc. 264, Κάδμον τε τὸν σπείραντα γηγενῆ στάχυν. For the passive, cf. 1055 infr.

1029. διαμμοιρηδά. Here only, 'watching for the middle of the night, when it divides,' intensifying μέσσην, 'when it divides exactly into half.' It is probably formed from Od. 14. 434, διεμοιρᾶτο: cf. Arat. 583, πλεῖον δίχα νυκτὸς ἰούσης, 'after midnight.'

1030. ἀκαμάτοιο, cf. 531; always epithet of fire in Homer. Apollonius extends the use in 765, 1343; here it is a variant of the commoner ἀενάοισιν, as in 860.

1031. κυανέοισι, 'dark blue,' properly, v. n. 140; here it is probably 'dark black,' cf. 1205.

1032. ὀρύξασθαι, imperative infinitive, as in Soph. Ph. 57, 1080, etc.: contrast πελέσθαι 700 supr.

περιηγέα, 'circular,' v. n. 138.

1033. ἀρνειόν, cf. Od. 10. 527, ἀρνειὸν ὄϊν θῆλύν τε μέλαιναν, 'a ram and a black ewe': ὄϊς is commoner as feminine.

αὐτῷ πυρκαϊὴν εὖ νηήσας ἐπὶ βόθρῳ.
μουνογενῆ δ᾽ Ἑκάτην Περσηίδα μειλίσσοιο, 1035
λείβων ἐκ δέπαος σιμβλήια ἔργα μελισσέων.
ἔνθα δ᾽ ἐπεί κε θεὰν μεμνημένος ἱλάσσηαι,
ἂψ ἀπὸ πυρκαϊῆς ἀναχάζεο· μηδέ σε δοῦπος
ἠὲ ποδῶν ὄρσῃσι μεταστρεφθῆναι ὀπίσσω,
ἠὲ κυνῶν ὑλακή, μή πως τὰ ἕκαστα κολούσας 1040
οὐδ᾽ αὐτὸς κατὰ κόσμον ἑοῖς ἑτάροισι πελάσσῃς.
ἦρι δὲ μυδήνας τόδε φάρμακον, ἠύτ᾽ ἀλοιφῇ
γυμνωθεὶς φαίδρυνε τεὸν δέμας· ἐν δέ οἱ ἀλκὴ
ἔσσετ᾽ ἀπειρεσίη μέγα τε σθένος, οὐδέ κε φαίης
ἀνδράσιν, ἀλλὰ θεοῖσιν ἰσαζέμεν ἀθανάτοισιν. 1045
πρὸς δὲ καὶ αὐτῷ δουρὶ σάκος πεπαλαγμένον ἔστω
καὶ ξίφος. ἔνθ᾽ οὐκ ἄν σε διατμήξειαν ἀκωκαὶ

1034 ἐννηήσας Pariss. quatt. 1036 μελισσέων Rzach: μελισσῶν codd.
1037 ἐπεί κε Vrat. in marg., et coni. Brunck: ἔπειτα vulg. 1038 ἂψ Brunck:
ἂψ δ᾽ codd. 1045 θεοῖς ἰσαζέμεν coni. Merkel.

For the qualification by θῆλυς, compare ὁ θῆλυς ὀρεύς, θῆλυς ἄνθρωπος in Aristotle. This female is actually called αὐτόν in 1209.

ἀδάετον, here only, schol. ἀδιαμέριστος, 'undivided.'

ὠμοθετῆσαι, 'sacrifice.' Properly to lay raw slices wrapped in fat on the fire, Od. 3. 458, μηρία...δίπτυχα ποιήσαντες, ἐπ᾽ αὐτῶν δ᾽ ὠμοθέτησαν; this is the regular ritual in Ouranian sacrifice before the worshippers themselves partake. It is here used loosely of a holocaust, which is the regular ritual to the nether powers.

1035. **μουνογενῆ**, v. crit. app. on 847.

μειλίσσοιο, 'propitiate,' v. n. 105. The change of construction should be noted; the infinitives mark the regular order of the ritual, the optative defines the part that applies particularly to the case in hand.

1036. **σιμβλήια**, compare 1. 880 of a hive in a rock, σιμβληὶς πέτρα, and Anth. Pal. 9. 226, σιμβληίδες μέλισσαι. Both words are Alexandrine; compare the still more pompous periphrasis for honey in Or. Arg. 574, μελισσορύτων ἀπὸ νασμῶν Λοιβάς.

1039. **μεταστρεφθῆναι**, 'drive thee to turn back': cf. Soph. O. C. 490, ἀφέρπειν

ἄστροφος, after offerings to the Eumenides: Aesch. Ch. 99, of καθάρματα, ἀστρόφοισιν ὄμμασιν: Theoc. 24. 95, ἂψ δὲ νέεσθαι Ἄστρεπτος, after casting away impure substances: and Ov. Fast. 6. 164, 'quique sacris adsunt respicere illa vetat.'

1040. **ὑλακή**, v. n. 749.

κολούσας, 'ruining everything': cf. Od. 8. 211, ἕο δ᾽ αὐτοῦ πάντα κολούει, 'ruins all his own interests.'

1041. **ἑοῖς**, 'thy,' v. n. 26.

1042. **μυδήνας**, 'soaking.' Here only and in Lyc. 1008, ἔνθα μυδαίνει ποτοῖς Ὠκίναρος γῆν; it is repeated infr. 1247. μυδαλέος in 2. 1106 is Homeric.

1043. **φαίδρυνε**, 'anoint thy body with it, as though with unguent,' v. n. 300.

οἱ, i.e. σοί, v. n. 26.

1045. **ἰσαζέμεν**, 'to be equal to.' This intransitive use is first in Plato and in late prose. In Homer it means either 'to liken one's self to,' Il. 24. 607, οὕνεκ᾽ ἄρα Λητοῖ ἰσάσκετο καλλιπαρήῳ, or 'to make equal,' Il. 12. 435, σταθμὸν ἔχουσα καὶ εἴριον ἀμφὶς ἀνέλκει Ἰσάζουσα.

1046. **πεπαλαγμένον**, 'sprinkled,' reminiscent of Od. 22. 184, σάκος εὐρὺ γέρον, πεπαλαγμένον ἄζῃ.

1047. **διατμήξειαν**, 'pierce thee,' Homeric, v. n. 343.

γηγενέων ἀνδρῶν, οὐδ' ἄσχετος ἀίσσουσα
φλὸξ ὀλοῶν ταύρων. τοῖός γε μὲν οὐκ ἐπὶ δηρὸν
ἔσσεαι, ἀλλ' αὐτῆμαρ· ὅμως σύγε μή ποτ' ἀέθλου   1050
χάζεο. καὶ δέ τοι ἄλλο παρὲξ ὑποθήσομ' ὄνειαρ.
αὐτίκ' ἐπὴν κρατεροὺς ζεύξῃς βόας, ὦκα δὲ πᾶσαν
χερσὶ καὶ ἠνορέῃ στυφελὴν διὰ νειὸν ἀρόσσῃς,
οἱ δ' ἤδη κατὰ ὦλκας ἀνασταχύωσι Γίγαντες
σπειρομένων ὄφιος δνοφερὴν ἐπὶ βῶλον ὀδόντων,   1055
αἵ κεν ὀρινομένους πολέας νειοῖο δοκεύσῃς,
λάθρῃ λᾶαν ἄφες στιβαρώτερον· οἱ δ' ἂν ἐπ' αὐτῷ,
καρχαλέαι κύνες ὥστε περὶ βρώμης, ὀλέκοιεν
ἀλλήλους· καὶ δ' αὐτὸς ἐπείγεο δηιοτῆτος
ἰθῦσαι. τὸ δὲ κῶας ἐς Ἑλλάδα τοῖο γ' ἕκητι   1060

1048 ἄσπετος Pariss. tres: ἄσπετον Koechly.   1054 ἀνασταχύωσι Paris. unus
et coni. Stephanus: ἀνασταχύουσι vulg.   1058 καρχαλέαι Ox. Pap. 10. 1243:
καρχαλέοι codd.: καρχαρέοι Brunck ex Et. Mag. 493. 1.   1060 τοῖο ῥ' ἕκητι vulg.:
τοῖο ἕκητι Paris. unus, Wellauer.

ἀκωκαί, 'spear points,' because the
men were born armed with spears.
1049. ἐπὶ δηρόν, 'for long': cf. Il. 9.
415, ἐπὶ δηρὸν δέ μοι αἰῶν Ἔσσεται.
1050. αὐτῆμαρ, 'for that one day,'
cf. 850.
1051. χάζεο, 'shrink not ever from
the contest,' v. n. 436.
παρέξ, 'in addition,' cf. 195; as
preposition, v. n. 743. 'I will tell thee
as well of another help.'
1053. ἀρόσσῃς, the aorist is commonly
used in Hesiod, etc. with a single -σ-;
cf. 497 supr.
1054. ὦλκας. Homer has only the
acc. singular; for the un-Homeric ὀλκός,
v. n. 141, cf. 413.
ἀνασταχύωσι, cf. 1338, 1354, lit.
'shoot up with ears' as of corn; the
verb is first in Ap.
1055. δνοφερήν, 'dark,' Homeric and
common in tragedy.
1056. νειοῖο, 'from the land,' ablatival
genitive, v. n. 954 and Goodwin, Gk. Gr.
1117.
δοκεύσῃς. Homeric, 'watch for their
rising': cf. Arg. 2. 1269, κῶας ὄφις
εἴρυτο δοκεύων.
1057. λᾶαν. This device occurs in
the story of Cadmus as related by
Pherecydes. The Sparti thought that

they were being attacked by one another
and fought fiercely until only five were
left.
στιβαρώτερον, 'heavy,' modelled
perhaps on Od. 8. 186, ἀναΐξας λάβε
δίσκον Μείζονα καὶ πάχετον, στιβαρώτερον
οὐκ ὀλίγον περ Ἡ οἵῳ Φαίηκες ἐδίσκεον
ἀλλήλοισι. The force of the comparative
is that of μείζονα, 'greater' than those
among which it lay, and here 'heavier'
than Jason would normally have picked
up; cf. θηλυτέρας n. 209, αἰπύτεροι
n. 238.
1058. καρχαλέαι, v. crit. app. p. 141.
The Greeks tend to use the masculine of
a dog when complimentary, the feminine
when the reverse; compare Peisander's
abuse of the Trojans, in Il. 13. 623, as
κακαὶ κύνες. So the feminine is in order
here of 'fierce' dogs. The adj. is
Homeric, Il. 21. 541 δίψῃ καρχαλέοι,
repeated in singular in Arg. 4. 1442.
For the internecine strife of the Earth-
born Men, cf. Seneca, Medea 469–70,
'Cum iussu meo Terrigena miles mutua
caede occidit.'
1060. ἰθῦσαι, 'rush into': for the
genitive, v. n. 629.
τοῖο ἕκητι, 'as far as this trial is
concerned.' Way takes τοῖο to refer to
κῶας, 'as far as the Fleece is in question.'

οἴσεαι ἐξ Αἴης τηλοῦ ποθί· νίσσεο δ᾽ ἔμπης,
ᾗ φίλον, ᾗ τοι ἔαδεν ἀφορμηθέντι νέεσθαι.᾽
῾Ως ἄρ᾽ ἔφη, καὶ σῖγα ποδῶν πάρος ὄσσε βαλοῦσα
θεσπέσιον λιαροῖσι παρηίδα δάκρυσι δεῦεν
μυρομένη, ὅ τ᾽ ἔμελλεν ἀπόπροθι πολλὸν ἑοῖο   1065
πόντον ἐπιπλάγξεσθαι· ἀνιηρῷ δέ μιν ἄντην
ἐξαῦτις μύθῳ προσεφώνεεν, εἷλέ τε χειρὸς
δεξιτερῆς· δὴ γάρ οἱ ἀπ᾽ ὀφθαλμοὺς λίπεν αἰδώς·
῾Μνώεο δ᾽, ἢν ἄρα δή ποθ᾽ ὑπότροπος οἴκαδ᾽ ἵκηαι,
οὔνομα Μηδείης· ὣς δ᾽ αὖτ᾽ ἐγὼ ἀμφὶς ἐόντος   1070
μνήσομαι. εἰπὲ δέ μοι πρόφρων τόδε, πῇ τοι ἔασιν
δώματα, πῇ νῦν ἔνθεν ὑπεὶρ ἅλα νηὶ περήσεις·
ἢ νύ που ἀφνειοῦ σχεδὸν ἵξεαι Ὀρχομενοῖο,

1061 νίσσεο edd.: νείσεο Pap., codd.   1062 ἥτοι L: ἡ τοι Pap.: εἴ τι G: ᾗ τοι Pariss., Vrat., Brunck, Wellauer, Platt: εἴ τοι vulg.   ἔαδεν Mooney: ἔαδεν codd.   1065 ὅ τ᾽ Merkel: ὅτ᾽ codd.   1066 ἐπιπλάγξασθαι Vatt. duo, Pariss. quatt., Brunck, Wellauer.   1067 μῦθον G.   1068 δὴ Brunck: ἤδη codd.

1061. νίσσεο. νείσεο is given by the
MSS. and the papyrus; but forms of
νείσομαι, νείσσομαι have been removed
by editors from our texts.

1062. ᾗ τοι, 'depart, then, wherever
thou wilt, wherever it is thy pleasure to
go when thou art gone forth from here.'
For the form, against the MSS. and
papyrus, v. crit. appendix on 991, p. 141;
for the repetition ᾗ...ᾗ, cf. 1071 infr.
ἔαδεν, v. n. 568.

1063-1145. Jason swears eternal
gratitude, and begs Medea to return to
Iolcus as his bride.

1064. θεσπέσιον, v. n. 443.
λιαροῖσι, v. n. 300. From this passage,
Brunck restored *tepido* for *tepidos* in Ov.
Am. 3. 6. 68, which is a clear imitation:
'illa oculos in humum directa modestos
Spargebat tepido flebilis imbre sinus.'

1065. μυρομένη, v. n. 463.
ὅ τ᾽. Read this rather than MSS. ὅτ᾽. ὅτε
cannot mean 'because,' and ὅτι cannot
be elided. This follows Aristophanes on
Od. 5. 357, ὅ τέ με σχεδίης ἀποβῆναι
ἀνώγει, where Merry and Riddell keep
ὅτε on the grounds that, like the Latin
cum, it can have a causal sense. Bekker
has restored ὅ τε and ὅ τ᾽ in several
passages of Homer, giving τε a general-

ising sense, and ὅ the force that it has
in *Od.* 1. 382, ὅ θαρσαλέως ἀγόρευεν, 'in
that he spake with boldness.'
ἀπόπροθι πολλόν, v. n. 313.
ἑοῖο, v. n. 26.
1066. ἐπιπλάγξεσθαι, cf. *Od.* 8. 14,
πόντον ἐπιπλαγχθείς.
ἄντην, v. n. 100.
1069. μνώεο. For the accusative, v. n.
639. Cf. Verg. (?) *Cat.* 4. 1–4, 'quocunque ire ferunt variae nos tempora vitae,
Tangere quos terras quosque videre
homines, Dispeream si te fuerit mihi
carior alter, Alter enim quis te dulcior
esse potest?' It is imitated in Val.
Flacc. 7. 477 f.; 'sis memor, oro, mei,
contra memor ipse manebo, Crede, tui.
Quantum hic aberis, dic quaeso, profundi? Quod caeli spectabo latus? Sed
te quoque tangat Cura mei quocumque
loco, quoscumque per annos; Atque
hunc te meminisse velis et nostra fateri
Munera, servatum pudeat nec virginis
arte.'
ὑπότροπος, adapted from *Od.* 21.
211, ὑπότροπον οἴκαδ᾽ ἱκέσθαι: 20. 332,
ὑπότροπος ἵκετο δῶμα.
1073. σχεδόν, 'near,' as in *Od.* 4. 439;
in Apollonius it can mean also 'at once,'
v. n. 947.

ἠὲ καὶ Αἰαίης νήσου πέλας; εἰπὲ δὲ κούρην,
ἥντινα τήνδ᾽ ὀνόμηνας ἀριγνώτην γεγαυῖαν   1075
Πασιφάης, ἢ πατρὸς ὁμόγνιός ἐστιν ἐμεῖο.᾽
῾Ὡς φάτο· τὸν δὲ καὶ αὐτὸν ὑπήιε δάκρυσι κούρης
οὖλος Ἔρως, τοῖον δὲ παραβλήδην ἔπος ηὔδα·
῾Καὶ λίην οὐ νύκτας ὀίομαι, οὐδέ ποτ᾽ ἦμαρ
σεῦ ἐπιλήσεσθαι, προφυγὼν μόρον, εἰ ἐτεόν γε   1080
φεύξομαι ἀσκηθὴς ἐς Ἀχαιίδα, μηδέ τιν᾽ ἄλλον
Αἰήτης προβάλῃσι κακώτερον ἄμμιν ἄεθλον.
εἰ δέ τοι ἡμετέρην ἐξίδμεναι εὔαδε πάτρην
ἐξερέω· μάλα γάρ με καὶ αὐτὸν θυμὸς ἀνώγει.
ἔστι τις αἰπεινοῖσι περίδρομος οὔρεσι γαῖα,   1085
πάμπαν ἐύρρηνός τε καὶ εὔβοτος, ἔνθα Προμηθεὺς
Ἰαπετιονίδης ἀγαθὸν τέκε Δευκαλίωνα,
ὃς πρῶτος ποίησε πόλεις καὶ ἐδείματο νηοὺς

1076 Πασιφάης ed. Paris., Stephanus: Πασιφάην codd. omnes (exceptis fort. Pariss.).   1081 κεν pro τιν᾽ Brunck.   1083 εἰ δέ τι G, vulg.   1084 versum pro institicio habuit Platt.   1086 ἐύρρειτος Paris. unus, Brunck.

Ὀρχομενοῖο, cf. 265–6. Medea would know the name, having heard it from Chalciope and her sons.
1074. Αἰαίης, the home of Circe in *Od.* 10. 135; Αἰαίην δ᾽ ἐς νῆσον ἀφικόμεθ᾽, ἔνθα δ᾽ ἔναιε Κίρκη ἐυπλόκαμος, v. n. 312.
1075. ἀριγνώτην, 'far-famed.' In Homer, it is either 'easily recognised,' as in *Il.* 13. 72, or, ironically, 'famous,' *Od.* 17. 375. For the feminine, cf. *Od.* 6. 108, ῥεῖα δ᾽ ἀριγνώτη πέλεται.
1076. ὁμόγνιος, 'of the same race.' Pasiphae was the mother of Ariadne and daughter of Helios, and therefore sister of Aeetes. The word is first in tragedy of the *dï genitales*, Soph. *O.C.* 1333, πρὸς νῦν σε κρηνῶν καὶ θεῶν ὁμογνίων.
1077. ὑπήιε, 'stole over him,' cf. Eur. *Med.* 57, Soph. *O.T.* 386.
1078. οὖλος, v. n. 297.
παραβλήδην, 'in answer,' v. n. 107.
1079. With these formal protestations, formal for all that he is under the influence of Love, compare the still more formal protests of Aeneas in *Aen.* 4. 333 f.: 'ego te, quae plurima fando Enumerare vales, nunquam, regina, negabo Promeritam, nec me meminisse

pigebit Elissae Dum memor ipse mei, dum spiritus hos regat artus.'
1081. ἀσκηθής, here, as always in Homer, of persons, v. n. 787.
1084. αὐτόν. The end of this line recalls *Il.* 10. 389, ἦ σ᾽ αὐτὸν θυμὸς ἀνῆκεν: for the violation of 'Wernicke's Law,' v. crit. appendix, p. 141.
1085. περίδρομος, 'surrounded by'; the word is Homeric, but this passive use is rare; cf. Eur. *frag.* 542, ap. Strabo 8. 563, of Messenia, ὄρεσι περίδρομος.
1086. ἐύρρηνος, 'rich in sheep,' cf. *Anth. Pal.* 14. 149. ἐύρρην is in *Arg.* 1. 49, and the Homeric πολύρρηνες in 2. 377; cf. Hes. *Op.* 308, πολύμηλοι. This passage is presumably meant to recall *Od.* 11. 256, Πελίης μὲν ἐν εὐρυχόρῳ Ἰαωλκῷ Ναῖε πολύρρηνος, cf. 15. 406, εὔβοτος, εὔμηλος of Ortygia.
1087. Ἰαπετιονίδης, cf. 865.
τέκε, v. n. 32. Deucalion is mentioned as a son of Pandora and Prometheus in the Hesiodic catalogues; our scholia say that Hellanicus wrote of him as a king of Thessaly, and builder of an altar to the twelve gods.
1088. ἐδείματο. In Aesch. *Prom.* 451 f., it is Prometheus and not his son

ἀθανάτοις, πρῶτος δὲ καὶ ἀνθρώπων βασίλευσεν.
Αἱμονίην δὴ τήνγε περικτίονες καλέουσιν.　　　　1090
ἐν δ' αὐτῇ Ἰαωλκός, ἐμὴ πόλις, ἐν δὲ καὶ ἄλλαι
πολλαὶ ναιετάουσιν, ἵν' οὐδέ περ οὔνομ' ἀκοῦσαι
Αἰαίης νήσου· Μινύην γε μὲν ὁρμηθέντα,
Αἰολίδην Μινύην ἔνθεν φάτις Ὀρχομενοῖο
δή ποτε Καδμείοισιν ὁμούριον ἄστυ πολίσσαι.　　　1095
ἀλλὰ τίη τάδε τοι μεταμώνια πάντ' ἀγορεύω,
ἡμετέρους τε δόμους τηλεκλείτην τ' Ἀριάδνην,
κούρην Μίνωος, τόπερ ἀγλαὸν οὔνομα κείνην
παρθενικὴν καλέεσκον ἐπήρατον, ἥν μ' ἐρεείνεις;
αἴθε γάρ, ὡς Θησῆι τότε ξυναρέσσατο Μίνως　　　1100
ἀμφ' αὐτῆς, ὣς ἄμμι πατὴρ τεὸς ἄρθμιος εἴη.'
Ὣς φάτο, μειλιχίοισι καταψήχων ὀάροισιν.

1089 ἀθανάτων G.　　　1091 αὐτῇ LG.　　　Ἰαωλκός G, Vat. unus : Ἰωλκός vulg.
1102 καταψύχων vulg.

who teaches men to build and live in cities. Note the metrical echo of *Od.* 6. 9, πόλει καὶ ἐδείματο οἴκους.

1089. βασίλευσεν, ' was the first ruler of men.' Here only in Ap.; in Homer it is c. gen. in *Od.* 1. 401, c. dat. in *Od.* 7. 59.

1090. Αἱμονίην. Thessaly was known as Haemonia from Haemon the son of Ares, before it was called Thessaly from Thessalus the son of Haemon. The name is Alexandrine, cf. Call. *frag.* 9 B (Mair), ἀρχμενος ὡς ἥρωες ἀπ' Αἰήταο Κυταίου Αὖτις ἐς ἀρχαίην ἔπλεον Αἱμονίην.

1091. Ἰαωλκός, for the form, v. n. 2.

1092. ναιετάουσιν, 'are situated,' v.n. 313 : cf. *Od.* 9. 23, νῆσοι Πολλαὶ ναιετάουσιν.

ἀκοῦσαι. This is simply an ellipse of ἔστι, cf. 680, and 4. 262, γένος ἦεν ἀκοῦσαι. It is quite unnecessary to emend to ἀκούσαις, or to regard it as a strange use in *oratio recta* of the infinitive of *oratio obliqua*, as in Plat. *Rep.* 614 B, ἀφικνεῖσθαι ἔφη εἰς τόπον ἐν ᾧ δύο εἶναι χάσματα.

1094. Αἰολίδην, grandson of Sisyphus the son of Aeolus.

Ὀρχομενοῖο. Orchomenos was so called from Orchomenos the son of Minyas, and our scholia on 2. 1186

point out that οἱ Ὀρχομένιοι ἄποικοί εἰσι Θεσσαλῶν. It is called Ὀρχομενὸς Μινύειος in *Il.* 2. 511, *Od.* 11. 284.

1095. Καδμείοισιν. Thebans, v. infr. 1179.

ὁμούριον, 'that borders on,' Alexandrine form of prose ὅμορος : cf. Call. *frag.* 50 (Mair), Βρισήλου λαγόνεσσιν ὁμούριον ἐκτίσσαντο.

1097. τηλεκλείτην, ' far-famed ' : Homeric, but here only of three terminations.

1100. ξυναρέσσατο, 'was well inclined to...,' v. nn. 301, 901. This, however, is hardly the truth of the matter: cf. n. 1000 supr.

1101. ἄρθμιος, 'be joined to us': cf. *Od.* 16. 427, οἱ δ' ἡμῖν ἄρθμιοι ἦσαν.

1102. καταψήχων, un-Homeric, properly of 'rubbing down horses,' Eur. *Hipp.* 110, καὶ καταψήχειν χρεὼν Ἵππους. It is intransitive in Soph. *Tr.* 698, 'crumble away,' ῥεῖ πᾶν ἄδηλον καὶ κατέψηκται χθονί.

ὀάροισιν, 'with gentle words.' Homer has ὀαριστύς, *Il.* 14. 216; this form is first in Hes. *Th.* 205, παρθενίους τ' ὀάρους μειδήματά τε; in H. Hom. *Aph.* 249, it means 'wiles.' This meaning 'discourse,' 'words,' is first in Emped. 120.

τῆς δ' ἀλεγεινόταται κραδίην ἐρέθεσκον ἀνῖαι,
καί μιν ἀκηχεμένη ἀδινῷ προσπτύξατο μύθῳ·
  ''Ελλάδι που τάδε καλά, συνημοσύνας ἀλεγύνειν·   1105
Αἰήτης δ' οὐ τοῖος ἐν ἀνδράσιν, οἷον ἔειπας
Μίνω Πασιφάης πόσιν ἔμμεναι· οὐδ' Ἀριάδνη
ἰσοῦμαι· τῷ μήτι φιλοξενίην ἀγόρευε.
ἀλλ' οἷον τύνη μὲν ἐμεῦ, ὅτ' Ἰωλκὸν ἵκηαι,
μνώεο· σεῖο δ' ἐγὼ καὶ ἐμῶν ἀέκητι τοκήων   1110
μνήσομαι. ἔλθοι δ' ἧμιν ἀπόπροθεν ἠέ τις ὄσσα,
ἠέ τις ἄγγελος ὄρνις, ὅτ' ἐκλελάθοιο ἐμεῖο·
ἢ αὐτήν με ταχεῖαι ὑπὲρ πόντοιο φέροιεν
ἐνθένδ' εἰς Ἰαωλκὸν ἀναρπάξασαι ἄελλαι,
ὄφρα σ', ἐν ὀφθαλμοῖσιν ἐλεγχείας προφέρουσα,   1115
μνήσω ἐμῇ ἰότητι πεφυγμένον. αἴθε γὰρ εἴην
ἀπροφάτως τότε σοῖσιν ἐφέστιος ἐν μεγάροισιν.'
  Ὣς ἄρ' ἔφη, ἐλεεινὰ καταπροχέουσα παρειῶν

1113 γε pro με Pariss., Brunck.   1114 Ἰαωλκὸν Brunck : Ἰωλκὸν vulg.
1117 τόσσοισιν pro τότε σοῖσιν G.

1103. **ἀλεγεινόταται**, un-Homeric superlative, v. n. 582, cf. 764.
ἐρέθεσκον, 'stirred her heart': for the Ionic imperfect, v. n. 618.
1104. **ἀδινῷ**, 'miserable,' v. n. 616.
προσπτύξατο, 'addressed': cf. *Od.* 4. 647, προσπτύξατο μύθῳ, v. n. 782.
1105. **συνημοσύνας**, 'compacts,' an echo of *Il.* 22. 261, μή μοι συνημοσύνας ἀγόρευε, *i.e.* κοινοβουλίαι (schol. *ad loc.*). The singular is in Theognis 284 with *var. lect.* φιλημοσύνῃ. Herodian interaspirates it, συνήμοσύνας.
1108. **ἰσοῦμαι**, 'I do not liken myself to': cf. *Od.* 7. 212, ἀνθρώπων τοῖσιν κεν ἐν ἀλγεσιν ἰσωσαίμην, Soph. *O.T.* 31, etc.
φιλοξενίην, 'friendship with a stranger,' first in Theog. 1358 of courtesans, ἀργαλέον μνῆμα φιλοξενίης; the adj. **φιλόξεινος** is Homeric: cf. *Il.* 22. 261, cited on 1105 supr.
1110. **μνώεο**, 'remember,' v. n. 639: cf. the farewell of Nausicaa to Odysseus in *Od.* 8. 461, χαῖρε, ξεῖν', ἵνα καί ποτ' ἐὼν ἐν πατρίδι γαίῃ Μνήσῃ ἐμεῦ.
ἀέκητι, 'in spite of,' common in Homer.
1111. **ὄσσα**, 'rumour,' called in *Il.* 2. 94, because of its mysterious move-

ments, Διὸς ἄγγελος: Ap. has adapted this to the ὄρνις in the next line. The sense of 'omen,' of the utterance of a bird, as in 1. 1087, 1095, is first in Pind. *Ol.* 6. 62 (106).
1112. **ἄγγελος**, cf. 1121 infr.: it is adapted from *Il.* 24. 292, οἰωνόν, ταχὺν ἄγγελον.
ἐκλελάθοιο, 'when thou hast utterly forgotten me,' v. n. 280; it is attracted into the mood of ἔλθοι, cf. 788 supr.
1114. **ἀναρπάξασαι**. Typical variant of *Od.* 4. 515, 5. 419, ἀναρπάξασα θύελλα.
1115. **ἐν ὀφθαλμοῖσιν**, v. n. 93: here it is 'face to face.'
1116. **ἰότητι**, 'by my good will': cf. *Il.* 15. 41, and note on 545 supr.
1117. **ἐφέστιος**, either in the Homeric sense, 'a guest in your halls,' or the post-Homeric, 'a suppliant'; v. n. 585. Medea is not threatening here as in 4. 383; compare the threats of Dido in *Aen.* 4. 384, 'sequar atris ignibus absens, Et cum frigida mors anima seduxerit artus Omnibus umbra locis adero; dabis, improbe, poenas, Audiam, et haec Manis veniet mihi fama sub imos.'
1118. **καταπροχέουσα**, 'with tears of pity streaming down her cheeks.'

δάκρυα· τὴν δ᾽ ὅγε δῆθεν ὑποβλήδην προσέειπεν·
'Δαιμονίη, κενεὰς μὲν ἔα πλάζεσθαι ἀέλλας, 1120
ὡς δὲ καὶ ἄγγελον ὄρνιν, ἐπεὶ μεταμώνια βάζεις.
εἰ δέ κεν ἤθεα κεῖνα καὶ Ἑλλάδα γαῖαν ἵκηαι,
τιμήεσσα γυναιξὶ καὶ ἀνδράσιν αἰδοίη τε
ἔσσεαι· οἱ δέ σε πάγχυ θεὸν ὣς πορσανέουσιν,
οὕνεκα τῶν μὲν παῖδες ὑπότροποι οἴκαδ᾽ ἵκοντο 1125
σῇ βουλῇ, τῶν δ᾽ αὖτε κασίγνητοί τε ἔται τε
καὶ θαλεροὶ κακότητος ἅδην ἐσάωθεν ἀκοῖται.
ἡμέτερον δὲ λέχος θαλάμοις ἔνι κουριδίοισιν
πορσυνέεις· οὐδ᾽ ἄμμε διακρινέει φιλότητος
ἄλλο, πάρος θάνατόν γε μεμορμένον ἀμφικαλύψαι.' 1130
Ὣς φάτο· τῇ δ᾽ ἔντοσθε κατείβετο θυμὸς ἀκουῇ,
ἔμπης δ᾽ ἔργ᾽ ἀίδηλα κατερρίγησεν ἰδέσθαι.

1121 ἄλλον ὄρνιν G. 1124 ἠδέ σε Paris. unus, Brunck. 1129 πορσανέεις G,
vulg.   φιλότητας Madvig : φιλέοντας Cobet.

This compound is here only; Homer
has προχέω in a similar sense in *Il.* 21.
219. Apollonius has προχέουσιν transitive in 4. 606, intr. *ib.* 135.
1119. δῆθεν, as in 354, a stronger
form of δή; no irony is meant.
ὑποβλήδην, 'in answer,' v. nn. 107,
400.
1120. δαιμονίη, v. n. 711.
κενεάς, for the form, v. n. 126.
1122. ἤθεα, cf. *Arg.* 1. 1177, ἤθεα
γαίης, as here in the Homeric sense of
'places.' In the sense of 'customs,' it is
first in Hesiod.
1124. θεὸν ὣς, reminiscent of *Il.* 9.
302, οἵ σε θεὸν ὣς Τίουσι.
πορσανέουσιν. This is persistently
found as a *var. lect.* with πορσύνω, and
in Pindar and Ap. it is impossible to
lay down a rule. Here it is 'adore,'
but Pindar uses it also of 'tending' a
child, and 'esteeming' a saying.
1125. ὑπότροπος, cf. 1069.
1126. ἔται, 'kinsmen,' the original
meaning. It is used in the wider sense
of 'clansmen,' those of the same φυλή,
in 1. 305; cf. *Il.* 6. 239, 16. 456,
κασίγνητοί τε ἔται τε.
1127. ἅδην, probably 'many,' v. n.
ἅλις 272, and Leaf on *Il.* 13. 315.
ἐσάωθεν, 'were saved from,' with
genitive. The Homeric use is with ἐκ,
as in *Arg.* 2. 610: cf. n. 596, τιμῆς.

1128. θαλάμοις, 'bridal-chamber,'
v. n. 799.
κουριδίοισιν, cf. 243, 623, and of
λέχος, δῶμα in *Il.* 15. 40, *Od.* 19. 580.
1129. πορσυνέεις, *i.e* 'share,' cf. 840,
v. n. 40. Compare of Jason and Medea
in Pind. *Pyth.* 4. 223, καταίνησάν τε
κοινὸν γάμον Γλυκὺν ἐν ἀλλάλοισι μῖξαι.
The following phrase here is based on
Od. 4. 178, οὐδέ κεν ἡμέας Ἄλλο διέ-
κρινεν φιλέοντέ τε τερπομένω τε Πρίν γ᾽
ὅτε δὴ θανάτοιο μέλαν νέφος ἀμφεκά-
λυψεν. For the passive, διακρίνεσθαι
ἀπό, cf. Thuc. 1. 105. 5.
1130. μεμορμένον, late and false form,
v. n. 4.
1131. κατείβετο, v. n. 290, cf. *Il.* 24.
794, θαλερὸν δὲ κατείβετο δακρὺ παρειῶν :
Od. 5. 152, κατείβετο δὲ γλυκὺς αἰών.
1132. ἀίδηλα, 'pernicious,' cf. 4.
1672, ἐκ δ᾽ ἀίδηλα Δείκηλα προίαλλεν.
Apollonius would appear to have read
in *Il.* 5. 757, 872, the pre-Aristarchean
ἔργ᾽ ἀίδηλα, not κρατερ᾽ ἔργα of the MSS.;
Ameis retains this in both places,
Buttmann in the former only. Ap. has
the word twice meaning 'unexpectedly,'
cf. Sextus ap. Porph. on *Il.* 11. 155, πῦρ
ἀίδηλον; thrice meaning 'unseen,' 1.
102, etc.: and once 'ambiguous,' 4.
681, φυὴν ἀίδηλοι. These are confusions
from *Il.* 2. 318, τὸν μὲν ἀρίζηλον θῆκεν
θεός, and the variant ἀίδηλον.

σχετλίη· οὐ μὲν δηρὸν ἀπαρνήσεσθαι ἔμελλεν
Ἑλλάδα ναιετάειν. ὡς γὰρ τόδε μήδετο Ἥρη,
ὄφρα κακὸν Πελίῃ ἱερὴν ἐς Ἰωλκὸν ἵκοιτο   1135
Αἰαίη Μήδεια, λιποῦσ᾽ ἄπο πατρίδα γαῖαν.
Ἤδη δ᾽ ἀμφίπολοι μὲν ὀπιπεύουσαι ἄπωθεν
σιγῇ ἀνιάζεσκον· ἐδεύετο δ᾽ ἤματος ὥρη
ἂψ οἰκόνδε νέεσθαι ἐὴν μετὰ μητέρα κούρην.
ἡ δ᾽ οὔπω κομιδῆς μιμνήσκετο, τέρπετο γάρ οἱ   1140
θυμὸς ὁμῶς μορφῇ τε καὶ αἱμυλίοισι λόγοισιν,
εἰ μὴ ἄρ᾽ Αἰσονίδης πεφυλαγμένος ὀψέ περ ηὔδα·
'Ὥρη ἀποβλώσκειν, μὴ πρὶν φάος ἠελίοιο
δύῃ ὑποφθάμενον, καί τις τὰ ἔκαστα νοήσῃ
ὀθνείων· αὖτις δ᾽ ἀβολήσομεν ἐνθάδ᾽ ἰόντες.'   1145
Ὡς τώγ᾽ ἀλλήλων ἀγανοῖς ἐπὶ τόσσον ἔπεσσιν

1133 ἀπαρνήσασθαι G.   1135 ἵκοιτο Brunck : ἵκητο L : ἵκηται vulg.
1136 λιποῦσ᾽ ἄπο Merkel : λιποῦσα LG, Vatt. tres, Pariss. tres, Vrat., Vind. :
λιποῦσά γε vulg.   1137 ὀπιπεύουσαι Vatt. duo, Merkel, Mooney : ὀπιπτεύουσαι
LG, Seaton.   1138 ἐδύετο Samuelsson.   1139 ἂψ ἐς οἰκόνδε G : εἰς οἰκόνδε
Pariss. tres.

κατερρίγησεν, 'shuddered to see.'
The simple verb is Homeric, of 'shud-
dering with horror'; it is post-Homeric
in a physical sense, 'shudder with cold.'
1133. **ἀπαρνήσεσθαι**, 'refuse,' post-
Homeric.
ἔμελλεν, 'was not destined,' v. n.
260.
1136. **λιποῦσ᾽ ἄπο**, cf. 832: for the
enmity between Here and Pelias, v. n.
65.
1137. **ὀπιπεύουσαι**, cf. Il. 7. 243,
λάθρῃ ὀπιπεύσας, 'watching.' This form,
rather than ὀπιπτ-, is supported by the
best MSS. in Homer; cf. also such words
as παρθενοπίπης.
1138. **ἀνιάζεσκον**, 'were beginning
to grieve.' This is only intransitive in
Ap.; in Homer it is also transitive.
ἐδεύετο. The infinitive is epexegetic,
'the time of day was failing for her to
return.' The schol. explains ἐδέετο,
ἐνελείπετο. Coleridge follows the former; but Ap. must have read the
dative rather than the genitive in Il.
20. 121, μηδέ τι θυμῷ Δενέσθω, v. Leaf
ad loc.

1140. **κομιδῆς**, 'return.' This sense
is first in Herodotus; in Homer, it is
'care,' attention,' in Pind. Pyth. 6. 39
'rescue.' In a strict condition, this
would have ἄν or κεν; but it is loose
here, and the first half can be reckoned
as a statement rather than an apodosis,
v. n. 377.
1141. **αἱμυλίοισι**. This phrase is also
in Od. 1. 56; and v. n. 51. Similarly it
is with αἱμυλίοισι λόγοισι, in Theog. 704,
that Sisyphus obtains permission to return to earth in order to punish his
wife.
1143. **ἀποβλώσκειν**. Here only:
Homer has μέμβλωκε from the simple
verb in Od. 17. 190.
1144. **ὑποφθάμενον**, 'before we know
it': cf. Od. 4. 547, κτεῖνεν ὑποφθάμενος:
15. 171, ὑποφθαμένη φάτο μῦθον.
1145. **ὀθνείων**, 'some one not concerned in the matter,' v. nn. 389, 403.
ἀβολήσομεν, 'meet': Alexandrine,
v. n. 179.
1146-1162. Jason returns to the ship;
Medea goes to the palace and ponders
over her promise.

πείρηθεν· μετὰ δ᾽ αὖτε διέτμαγον. ἤτοι Ἰήσων
εἰς ἑτάρους καὶ νῆα κεχαρμένος ὦρτο νέεσθαι·
ἡ δὲ μετ᾽ ἀμφιπόλους· αἱ δὲ σχεδὸν ἀντεβόλησαν
πᾶσαι ὁμοῦ· τὰς δ᾽ οὔτι περιπλομένας ἐνόησεν.   1150
ψυχὴ γὰρ νεφέεσσι μεταχρονίη πεπότητο.
αὐτομάτοις δὲ πόδεσσι θοῆς ἐπεβήσατ᾽ ἀπήνης,
καί ῥ᾽ ἑτέρῃ μὲν χειρὶ λάβ᾽ ἡνία, τῇ δ᾽ ἄρ᾽ ἱμάσθλην
δαιδαλέην, οὐρῆας ἐλαυνέμεν· οἱ δὲ πόλινδε
θῦνον ἐπειγόμενοι ποτὶ δώματα. τὴν δ᾽ ἄρ᾽ ἰοῦσαν   1155
Χαλκιόπη περὶ παισὶν ἀκηχεμένη ἐρέεινεν·
ἡ δὲ παλιντροπίῃσιν ἀμήχανος οὔτε τι μύθων
ἔκλυεν, οὔτ᾽ αὐδῆσαι ἀνειρομένῃ λελίητο.
ἷζε δ᾽ ἐπὶ χθαμαλῷ σφέλαϊ κλιντῆρος ἔνερθεν
λέχρις ἐρεισαμένη λαιῇ ἐπὶ χειρὶ παρειήν·   1160
ὑγρὰ δ᾽ ἐνὶ βλεφάροις ἔχεν ὄμματα, πορφύρουσα
οἷον ἑῇ κακὸν ἔργον ἐπιξυνώσατο βουλῇ.

1147 διέτμαγον Platt, codd.: διέτμαγεν Spitzner, edd.   1151 μεταχθονίη Vat.
unus, vulg.   1152 αὐτομάτη Pariss.   1155 τὴν δ᾽ ἀνιοῦσαν Paris. unus,
Brunck.

1147. **διέτμαγον**, intransitive, v. n.
343, and crit. note.
1149. **σχεδόν**, 'drew near to meet
her,' the Homeric use; v. nn. 947, 1073.
1150. **περιπλομένας**, 'surrounding
her,' v. n. 25.
1151. **μεταχρονίη**, 'soaring aloft':
for the form, v. crit. appendix, p. 141.
The line is a clear echo of *Od.* 11. 222,
ψυχὴ δ᾽ ἠΰτ᾽ ὄνειρος ἀποπταμένη πεπότηται.
1152. **ἐπεβήσατο**, repeated from 869;
v. n. *ad loc.* for form, and Homeric
echo.
1155. **ἰοῦσαν**, *i.e.* on her arrival at
the palace, as she went from the chariot
into the palace.
1157. **παλιντροπίῃσιν**, 'changes of
mind,' first in Ap., cf. n. 144. It is used
in Polybius of 'changes of fortune'; cf.
the tragic παλίντροπος, and *Od.* 15. 404,
τροπαὶ ἠελίοιο.
1158. **λελίητο**, 'was not eager to
speak in answer to her questions.' This
form and the use with infinitive belong
to late epic, v. n. 80.

1159. **χθαμαλῷ**, 'low': cf. *Od.* 11.
194, χθαμαλαί...εὐναί.
σφέλαϊ, 'footstool': Homer has the
singular in *Od.* 18. 394, the plural in
17. 231.
κλιντῆρος, 'at the foot of her couch.'
This is in Homer only in *Od.* 18. 190,
αὐτοῦ ἐνὶ κλιντῆρι, where Munro doubts
the authenticity of the passage.
1160. **λέχρις**, v. n. 238.
1161. **βλεφάροις**, 'her eyes in her eye-
lids were wet': cf. *Od.* 23. 33, βλεφάρων
ἀπὸ δάκρυον ἧκε. It is an unnecessary,
but typically Alexandrine, particulari-
sation.
πορφύρουσα, v. n. 23.
1162. **ἐπιξυνώσατο**, 'in what an evil
deed she was a sharer by her counsels.'
This compound is first here; the active
voice is first in Nonn. *Dion.* 26. 290,
ἐπεξύνωσεν ἑκάστῳ. This passage recalls
Eur. *Med.* 1078, καὶ μανθάνω μὲν οἷα
δρᾶν μέλλω κακά, Θυμὸς δὲ κρείσσων τῶν
ἐμῶν βουλευμάτων. There too Medea is
ἀρτίδακρυς, 903, ὦ τάλαιν᾽ ἐγώ, Ὡς ἀρτί-
δακρύς εἰμι καὶ φόβου πλέα.

Αἰσονίδης δ' ὅτε δὴ ἑτάροις ἐξαῦτις ἔμικτο
ἐν χώρῃ, ὅθι τούσγε καταπρολιπὼν ἐλιάσθη,
ὦρτ' ἰέναι σὺν τοῖσι, πιφαυσκόμενος τὰ ἕκαστα,　　1165
ἡρώων ἐς ὅμιλον· ὁμοῦ δ' ἐπὶ νῆα πέλασσαν.
οἱ δέ μιν ἀμφαγάπαζον, ὅπως ἴδον, ἔκ τ' ἐρέοντο.
αὐτὰρ ὁ τοῖς πάντεσσι μετέννεπε δήνεα κούρης,
δεῖξέ τε φάρμακον αἰνόν· ὁ δ' οἰόθεν οἶος ἑταίρων
Ἴδας ἧστ' ἀπάνευθε δακὼν χόλον· οἱ δὲ δὴ ἄλλοι　　1170
γηθόσυνοι τῆμος μέν, ἐπεὶ κνέφας ἔργαθε νυκτός,
εὔκηλοι ἐμέλοντο περὶ σφίσιν. αὐτὰρ ἅμ' ἠοῖ
πέμπον ἐς Αἰήτην ἰέναι σπόρον αἰτήσοντας
ἄνδρε δύω, πρὸ μὲν αὐτὸν ἀρηίφιλον Τελαμῶνα,
σὺν δὲ καὶ Αἰθαλίδην, υἷα κλυτὸν Ἑρμείαο.　　1175
βὰν δ' ἴμεν, οὐδ' ἁλίωσαν ὁδόν· πόρε δέ σφιν ἰοῦσιν

1166 ἡρώων ἐς ὅμιλον G, L in marg.: ἡρώων ἐς ἕκαστα L.　οἱ δ' ἔκλυον ἕκαστα
Vat. unus, Pariss. tres: οἱ δ' ἔκλυον τὰ ἕκαστα Gerhard.　　1172 ἐμέλοντο Paris.
unus, schol. Par.: μέλλοντο LG, vulg.　　1174 πρόμον O. Schneider.

1163–1190. Telamon and Aethalides
go to the palace for the dragon's teeth.
1163. ἔμικτο, 'joined': cf. Il. 11.
354, μίκτο δ' ὁμίλῳ, and 1223 infr.
1164. καταπρολιπών, here only,
'where he had left them': L. and S.
curiously take it as 'forsaking utterly.'
Homer has the single compound in Od.
3. 314, κτήματά τε προλιπών.
ἐλιάσθη, v. n. 827.
1166. ἐπι...πέλασσαν, probably ἐπι-
πελάζω in tmesi, 'approached the ship.'
L. and S. take it as trans. in Eur. I. T.
880, πρὶν ἐπὶ ξίφος αἵματι σῷ πελάσαι,
but it may be intr. there also. For the
accusative, cf. Eur. Andr. 1167, δῶμα πε-
λάζει: contrast Il. 12. 112, πέλασεν νήεσσι.
1167. ἀμφαγάπαζον, v. n. 258 supr.:
an echo of Od. 14. 381, ἐγὼ δέ μιν ἀμφαγάπαζον.
1168. μετέννεπε, Alexandrine.
δήνεα, 'cunning plans,' as in Homer;
but v. n. 661.
1169. οἰόθεν. Homer uses this only
in the phrase οἰόθεν οἶος, as here. Ap.
has it also alone, 1. 270; v. n. 945
οἰόθι.
1170. ἀπάνευθε, preposition governing ἑταίρων, v. n. 114.
δακών, 'biting back his anger': cf.

Arist. Nub. 1369, θυμὸν δακών. For the
reason, v. 556 f.
1171. ἔργαθε, 'at the hour when the
darkness of night stayed them.' This is
the tragic meaning; in Homer it is
'sever.' For the form, which is strictly
a poetical second aorist of εἴργω, cf.
διωκαθεῖν, εἰκαθεῖν, etc.
1172. εὔκηλοι, 'at their ease,' as in
Homer: for the later meaning 'silent,'
v. n. 219.
ἐμέλοντο. Ap. uses this also with
ἀμφί c. acc. 2. 376, c. gen. 4. 491, but
elsewhere with the genitive alone.
Homer has the perfect participle only
in this sense, μεμηλώς, c. gen.
1173. αἰτήσοντας ἄνδρε. Another
example of the indiscriminate use of
dual and plural, in which Ap. seems to
have followed Zenodotus, v. n. 206, cf.
410, 1327.
1174. πρό...σύν. 'First...and with
him': cf. Il. 13. 799, πρό...ἐπί.
1175. Αἰθαλίδην, son of Hermes,
and so well qualified to act as herald,
as he did in Arg. 1. 640, on the visit to
Lemnos; contrast n. 198 supr.
1176. ἁλίωσαν, 'did not journey in
vain.' This may be an echo of Il. 16.
737, οὐδ' ἁλίωσε βέλος, cf. Od. 5. 104,

κρείων Αἰήτης χαλεποὺς ἐς ἄεθλον ὀδόντας
Ἀονίοιο δράκοντος, ὃν Ὠγυγίῃ ἐνὶ Θήβῃ
Κάδμος, ὅτ' Εὐρώπην διζήμενος εἰσαφίκανεν,
πέφνεν Ἀρητιάδι κρήνῃ ἐπίουρον ἐόντα·   1180
ἔνθα καὶ ἐννάσθη πομπῇ βοός, ἥν οἱ Ἀπόλλων
ὤπασε μαντοσύνῃσι προηγήτειραν ὁδοῖο.
τοὺς δὲ θεὰ Τριτωνὶς ὑπὲκ γενύων ἐλάσασα
Αἰήτῃ πόρε δῶρον ὁμῶς αὐτῷ τε φονῆι.
καί ῥ' ὁ μὲν Ἀονίοισιν ἐνισπείρας πεδίοισιν   1185
Κάδμος Ἀγηνορίδης γαιηγενῆ εἴσατο λαόν,

1180 Ἀρητιάδι Pariss. tres et coni. Stephanus: Ἀρητιάδη vulg.   1186 γαιηγενῆ
G, vulg.: γεηγενῆ L: ἐπὶ γηγενῆ Pariss., Brunck.   εἴσατο Stephanus:
εἴσατο vulg.

138, and οὐχ ἥλιωσε τοῦτος, Soph. *Tr.* 258.

1178. **Ἀονίοιο**, Boeotian. The Aones, descended from Aon son of Poseidon, are mentioned among the oldest inhabitants of Boeotia by Paus. 9. 5. 1.

Ὠγυγίη. Thebes is ὠγυγίη πόλις in Aesch. *Th.* 321, which Verrall *ad loc.* takes to mean 'prehistoric.' It was explained with reference to a hero Ogygus, who was called a son of Boeotus by Corinna, according to our scholiast.

1179. **Κάδμος.** Cadmus was bidden by the oracle to follow a cow, and to found a city where it lay down (Apollod. 3. 4. 1, Paus. 9. 12. 1, Hyg. 178). Here Apollonius follows the account of Pherecydes and Hellanicus, that he sowed the teeth at the spring of Ares by the command of Ares. This must belong to the legend of the wooing of Harmonia daughter of Ares, rather than to that of Europa; v. n. 414.

εἰσαφίκανεν, Homeric, v. n. 888.

1180. **ἐπίουρον**, 'guardian': this takes dative in *Il.* 13. 450. Ap. has also the genitive in this sense in 1. 87, with which cf. *Od.* 13. 405 of a herdsman, ὑῶν ἐπίουρος.

1181. **ἐννάσθη**, 'settled.' Homer does not use the middle of this verb, but Ap. does, either abs., as here, or with the accusative ἄστη νάσσατο, 4. 275, 'founded.' It is with the accusative of the person, 'make to dwell,' in 1. 1356, and of the place νάσσεσθαι ἔμελλον γῆν, 2. 747, 'settle in, dwell in.'

1182. **προηγήτειραν**, 'to guide him on his way.' This is first in Ap., and recurs in Nonn. *Dion.* 35. 304; cf. Eur. *Bacc.* 1159, ταῦρον προηγητῆρα συμφορᾶς ἔχων. Other Alexandrine inventions of this termination are in Callimachus, *H. Art.* 237, ἐπιθυμήτειρα: *H. Del.* 230, θηρήτειρα: *frag.* 18 (Mair), λήτειρα: *frag.* 136, ὀπτήτειρα.

1183. **Τριτωνίς**, Athene. According to the scholiast, there are three rivers called Tritonis, in Boeotia, Thessaly, and Libya, all connected with the birth of Athena. The Tritonian lake is mentioned in this connection in *Arg.* 4. 1391.

ὑπὲκ...ἐλάσασα. Transitive, 'forcing out of its jaws,' but in Hdt. 4. 130 ὑπεξελαύνω is to 'march away.' This is probably *in tmesi*: Homer has the simple compound. For the genitive, cf. Eur. *Med.* 70, γῆς ἐλᾶν.

1184. **ὁμῶς**, 'in equal parts': cf. Hes. *Th.* 74, ἀθανάτοις διέταξεν ὁμῶς καὶ ἐπέφραδε τιμάς.

φονῆι. Epic form, as in Homer.

1185. **ἐνισπείρας.** This is first here with certainty; the passive occurs as a *var. lect.* in Xen. *Cyr.* 5. 2. 30, καὶ αὐτὸς ὁ λόγος πολὺς ἤδη ἐνέσπαρται.

1186. **γαιηγενῆ.** Here only for γηγενῆ: cf. Eur. *Bacc.* 265, Κάδμον τε τὸν σπείραντα γηγενῆ στάχυν.

εἴσατο. Here only of 'founding a people'; but Homer has the active in this sense, *Od.* 6. 8, εἶσεν δὲ Σχερίῃ. Elsewhere it is of temples.

8-2

Ἄρεος ἀμώοντος ὅσοι ὑπὸ δουρὶ λίποντο·
τοὺς δὲ τότ' Αἰήτης ἔπορεν μετὰ νῆα φέρεσθαι
προφρονέως, ἐπεὶ οὔ μιν ὀίσσατο πείρατ' ἀέθλου
ἐξανύσειν, εἰ καί περ ἐπὶ ζυγὰ βουσὶ βάλοιτο.   1190
  Ἥλιος μὲν ἄπωθεν ἐρεμνὴν δύετο γαῖαν
ἑσπέριος, νεάτας ὑπὲρ ἄκριας Αἰθιοπήων·
Νὺξ δ' ἵπποισιν ἔβαλλεν ἔπι ζυγά· τοὶ δὲ χαμεύνας
ἔντυον ἥρωες παρὰ πείσμασιν. αὐτὰρ Ἰήσων
αὐτίκ' ἐπεί ῥ' Ἑλίκης εὐφεγγέος ἀστέρες Ἄρκτου   1195
ἔκλιθεν, οὐρανόθεν δὲ πανεύκηλος γένετ' αἰθήρ,
βῆ ῥ' ἐς ἐρημαίην, κλωπήιος ἠύτε τις φώρ,
σὺν πᾶσιν χρήεσσι· πρὸ γάρ τ' ἀλέγυνεν ἕκαστα
ἡμάτιος· θῆλυν μὲν ὄιν, γάλα τ' ἔκτοθι ποίμνης
Ἄργος ἰὼν ἤνεικε· τὰ δ' ἐξ αὐτῆς ἕλε νηός.   1200

1187 ἀμώωντος coni. Merkel.   1195 εὔφεγγέες Brunck.   1198 πᾶσιν L: πᾶσι G, vulg.

1187. **ἀμώοντος**, 'all who were left, when Ares was the reaper with his spear.' ὑπὸ...λίποντο is probably *in tmesi* for ὑπελίποντο; this passive sense of the 2nd aorist is Homeric. For this legend that Ares himself slew the men, cf. Eur. *H.F.* 252, ὦ γῆς λοχεύμαθ', οὓς Ἄρης σπείρει ποτέ, Λαβρὸν δράκοντος ἐξερημώσας γένυν,and Roscher, *Lex.* 2. 1. 835.
1189. **ὀίσσατο**, 'did not think'; for the form, v. n. 456, cf. 926.
πείρατα, pleonastic for ἄεθλος, like νίκης πείρατα for νίκη in *Il.* 7. 102: cf. 680 supr., and Pind. *Pyth.* 4. 220.
1190. **ἐξανύσειν**, v. n. 788.
εἰ καί περ, 'even granting that': cf. *Od.* 9. 35, εἴ περ καί.
1191–1224. Jason, in obedience to Medea's instructions, sacrifices at dead of night to Hecate.
1191. **ἐρεμνήν**, epithet in Homer of γαῖα, v. n. 864.
δύετο, 'was sinking beneath.' For the quantity, v. nn. 225, 764; cf. *Od.* 7. 18, πόλιν δύσεσθαι, 'enter,' and *Il.* 6. 19, γαῖαν ἐδύτην, i.e. 'died.'
1192. **νεάτας**, v. n. 763.
ἄκριας, v. n. 166.
Αἰθιοπήων, cf. *Od.* 1. 23, Αἰθίοπες, τοὶ διχθὰ δεδαίεται, ἔσχατοι ἀνδρῶν, Οἱ μὲν δυσομένου Ὑπερίονος, οἱ δ' ἀνίοντος.
1193. **ἔβαλλεν ἔπι**, cf. *Od.* 14. 520, ἐπὶ

δὲ χλαῖναν βάλεν αὐτῷ, and n. 832 supr. For the chariot of Night, cf. Theoc. 2. 166, κατ' ἄντυγα Νυκτὸς ὀπαδοί.
χαμεύνας, contracted for χαμαὶ εὐνή. It is first in tragedy, though Homer has the adj. χαμαιεύνης, *Il.* 16. 235, 'sleeping on the ground.'
1195. **εὐφεγγέος**, cf. Arat. 518, ζώνη εὐφεγγέος Ὠρίωνος: for the connection of Orion and Helice, v. 745 supr.
1196. **ἔκλιθεν**, 'had set,' post-Homeric. *Arg.* 1. 452, κλίνοντος ἠελίου, is a new use; cf. ἀποκλίναι 'fall away,' in Soph. *O.T.* 1192.
πανεύκηλος. This compound is here only. Homer has the simple adjective of mental tranquility of persons; the Alexandrines use it of things also, cf. 219 supr.
1197. **κλωπήιος**, first here for the tragic κλοπαῖος.
1198. **χρήεσσι**, 'with all things needful.' Here only in this form; the proper form χρέεσι does not occur till Manetho.
1199. **ἡμάτιος**, the Homeric form; cf. 895 ἐπημάτιαι.
ἔκτοθι, 'from the flock'; in Homer, this is 'outside of.' The absolute use, as in 255, is likewise un-Homeric.
1200. **ἤνεικε**, 'had already brought': Argos did not accompany Jason.

ἀλλ' ὅτε δὴ ἴδε χῶρον, ὅτις πάτου ἔκτοθεν ἦεν
ἀνθρώπων, καθαρῇσιν ὑπεύδιος εἰαμενῇσιν,
ἔνθ' ἤτοι πάμπρωτα λοέσσατο μὲν ποταμοῖο
εὐαγέως θείοιο τέρεν δέμας· ἀμφὶ δὲ φᾶρος
ἕσσατο κυάνεον, τό ῥά οἱ πάρος ἐγγυάλιξεν   1205
Λημνιὰς Ὑψιπύλη, ἀδινῆς μνημήιον εὐνῆς.
πήχυιον δ' ἄρ' ἔπειτα πέδῳ ἔνι βόθρον ὀρύξας
νήησεν σχίζας, ἐπὶ δ' ἀρνειοῦ τάμε λαιμόν,
αὐτόν τ' εὖ καθύπερθε τανύσσατο· δαῖε δὲ φιτροὺς
πῦρ ὑπένερθεν ἱείς, ἐπὶ δὲ μιγάδας χέε λοιβάς,   1210
Βριμὼ κικλήσκων Ἑκάτην ἐπαρωγὸν ἀέθλων.
καί ῥ' ὁ μὲν ἀγκαλέσας πάλιν ἔστιχεν· ἡ δ' ἀίουσα
κευθμῶν ἐξ ὑπάτων δεινὴ θεὸς ἀντεβόλησεν
ἱροῖς Αἰσονίδαο· πέριξ δέ μιν ἐστεφάνωντο

1205 ῥά Hermann: μὲν codd.   1208 νήησεν L: νήησε G, vulg.

1201. πάτου, 'away from the beaten track': cf. *Il.* 20. 137, ἐκ πάτου.
1202. ὑπεύδιος, Alexandrine, 'under a clear sky,' cf. *Arg.* 1. 584, 4. 1731. εὔδιος, as in 1. 521, is first in Pind. *Pyth.* 5. 10.
εἰαμενῇσιν, 'meadow,' Homeric.
1203. πάμπρωτα, cf. *Il.* 17. 568, οἱ πάμπρωτα θεῶν ἠρήσατο πάντων.
λοέσσατο, for the genitive, v. n. 877.
1204. εὐαγέως, 'with proper reverence,' cf. 2. 699. The adverb is first in H. Hom. *Dem.* 274: the adjective is in tragedy and in a law of Solon ap. Andoc. 13. 8, ὁ ἀποκτείνας...ὅσιος ἔστω καὶ εὐαγής.
θείοιο, for the holiness of rivers, v. n. 165.
1205. κυάνεον, v. n. 140.
ἐγγυάλιξεν, 'gave,' v. n. 1016. The visit to Lemnos is described in *Arg.* 1. 609 f.
1206. ἀδινῆς, 'frequent,' schol. 'miserable,' v. n. 616. Here it may possibly be 'sweet,' a use attested as that of οἱ παλαιοί by Eustathius on *Il.* 2. 87.
1207. πήχυιον, v. n. 854.
1208. νήησεν, v. n. 290 and crit. note.
σχίζας, 'wood cleft small.' Homer has σχίζῃς in *Il.* 1. 462, *Od.* 3. 459, σχίζῃ in *Od.* 14. 425.
1210. μιγάδας, *i.e.* of milk, 1199, and

honey, 1036: the adj. is first in tragedy, Eur. *Bacc.* 18, *Andr.* 1142.
1211. Βριμώ, v. n. 861.
ἐπαρωγόν, 'helper.' It is feminine here and in 4. 196; masculine in 1. 32 and *Od.* 11. 498, the only Homeric instance.
1213. κευθμῶν. Apollonius is using a form found only once in Homer, *Il.* 13. 28, πάντοθεν ἐκ κευθμῶν; it is elsewhere only in Call. *H. Zeus* 34, Lyc. 317. κευθμῶνος is in 1290 infr., as in *Od.* 13. 367, of a cave: cf. of a pig-sty, *Od.* 10. 283.
ὑπάτων. Apollonius is unique in using this to mean 'lowest,' cf. 2. 207, μόλις ἐξ ὑπάτοιο Στήθεος. It is in the Homeric sense *summus* in 1. 222, κράατος ἐξ ὑπάτοιο, extended to mean 'furthest' in 4. 282, ὕπατον κέρας Ὠκεανοῖο. In Soph. *Ant.* 1331, it is 'best of all'; the meaning 'last' is of the Roman period.
ἀντεβόλησεν, 'came to receive,' v. n. 179.
1214. πέριξ, cf. 1291. Un-Homeric adverb, but common in tragedy.
ἐστεφάνωντο, cf. *Il.* 5. 739 of the aegis, ἣν περὶ μὲν πάντῃ φόβος ἐστεφάνωται: *ib.* 11. 36, 18. 485 τείρεα... τά τ' οὐρανὸς ἐστεφάνωται, 'has set in it as in a crown': and Hes. *Th.* 382 for the same phrase. This may be modelled on *Il.* 11. 36, τῇ δ' ἐπὶ μὲν Γοργὼ βλοσυρῶπις ἐστεφάνωτο Δεινὸν δερκομένη.

σμερδαλέοι δρυΐνοισι μετὰ πτόρθοισι δράκοντες·   1215
στράπτε δ' ἀπειρέσιον δαΐδων σέλας· ἀμφὶ δὲ τήνγε
ὀξείῃ ὑλακῇ χθόνιοι κύνες ἐφθέγγοντο.
πίσεα δ' ἔτρεμε πάντα κατὰ στίβον· αἱ δ' ὀλόλυξαν
νύμφαι ἑλειονόμοι ποταμηΐδες, αἳ περὶ κείνην
Φάσιδος εἰαμενὴν 'Αμαραντίου εἰλίσσονται.   1220
Αἰσονίδην δ' ἤτοι μὲν ἕλεν δέος, ἀλλά μιν οὐδ' ὣς
ἐντροπαλιζόμενον πόδες ἔκφερον, ὄφρ' ἑτάροισιν

1219 ποταμηΐδες L 16, Vat. unus, vulg.: ποταμηΐδες LG, Wellauer: ποταμΐτιδες
O. Schneider, Merkel.

1215. **σμερδαλέοι**, epithet of δράκων in *Il*. 2. 309, cf. 1257 infr. and n. 433. Dionysus received a similar crown from Zeus, Eur. *Bacc*. 101, στεφάνωσέν τε δρακόντων Στεφάνοις. Likewise the Bacchanals wore crowns of serpents, *ib*. 698, 768.

δρυΐνοισι. The sole authority for the crowning of Hecate with oakleaves, apart from this passage, is a fragment of Sophocles 'Ριζοτόμοι quoted in the scholia (Jebb and Pearson, 2. 176, *frag*. 535): στεφανωσαμένη δρυΐ καὶ πλεκτοῖς Ὠμῶν σπείραισι δρακόντων. Blaydes curiously reads κυσί, giving the goddess a truly terrifying crown of hell-hounds. There is no representation in art of Hecate either crowned with serpents, or in serpent form.

1216. **στράπτε**, v. n. 1018.

ἀπειρέσιον, either adjective, as in Homer, or better as adverb, cf. Qu. Sm. 2. 179, ἀπειρέσιον τρομέεσκον, *i.e.* 'gleam of countless torches,' or 'torches flashed unspeakably like lightning.' For the torches, cf. the meeting of Demeter and Hecate in H. Hom. *Dem*. 52, 61, σέλας ἐν χείρεσσιν ἔχουσα, αἰθομένας δαΐδας μετὰ χερσὶν ἔχουσα.

1217. **ἐφθέγγοντο**, 'the hounds of hell were baying.' Homer uses this of persons, as in 972 supr. The philosophers applied it to various animals, including worms and fishes. The usual offering to Hecate was a dog; this sacrifice is peculiar and marks the importance of the occasion. The hounds of Hecate are described in Lucian, *Phil*. 22. 24, as ἐλεφάντων ὑψηλότεροι, καὶ μέλανες καὶ λάσιοι, πιναρᾷ καὶ αὐχμώσῃ τῇ λάχνῃ.

1218. **κατὰ στίβον**, 'at her tread,' v. n. 534: cf. Soph. *Ph*. 487, χωρὶς

ἀνθρώπων στίβου. So too at the appearance of Hecate in *Aen*. 6. 256, 'sub pedibus mugire solum et iuga coepta moveri Silvarum, visaeque canes ululare per umbram Adventante dea.' Note the female dogs in the Latin, v. n. 1058. The theme is as old as Homer; cf. *Il*. 13. 18, τρέμε δ' οὔρεα μακρὰ καὶ ὕλη Ποσσὶν ὑπ' ἀθανάτοισι Ποσειδάωνος ἰόντος.

ὀλόλυξαν. Used always of women. In Homer it is either of triumph, *Od*. 22. 408, or raising the ritual cry at a sacrifice, *Od*. 3. 450. This cry may be either the latter, or a cry of fear; cf. H. Hom. *Ap*. 445, ὀλόλυξαν...Φοίβου ὑπὸ ῥιπῆς, μέγα γὰρ δέος εἷλεν ἕκαστον. With the passage of Ap., cf. *Aen*. 4. 168, 'summoque ulularunt vertice nymphae.' For the use by other divinities of the ritual cry to a god or goddess, cf. Ar. *Av*. 222, where all the gods of Olympus accompany the song of the nightingale with the ὀλολυγή. For the ὀλολυγή in general, v. Eitrem, *Beitr. zur gr. Religionsgeschichte* 3. 44 f.

1219. **ἑλειονόμοι**, cf. *Arg*. 2. 821. This form is first in Ap.; Hippocrates has ἑλονόμος.

ποταμηΐδες. First in Ap., also in Nicander and Nonnus. There are three kinds of nymphs in *Il*. 20. 8, αἵ τ' ἄλσεα καλὰ νέμονται Καὶ πηγὰς ποταμῶν καὶ πίσεα ποιήεντα.

1220. **εἰαμενήν**, v. n. 1202.

'Αμαραντίου, cf. *Arg*. 2. 399, 'Αμαραντῶν Τηλόθεν ἐξ ὀρέων πεδίοιό τε Κιρκαίοιο Φᾶσις δινήεις εὐρὺν ῥόον εἰς ἅλα βάλλει.

1222. **ἐντροπαλιζόμενον**, 'without one backward turn': cf. 1337 infr., and *Il*. 6. 496, ἄλοχος δὲ φίλη οἶκόνδε βεβήκει 'Εντροπαλιζομένη.

μίκτο κιών· ἤδη δὲ φόως νιφόεντος ὕπερθεν
Καυκάσου ἠριγενὴς Ἠὼς βάλεν ἀντέλλουσα.
Καὶ τότ' ἄρ' Αἰήτης περὶ μὲν στήθεσσιν ἕεστο   1225
θώρηκα στάδιον, τόν οἱ πόρεν ἐξεναρίξας
σφωιτέραις Φλεγραῖον Ἄρης ὑπὸ χερσὶ Μίμαντα·
χρυσείην δ' ἐπὶ κρατὶ κόρυν θέτο τετραφάληρον,
λαμπομένην οἷόν τε περίτροχον ἔπλετο φέγγος
ἠελίου, ὅτε πρῶτον ἀνέρχεται Ὠκεανοῖο.   1230
ἂν δὲ πολύρρινον νῶμα σάκος, ἂν δὲ καὶ ἔγχος
δεινόν, ἀμαιμάκετον· τὸ μὲν οὔ κέ τις ἄλλος ὑπέστη

1227 σφωιτέραις schol. Flor. et Par. : σφωιτέρῃς codd.   1229 περιτρόχου
Hoelzlin.

1223. μίκτο, 'joined': cf. Il. 5. 134, ἰὼν προμάχοισιν ἐμίχθη, and 1163 supr.

1224. ἠριγενής, v. n. 824.

ἀντέλλουσα, v. n. 520. This is an amplification of Homer typical of Apollonius at his best, cf. n. 166 supr. In Homer, the sun rises only to give light to men; Apollonius has five descriptions, each amplified by some touch adding to the beauty of the picture, and all different; viz. 162 supr.: 1. 519, αὐτὰρ ὅτ' αἰγλήεσσα φαεινοῖς ὄμμασιν ἠὼς Πηλίου αἰπεινὰς ἴδεν ἄκριας: ib. 1280: 2. 164: and 4. 1170, Ἠὼς δ' ἀμβροσίοισιν ἀνερχομένη φαέεσσιν λῦε κελαινὴν νύκτα δι' ἠέρος. It is worth while noticing that the Alexandrine interest in the order of nature is not confined to literature, but has its counterpart in contemporary art, in the general tendency towards atmospheric effects, images shining through transparent media, and the representation of stars: cf. Butcher, *Some Aspects of the Greek Genius*, pp. 298 f.

1225–1245. Aeetes and the Colchians go forth to attend the trials.

1225. ἕεστο, v. n. 454.

1226. στάδιον, cf. Call. *Hec. frag.* 19 (Mair), στάδιον δ' ὑφέεστο χιτῶνα. It is 'stiff,' because it was made of stiff plates of metal and could stand by itself; it sounds like the ancestor of the modern evening-dress shirt! Callimachus used this adj. of a tunic, in the sense of ὀρθοστάδιος, ungirdled, and falling straight from the neck to the feet: cf. Arist. *Lys.* 45, ὀρθοστάδια.

1227. σφωιτέραις, 'his,' v. n. 26.

Φλεγραῖον, 'at the battle of Phlegra,' v. n. 234. In Eur. *Ion* 216, he was slain by the thunderbolt of Zeus : in Apollod. 1. 6. 2, by Hephaestus : in Horace, *Carm.* 3. 4. 53, by Athena. The version followed by Apollonius is attested by the Berlin vase: v. Roscher, *Lex. s.v.* Mimas.

ὑπὸ χερσί, cf. *Il.* 2. 374, χερσὶν ὑφ' ἡμετέρῃσιν ἁλοῦσα.

1228. κόρυν. This accusative is in *Il.* 13. 131; Homer has also κόρυθα.

τετραφάληρον, cf. *Il.* 5. 743, κρατὶ δ' ἐπ' ἀμφίφαλον κυνέην θέτο τετραφάληρον: Buttmann assumes φάληρος from φαληριάω in *Il.* 13. 799, κύματα...φαληριόωντα, *i.e.* 'with four plumes.' Leaf on *Il.* 22. 315, cf. *Arg.* 2. 920, explains τετράφαλος in terms of φάλοι, 'metal projections.' The meaning of both words is uncertain.

1229. περίτροχον, 'round': cf. *Il.* 23. 455, σῆμα περίτροχον ἠΰτε μήνης. It has a passive force in Dion. Perieg. 987, περίτροχος ὕδασι λίμνη.

1230. ἀνέρχεται: elsewhere this is used with a preposition, and not the direct genitive: cf. Aesch. *Ag.* 658, ἀνῆλθε λαμπρὸν ἡλίου φάος: id. *Cho.* 536, ἀνῆλθον λαμπτῆρες, which is altered unnecessarily by some to ἀνῆθον.

1231. πολύρρινον, 'of many hides,' here only: cf. infr. 1299, εὔρινοι, and the ἑπταβόειον shield of Ajax in *Il.* 7. 222.

1232. ἀμαιμάκετον, 'irresistible,' common in Homer. It is either a reduplicated form of ἄμαχος, or from root μαιμακ-, μαιμάω.

ἀνδρῶν ἡρώων, ὅτε κάλλιπον Ἡρακλῆα
τῆλε παρέξ, ὅ κεν οἶος ἐναντίβιον πολέμιξεν.
τῷ δὲ καὶ ὠκυπόδων ἵππων εὐπηγέα δίφρον   1235
ἔσχε πέλας Φαέθων ἐπιβήμεναι· ἂν δὲ καὶ αὐτὸς
βήσατο, ῥυτῆρας δὲ χεροῖν ἔλεν. ἐκ δὲ πόληος
ἤλασεν εὐρεῖαν κατ᾽ ἀμαξιτόν, ὥς κεν ἀέθλῳ
παρσταίη· σὺν δέ σφιν ἀπείριτος ἔσσυτο λαός.
οἶος δ᾽ Ἴσθμιον εἶσι Ποσειδάων ἐς ἀγῶνα   1240
ἅρμασιν ἐμβεβαώς, ἢ Ταίναρον, ἢ ὅγε Λέρνης
ὕδωρ, ἠὲ κατ᾽ ἄλσος Ταντίου Ὀγχηστοῖο,
καί τε Καλαύρειαν μετὰ δαῖθ᾽ ἅμα νίσσεται ἵπποις,

1234 πολέμιξεν Merkel: πτολέμιξεν vulg.: πελέμιξε Paris. unus, Brunck. versum pro institicio habuit Herwerden.   1235 εὐπηγέα Brunck.   1237 ἔλεν Brunck, Platt: ἔχεν codd.   1238 ἀέθλῳ Vatt., Pariss. quatt.: ἀέθλων LG: ἀέθλων προσταίη Samuelsson.   1243 δαῖθ᾽ Wilamowitz: δῆθ᾽ codd.: δὴ θάμα Brunck.

ὑπέστη, 'none could have withstood its shock': cf. Eur. H.F. 1350, ὑποστῆναι βέλος. The account of the desertion of Heracles in Mysia is at the end of Book 1.

1234. τῆλε παρέξ, cf. Arg. 2. 272, ὑπὲρ πόντοιο φέροντο Τῆλε παρέξ: παρέξ is Homeric.

ἐναντίβιον, 'alone could have met it in the battle': cf. Il. 8. 168, ἐναντίβιον μαχέσασθαι, etc. It is once in Anth. Pal. 10. 8, as adj. The Homeric ἀντίβιον, abs. and with dative, is not in Ap., but he has ἀντιβίην, v. n. 384 supr.

1235. εὐπηγέα, v. n. 236.
1236. ἔσχε πέλας. This should be taken, with Platt, in the Homeric sense 'drove,' and ἔλεν should be read with him and Brunck in the next line. Phaethon was the charioteer of the sun, and Absyrtus-Phaethon in the same capacity follows his father into the chariot and takes the reins.

αὐτός, i.e. Phaethon: this is an echo of Od. 2. 419, ἂν δὲ καὶ αὐτοὶ βάντες ἐπὶ κληῖσι κάθιζον.

1237. ῥυτῆρας, 'reins': the Homeric sense is 'traces.' This is first found in tragedy; but in Il. 16. 475, ἐν δὲ ῥυτῆρσι τάνυσθεν, Leaf takes it in the former meaning, though he considers the other more natural. ῥυτά as 'reins' is first in Hes. Sc. 308: cf. Soph. O.C. 900, σπεύδειν ἀπὸ ῥυτῆρος.

1238. ἤλασεν, cf. n. 872, ἔλαεν.
1239. παρσταίη, cf. Il. 20. 120, Ἀχιλῆι Παρσταίη.
σφιν, commoner than σφίσι in Homer, and exclusively used by the Attic poets. Apollonius uses both freely.
ἀπείριτος, cf. H. Hom. Aph. 120, ὅμιλος ἀπείριτος: v. n. 971.
1240. Ἴσθμιον. The Isthmian games, held in the precinct of Poseidon.
1241. ἐμβεβαώς, cf. Il. 5. 199, ἅρμασιν ἐμβεβαῶτα.
Ταίναρον. Taenarus in Laconia had a famous temple of Poseidon.
ὅγε, v. n. 399.
Λέρνης, a marsh near Argos, famous on account of the hydra slain there by Heracles. For Poseidon's affaire with Amymone there, v. Apollod. 2. 1. 4.
1242. Ὀγχηστοῖο, this is mentioned in Il. 2. 506, Ὀγχηστὸν θ᾽ ἱερόν, and Paus. 9. 26. 5; but Strabo, 354. 31, considers it to be a fiction of the poets. Onchestus was the son of Poseidon, according to Paus. 9. 25. 5, or grandson, Eustath. 270. 14. The Hyantes were the primitive inhabitants of Boeotia, and were expelled by Cadmus or the Boeotians; they wandered thence to Phocis and Aetolia.
1243. Καλαύρειαν, an island in the Saronic gulf, which Poseidon received from Apollo in exchange for Delphi, Paus. 2. 33. 2, 10. 5. 6. Strabo, 8,

πέτρην θ' Αἱμονίην, ἢ δενδρήεντα Γεραιστόν·
τοῖος ἄρ' Αἰήτης Κόλχων ἀγὸς ἦεν ἰδέσθαι.　　　　1245
Τόφρα δὲ Μηδείης ὑποθημοσύνῃσιν Ἰήσων
φάρμακα μυδήνας ἠμὲν σάκος ἀμφεπάλυνεν
ἠδὲ δόρυ βριαρόν, περὶ δὲ ξίφος· ἀμφὶ δ' ἑταῖροι
πείρησαν τευχέων βεβιημένοι, οὐδ' ἐδύναντο
κεῖνο δόρυ γνάμψαι τυτθόν γέ περ, ἀλλὰ μάλ' αὔτως　　1250
ἀαγὲς κρατερῇσιν ἐνεσκλήκει παλάμῃσιν.
αὐτὰρ ὁ τοῖς ἄμοτον κοτέων Ἀφαρήιος Ἴδας
κόψε παρ' οὐρίαχον μεγάλῳ ξίφει· ἆλτο δ' ἀκωκὴ
ῥαιστὴρ ἄκμονος ὥστε, παλιντυπές· οἱ δ' ὁμάδησαν

1244 Πέτρην littera maiuscula scripsit Beck.　　　1249 λελιημένοι Naber.
1254-6 om. G.

p. 373, says that Poseidon gave Delos
to Leto in exchange for Calauria, and
Pytho to Apollo for Taenarus.
μετά...νίσσεται. In Homer only of
the declining sun, Il. 16. 779, μετενίσ-
σετο βουλυτόνδε. In this sense of 'going
in quest of,' it is first in Eur. Tr. 131,
μετανισσόμεναι...ἄλοχον.
δαῖθ'. So Wilamowitz for the trivial
δῆθ' of the MSS., cf. the simile in 876
supr. of Artemis in quest of a sacrifice.
This recalls Poseidon's visit to the
Aethiopians in Od. 1. 25, ἀντιόων ταύρων
τε καὶ ἀρνειῶν ἑκατόμβης.
1244. Αἱμονίην, v. n. 1090: the
scholiast on Pind. Pyth. 4. 139 refers to
games held there.
Γεραιστόν, in Euboea. Homer knows
of a famous temple there, Od. 3. 177,
ἐς δὲ Γεραιστὸν Ἐννύχιαι κατάγοντο·
Ποσειδάωνι δὲ ταύρων Πόλλ' ἐπὶ μῆρ'
ἔθεμεν. This list of sanctuaries is typical
of Alexandrine poetry, and is rather
alien to the spirit of Homer, who is
generally content with fewer instances.
In a religious sphere, it is parallel to
the ritual accumulation of epithets as
seen in 862 supr. in the case of Hecate.
1245. ἀγός, 'chief,' Homeric; dis-
tinguish from ἄγος, 203, 338.
1246-1277. Jason sprinkles his
weapons with the magic drugs, and
goes in the Argo to the scene of the
ordeal.
1246. ὑποθημοσύνῃσιν, 'instructions,'
as in Homer: the dative sing. is in
Xenophon.
1247. μυδήνας, v. n. 1042.

ἀμφεπάλυνεν, 'sprinkled.' The compound is here only; for the simple verb,
which is Homeric, cf. 69, 1256.
1249. πείρησαν, the normal use c.
gen.: for the accusative, v. n. 10.
βεβιημένοι, 'with might and main.'
This is formed by Ap. from the Homeric
βεβίηκεν of Il. 10. 145, etc.: v. n. 168.
1250. γνάμψαι, 'bend,' cf. 1350. This
is in Homer only in the dubious phrase
ἐν δὲ γόνυ γνάμψεν, Il. 23. 731.
1251. ἀαγές, 'unbroken.' The ἀ- is
long here and in Qu. Sm. 6. 596,
lengthened on the false analogy of
ἀθάνατος: it is short in Od. 11. 575, and
Theoc. 24. 123.
ἐνεσκλήκει, pluperfect of ἐνσκέλλω,
which is in Nicander and the Corpus
Hippocraticum. It was dry through
being seasoned, and therefore hard.
σκήλειε from σκέλλω is transitive in
Il. 23. 191, 'wither'; contrast Arg.
2. 201, ἐσκλήκει.
1252. ἄμοτον, 'insatiably,' common
in Homer with verbs of passion: for
Idas and his temper, v. n. 516.
1253. παρά, cf. Il. 4. 480, βάλε
στῆθος παρὰ μαζόν.
οὐρίαχον, 'butt-end,' Homeric. Compare the criticism in Aristotle, Poet.
1461 A, of Il. 10. 153, ἔγχεα δέ σφιν
Ὀρθ' ἐπὶ σαυρωτῆρος ἐλήλατο.
ἆλτο, cf. Il. 4. 125, ἆλτο δ' ὀιστός:
for the genitive, cf. Eur. H.F. 1148,
ἅλματα πέτρας, contrast Ion 1268,
πετραῖον ἅλμα.
1254. ῥαιστήρ, 'hammer': once in
Homer, Il. 18. 477, v. n. 790.

γηθόσυνοι ἥρωες ἐπ' ἐλπωρῇσιν ἀέθλου.　　　　1255
καὶ δ' αὐτὸς μετέπειτα παλύνετο· δῦ δέ μιν ἀλκὴ
σμερδαλέη ἄφατός τε καὶ ἄτρομος· αἱ δ' ἑκάτερθεν
χεῖρες ἐπερρώσαντο περὶ σθένεϊ σφριγόωσαι.
ὡς δ' ὅτ' ἀρήιος ἵππος ἐελδόμενος πολέμοιο
σκαρθμῷ ἐπιχρεμέθων κρούει πέδον, αὐτὰρ ὕπερθεν　　1260
κυδιόων ὀρθοῖσιν ἐπ' οὔασιν αὐχέν' ἀείρει·
τοῖος ἄρ' Αἰσονίδης ἐπαγαίετο κάρτεϊ γυίων.
πολλὰ δ' ἄρ' ἔνθα καὶ ἔνθα μετάρσιον ἴχνος ἔπαλλεν,
ἀσπίδα χαλκείην μελίην τ' ἐν χερσὶ τινάσσων.
φαίης κεν ζοφεροῖο κατ' αἰθέρος ἀίσσουσαν　　　1265
χειμερίην στεροπὴν θαμινὸν μεταπαιφάσσεσθαι

1262 ἐπαγάλλετο Herwerden.　　　1264 ἐνὶ Paris. unus, Brunck, Gerhard.
1265 κεν L: κε G, edd.　　　1266 μεταπαιφάσσουσαν v.l. in schol.

παλιντυπές, 'beaten back': here only, on the analogy of the Homeric παλιμπετές.
1255. ἐλπωρῇσιν. Here first in the plural, cf. Maximus *de Auspiciis* 399, κενεῇσιν ἐπ' ἐλπωρῇσι γεγηθώς: the singular as in 488 is Homeric.
1256. δῦ κ.τ.λ., cf. *Il.* 17. 210, δῦ δέ μιν Ἄρης Δεινὸς ἐννάλιος. For Jason's acquisition of courage at last, v. n. 21.
1257. σμερδαλέη, 'terrible': v. nn. 433, 1215, and the promise in 1043.
1258. ἐπερρώσαντο, 'moved nimbly.' A favourite word of Ap.; cf. Hes. *Th.* 8, ἐπερρώσαντο δὲ ποσσίν: *Arg.* 1. 385, ἐπὶ δ' ἐρρώσαντο πόδεσσιν. For its use of hair 'flowing down the head,' cf. *Arg.* 2. 677, πλοχμοὶ βοτρυόεντες ἐπερρώοντο κιόντι, and *Il.* 1. 529, χαῖται ἐπερρώσαντο ἄνακτος, *ib.* 23. 367.
περὶ...σφριγόωσαι. Probably a compound, 'swelling all round,' as in schol. Nic. *Alex.* 62, μοσχαρίον κρέατα ἐψήσας περισφριγῶντος: the simple verb is used with dative by Plato and Euripides. Contrast the adverbial περί in *Il.* 17. 22, περὶ σθένεϊ βλεμεαίνων, on which this may be modelled.
1259. ἐελδόμενος, v. n. 383, and for the genitive cf. 766.
1260. σκαρθμῷ, 'prancing,' from σκαίρω, an Alexandrine verb: cf. Arat. 282, τὸν δὲ μετασκαίροντα, and 281, σκαρθμός.
ἐπιχρεμέθων, 'neighing and prancing,'

first in Ap.: cf. Qu. Sm. 11. 328, φορβῇ ἐπιχρεμέθοντες ἄδην. χρεμετίζω is Homeric, χρεμέθων is in Opp. *Cyn.* 1. 234, cf. *Anth. Pal.* 9. 295, μὴ θάμβει χρεμέθοντα (πῶλον).
1261. ὀρθοῖσιν, cf. *Arg.* 1. 514, ὀρθοῖσιν ἐπ' οὔασιν ἠρεμέοντες, and the simile of the steed in Soph. *El.* 26, ἐν τοῖσι δεινοῖς θυμὸν οὐκ ἀπώλεσεν Ἀλλ' ὀρθὸν οὖς ἵστησιν.
1262. ἐπαγαίετο, v. n. 470. This simile is founded on that in *Il.* 6. 506, of Paris going forth to battle: ὡς δ' ὅτε τις στατὸς ἵππος, ἀκοστήσας ἐπὶ φάτνῃ Δεσμὸν ἀπορρήξας θείῃ πεδίοιο προαίνων Εἰωθὼς λούεσθαι ἐϋρρεῖος ποταμοῖο, Κυδιόων· ὑψοῦ δὲ κάρη ἔχει, ἀμφὶ δὲ χαῖται Ὤμοις ἀίσσονται· ὁ δ' ἀγλαΐηφι πεποιθὼς Ῥίμφα ἑ γοῦνα φέρει μετά τ' ἤθεα καὶ νομὸν ἵππων, Ὣς υἱὸς Πριάμοιο Πάρις κ.τ.λ. It is imitated, of Turnus, in *Aen.* 11. 492.
1263. πολλά, 'often,' v. n. 313.
μετάρσιον, cognate accusative, 'up in the air,' 'aloft': first in Emped. 35. 9, and common in tragedy.
ἔπαλλεν. So too before the contest in *Arg.* 2. 45, Polydeuces πῆλε δὲ χεῖρας Πειράζων.
1265. ζοφεροῖο, 'gloomy.' ζόφος is Homeric, but the adj. is first in Hesiod, *Th.* 814, πέρην Χάεος ζοφεροῖο.
1266. θαμινόν, probably adverb, 'frequently,' rather than adj. with στεροπήν. The adj. is not elsewhere in

ἐκ νεφέων, ὅτε πέρ τε μελάντατον ὄμβρον ἄγωνται.
καὶ τότ' ἔπειτ' οὐ δηρὸν ἔτι σχήσεσθαι ἀέθλων
μέλλον· ἀτὰρ κληῖσιν ἐπισχερὼ ἱδρυθέντες
ῥίμφα μάλ' ἐς πεδίον τὸ Ἀρήιον ἠπείγοντο.   1270
τόσσον δὲ προτέρω πέλεν ἄστεος ἀντιπέρηθεν,
ὅσσον τ' ἐκ βαλβῖδος ἐπήβολος ἅρματι νύσσα
γίγνεται, ὁππότ' ἄεθλα καταφθιμένοιο ἄνακτος
κηδεμόνες πεζοῖσι καὶ ἱππήεσσι τίθενται.
τέτμον δ' Αἰήτην τε καὶ ἄλλων ἔθνεα Κόλχων,   1275
τοὺς μὲν Καυκασίοισιν ἐφεσταότας σκοπέλοισιν,
τὸν δ' αὐτοῦ παρὰ χεῖλος ἑλισσόμενον ποταμοῖο.

1267 ὅτε πέρ τε Ziegler: ὅτ' ἔπειτα codd.: ἅτ' ἔπειτα...ἄγονται Koechly.
ἄγονται vulg.   1269 ἱδρυνθέντες codd.   1277 ἑλισσομένου Herwerden.

Ap.; cf. Call. *H. Dem.* 64, θαμιναί...
εἰλαπίναι. Homer has adv. θαμά, cf. 954;
Pindar has θαμινά, *Ol.* 1. 53, and
θαμινῶς is mentioned in Hesychius.

μεταπαιφάσσεσθαι, 'flash,' here
only: the simple verb is in 4. 1442,
and *Il.* 2. 450. For the 'wintry lightning,'
cf. the simile infr. 1360.

1267. **ὅτε πέρ τε.** Ziegler's correction
of the MSS. from *Il.* 10. 7, ἠ νιφετόν,
ὅτε πέρ τε χιὼν ἐπάλυνεν ἀρούρας: the
corruption is from ἔπειτα in the next
line, cf. *Arg.* 1. 234.

ὄμβρον. Thunder rain, as opposed to
ὑετός, cf. *Il.* 10. 6.

1268. **σχήσεσθαι,** 'refrain from,'
common use c. gen.: v. n. 514.

1269. **κληῖσιν.** The benches on which
the rowers sat: in *Il.* 16. 170, it may
mean either this, or 'thole-pins.' For
the latter Ap. uses the post-Homeric
word σκαλμοί, 1. 379.

ἐπισχερώ, 'in order,' v. n. 170. For
ἱδρυθέντες rather than ἱδρυνθέντες, v.
crit. appendix, p. 141.

1271. **ἀντιπέρηθεν,** 'on the further
side of,' 'beyond.' The Argonauts rowed
the boat past the city, while Aeetes
drove, 1238. Similarly in *Arg.* 2. 1030,
they were rowing 'almost past the
island,' σχεδὸν ἀντιπέρηθεν νήσου, when
they decided to land: in 1. 977, it is
'from the mainland opposite.' The word
is first in Ap. and in the *Anthology.*

1272. **βαλβῖδος,** un-Homeric, used in
tragedy in sing. and pl. It is properly
the rope stretched between the posts,

and comes to be used for the posts
themselves, cf. Eur. *H.F.* 867, βαλβίδων
ἄπο.

ἐπήβολος, 'which a chariot must
reach.' Ap. seems to use only this
passive sense, 'attainable': but Homer
has also an active use, *Od.* 2. 319
νηὸς ἐπήβολος, *i.e.* 'in possession of the
ship.' There may possibly be something
of an active sense in *Arg.* 4. 1380,
μῆτις ἐπήβολος, *i.e.* 'hitting the mark,'
'fitting,' but it is more probably passive
as here. Apollonius is thinking of the
pillars at the opposite end of the
hippodrome, rather than of the Homeric
racecourse: 'it lay as far beyond, on
the other side of the city, as the winning
post at which a chariot aims is distant
from the starting post.'

νύσσα, 'winning post.' In Homer,
it may mean either the 'starting'
or the 'winning' post; actually, of
course, they were one and the same
post.

1273. **ἄεθλα,** compare the funeral
games of Pelias, mentioned in *Arg.* 1.
1304.

1274. **κηδεμόνες,** probably in the
Homeric sense, 'kindred mourners,'
v. n. 732.

1276. **ἐφεσταότας,** v. n. 121. The
Caucasus and the city were on one side
of the river, the plain and the grove
of Ares on the other.

1277. **ἑλισσόμενον,** not neut., but
masc., of Aeetes, 'wheeling about' in
his chariot, cf. *Il.* 18. 372 of Hephaestus,

Αἰσονίδης δ᾽, ὅτε δὴ πρυμνήσια δῆσαν ἑταῖροι,
δή ῥα τοτε ξὺν δουρὶ καὶ ἀσπίδι βαῖν᾽ ἐς ἄεθλον,
νηὸς ἀποπροθορών· ἄμυδις δ᾽ ἕλε παμφανόωσαν   1280
χαλκείην πήληκα θοῶν ἔμπλειον ὀδόντων
καὶ ξίφος ἀμφ᾽ ὤμοις, γυμνὸς δέμας, ἄλλα μὲν Ἄρει
εἴκελος, ἄλλα δέ που χρυσαόρῳ Ἀπόλλωνι.
παπτήνας δ᾽ ἀνὰ νειὸν ἴδε ζυγὰ χάλκεα ταύρων
αὐτόγυόν τ᾽ ἐπὶ τοῖς στιβαροῦ ἀδάμαντος ἄροτρον.   1285
χρίμψε δ᾽ ἔπειτα κιών, παρὰ δ᾽ ὄβριμον ἔγχος ἔπηξεν
ὀρθὸν ἐπ᾽ οὐριάχῳ, κυνέην δ᾽ ἀποκάτθετ᾽ ἐρείσας.
βῆ δ᾽ αὐτῇ προτέρωσε σὺν ἀσπίδι νήριτα ταύρων
ἴχνια μαστεύων· οἱ δ᾽ ἔκποθεν ἀφράστοιο

1283 χρυσαόρῳ G, L 16, Vatt. duo: χρυσάορι vulg.

ἐλισσόμενον περὶ φύσας. It cannot be applied to a bank, which is at rest, as in 138 supr. to a line which has been drawn, and then is at rest. This is a touch well in keeping with the restless character of Aeetes: cf. *Arg.* 4. 1198, of the nymphs at the marriage of Jason, ἐλισσόμεναι περὶ κύκλον.

1278-1329. Jason overcomes the fire-breathing bulls, and leads them under the yoke.

1280. ἀποπροθορών, 'leaping out of the ship.' The double compound is first here; προθορών is Homeric.

1281. θοῶν, 'swift' in Homer, and then used in a variety of senses: 'sharp,' infr. 1318: of fire, 1303: of dogs, 'fierce,' 1373.

ἔμπλειον, 'full,' the Homeric form; contrast the Alexandrine ἐνίπλεον, 119 supr.

1282. γυμνός, *i.e.* not enclosed like Aeetes in a στάδιος θώρηξ.

1283. χρυσαόρῳ, 'of the golden sword,' an obvious echo of *Il.* 5. 509, Φοίβου Ἀπόλλωνος χρυσαόρου, which is repeated probably without knowledge of the meaning. The difficulty is, that the sword is not the weapon of Apollo; and as the title is applied also to Artemis, Demeter and Orpheus, it is best with Leaf, on *Il. loc. cit.*, to regard it as an archaic title of unknown significance.

1285. αὐτόγυον, v. n. 232; the line is repeated from there with a slight alteration.

1286. χρίμψε, 'drew near.' Homer has only the compound ἐγχρίμπτω, which is not in Ap., in the transitive sense of 'bringing near': contrast the intransitive use in Soph. *El.* 898, μή πού τις ἡμῖν ἐγγὺς ἐγχρίμπτῃ βροτῶν.

1287. οὐριάχῳ, v. n. 1253.

κυνέην. Jason must have been carrying the teeth in another helmet, which here he props against the spear to prevent the teeth from falling out, and picks up in 1321: his own helmet, of course, he would be wearing all the time. Cf. in Verg.(?) *Moret.* 123, Simylus puts his helmet on before ploughing: 'ambit crura ocreis paribus tectusque galero Sub iuga parentes cogit lorata iuvencos.'

ἀποκάτθετο, put 'down,' 'away from' him; not 'off.' It takes the genitive, 817 supr.

ἐρείσας, *i.e.* 'leaning it against the spear.'

1288. αὐτῇ, 'shield and all,' not 'with shield alone.'

νήριτα, 'countless,' as in Homer: the Hesiodic meaning 'immense' is in *Arg.* 4. 158, cf. Hes. *Op.* 511. Derivations are given from νη-ἐρίζειν, νη-ἀριθμός.

1289. μαστεύων, 'tracking out,' not 'looking for,' since they must have been clear enough. The word is first in Hes. ap. schol. Pind. *Nem.* 4. 95.

ἔκποθεν ἀφράστοιο, 'from some unseen place': cf. 2. 224, 824, and v. n. 262.

ἀφράστοιο, post-Homeric. Either

κευθμῶνος χθονίου, ἵνα τέ σφισιν ἔσκε βόαυλα   1290
καρτερὰ λιγνυόεντι πέριξ εἰλυμένα καπνῷ,
ἄμφω ὁμοῦ προγένοντο πυρὸς σέλας ἀμπνείοντες.
ἔδδεισαν δ᾽ ἥρωες, ὅπως ἴδον. αὐτὰρ ὁ τούσγε,
εὖ διαβάς, ἐπιόντας, ἅ τε σπιλὰς εἰν ἁλὶ πέτρη
μίμνει ἀπειρεσίῃσι δονεύμενα κύματ᾽ ἀέλλαις.   1295
πρόσθε δέ οἱ σάκος ἔσχεν ἐναντίον· οἱ δέ μιν ἄμφω
μυκηθμῷ κρατεροῖσιν ἐνέπληξαν κεράεσσιν·
οὐδ᾽ ἄρα μιν τυτθόν περ ἀνώχλισαν ἀντιόωντες.
ὡς δ᾽ ὅτ᾽ ἐνὶ τρητοῖσιν ἐύρρινοι χοάνοισιν
φῦσαι χαλκήων ὁτὲ μέν τ᾽ ἀναμαρμαίρουσιν,   1300
πῦρ ὀλοὸν πιμπρᾶσαι, ὅτ᾽ αὖ λήγουσιν ἀυτμῆς,

1294 ἐπιόσσετ᾽ Damste.   1295 μίμνειν Vat. unus, unde μίμνεν Merkel.
1299 ἐύρρινοι Par. unus e corr.: ἐύρρινοις vulg.   1300 ἀναμορμύρουσιν Ruhnken:
ἀναμαιμάουσιν Merkel.

'unseen,' as here, or 'wonderful': cf.
H. Hom. *Herm.* 80, 353, Arat. 608.
κευθμῶνος is local genitive, governed
only indirectly by ἔκποθεν: like κευθμός,
it is Homeric, v. n. 1213.
1290. **βόαυλα**. Here only: cf. βόαυλος
in Theoc. 25. 108, βοαύλιον in *Or. Arg.*
438.
1291. **λιγνυόεντι**, 'murky,' only here
and in *Arg.* 2. 133, λιγνυόεντι Κάπνῳ
τυφόμεναι.
πέριξ, un-Homeric, v. n. 1214.
εἰλυμένα, 'enveloped in,' v. n. 281.
1292. **προγένοντο**, 'both rushed forward together,' v. n. 319. This recalls
οἱ δὲ τάχα προγένοντο of oxen, in *Il.*
18. 525: cf. Call. *H. Art.* 178 βόες...
κόπρον ἔπι προγένοιντο.
ἀμπνείοντες, v. n. 410.
1293. **ἔδδεισαν**, for the double -δδ-,
v. n. 318; cf. Call. *H. Art.* 51, αἱ
νύμφαι δ᾽ ἔδδεισαν, ὅπως ἴδον.
1294. **εὖ διαβάς**, 'with feet well
apart': cf. *Il.* 12. 458, *Arg.* 1. 1199.
ὅ τε. Platt, following Merkel, reads
μίμνεν, comparing infr. 1390, on the
grounds that ἅ τε cannot take a verb;
but the alteration is not required, as it
does so in *Arg.* 2. 70, ἅ τε κῦμα κορύσ-
σεται. μίμνεν for Jason can be assumed
from μίμνει, 'he awaited their onslaught
like....' The simile is founded on *Il.* 15.
618: ἴσχον γὰρ πυργηδὸν ἀρηρότες, ἠύτε
πέτρη Ἠλίβατος μεγάλη, πολιῆς ἁλὸς

ἐγγὺς ἐοῦσα Ἥτε μένει λιγέων ἀνέμων
λαιψηρὰ κέλευθα, Κύματά τε τροφόεντα,
τά τε προσερεύγεται αὐτήν: it is imitated
in *Aen.* 10. 693.
σπιλάς. Here adjective; in Homer
it is a noun. Πλαγκτῆσιν σπιλάδεσσιν
in *Arg.* 4. 932 may be either.
1295. **δονεύμενα**, of the waves, 'lashed
to fury.'
1297. **μυκηθμῷ**, v. n. 864: for the
double dative, v. n. 346.
1298. **ἀνώχλισαν**, 'disturbed him
not a jot by their onset.' The simple
verb is Homeric, but the compound is
first in Ap. and Oppian; cf. *Arg.* 4.
1677, ἂν δὲ βαρείας Ὀχλίζων λάιγγας.
1299. **ἐύρρινοι**. Here and in the
Anthology only: cf. 1231, πολύρρινος.
χοάνοισιν, 'melting pot.' The simile
is imitated from *Il.* 18. 470: φῦσαι δ᾽
ἐν χοάνοισιν ἐείκοσι πᾶσαι ἐφύσων,
Παντοίην εὔπρηστον ἀυτμὴν ἐξανιεῖσαι,
Ἄλλοτε μὲν σπεύδοντι παρέμμεναι, ἄλλοτε δ᾽ αὖτε, Ὅππως Ἥφαιστός τ᾽ ἐθέλοι
καὶ ἔργον ἄνοιτο: cf. Hes. *Th.* 863,
εὐτρήτοις χοάνοισι.
1300. **ἀναμαρμαίρουσιν**. Here only,
though the simple verb is common, from
Homer onwards; it is rightly supported
here by Mooney against various emen-
dations, for which v. crit. note. It
combines the two ideas of the flash of
the flame and the puff of the bellows.
1301. **ἀυτμῆς**, v. n. 531.

δεινὸς δ' ἐξ αὐτοῦ πέλεται βρόμος, ὁππότ' ἀίξῃ
νειόθεν· ὡς ἄρα τώγε θοὴν φλόγα φυσιόωντες
ἐκ στομάτων ὁμάδευν, τὸν δ' ἄμφεπε δήιον αἶθος
βάλλον ἅ τε στεροπή· κούρης δέ ἑ φάρμακ' ἔρυτο.   1305
καί ῥ' ὅγε δεξιτεροῖο βοὸς κέρας ἄκρον ἐρύσσας
εἷλκεν ἐπικρατέως παντὶ σθένει, ὄφρα πελάσσῃ
ζεύγλῃ χαλκείῃ, τὸν δ' ἐν χθονὶ κάββαλεν ὀκλάξ,
ῥίμφα ποδὶ κρούσας πόδα χάλκεον. ὡς δὲ καὶ ἄλλον
σφῆλεν γνὺξ ἐπιόντα, μιῇ βεβολημένον ὁρμῇ.   1310
εὐρὺ δ' ἀποπροβαλὼν χαμάδις σάκος, ἔνθα καὶ ἔνθα,
τῇ καὶ τῇ βεβαώς, ἄμφω ἔχε πεπτηῶτας
γούνασιν ἐν προτέροισι, διὰ φλογὸς εἶθαρ ἐλυσθείς.
θαύμασε δ' Αἰήτης σθένος ἀνέρος. οἱ δ' ἄρα τείως
Τυνδαρίδαι—δὴ γάρ σφι πάλαι προπεφραδμένον ἦεν—   1315

1302 αὐτῶν Pariss., Brunck, Wellauer: αὖ τοῦ Merkel: αἴθου Damste.
1304 ὁμόδευν Hermann: ὁμάδουν Stephanus: ὁμάδῳ vulg.   ἄμφεπε Merkel:
ἀμφὶ τε codd.: ἀμφί ἑ Hermann, Wilamowitz.   1305 βάλλον Merkel:
βάλλεν codd., Wilamowitz: βάλλε θ' ἅτε Ziegler.   1310 σφῆλε LG.   ἐριπόντα
Breidenbach, Wilamowitz, cf. Il. 8. 329.   1311 ita post ἔνθα atque βεβαώς
interpunxit Platt.   1313 δι' ἐκ O. Schneider.   1315 προπεφασμένον Hermann.

1302. **αὐτοῦ**, i.e. the fire, cf. πῦρ in
the line before; Damste reads αἴθου.
1303. **θοήν**, v. n. 1281.
φυσιόωντες, v. n. 410.
1304. **ὁμάδευν**, v. n. 564.
ἄμφεπε, 'played round him,' v.n. 547.
αἶθος, cf. n. 39. It is neuter here
only; the masculine is in Eur. *Supp.*
208, if the text is sound.
1307. **ἐπικρατέως**, 'with might and
main,' common in *Iliad*, but not in
Odyssey: cf. *Il.* 23. 863, ἦκεν ἐπικρατέως.
ὄφρα, v. n. 909: Homer uses the
optative after a past tense.
1308. **ζεύγλῃ**, 'yoke collar.' Leaf on
Il. 17. 440, ζεύγλης ἐξεριποῦσα, explains
it as a cushion round the yoke to prevent chafing of the neck: but the epithet
χαλκείη here shews that Ap. attached
no such meaning to it.
ὀκλάξ, 'on to its knees,' v. n. 122.
1310. **σφῆλεν**, cf. *Od.* 17. 464, οὐδ'
ἄρα μιν σφῆλεν βέλος Ἀντινόοιο: *Il.* 5.
357, ἡ δὲ γνὺξ ἐριποῦσα: 8. 329, στῆ δὲ
γνὺξ ἐριπών.

βεβολημένον, 'smitten with one swift
movement.' Homer uses this participle
in metaphorical, βεβλημένος in literal
sense: Ap. makes no such distinction,
cf. *Arg.* I. 262, μητὴρ ἀμφ' αὐτὸν
βεβολημένη.
1311. **ἀποπροβαλών**, the double compound is here only, the single compound
is Homeric.
1312. **βεβαώς**, 'standing,' cf. Qu.
Sm. 4. 252, στιβαροῖς ποσὶν ἐμβεβαῶτα.
Punctuate with Platt with a comma
after both ἔνθα and βεβαώς, i.e. 'held
the bulls down on right and left, standing with feet planted wide apart on
right and left.' Jason surely did not
'stride' from one side to another like
an acrobat!
πεπτηῶτας, from πίπτω, 'where they
had fallen': v. n. 321.
1313. **εἶθαρ**, 'in a moment,' frequent
in *Iliad*, but not in *Odyssey*.
ἐλυσθείς, 'enveloped in,' v. n. 281.
1315. **προπεφραδμένον**, 'previously
appointed as their task': first in Hes.
Op. 655, τά τε προπεφραδμένα πολλά.

ἀγχίμολον ζυγά οἱ πεδόθεν δόσαν ἀμφιβαλέσθαι.
αὐτὰρ ὁ εὖ ἐνέδησε λόφους· μεσσηγὺ δ' ἀείρας
χάλκεον ἱστοβοῆα, θοῇ συνάρασσε κορώνῃ
ζεύγληθεν. καὶ τὼ μὲν ὑπὲκ πυρὸς ἂψ ἐπὶ νῆα
χαζέσθην. ὁ δ' ἄρ' αὖτις ἑλὼν σάκος ἔνθετο νώτῳ   1320
ἐξόπιθεν, καὶ γέντο θοῶν ἔμπλειον ὀδόντων
πήληκα βριαρὴν δόρυ τ' ἄσχετον, ᾧ ῥ' ὑπὸ μέσσας
ἐργατίνης ὥς τίς τε Πελασγίδι νύσσεν ἀκαίνῃ
οὐτάζων λαγόνας· μάλα δ' ἔμπεδον εὖ ἀραρυῖαν
τυκτὴν ἐξ ἀδάμαντος ἐπιθύνεσκεν ἐχέτλην.   1325
οἱ δ' εἵως μὲν δὴ περιώσια θυμαίνεσκον,
λάβρον ἐπιπνείοντε πυρὸς σέλας· ὦρτο δ' ἀυτμὴ

1319 ὑπὲρ L, vulg.   1320 ἄνθετο vulg.   1324 αὖ G.   1326 οἱ δ' εἵως
Merkel: οἱ δ' ἤτοι εἵως LG: οἱ δὲ τέως edd. vett.: οἱ δ' ἤτοι εἵως περιώσια
O. Schneider.

1316. **ἀγχίμολον**, 'near by': cf. *Il.*
24. 352, ἐξ ἀγχιμόλοιο, 4. 529, ἀγχίμολον δέ οἱ ἦλθε.
πεδόθεν, 'from the ground.' For this
literal meaning, cf. Eur. *Tro.* 98, ἄνα,
δύσδαιμον, πεδόθεν κεφαλήν. Homer uses
it metaphorically, *Od.* 13. 295, οἵ τοι
πεδόθεν φίλοι εἰσίν: contrast Hes.
Th. 680, πεδόθεν δὲ τινάσσετο μακρὸς
Ὄλυμπος. Hesychius explains it as
ἀρχῆθεν, etc., or παιδόθεν. Merkel finds
the former here, and the latter in *Arg.*
I. 1199, πεδόθεν δὲ βαθύρριζόν περ
ἐοῦσαν *sc.* ἐλάτην: but it has probably
the literal meaning in both cases.
1317. **λόφους**, the necks of the bulls.
1318. **ἱστοβοῆα**, 'plough-tree': first
in Hes. *Op.* 431, γόμφοισιν πελάσας
προσαρήρεται ἱστοβοῆι.
θοῇ, 'sharp,' v. n. 1281.
συνάρασσε, 'made fast': in Homer
only *in tmesi.*
1319. **ζεύγληθεν**, *i.e.* ἐκ τῆς ζεύγλης,
here only: the English idiom is to
fasten *to*, rather than *from.* 'He lifted
the bronze pole and placed it between
them, and fastened it to the yoke by its
sharp tip.'
1320. **χαζέσθην**, *i.e.* the Tyndaridae:
for the verb, v. n. 436.
1321. **γέντο**, 'grasped,' as in Homer;
the verb exists only in this form.
ἔμπλειον, v. n. 119. This was the
second helmet, not his own: v. nn.
1281, 1287.

1322. **ἄσχετον**, cf. 606: Homer has
also ἀάσχετος, which is not in Ap.
1323. **ἐργατίνης**, Alexandrine,
'ploughman': cf. Theoc. 10. 1, ἐργατίνα
Βουκαῖε.
Πελασγίδι, 'Thessalian.' Apollonius
regards the Pelasgians as the Thessalians: Thessaly is αἶα Πελασγῶν in
Arg. 1. 580, cf. the Homeric Πελασγικὸν
Ἄργος, *Il.* 2. 681.
ἀκαίνῃ, lit. 'thorn,' *i.e.* 'goad': cf.
Agathias in *Anth. Pal.* 6. 41, βού-
πληκτρον ἄκανθαν. According to the
scholiast, it was a ten foot Thessalian
measure, or a shepherd's stick invented
by the Thessalians; cf. Call. *frag.* 67
(Mair), ἀμφότερον κέντρον τε βοῶν καὶ
μέτρον ἀρούρης. For the second meaning,
v. Olympiod. ad Arist. *Meteor.* 25 A.
1325. **ἐπιθύνεσκεν**, cf. Soph. *Ph.*
1059 of a bow, ἐπιθύνειν χερί.
ἐχέτλην, 'plough-handle': first in
Hes. *Op.* 465, ἄκρον ἐχέτλης Χειρὶ
λαβών.
1326. **εἵως**, *metri gratiâ*, as in Homer,
for ἕως.
περιώσια, post-Homeric as adverb,
v. n. 334.
θυμαίνεσκον, poetic only, first in Hes.
Sc. 262, ὄμμασι θυμήνασαι, and in
drama.
1327. **ἐπιπνείοντε**, 'breathing,'
modelled on the description of the
Chimaera in *Il.* 6. 182, δεινὸν ἀποπνείουσα πυρὸς μένος αἰθομένοιο: in 937 supr.,

ἠύτε βυκτάων ἀνέμων βρόμος, οὕς τε μάλιστα
δειδιότες μέγα λαῖφος ἁλίπλοοι ἐστείλαντο.
δηρὸν δ' οὐ μετέπειτα κελευόμενοι ὑπὸ δουρὶ   1330
ἦισαν· ὀκριόεσσα δ' ἐρείκετο νειὸς ὀπίσσω,
σχιζομένη ταύρων τε βίῃ κρατερῷ τ' ἀροτῆρι.
δεινὸν δ' ἐσμαράγευν ἄμυδις κατὰ ὦλκας ἀρότρῳ
βώλακες ἀγνύμεναι ἀνδραχθέες· εἵπετο δ' αὐτὸς
λαῖον ἐπὶ στιβαρῷ πιέσας ποδί· τῆλε δ' ἑοῖο   1335
βάλλεν ἀρηρομένην αἰεὶ κατὰ βῶλον ὀδόντας
ἐντροπαλιζόμενος, μή οἱ πάρος ἀντιάσειεν
γηγενέων ἀνδρῶν ὀλοὸς στάχυς· οἱ δ' ἄρ' ἐπιπρὸ
χαλκείῃς χηλῇσιν ἐρειδόμενοι πονέοντο.
ἦμος δὲ τρίτατον λάχος ἤματος ἀνομένοιο   1340
λείπεται ἐξ ἠοῦς, καλέουσι δὲ κεκμηῶτες

1330 δηναιὸν G.   1331 ὀκριόεσσα G: ὀκρυόεσσα L, vulg.   1333 ἀρότρῳ
Damste: ἀρότρου codd.   1335 λαῖον supr. γρ. βαθμὸν L: λαῖον G:
βαθμὸν vulg.: λαιῷ...στιβαρῶς Samuelsson.   1340 λέχος G.   1341 χατέουσι
Naber.

it is 'inspire,' 'breathe upon.' For the
mixture of dual and plural, cf. 410,
1173, v. n. 206.
ἀντμή, v. n. 531.
1328. βυκτάων ἀνέμων, 'blustering':
cf. *Od.* 10. 20, ἔνθα δὲ βυκτάων ἀνέμων
κατέδησε κέλευθα, and *Or. Arg.* 1103.
1329. δειδιότες. Homeric; for the
un-Homeric form, v. n. 753.
ἁλίπλοοι, 'sailors': cf. Call. *H. Del.*
15, ἰχθυβοληῆες ἁλίπλοοι. In *Il.* 12.
26, ἁλίπλοα τείχεα is 'covered with
water.'
1330–1353. Jason ploughs the field
of Ares and sows the dragon's teeth.
1331. ἐρείκετο, 'was broken up': cf.
Hes. *Sc.* 286, ἀροτῆρες Ἥρεικον χθόνα.
In *Il.* 13. 441, ἐρεικομένης περὶ δουρὶ is
of a tunic, 'torn.'
1332. ἀροτῆρι. Homeric, 'ploughman.'
1333. ὦλκας, v. n. 1054.
ἀρότρῳ. Emend from the genitive
with Damste, who reasonably comments
'miror aratrum sulcum habens': *i.e.*
'broken up by the plough along the
furrows.' Compare Hdt. 2. 14, ἀρότρῳ
ἀναρήγνυντες αὔλακας.
1334. ἀνδραχθέες, 'as heavy as a man

could lift': cf. *Od.* 10. 121, ἀνδραχθέσι
χερμαδίοισιν.
1335. λαῖον. This, if genuine, must
be the ploughshare, though the lexicographers explain it as a sickle.
Samuelsson suggests λαιῷ...στιβαρῶς,
and that the vulgate βαθμόν, 'step,'
has been introduced to give an object
to the verb.
1336. ἀρηρομένην, from ἀρόω: cf.
Il. 18. 548, ἀρηρομένη. The aorist is
peculiar to Ap., v. n. 497.
1337. ἐντροπαλιζόμενος, 'frequently
turning round,' v. n. 1222.
1338. στάχυς, v. n. 1054.
ἐπιπρό, common in Ap., v. n. 665.
1340. τρίτατον. Like Homer, Apollonius divides the day and the night
each into three watches. This may be
modelled on *Il.* 10. 251, μάλα γὰρ νὺξ
ἄνεται, ἐγγύθι δ' ἠώς, Ἄστρα δὲ δὴ
προβέβηκε, παροίχωκεν δὲ πλέων νὺξ Τῶν
δύο μοιράων, τριτάτη δ' ἐπὶ μοῖρα λέλειπται.
Compare also Moschus, *Europa*, 2,
νυκτὸς ὅτε τρίτατον λάχος ἵσταται.
ἀνομένοιο, 'as it wanes from dawn,'
cf. 2. 494. The ἀ- is long in Homer,
except in the disputed ἔργον ἄνοιτο, or
ἄνυτο, of *Il.* 18. 473, cited on 1299 supr.

ἐργατίναι γλυκερόν σφιν ἄφαρ βουλυτὸν ἱκέσθαι,
τῆμος ἀρήροτο νειὸς ὑπ' ἀκαμάτῳ ἀροτῆρι,
τετράγυός περ ἐοῦσα· βοῶν τ' ἀπελύετ' ἄροτρα.
καὶ τοὺς μὲν πεδίονδε διεπτοίησε φέβεσθαι·   1345
αὐτὰρ ὁ ἂψ ἐπὶ νῆα πάλιν κίεν, ὄφρ' ἔτι κεινὰς
γηγενέων ἀνδρῶν ἴδεν αὔλακας. ἀμφὶ δ' ἑταῖροι
θάρσυνον μύθοισιν. ὁ δ' ἐκ ποταμοῖο ῥοάων
αὐτῇ ἀφυσσάμενος κυνέῃ σβέσεν ὕδατι δίψαν·
γνάμψε δὲ γούνατ' ἐλαφρά, μέγαν δ' ἐμπλήσατο θυμὸν 1350
ἀλκῆς, μαιμώων συῒ εἴκελος, ὅς ῥά τ' ὀδόντας
θήγει θηρευτῇσιν ἐπ' ἀνδράσιν, ἀμφὶ δὲ πολλὸς
ἀφρὸς ἀπὸ στόματος χαμάδις ῥεῖ χωομένοιο.

1351 εἴκελος Stephanus : ἴκελος codd.   1353 ῥεῖ Samuelsson : ῥέε codd.

1342. ἐργατίναι, v. n. 1323.
βουλυτόν, sc. καιρόν, 'the time of unyoking': cf. Arat. 583, βουλυτῷ. In Homer it is only an adverb, βουλυτόνδε, Il. 16. 779, Od. 9. 58: cf. Arat. 826, 1119, βουλύσιος ὥρη. Compare the description of evening in Arg. 4. 1629, ἦμος δ' ἠέλιος μὲν ἔδυ, ἀνά τ' ἤλυθεν ἀστὴρ Αὔλιος, ὅς τ' ἀπέπαυσεν ὀϊζύρους ἀροτῆρας: Call. frag. 160 (Mair), ἀστὴρ Αὔλιος, ὃς δυθμὴν εἶσι μετ' ἠελίου: Arg. 1. 1172, ἦμος δ' ἀγρόθεν εἶσι φυτοσκάφος ἤ τις ἀροτρεὺς Ἀσπασίως εἰς αὖλιν ἑήν.

1343. ὑπό. The dative has something of the sense of 'under,' i.e. 'was ploughed under his feet,' which would be lacking in the genitive: cf. Call. H. Art. 176, τετράγυον τέμνοιεν ὑπ' ἀλλοτρίῳ ἀροτῆρι.

1344. τετράγυος, v. n. 412.
ἀπελύετο. The genitive is usual: cf. Od. 21. 46, ἱμάντα θοῶς ἀπέλυσε κορώνης. The force of the middle and imperfect, if any, is that it was a slow process, 'began to unloose,' i.e. quickly done but not so quickly undone.

1345. διεπτοίησε, 'scared': cf. Od. 18. 340, ἐπέεσσι διεπτοίησε γυναῖκας.
φέβεσθαι, 'in startled flight': cf. Il. 8. 107, ἔνθα καὶ ἔνθα διωκέμεν ἠδὲ φέβεσθαι. It is used only in the present and imperfect.

1346. κεινάς, 'empty of...,' for the form, v. n. 126.

1349. κυνέῃ, i.e. in the same helmet as he had used to carry the teeth.

1350. γνάμψε, 'bent to make them supple,' not in weariness as in Il. 7. 118, cf. Arg. 1. 1174, γούνατ' ἔκαμψεν. It is modelled on Il. 13. 61, γυῖα δ' ἔθηκεν ἐλαφρά.

ἐμπλήσατο, 'filled his mighty soul with courage': varied from Il. 22. 312, μένεος δ' ἐμπλήσατο θυμὸν Ἀγρίου. Homer uses the forms ἐμ- and ἐνι- indifferently, but Ap. has only the former: cf. also Il. 13. 60, πλῆσεν μένεος κρατεροῖο.

1351. μαιμώων, v. n. 351: cf. Il. 17. 281, συῒ εἴκελος ἀλκήν. This passage is founded on the simile in Il. 13. 471 f.: ὡς ὅτε τις σῦς οὔρεσιν ἀλκὶ πεποιθὼς Ὃς τε μένει κολοσυρτὸν ἐπερχόμενον πολὺν ἀνδρῶν Χώρῳ ἐν οἰοπόλῳ, φρίσσει δέ τε νῶτον ὕπερθεν· Ὀφθαλμὼ δ' ἄρα οἱ πυρὶ λάμπετον· αὐτὰρ ὀδόντας Θήγει, ἀλέξασθαι μεμαὼς κύνας ἠδὲ καὶ ἄνδρας.

1352. θήγει, cf. Il. loc. supr. cit., and contrast Xen. Cyr. 1. 2. 10, καὶ τὴν ψυχὴν ἀνάγκη πολλάκις θήγεσθαι ὅταν τι τῶν ἀλκίμων θηρίων ἀνθίστηται.

θηρευτῇσιν, adjective, as in Homer, who has it in the Iliad only.

1353. ῥεῖ, Samuelsson's emendation of MSS. ῥέε, which could only refer to Jason: moreover neither Homer nor Ap. uses the imperfect in similes. For the MSS. reading, cf. Il. 17. 437, δάκρυα δέ σφιν θερμὰ κατὰ βλεφάρων χαμάδις ῥέε μυρομένοισιν: for that as emended, cf. Il. 17. 663, likewise in a simile, τάς τε τρεῖ ἐσσύμενός περ. Compare also the

οἱ δ' ἤδη κατὰ πᾶσαν ἀνασταχύεσκον ἄρουραν
γηγενέες· φρίξεν δὲ περὶ στιβαροῖς σακέεσσιν   1355
δούρασί τ' ἀμφιγύοις κορύθεσσί τε λαμπομένῃσιν
Ἄρηος τέμενος φθισιμβρότου· ἵκετο δ' αἴγλη
νειόθεν Οὔλυμπόνδε δι' ἠέρος ἀστράπτουσα.
ὡς δ' ὁπότ' ἐς γαῖαν πολέος νιφετοῖο πεσόντος
ἂψ ἀπὸ χειμερίας νεφέλας ἐκέδασσαν ἄελλαι   1360
λυγαίῃ ὑπὸ νυκτί, τὰ δ' ἀθρόα πάντ' ἐφαάνθη
τείρεα λαμπετόωντα διὰ κνέφας· ὣς ἄρα τοίγε
λάμπον ἀναλδήσκοντες ὑπὲρ χθονός. αὐτὰρ Ἰήσων
μνήσατο Μηδείης πολυκερδέος ἐννεσιάων,

1355 φρίξαν L, vulg. : φράξαν Samuelsson.   1360 ἆται L ex corr., Paris. unus
in marg., Brunck.   1361 πάντ' ἐφαάνθη Brunck : πάντα φαάνθη codd.

simile in Hes. *Sc.* 386–91, and Qu. Sm.
4. 245, πουλὺς δ' ἐκ στομάτων χαμάδις
καταχεύεται ἀφρός.
1354–1404. The Earthborn Men
spring up, and Jason casts a stone
among them. While they fight among
themselves, he leaps among them and
mows them down.
1354. ἀνασταχύεσκον, v. n. 1054.
1355. φρίξεν. This is clearly based on
Il. 13. 339, ἔφριξεν δὲ μάχη φθισίμ-
βροτος ἐγχείῃσι, cf. Aesch. *Supp.* 607,
χερσὶ δεξιωνύμοις Ἔφριξεν αἰθήρ. Platt
has restored to this passage the scholium
on 1372, and the quotation therein from
Sophocles, καὶ κάρτα φρίξας εὐλόφῳ
σφηνώματι. Compare the imitation in
Aen. 7. 525: 'atraque late Horrescit
strictis seges ensibus aeraque fulgent
Sole lacessita et lucem sub nubila
iactant.'
1356. ἀμφιγύοις. Leaf on *Il.* 13. 147,
ἔγχεσιν ἀμφιγύοισιν, gives four inter-
pretations: (1) with a limb, γυῖον, on
each end, (2) with a curve at both sides,
(3) bending to each side, elastic,
(4) wielded with both hands. The last
is preferable. Jebb on Soph. *Tr.* 505,
τίνες ἀμφίγυοι κατέβαν πρὸ γάμων, says
that there ἀμφί- means 'two,' -γυοι
means 'stalwart,' *i.e.* 'stalwart rivals':
cf. also n. 37 supr. ἀμφιγυήεις.
1357. φθισιμβρότου, v. on 1355 supr.:
it is an epithet also in Homer of the
aegis of Athene.
1358. ἀστράπτουσα. The reverse of

the Homeric use of Zeus sending lightning from above, cf. 1018, and Eur.
Phoen. 110, κατάχαλκον ἅπαν πεδίον
ἀστράπτει. This is an obvious paraphrase of *Il.* 2. 457–8, ὣς τῶν ἐρχομένων
ἀπὸ χαλκοῦ θεσπεσίοιο Αἴγλη παμφανό-
ωσα δι' αἰθέρος οὐρανὸν ἷκεν.
1359. ὡς κ.τ.λ. Compare *Il.* 8. 555f.,
ὡς δ' ὅτ' ἐν οὐρανῷ ἄστρα φαεινὴν ἀμφὶ
σελήνην Φαίνετ' ἀριπρεπέα, ὅτε δ' ἔπλετο
νήνεμος αἰθήρ, Ἐκ δ' ἔφανεν πᾶσαι σκοπιαὶ
καὶ πρώονες ἄκροι Καὶ νάπαι· οὐρανόθεν
δ' ἄρ' ὑπερράγη ἄσπετος αἰθήρ, Πάντα δὲ
εἴδεται ἄστρα. There is an implied interpretation as a night scene of *Il.* 16.
297 f.: ὡς δ' ὅτ' ἀφ' ὑψηλῆς κορυφῆς
ὄρεος μεγάλοιο Κινήσῃ πυκινὴν νεφέλην
στεροπηγερέτα Ζεύς, Ἐκ δ' ἔφανεν πᾶσαι
σκοπιαὶ κ.τ.λ.
1360. ἂψ...ἐκέδασσαν, v. n. 996.
1361. λυγαίῃ, 'dark,' v. n. 323.
ὑπό, v. n. 323.
1362. τείρεα, 'stars.' Once in Homer,
Il. 18. 485, τά τε τείρεα πάντα τά τ'
οὐρανὸς ἐστεφάνωται, imitated in *Arg.* 4.
261, τείρεα πάντα τά τ' οὐρανῷ εἰλίσσονται.
λαμπετόωντα, used only in the participle, *Il.* 1. 104, πυρὶ λαμπετόωντι :
cf. Hes. *Th.* 110, ἄστρα τε λαμπετόωντα.
1363. ἀναλδήσκοντες, 'growing up,'
v. n. 414.
1364. πολυκερδέος, 'full of cunning.'
Here only in Ap., and once in Homer
of Odysseus νόον πολυκερδέα νωμῶν, *Od.*
13. 255.

λάζετο δ' ἐκ πεδίοιο μέγαν περιηγέα πέτρον, 1365
δεινὸν Ἐνυαλίου σόλον Ἄρεος· οὔ κέ μιν ἄνδρες
αἰζηοὶ πίσυρες γαίης ἄπο τυτθὸν ἄειραν.
τόν ῥ' ἀνὰ χεῖρα λαβὼν μάλα τηλόθεν ἔμβαλε μέσσοις
ἀΐξας· αὐτὸς δ' ὑφ' ἑὸν σάκος ἕζετο λάθρῃ
θαρσαλέως. Κόλχοι δὲ μέγ' ἴαχον, ὡς ὅτε πόντος 1370
ἴαχεν ὀξείῃσιν ἐπιβρομέων σπιλάδεσσιν·
τὸν δ' ἕλεν ἀμφασίη ῥιπῇ στιβαροῖο σόλοιο
Αἰήτην. οἱ δ' ὥστε θοοὶ κύνες ἀμφιθορόντες
ἀλλήλους βρυχηδὸν ἐδήιον· οἱ δ' ἐπὶ γαῖαν
μητέρα πῖπτον ἑοῖς ὑπὸ δούρασιν, ἠύτε πεῦκαι 1375
ἢ δρύες, ἅς τ' ἀνέμοιο κατάικες δονέουσιν.
οἷος δ' οὐρανόθεν πυρόεις ἀναπάλλεται ἀστὴρ
ὁλκὸν ὑπαυγάζων, τέρας ἀνδράσιν, οἵ μιν ἴδωνται

1367 ὑπὸ Paris. unus, Brunck.   1374 ἐπήιον Struve.   1377 ἀπολάμπεται v.l.
in schol., Et. Mag. 697. 50: ἀποπάλλεται O. Schneider.

1365. λάζετο, 'took,' Homeric, cf.
1394.
περιηγέα, 'round,' v. n. 138.
1366. Ἐνυαλίου. Here, as in Il. 17.
211, an epithet of Ares; it is usually a
substantive. For the connection with
Ἐνυώ, v. Jessen ap. Pauly-Wissowa s.v.
σόλον. In Il. 23. 826, this is a mass
of iron used for throwing, distinct from
the discus. Here it is either 'a quoit
of Ares,' i.e. 'a weapon of war,' or a
sort of extension of μέγαν, 'a quoit that
Ares himself might be proud to throw.'
The latter is more probable.
1367. αἰζηοί, v. n. 518.
πίσυρες, v. n. 222. Tydeides in Il. 5.
302 takes up a stone that two ordinary
men could not lift, likewise Ajax in
Il. 12. 381: with typical Alexandrine
exaggeration, Apollonius doubles the
Homeric number.
1368. ἀνά, cf. ἀνὰ στόμ' ἔχειν, 'took
up on to his hand': Jason takes the
attitude of a shot-putter.
1369. ἀΐξας, 'with a rush.'
1371. ἐπιβρομέων, a late form of the
Homeric ἐπιβρέμω, cf. Arg. 4. 240, 908.
For the simile, cf. Il. 2. 394 f.: ὡς ὅτε
κῦμα Ἀκτῆ ἐφ' ὑψηλῇ, ὅτε κινήσῃ Νότος
ἐλθών, Προβλῆτι σκοπέλῳ· τὸν δ' οὔποτε
κύματα λείπει Παντοίων ἀνέμων, ὅτ' ἂν
ἔνθ' ἢ ἔνθα γένωνται.

1372. ἀμφασίη, 'speechlessness,' v. n.
76.
ῥιπῇ. For the typical alteration of a
Homeric phrase, λαὸς ὑπὸ ῥιπῆς in Il.
12. 462, cf. 43, 970 supr.
1373. θοοί, v. n. 1281.
ἀμφιθορόντες, 'leaping about': the
compound is here only, but the simple
verb is Homeric.
1374. βρυχηδόν, 'with hoarse shouts,'
from the Homeric βρυχάομαι: cf. Anth.
Pal. 9. 371, τὸν δ' αἶψα κύων βρυχηδὸν
ὀδοῦσιν Μάρψε. Platt takes it here to
mean 'bit one another like dogs,' but
that would rather imply that βρυχήσατ'
ἀνίῃ of Medea in 4. 19 means 'bit herself
in her despair'(!). The construction is
rather compressed; 'they, the earthborn
men, leapt about like fierce hounds.
Some with loud shouts slew each other;
others fell to mother Earth under their
own spears, like pines or oaks shaken
by the storms of wind.' Contrast the
simile in 967 of the trees waving gently
in the breeze.
1376. κατάικες, like the simple ἄιξ
of 4. 820, 'storms'; cf. καταιγίς in
Aristotle.
1378. ὑπαυγάζων, 'trailing a furrow
of light,' first here. The Homeric
αὐγάζομαι in Arg. 1. 155, 2. 682, like
καταυγάζομαι of Arg. 4. 1248 and the

μαρμαρυγῇ σκοτίοιο δι' ἠέρος ἀίξαντα·
τοῖος ἄρ' Αἴσονος υἱὸς ἐπέσσυτο γηγενέεσσιν·   1380
γυμνὸν δ' ἐκ κολεοῖο φέρεν ξίφος, οὖτα δὲ μίγδην
ἀμώων, πολέας μὲν ἔτ' ἐς νηδὺν λαγόνας τε
ἡμίσεας ἀνέχοντας ἐς ἠέρα· τοὺς δὲ καὶ ἄχρις
ὤμων τελλομένους· τοὺς δὲ νέον ἑστηῶτας,
τοὺς δ' ἤδη καὶ ποσσὶν ἐπειγομένους ἐς ἄρηα.   1385
ὡς δ' ὁπότ', ἀμφ' οὔροισιν ἐγειρομένου πολέμοιο,
δείσας γειομόρος, μή οἱ προτάμωνται ἀρούρας,
ἅρπην εὐκαμπῆ νεοθηγέα χερσὶ μεμαρπὼς
ὠμὸν ἐπισπεύδων κείρει στάχυν, οὐδὲ βολῆσιν
μίμνει ἐς ὡραίην τερσήμεναι ἠελίοιο·   1390

1381 φέρεν L : φέρει G.   οὖτα Brunck : οὕτα codd.   1384 γούνων Struve :
κώλων Merkel.   στελλομένους vulg.   1386 ἀγχούρουσιν Pierson.

Anthology, means 'to see'; but here and in 1. 1231, αὐγάζουσα Βάλλε σεληναίη, the idea of 'making radiant' is prominent.

1379. μαρμαρυγῇ, v. n. 288.

1380. ἐπέσσυτο, cf. *Il.* 15. 347, νηυσὶν ἐπὶ...σεύεσθαι: for the simile, cf. *Il.* 4. 75: οἷον δ' ἀστέρα ἧκε Κρόνου πάϊς ἀγκυλομήτεω, Ἢ ναύτῃσι τέρας ἠὲ στρατῷ εὐρέϊ λαῶν, Λαμπρόν· τοῦ δέ τε πολλοὶ ἀπὸ σπινθῆρες ἵενται, Τῷ εἰκυῖ' ἤϊξεν ἐπὶ χθόνα Παλλὰς Ἀθήνη.

1381. οὖτα, from οὐτάω, as though from οὖτημι, cf. *Il.* 4. 525, etc.

μίγδην. First in H. Hom. *Her.* 494. The Homeric form is μίγδα: μίγα, as in 4. 1345, is first in Pindar.

1383. ἀνέχοντας, intransitive, 'rising up': cf. 851, v. n. 161.

ἄχρις, 'as far as,' v. n. 763.

1384. ἑστηῶτας. For the form, v. n. 121. Some suspect a corruption of ὤμων from 1389 infr.; and the fact that Val. Flacc. 7. 619 mentions those of whom 'necdum humeri videre diem' may only shew that the corruption is of early standing. The three stages, (1) 'halfway,' (2) 'as far as the shoulders,' (3) 'completely,' are naturally expected in the order 2. 1. 3. Platt accepts Struve's γούνων; but it is best with Seaton to keep the text as it stands, and to regard the second group as parenthetical.

1386. ἀμφί, 'concerning': cf. *Il.* 3. 70, ἀμφ' Ἑλένῃ. De Mirmont takes it in a local sense, v. n. 117.

1387. γειομόρος, *lit.* 'earth cleaver,' cf. 4. 1453, an Alexandrine form of the Attic γεωμόρος, which is in 1. 1214; cf. Call. *frag.* Mair 148, τέμνοντα σπορίμην αὔλακα γειομόρον.

προτάμωνται, 'ravage it before he has time to reap it.' Compare *Od.* 18. 375, ὦκα διηνεκέα προταμοίμην, the sole instance of the middle in Homer, which is 'anticipate in cutting,' as here, not as with Ellis on Catullus 64. 353. This passage and 2. 794 give some support to Aristarchus and most MSS. for ἀπουρίσσουσιν in *Il.* 22. 489, rather than ἀπαυρήσουσιν of Bekker, Ameis, etc.

1388. ἅρπην. Here and in 4. 987, as in Hes. *Op.* 573, a 'sickle': in *Il.* 19. 350, a 'kite.'

εὐκαμπῆ, 'curved,' epithet of δρέπανον in *Od.* 18. 368; cf. Moschus, *Europa* 81, εὐκαμπὲς ἄροτρον.

νεοθηγέα, 'newly-whetted,' here and in *Anth. Plan.* 124 only: νεόθηκτος is in Suidas.

1389. ἐπισπεύδων, 'in haste,' intransitive as in Eur. *Tr.* 1275: it is tr. in Sophocles and Herodotus.

1390. ὡραίην, formed like ἀναγκαίη, σεληναίη, Ἀθηναίη, etc.: cf. Hdt. 4. 28, τὴν μὲν ὡραίην οὐχ ὕει.

τερσήμεναι, 'does not wait for it till harvest time, to be ripened by the rays of the sun': this is founded on *Od.* 6. 98, εἵματα δ' ἠελίοιο μένον τερσήμεναι αὐγῇ.

ὡς τότε γηγενέων κεῖρεν στάχυν· αἵματι δ᾽ ὁλκοὶ
ἠύτε κρηναῖαι ἀμάραι πλήθοντο ῥοῇσιν.
πῖπτον δ᾽, οἱ μὲν ὀδὰξ τετρηχότα βῶλον ἀρούρης
λαζόμενοι πρηνεῖς, οἱ δ᾽ ἔμπαλιν, οἱ δ᾽ ἐπ᾽ ἀγοστῷ
καὶ πλευροῖς, κήτεσσι δομὴν ἀτάλαντοι ἰδέσθαι.   1395
πολλοὶ δ᾽ οὐτάμενοι, πρὶν ὑπὸ χθονὸς ἴχνος ἀεῖραι,
ὅσσον ἄνω προύτυψαν ἐς ἠέρα, τόσσον ἔραζε
βριθόμενοι πλαδαροῖσι καρήασιν ἠρήρειντο.
ἔρνεά που τοίως, Διὸς ἄσπετον ὀμβρήσαντος,
φυταλιῇ νεόθρεπτα κατημύουσιν ἔραζε   1400
κλασθέντα ῥίζηθεν, ἀλωήων πόνος ἀνδρῶν·

1391 ὡς ὅγε Koechly.   κεῖρεν L : κεῖρε G.   1393 ὀκλὰξ Abresch.   ἀρούρης
pro ὀδοῦσιν, Hermann, Seaton : ὅπλοισιν Pierson : ὅλοξιν Merkel.   1396 ἀπὸ
Vatt. duo, et coni. Struve.

1392. ἀμάραι, 'channels,' for irriga-
tion of fields, as in *Il.* 21. 259, χερσὶ
μάκελλαν ἔχων, ἀμάρης ἐξ ἔχματα βάλλων.
πλήθοντο. Ap. alone uses the passive:
Homer has the active in passive sense,
'to be filled,' as in 67 supr. It is transitive in Qu. Sm. 6. 345, πλήθει δ᾽ αὖτε
κύπελλα βοῶν γλάγος.
1393. τετρηχότα, v. n. 276: *schema
Atticum,* for βῶλος elsewhere is feminine,
v. n. 21.
ἀρούρης. Read this with Hermann
for MSS. ὀδοῦσιν, v. crit. appendix, p. 142.
1394. λαζόμενοι, cf. 1365. This is a
typical adaptation of *Il.* 2. 418, πρηνέες
ἐν κονίῃσιν ὀδὰξ λαζοίατο γαῖαν, combined with *Il.* 11. 425, ἕλε γαῖαν ἀγοστῷ,
for which v. n. 120.
ἔμπαλιν, 'on their backs,' un-
Homeric; cf. Plat. *Theaet.* 193 C,
ἔμπαλιν ὑποδεῖσθαι, 'put one's shoes on
the wrong feet.'
ἀγοστῷ, probably 'crook of the elbow',
v. n. 120.
1395. δομήν, 'like,' Alexandrine for
δέμας: cf. Lyc. 334, Μαίρας ὅταν φαιουρὸν
ἀλλάξῃς δομήν and *ib.* 783, for use as
substantive.
1396. ὑπό, cf. *Il.* 21. 56, ὑπὸ ζόφου,
'from under the gloom.'
ἴχνος, cf. Eur. *Phoen.* 105, ἴχνος
ἐπαντέλλων.
1397. προύτυψαν, 'shot up,' but in
1. 953, 'sped forward': cf. *Il.* 13. 136,
Τρῶες δὲ προύτυψαν ἀολλέες.

1398. βριθόμενοι, 'weighed down
with their limp heads,' Homeric.
πλαδαροῖσι, 'clammy': in Hippocrates, 'flabby.'
ἠρήρειντο, 'rested there,' from ἀραρίσκω, v. n. 833. From this line, and 4. 35,
διειλυσθεῖσα δόμοιο, Nonnus concocted
Dion. 4. 364, αὐτομάτη πλαδαροῖο διειλυσθεῖσα καρήνου.
1399. ὀμβρήσαντος, un-Homeric:
cf. Hes. *Op.* 415, μετοπωρινὸν ὀμβρήσαντος Ζηνός.
1400. φυταλιῇ, 'vineyard,' as in
Homer: *Arg.* 2. 1003 is a curious use,
the 'act of planting,' οὐδέ τις ἄλλη
Φυταλιὴ καρποῖο.
νεόθρεπτα, 'newly grown,' peculiar
to Apollonius.
κατημύουσιν, compound peculiar to
Ap.; the simple verb is Homeric, 'bow
down.' *Arg.* 2. 862, κατήμυσαν...Θυμόν,
is a cognate accusative, not a transitive
use as in L. & S.
1401. ῥίζηθεν, 'from the roots,' here
only. Alexandrine poetry has also
ῥιζόθεν, on the analogy of Homeric
adverbs like ἄλλοθεν, οἴκοθεν.
ἀλωήων. Ἀλωεύς is a proper name in
Homer, and is first as a noun in Arat.
1045, and often in Nonnus; but there
is clearly a metrical resemblance here
to *Il.* 5. 90, ἀλωάων ἐριθηλέων.
πόνος, 'the work of men who labour
in vineyards,' cf. ἔργα ἀνδρῶν as a
description of gardens in *Od.* 10. 98;

τὸν δὲ κατηφείη τε καὶ οὐλοὸν ἄλγος ἱκάνει
κλήρου σημαντῆρα φυτοτρόφον· ὡς τότ᾽ ἄνακτος
Αἰήταο βαρεῖαι ὑπὸ φρένας ἦλθον ἀνῖαι.
ἤιε δ᾽ ἐς πτολίεθρον ὑπότροπος ἄμμιγα Κόλχοις,   1405
πορφύρων, ᾗ κέν σφι θοώτερον ἀντιόῳτο.
ἦμαρ ἔδυ, καὶ τῷ τετελεσμένος ἦεν ἄεθλος.

1406 κε codd., edd.

others take πόνος here to mean 'to the vexation of,' which is less probable.

This simile is clearly modelled on that in *Il.* 8. 306, of a hero slain by Hector: μήκων δ᾽ ὡς ἑτέρωσε κάρη βάλεν, ἥ τ᾽ ἐνὶ κήπῳ Καρπῷ βριθομένη νοτίῃσί τε εἰαρινῇσιν 'Ὡς ἑτέρωσ᾽ ἤμυσε κάρη πήληκι βαρυνθέν. It is imitated in Verg. *Aen.* 9. 435: 'purpureus veluti cum flos succisus aratro Languescit moriens lassoque papavera collo Demisere caput pluvia cum forte gravantur.' There is a still closer imitation in Qu. Sm. 14. 75 f.: ὡς δ᾽ ὅτε λήιον αὖον ἐπιβρίσασα χάλαζα Τυτθὰ διατμήξῃ, στάχυας δ᾽ ἀπὸ πάντας ἀμέρσῃ, 'Ριπῇ ὑπ᾽ ἀργαλέῃ, καλάμη δ᾽ ἄρα χεύατ᾽ ἔραζε Μαψιδίη καρποῖο κατ᾽ οὔδεος ὀλλυμένοιο, Λευγαλέως, λυγρῷ δὲ πέλει μέγα πένθος ἄνακτι, 'Ὡς ἄρα καὶ Ξάνθοιο περὶ φρένας ἤλυθεν ἄλγος.

1402. **κατηφείη**, v. n. 123.

οὐλοόν. Peculiar to Ap., v. n. 297.

1403. **σημαντῆρα**, 'owner,' and 1. 575 'herdsman': elsewhere only in Josephus, in the sense of 'seal.' Homer has σημάντορες, *Od.* 19. 314, cf. *Arg.* 1. 175, in the sense of 'masters': in *Il.* 15. 325, it means 'herdsman.'

φυτοτρόφον, 'who planted them,' here only.

1404. **ὑπό**, un-Homeric use, cf. 675, and v. n. 288; for the Homeric use, cf. 1077.

1405–1407. Aeetes returns to the palace to devise further trouble for the Argonauts.

1406. **πορφύρων**, v. n. 23.

ᾗ, 'how,' first in tragedy: this is never in Homer, where ἦ should be read, as in *Il.* 2. 73, etc., ἦ θέμις ἐστίν, and v. n. 991 supr.

ἀντιόῳτο, 'thwart them': cf. *Il.* 21. 151, ἐμῷ μένει ἀντιόωσι, 'face my might.'

1407. **ἔδυ**, 'the day died, and Jason's task was at an end.' The book ends appropriately with a variant of *Od.* 5. 262, τέτρατον ἦμαρ ἔην καὶ τῷ τετέλεστο ἄπαντα: cf. *Il.* 7. 465, δύσετο δ᾽ ἠέλιος τετέλεστο δὲ ἔργον Ἀχαιῶν.

APPENDIXES.

(a) THE PALACE OF AEETES (with plan).

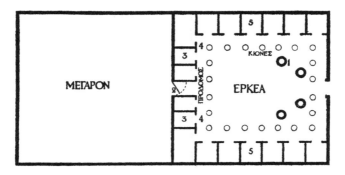

THE PALACE OF AEETES

THE description of the Palace of Aeetes, though elaborate with regard to individual points, is exceedingly vague in outline; none the less it appears to agree in essentials with the formula of the Homeric palace in *Il.* 6. 316, θάλαμος καὶ δῶμα καὶ αὐλή.

Wide gates, εὐρεῖαι πύλαι, form the entrance, προμολαί, to an open court, ἔρκεα, near the threshold of which, οὐδός, are four fountains (1), κρῆναι, surrounded by vines; pillars, κίονες, run from right and left of the entrance round all four sides of the court. Directly facing the entrance is the μέσσαυλος (2), an imposing door of wrought metal, ἐλήλατο, giving access to the μέγαρον. To right and left of this central door are a number of rooms (3), θάλαμοι, of which the doors, δικλίδες, open on to the πρόδομος (4), and seem to have been visible from the outer entrance of the court.

The πρόδομος is formed by the αἴθουσα, 237, which runs παρὲξ ἑκάτερθε from either side of the main door; it is here that Eros stops to string his bow, 278, before entering the μέγαρον. Behind and above the πρόδομος rise the walls of the μέγαρον; the bronze γλυφίδες, 218, which support the θριγκός, are visible from the threshold of the court.

One side of the court is thus occupied by the πρόδομος; those to right and left of it are taken up by higher buildings or suites (5), αἰπύτεροι δόμοι. The number and order of these are not specified, but at any rate those occupied by Medea and Chalciope must have been on opposite sides, as Medea has to cross the court, 647, to reach her sister.

For the above plan no greater authority is claimed than that of a rough sketch. The vagueness of the text leaves much to the imagination of the reader, and no interpretation of it can be other than arbitrary at many points.

(b) CRITICAL APPENDIX.

1. ἔνισπε. Here and in 4. 1565 Merkel reads ἔνισπες, which is given by the MSS. in 1. 832, and indicated in 1. 487 by L ἔνισπες, G ἔνισπε. Both are Homeric, and Ap. doubtless made a point of using both forms; ἔνισπε is considered spurious by Buttmann and la Roche, but defended by Curtius, *G.V.* 1. 195.

33. θελκτήριον. This accusative has given unnecessary trouble to recent critics. χρειὼ πόθοιο can be accompanied by an adjective in agreement with either word; cf. Aesch. *Sept.* 348 f. βλαχαὶ δ᾽ αἱματόεσσαι Τῶν ἐπιμαστιδίων Ἀρτιτρεφεῖς βρέμονται, where in English the adjectives would agree with ἐπιμαστιδίων. Damste needlessly emends θελκτήριον to the genitive, and translates 'neque ullum blandi amoris desiderium sentio.' Platt feels that if it is an adjective, some noun meaning 'charm' is required; if a noun, some adjective agreeing with πόθοιο. His suggestion ἀχρείου θελκτήρια, 'to suit Athene's contempt for the sentimental,' is unfortunate; she is not contemptuous, but merely, as she herself says, ignorant, and in fact gives her whole support to the idea.

Πόθοιο. I write this, against MSS. and edd., with a capital; it is not quite the same as 86 infr., θέλξαι πόθῳ Αἰσονίδαο. Mention of Eros, τοῖο, 32, leads Athene as a good Alexandrine to speak of Πόθος also. For the conjunction of this pair, cf. *Anth. Pal.* 5. 214, σφαιριστὰν τὸν Ἔρωτα τρέφω... Ἀλλ᾽ ἄγε συμπαίκταν δέξαι Πόθον: *ib.* 12. 54, ἀλλὰ νέοι στέργοιτε νέον Πόθον· ἦ γὰρ ὁ κοῦρος Εὕρηται κρείσσων οὗτος Ἔρωτος Ἔρως. Πόθος is first found in Aesch. *Supp.* 1038, μετάκοινοι δὲ φίλα ματρὶ πάρεισιν Πόθος ᾷ τ᾽ οὐδὲν ἄπαρνον Τελέθει θελκτορι Πειθοῖ: cf. Nonnus, *Dion.* 25. 154, Πόθος ἱμεροείς. Peitho, etc., as a religious figure is probably an offshoot of Aphrodite; cf. the worship of Aphrodite-Peitho at Pharsalus in the 5th century, Farnell, *Cults*, 2. 731. 2; 4. 444. 247.

61. ναυτίληται. Platt reads aorist ναυτίληται, citing *Od.* 4. 672, ὡς ἂν ἐπισμυγερῶς ναυτίλεται εἵνεκα πατρός, where, according to Curtius, *G.V.* p. 322, we must either assume an Aeolic form like ὀφέλλειεν in *Il.* 16. 651, or read aor. subj. ναυτίληται. Monro, *H.G.* 82, reads the latter, as no thematic stem forms the subjunctive with a short vowel; Platt considers the present impossible, and reads aor. as preserved, perhaps only by haplography, in one MS. ναυτίληται would accordingly be the correct aorist form for Ap.; but there is no need whatever to depart from the present.

75. ὀπάσσῃς. Wellauer and Mooney condemn the subjunctive, and read ὀπάσσεις with G, in support of which the former cites Arist. *Eccl.* 162, οὐκ ἂν προβαίην ... εἰ μὴ ταῦτ᾽ ἀκριβωθήσεται, and Eur. *Hipp.* 480, ὀψέ γ᾽ ... ἐξεύροιεν ἄν, Εἰ μὴ ... εὑρήσομεν. Brunck and Beck read ὀπάσσοις with a single Paris. MS. But Ap. uses the subjunctive both after κεν, 437 infr., and ἄν, 1. 334, and after the optative alone, 79 infr.: there is no need to alter it here.

158. Here, for the MSS. διὲκ μεγάροιο Διός, I read Διὸς μεγάλοιο θέων, as indicated by *Stras. Pap.* 193, .ΗΔΕΔΙΟΣΜΕΓΑΛΟΙΟΘ..., for which v. Reitzenstein in *Hermes* 35 (1900), 605–7, and Seaton in *Class. Quart.* 9 (1915), 10. Probably Διός was misread as διέκ; then Διός was put in the margin as a variant of διέκ, and finally taken as a variant of θέων, misread as θεῶν, which it has displaced in the MSS. Gerhard's μεγάλοιο is thus confirmed. It should be noticed that, whereas an *epitheton ornans* properly precedes, as in 1. 1315 μεγάλοιο Διός, those ending in -οιο end a line or hemistich so handily that they often follow; cf. Διὸς μεγάλοιο, ἀθανάτοιο Qu. Sm. 1. 502, 715, and in Latin, *Iovis omnipotentis*. The MSS. διὲκ μεγάροιο is a common Homeric phrase, *e.g. Od.* 17. 61.

161. Read πόλον with Platt for MSS. πόλοι. The latter requires the explanation of δέ as γάρ by parataxis, and further obfuscation of a sufficiently meaningless text by the adjustment of Homeric ideas of Olympus to those of the Aristotelian poles, ὁ ἄνω and ὁ κάτω πόλος ap. Arist. *de Mundo*, 2. 5. Platt tentatively identifies the two mountains with the half-legendary Parnassus and Caucasus of Arist. *Meteor.* 1. 350a, 18–33; Apollonius should have known better after the conquests of Alexander had opened up the further seas, but he shews ignorance even of Aegean geography.

166. ἀν᾽ αἰθέρι. The dative of L and G is open to suspicion. The Homeric ἀνά c. dat. does not occur elsewhere in Ap. (ἀνὰ βωμῷ καῖον 2. 699 is probably *in tmesi*), hence presumably the vulgate ἐν αἰθέρι. The dative is probably due to forced agreement with ἰόντι by a scribe who did not realise the dependence of the participle on φαίνετο. A dative after ἰόντι is unlikely, and there is further support for the acc. in πολλὸν, which, though of course it *may* be adverbial, is probably an adjective, cf. *Il.* 4. 244, πολέος πεδίοιο θέουσαι, *Od.* 4. 709, περόωσι δὲ πουλὺν ἐφ᾽ ὑγρήν. Platt's suggestion, ἀν᾽ αἰθέρι παπταίνοντι, 'standing on ether and looking around,' is attractive, but too great a departure from the MSS.

248. τῇ μὲν ἄρ᾽ οἵγε ... μετιοῦσαν ... ἀνίαχεν. This very harsh anacolouthon as it appears in L and G has been freely emended. The main

fault, as Gerhard realised, may consist in the attraction into the case of κασιγνήτην of an original nom. μετιοῦσα. But his βῆ μὲν ἄρ' ἥγε... μετιοῦσα is rightly rejected by Wellauer as too far ignoring the best MSS. authority, τῇ μὲν ἄρ' οἵγε subsequently corrupted into τὴν μὲν in sympathy with μετιοῦσαν. The abrupt οἵγε, resumptive after 30 lines and needlessly anticipating σφεας in 253, is to my mind suspect as being an addition of an extraneous nominative made necessary only through the corruption into the accusative of μετιοῦσα; and I would accept as the most faithful and convincing emendation of an awkward passage Platt's τῇ μὲν ἄρ' ἥγε...μετιοῦσα, which is supported by similar anacoloutha beginning with the nominative in *Arg.* 4. 435, 852.

290. Here and in 744, 827, 1198, 1208, 1265, 1381, 1391, G lengthens the final vowel before two consonants, L reads final -ν; in 1381 G reads φέρει, L φέρεν. In 655 G gives and L omits the -ν; both give it in 359 and both omit in 1310, 1406; 744 does not appear in the papyrus. It is best to read the -ν consistently, assuming that Apollonius follows Aristophanes rather than the view of Aristarchus, cf. schol. *Il.* 13. 713, Merkel, *Proleg.* 106. It is clear, however, from 316, 410, 496, 1180, that Apollonius had no objection to the lengthening of a final vowel before two consonants.

295. ἀναιθόμενον. Platt is probably right in restoring this for the MSS. ἀνεγρόμενον, answered, as so often in similes, by αἴθετο in the second half. This may underlie the obscure ἀνερθόμενον of a single Paris. MS. Correspondence in a simile is more likely to exist between the two parts than between two subsidiary verbs in a single half. Moreover, Wellauer is hardly justified in supporting the sequence of a simple and a compound verb by such examples of direct repetition of the same word in the same place as 1. 234–5, 375–6, 2. 602–5, 1007–8, 4. 1522–3. Brunck's horror of tautology led him to alter all these save the second, and in this case to evolve from the Paris. MS. the singularly infelicitous ἀνερχόμενον. Damste finds a cure in ἐργομένη for ἐγρομένη, with which might be compared Vergil (?) *Moretum* 14: 'oppositaque manu lumen defendit ab aura.'

404. ἤν κ' ἐθέλησθα. Cf. Arat. 562, ἄν κε περισκέψαιο. Brunck, followed by editors, reads αἴ κε with D in this passage, and in Arat. *loc. cit.* But the vulgate is supported by A in *Il.* 4. 353, ἤν κ' ἐθέλησθα, and by *Brit. Mus. Pap.* 136, repeated in Plato, *Hipp. Min.* 370B. It is likewise read by all MSS. except F, which has εἰ, in *Od.* 18. 318; cf. Qu. Sm. 7. 215, 12. 226. It is best, with Platt, to regard *Il. loc. cit.* A as preserving the reading of Aristarchus, and to believe,

whatever the modern philologist may think of it, that Apollonius and Quintus Smyrnaeus likewise read ἦν κε in their Homer.

551. πότμον L, vulg.: μόρον G. Platt is probably right in regarding as more than a casual emendation οἶτον of the *Ed. Flor.*; Lascaris can hardly have had μόρον before him, and both it and the more metrical effort of L look rather like glosses. Ap. makes considerable use of οἶτος, cf. in particular 2. 172, φεύξεσθαι κακὸν οἶτον, and 64 of this book.

741. τὴν δέ μιν αὖθις. This astonishing use of the pronoun can hardly be genuine. Samuelsson, in view of the Homeric μιν αὐτόν, would defend it by αὐτόν μιν in 4. 1316, cf. Arat. 160; he would even read τὰς δέ σφε for τὰς δέ σφι in 4. 1410, thus supporting a doubtful reading by a still more doubtful conjecture. Damste's κὰδ δέ μιν is too far from the mss. Brunck more reasonably proposed μέν, or alternatively τὴν δέ τοι. It is best with Platt to read τήν γε μὲν αὖτις, cf. Headlam's restoration at 4. 49 of τήν γε for τήνδε, the variation of δέ and γε at 1. 15, 2. 151, 4. 1023, and of μέν and μίν at 2. 8, 4. 880, 1489, 1718. For μέν used without a δέ to follow, cf. Soph. *El.* 516, ἀνειμένη μέν, ὡς ἔοικας, αὖ στρέφει, where the antithesis is implied but not expressed, and L. & S. *sub voc.* A. 1.

847. κούρην. Following de Mirmont and Seaton (*Class. Rev.* 1903, 393B), I read this without the capital. All mss. have Κούρην, *i.e.* Persephone, except G, which with the scholiast has Δαῖραν, a title of Persephone in Lyc. 710, Aesch. *Psychagogoi* frag. 277, and of Demeter at the Eleusinian mysteries. The scholiast says that this is clearly Persephone because of μουνογένειαν; but to Hecate also as a chthonian goddess apply most of the epithets of Demeter and Persephone. She also is μουνογενής, infr. 1035, Hes. *Th.* 426, *h. mag.* ed. Abel, 3. 23, etc., and κουροτρόφος, infr. 861, Hes. *Th.* 450. It is to her exclusively that this ritual is addressed, and it has nothing to do with τῇ Μητρὶ καὶ τῇ Κούρῃ, Hdt. 8. 65. Probably Δαῖραν of the earlier recension was altered for this very reason to κούρην-Hecate, which in time, through the more familiar association of the word with Κούρη-Persephone, would be written with a capital K. That Hecate is both μουνογενῆ and μουνογένειαν need cause no difficulty; Apollonius is quite capable of using double forms as close to each other as this without any deep cult significance.

859. Κασπίῃ ἐν κόχλῳ ἀμήσατο. In Homer, the ἀ- of this verb is short *in thesi* and long *in arsi*, with the exception of *Od.* 9. 135, εἰς ὥρας ἀμῷεν, where probably ἀμμῷεν should be read. So it is best, with Rzach and Gerhard, to accept ἐνί of two Pariss. mss., and to lengthen

the -ι- of Κασπίη, as is legitimate in a proper name. Nonnus, however, has Κάσπιον as a dactyl in *Dion.* 6. 123.

892. οὐδ' ἐνόησα Μὴ ἴμεν. This hiatus in the first foot is unique in Ap. Neither 81 supr., ἢ ἔπος, nor 2. 279, ἢ αἶγας, is parallel, since both may have the digamma; with the latter, however, contrast *Od.* 14. 530, ἔλετ' αἰγός. Samuelsson's ἔμμεναι is tame and unconvincing; Platt's δὴν ἔμεν, cf. 2. 870 δὴν ἔμμεναι, 'I did not mean to be so long among the strangers,' is unlikely, since Medea has only just arrived. Punctuate with a full stop after ἐνόησα with Schneider, and read βῆν ἴμεν with Prescott. The latter supports his emendation with 11 other examples of ἴμεν; ten of these form the *arsis* of the first foot or overlap into the second, nine are preceded by a verb of motion, which in no less than six cases is the aorist of βαίνω.

991. ἤ MSS. edd.: ᾗ Platt. The MSS. cannot be taken seriously with regard to this word where it occurs; on the whole L favours the Homeric ἤ, G the tragic ᾗ. Even if Apollonius knew the former to be the correct Homeric usage, we are not entitled to assume that he would follow it. Read, with Platt, ᾗ here and in 1406, likewise in 189, 1062, and the demonstrative ἥ in 209.

1058. καρχαλέαι. This feminine is defended at greater length in my article on καρχαλέαι κύνες, in the *Liverpool Annals of Archaeology and Anthropology*, Vol. 14 (1927), pp. 51–54.

1084. αὐτὸν θυμὸς ἀνώγει. This, since the emendation of 517 (*q.v.*), makes the only real violation in the *Argonautica* of 'Wernicke's Law' as qualified by Platt, that 'a syllable naturally short cannot be lengthened by position at the end of the fourth foot, unless it forms part of a monosyllabic word, and unless the consonant or consonants lengthening it are part of the same word.' The combination with a spondaic word in the fourth foot, which is rare in Ap., suggests to Platt that the line is an interpolation.

1151. μεταχρονίη. MSS. vary between -θ- and -ρ- in this word; Merkel uniformly writes the latter, Brunck the former. Schol. Flor. 2. 300 recognises both forms as meaning μετέωρος, τὸ δὲ μεταχθονίη γράφεται καὶ μεταχρονίη, καὶ σημαίνει ἑκατέρως τὴν μετέωρον. In 4. 1269, -θ- seems right of a ship, carried ἐκ πόντοιο μεταχθονίην, 'up to the land.' -ρ- is first found in Hes. *Th.* 269 of the Harpies, μεταχρόνιαι γὰρ ἴαλλον.

1269. ἰδρυθέντες. Better than ἰδρυνθέντες. The form without -ν- is in the best MSS. of Theoc. 13. 28, and in the papyrus text of *Il.* 3. 78. Our MSS. have it in 4. 723, and L supports it at 4. 532, but not here.

1393. ἀρούρης. It is best with Lehrs to accept this emendation of Hermann's, and to regard the MSS. ὀδοῦσιν as a gloss on ὀδάξ, though such a familiar word, as Mooney reasonably objects, should stand in no need of a gloss. It is difficult to accept as a deliberate extension of the Homeric λὰξ ποδί the pleonastic ὀδάξ...ὀδοῦσιν, even in the light of Mooney's plea that they are probably from different roots, or to regard ὀδοῦσιν, in the light of 1336, as referring to the dragon's teeth, 'for which' the soil was broken up. Merkel's conjecture ὄλοξιν, from ὄλοκες 'furrows' in Hesychius, is more ingenious than probable.

INDEX OF PROPER NAMES

INDEX TO NOTES. I. WORDS

*Verbs are indexed under the 1st sing. present
indicative; other words as they occur in the text*

ἐκλανθάνω—ἐκ/λαθών 280
  „   (ἐκλελάθοιο 1112) 280
ἐκπίπτω—ἐκ/πέσεν 962
ἔκποθεν 262, 1289
ἔκτοθι (373) 255
ἐκφαίνω—ἐξεφαάνθη 855
ἐλαύνω—ἐλήλατο 235
  „   —ἤλασεν 233, 1238
ἐλάω—ἔλαεν 872
  „   —ἐλάουσα 888
ἔλδομαι—ἐέλδετο (747) 383
  „   (ἐελδομένη 956) 383
  „   (ἐελδόμενος 1259) 383
  „   (ἐελδομένους 601) 383
ἐλέγχεα 800
ἐλειονόμοι 1219
ἐλελίζω—ἐλελίζετο 760
ἐλέῳ 462, 761
ἔλιξ 139
ἑλίσσω—ἐλισσόμενον 1277
  „   —εἰλιχθεῖσα 655
ἕλος 489
ἐλπωρῆσιν 1255
ἐλύω—ἐλυσθείς (1313) 281
ἐμβαίνω—ἐμβεβαώς 1241
ἐμβάλλω—ἐνιβάλλομαι 413
ἔμμορες (208) 4
ἔμπα 641
ἔμπαλιν 1394
ἔμπεδον 773
ἐμπίμπλημι—ἐμπλήσατο 1350
ἔμπλειον (1281, 1321) 119
ἐμὸν αὐτῆς 151
ἐν ὄμμασιν 93
ἐν ὀφθαλμοῖσιν (1115) 93
ἐν ποσίν 314, 836
ἐναίσιμον 524
ἐναντίβιον 1234
ἐναρίθμιος 518
ἐνδαίω—ἐνεδαίετο 286
ἐνεοστασίη 76
ἐνέπω—ἔνισπε 1
  „   —ἐνισπεῖν 685
ἐνέροισιν 862
ἔνθα 771
ἐνίημι—ἐν/ῆκεν 959
ἐνικλάω—ἐνέκλασεν 307
ἐνιπήν 677
ἐνίπλεον 119
ἐνίπτω—ἠνίπαπε 931
ἐνίσχω—ἐνί/ίσχεται 343
ἐννεσίῃσιν (478, 818, 942) 29
ἕννυμι (ἕεστο 1225) 454
  „   —ἕστο 454
ἐνσκέλλω—ἐνεσκλήκει 1251
ἐνσκίμπτω—ἐνισκίμψῃς (765) 153
ἐνσπείρω—ἐνισπείρας 1185
ἐντίθημι—ἐνθεμένη 804

ἐντροπαλίζω—ἐντροπαλιζόμενον (1337) 1222
ἐντύνω—ἐντύναιο 510
  „   —ἐντύνεσκε 40
  „   (ἐντύνουσα 737) 510
ἐξ ἀνέμοιο 345
ἐξ ἐμέθεν 904
ἐξαλέομαι—ἐξαλέασθαι (600) 466
ἐξαναιρέω—ἐξανελοῦσα 867
ἐξάνειμι—ἐξανιοῦσα 757
ἐξανύω—ἐξανύσειεν (788) 188
  „   (ἐξανύσειν 1190) 188
ἐξαποβαίνω—ἐξαποβάντες 326
ἐξαῦτις 482
ἐξεναρίζω—ἐξεναρίζοι 398
ἐξέρχομαι—ἐξήλυθεν 159
ἔοικα—ἔοικεν 172
  „   —ἐοικότα 594
  „   —ἐῴκει 189
ἐολέω—ἐόλητο 471
ἑός 26
ἐπαγαίομαι (1262) 470
ἐπαινέω—ἐπί/ῄνεον 947
ἐπαλδομαι—ἐπαληθείς 348
ἐπαλαστέω—ἐπαλαστήσας (557) 369
ἐπανθιάω—ἐπανθιόωντας 519
ἐπαρτέα 299
ἐπαρωγόν 1211
ἐπαυλίζομαι—ἐπηυλίζοντο 929
ἐπεί 54
ἐπέοικα—ἐπέοικε 991
ἐπερύω—ἐπειρύσασα 149
ἐπέρχομαι—ἔπεισιν 896
ἐπέτις 666
ἐπήβολος 1272
ἐπήλυδες 935
ἐπημάτιαι 895
ἐπήορον 856
ἐπήρατον 5
ἐπηετείῃσι 1007
ἐπί 28, 235, 288, 405, 643, 780, 919
ἐπὶ δηρόν (1049) 950
ἐπὶ τοῖσιν 497
ἐπιανδάνω—ἐπιανδάνει 171
ἐπιβαίνω—ἐπεβήσατο (1152) 869
ἐπιβάλλω—ἔβαλλεν ἔπι 1193
ἐπιβρίθω—ἐπιβρίσωσιν 344
ἐπιβρομέω—ἐπιβρομέων 1371
ἐπιγουνίδος 875
ἐπιδεύομαι—ἐπιδευήσεσθαι 717
ἐπιδοιάζω—ἐπεδοίασα 21
ἐπιδρομῇσι (593) 144
ἐπιθύνω—ἐπιθύνεσκεν 1325
ἐπιθύω—ἐπιθύεις 354
ἐπικείμαι—ἐπικείσεται 430
ἐπικέλλω—ἐπέκελσαν 575
ἐπικεύθω—ἐπικεύσω 332
ἐπικλείω—ἐπικλείοντες 553

INDEX TO NOTES. II. SUBJECTS

Roman Numbers denote pages of Introduction,
Arabic Numbers lines as cited in the Commentary

For EU product safety concerns, contact us at Calle de José Abascal, 56–1°,
28003 Madrid, Spain or eugpsr@cambridge.org.

www.ingramcontent.com/pod-product-compliance
Ingram Content Group UK Ltd.
Pitfield, Milton Keynes, MK11 3LW, UK
UKHW010046140625
459647UK00012BB/1635